GENERAL GORDON

Charles George Gordon in 1862

GENERAL GORDON

By
LORD ELTON
Author of ' St. George or the Dragon'
' Imperial Commonwealth' etc.

COLLINS
ST JAMES'S PLACE, LONDON
1954

To my Wife

PRINTED IN GREAT BRITAIN
COLLINS CLEAR-TYPE PRESS: LONDON AND GLASGOW

CONTENTS

ILLUSTRATIONS

MAPS

FOREWORD

GORDON WAS a prolific correspondent and much the most important source for a biography of him is his own letters, of which by far the greater number are unpublished. Of these, thanks to the generosity of their owners, I have been fortunate enough to examine many hundreds, I could almost say many thousands. Much the largest accumulation is that which was in the possession of his nephew, the late Colonel Moffitt, who most generously placed it at my disposal not long before his death. It consists mainly, though by no means solely, of correspondence with his sister Augusta. From the close of the Chinese war onwards the series is almost continuous. Miss Gordon published selections from these letters in the volume which she edited in 1888. But she lavishly bowdlerised the texts, omitting, adding, and even altering, to suit her own notions of propriety, and even of grammar, and often for no discernible reason whatever. Moreover, she was chiefly concerned to present Gordon's religious opinions and resolutely omitted precisely those more personal passages which throw most light on his eccentric and attractive personality. And in any case, the extent of the correspondence is such—Gordon wrote to her weekly for many years from all over the world, often ten or fifteen sheets at a time —that her selection could only hope to represent an insignificant fraction of it. The same difficulty confronted Dr. Birkbeck Hill, who in 1881 published an earlier selection from letters which Gordon wrote to Augusta from the Sudan and Equatoria. Moreover, at that date Gordon was still alive and even more than Augusta

9

Dr. Birkbeck Hill felt himself under compulsion to omit what was personal. Unfortunately, as will appear, he failed to omit, or to disguise adequately, one or two of Gordon's strictures on a sensitive and ill-conditioned subordinate, and thereby unwittingly earned him a bitter enemy, whose subsequent autobiography, though demonstrably a tissue of egoistic fantasies, provided the opportunity, though not the justification, for the best-known innuendo in the entertaining caricature of Gordon in Lytton Strachey's *Eminent Victorians*. Colonel Moffitt died recently, and I understand that he has bequeathed his most valuable collection to the British Museum.

Another source of the greatest importance is the large collection of letters written to Mrs. Freese, the lady who may be said to have introduced Gordon to the slums of Gravesend and corresponded with him at intervals for the rest of his life. This correspondence throws a flood of light on what I have called Gordon's apostolate to the poor, and I am most grateful to Mr. H. W. Freese-Penne-father for lending it to me. Mrs. Freese printed selections from a few of the letters in her anonymous booklets, but by far the greater part of it has never been published. It is of the highest value, for the Gravesend period was not only an extraordinary interlude in Gordon's career but the watershed of his spiritual development. The collection also includes Gordon's Crimean diary, which he gave to Mrs. Freese, and some reminiscences of Gordon by members of her family.

For the use of three other most interesting collections not hitherto known to biographers I must express my gratitude to Major Gordon H. Donnelly, Brigadier G. C. Gordon Blunt and Mr. G. R. F. Bredin, C.M.G. The Donnelly papers consist of Gordon's intermittent correspondence over many years with Major-General Sir John D. Donnelly, K.C.B.; Brigadier Gordon Blunt's collection contains a number of Gordon letters and valuable family notes; the Bredin papers include a number of letters to and from several of Gordon's military colleagues. I am also most grateful to Sir Kenneth Barnes for lending me typescript copies of the whole of Gordon's lengthy correspondence with his father, the Rev. R.

H. Barnes, vicar of Heavitree near Exeter. And to Mr. Martin Parr, C.B.E., for his study of the paper money issued by Gordon during the siege of Khartoum. I must also mention the Waller papers, an important collection of 127 letters, now in Rhodes House Library. In addition, I owe thanks, for the opportunity of examining smaller collections, or isolated letters, notes and photographs, to a number of institutions, individual owners and correspondents: Mr. J. J. Baker, Mr. Albert Bolton, Mr. George F. S. Bowles, The Dean of Bristol, Lt.-Col. L. Cockcroft, D.S.O., M.V.O., Mr. J. R. Danson, Mr. J. D. Donaldson, Lt.-Col. T. Donnelly, Major R. P. S. Elderton, Mrs. E. FitzGerald, Mr. W. T. Fulstow, Mrs. Florence Gordon, The Gordon Boys' School, Woking, Mr. F. G. Grigsby, Mrs. M. M. Hake, Mr. F. G. Hawley, Mr. Richard Hill, Mr. F. B. Horlock (of the Gordon Mission, Gravesend), Mr. Derek Hudson, Alderman S. J. Johnson, Miss G. E. Jones, Mr. A. J. McKillop, Col. G. E. B. Mackintosh, Col. J. MacNair-Smith, Mr. W. Miles Mason, Mrs. Megson, Mr. Henry J. Niblett, Mr. J. H. P. Pafford (Goldsmiths' Librarian, University of London), Mr. David H. Palmer, Mrs. C. Pinsent, Col. R. M. Powell, Mrs. Roberson, Mrs. Rogers, The Shaftesbury Society, Mr. Harry K. Strachan, Mrs. D. H. Taylor, Mrs. M. A. Taylor, Lt.-Col. Trenchall, Miss Mary Trotter, Miss F. M. Ward, Miss W. Warr, Mr. John Whitton, Lt.-Col. Williams and the Rev. P. Gordon Williams.

For permission to reproduce the photographs in this book, I must express thanks to Mrs. Wroughton, The National Portrait Gallery, Rhodes House Library and the Picture Post Library.

Gordon wrote his letters very rapidly, so that his grammar is frequently at fault, and grammatical lapses I have naturally left uncorrected; his punctuation, too, however was sketchy in the extreme, and here, for the sake of clarity, I have found it necessary to claim the privileges of an editor. In general, there seemed to be little purpose in burdening the pages of this biography with footnote references, particularly since my authority is so often an unpublished and inaccessible correspondence. In one section of the book, however, since it analyses the responsibility of Mr. Gladstone and his government for the catastrophe at Khartoum and may therefore be considered controversial, I have cited my printed authorities, whenever it seemed necessary. A bibliography of the chief works I have consulted will be found at the end of the book. I owe much, as must any student of Gordon, to the painstaking scholarship of the late Dr. B. M. Allen's two works, *Gordon in China* and *Gordon and the Sudan*. And I am most grateful for the kindness of Mr. Frewer, the Superintendent of Rhodes House Library, Oxford and of Mrs. Wroughton.

BOOK ONE

FOUNDATIONS

THE DEATH of Charles George Gordon at Khartoum in 1885 was the signal for a spate of biographies, essays, monographs and sermons, varying considerably in accuracy and bulk but all composed in a mood of solemn or ecstatic reverence. Queen Victoria's tribute, in an emotional autograph letter to the dead man's sister, to " your dear, noble, heroic Brother " struck the note subsequently sounded by scores of panegyrics from obscurer hands, of the soldier saint, the Christian warrior *sans peur et sans reproche*. Even Mr. Gladstone, whom many, including his Queen, regarded as personally responsible for Gordon's death, let " a hero of heroes " stand as his final estimate, after the disaster, of the man on whom, during the months of mounting tension which preceded it, he had delivered himself of not a few short-sighted and astringent criticisms. Twenty years later the flood of public eulogy had shrunk to a trickle, for the twentieth century was not greatly interested in soldier saints or Christian warriors. Indeed, with one exception even the iconoclasts of the nineteen-twenties, whether through discretion or indifference, left Gordon severely alone. Their prototype, Lytton Strachey, it is true, included him, as was almost inevitable, among the Eminent Victorians whose boundless energies and irrational beliefs he discreetly ridiculed; and he even contrived, in a characteristically feline and unfounded innuendo, to convey the suggestion that Gordon was a drunkard.

But Strachey's miniature caricature leaves out at least as much

13

as did the cruder full-length sketches of the nineteenth century. If Gordon was something a great deal more self-contradictory than the orthodox Christian warrior of the original hagiographers he was also something both much more formidable and much more mysterious than Strachey's pious, tripping Eminent Victorian. His courage was uncanny, his energy boundless; as a ruler of primitive peoples and as a commander of irregular troops he has had few equals in history. Yet, to say only this is to ignore his essential and distinctive quality. For though Gordon's strange unorthodoxies are scarcely to be found among the canonised, few, even of the canonised, have displayed a simpler, or a surer, faith. Often, it is true, he was impatient, often intolerant, prone to brief fits of passionate anger. But, once established, his faith, uncompromising and all-embracing, did not falter. And since to those who achieve an abundance of any one of the basic sanctities, faith, humility and love, a large measure of the other two is commonly permitted, it is natural to account Gordon a saint. And yet there remains an interrogation mark. For when all the qualities, all the defects and all the achievements, whether of saint or soldier, have been reckoned up the sum total cannot be said to be, quite simply, soldier-saint. The truth is that there was a further, and less easily definable, quality by which every other aspect of Gordon was transfused, and on occasion distorted. He was also one of the last, and one of the strangest, in the long line of British eccentrics.

2

Biographers rarely resist the initial temptation of ascribing the salient characteristics of their hero to his ancestry. But the conventional fumble through the family archives must, nine times out of ten, be almost wholly irrelevant. For whereas we sometimes know a good deal of the parentage and nursery lispings of a historical personage, we can in the nature of things seldom know anything of the remote forebears of Elizabethan or Plantagenet days who, for all we can tell, may have transmitted the rare aptitudes, the strange kinks of character which distinguished him. And all that it would be safe to read into what is known of Gordon's ancestry is the possibility that some at least of the enigmatic contradictions in his character may be ascribed to the fact that while his father, himself a Lieutenant-General, descended from a warrior Highland clan, his mother was the daughter of Samuel Enderby, a shrewd shipowner in London and New England.

Charles George Gordon was born, on 28th January, 1833, a younger son of one of those large peripatetic military families to whom life must have seemed an almost continual transit from garrison to garrison. The Pigeon House Fort in Dublin Bay, Leith Fort, the island of Corfu—from each in turn the small boy was carried off before he could learn to think of it as home. The restlessness, the complete indifference to comfort which he displayed in later life was being implanted early. At Leith he was easily frightened by the discharge of guns. But what after all, did being frightened matter so long as one was careful to behave as though one were not frightened? In which difficult art he seems to have displayed a precocious proficiency, frequently flinging himself into deep water at Corfu when nine years old and still unable to swim. If during the siege of Khartoum the harassed Mr. Gladstone had been informed of these early incidents he would doubtless have found something symbolical in the confidence with which the child had relied on others to rescue him from an unauthorised venture out of his depth.

At Woolwich, at which as Inspector of the Carriage Department their father occupied an official residence overrun with mice, the family made a longer stay, and when in later years Gordon spoke of his youth it was usually Woolwich that he recalled. The surreptitious opening of the front door of the Commandant's house, which was opposite their own, and the release of a liberal sample of their own abundant supply of mice; how he and William would push their young brother, Freddy, through the front doors of other Woolwich notabilities, and hold the door handle to prevent the

embarrassed child's escape; how their neighbours' servants would
be " kept at the doors by continual bell-ringing; " the readiness of
the workmen in the great arms factory to divert their attention to
the manufacture, during working hours, of juvenile but lethal
weapons of offence—formidable squirts and crossbows firing heavy
screws—thanks to which twenty-seven panes of glass in the Arsenal
storehouses were broken in the course of a single Sunday afternoon,
and the astonished Captain Soady narrowly escaped an untimely
end; how an evening lecture at the Academy was interrupted by so
prodigious a splintering of glass that the audience swarmed out like
startled wasps, only to find that the fleetfooted culprits, more
familiar with the tortuosities of the earthworks outside than were the
cadets for whose edification they had been constructed, had vanished
into the darkness; such were the memories over which twenty-six
years later, writing to a young niece from the Sudan, Gordon
would affectionately linger. He did not on this occasion recall how
William and he would plant their sister Helen on a chair by a
window overlooking the main street, pin her arms behind her back
and tap on the window as the workers were pouring out of the
Arsenal, so that the unhappy child was compelled to grin and
grimace in the hope of being taken for an imbecile. Or how, when
the Enderby uncles arrived lugubriously to report the collapse of
their whaling business, Freddy and he spat into the top-hats which
they had left in the hall. But it is scarcely surprising that his father,
a kindly man, if, like most generals and most Victorian parents,
a strict disciplinarian, should have been heard to observe " I feel
I am like a man sitting on a powder-barrel," a sensation with which
in later years most of those who were brought into close contact
with his famous son were destined sooner or later to become only
too familiar.

    Mrs. Gordon too may well have felt as if she were sitting on a
powder-barrel. She had after all to preserve friendly relations with
her military neighbours amid the incessant splintering of glass and
jangling of front-door bells, and despite the unwelcome irruptions
of mice, the unexplained intrusions of the reluctant Freddy and the

recurrent reports that that queer child Helen had been mopping and mowing at the window again. At home, moreover, there was always the prospect of an outbreak of the exhilarating game of " Crowds," in which by its very nature she involuntarily played the central role. As their mother entered or left a room one of the children would shout " Crowds," and instantly they would all rush for the door, elbowing and struggling in a mêlée punctuated by appropriate cries of " Don't push," " There's no hurry," and " You're hurting me." Certainly the young Gordons were re- markably unlike the grimly repressed Victorian family of tradition, but what Mrs. Gordon thought of it all has not been recorded. We know that she was cheerful and extremely pious, in the Puritan tradition of the Enderbys, and we have her son's later testimony that she loved him deeply. But she had a modest income and eleven uproarious children, and in course of time she not unnaturally delegated a good deal of her authority over the younger members of the family to her daughter Augusta, a strong-minded young lady twelve years Charles's senior. Throughout almost the whole of his adult life, Augusta was to be the confidante to whom in a voluminous correspondence from a variety of remote and savage lands he regularly poured out his inmost musings on life and eternity. But although later on she doubtless exercised some influence on the early growth of her brother's home-made religion, and although she has recorded that in due course his influence changed her own " whole inner life," it is clear that she was not at present in a position to suppress his aggressive instincts or his passion for squirts and crossbows.

It was when in 1848, before he was sixteen, the boy himself became an officer-cadet at Woolwich that for the first time he encountered a discipline more rigorous than any forthcoming from his own home or the school at Taunton to which he had been sent as a boarder, apparently for no better reason than that its headmaster was related to a lady who had been a governess in the Gordon family. The veteran General Parker who presided over the Academy at this time had lost a leg at Waterloo, and in later life Gordon would observe that one should "never employ a man minus a limb to be in authority over boys; they are apt to be irritable and unjust." But although this somewhat sweeping generalisation doubtless reflected his youthful impressions of his first commanding officer it is probable that at this time, as indeed at most others, his relations with authority would have been uneasy, even if authority had been represented by an official with the normal complement of limbs. Young Gordon's qualifications for the army, or at any rate, for fighting, were already undeniable, but they hardly seemed likely to render him a model cadet. He possessed hundreds of lead soldiers, it is true, and drilled them for hours on end. And at school at Taunton he had displayed an unusual proficiency, which he retained throughout life, in map-making and drawing. As a child in the Mediterranean at Corfu he had shown himself indifferent to fear. Above all, he came of a family with a long military tradition; his father, grandfather and great-grandfather had all been officers in the British army, and the Gordon tradition of irregular or illicit warfare stretched far back beyond their day into the mists of the ancient Highlands. On the other hand, the years at Woolwich before he entered the Academy himself had shown him to possess boisterous high spirits, and little proper respect for elderly officers and their wives. And there had already been hints of a peculiarly sensitive resentment at the least suspicion of injustice, so that on one occasion, when threatened, as retribution for some *contretemps* for which he considered himself not to blame, with exclusion from a family excursion to Astley's circus in London he had stubbornly insisted, even after the ban had been lifted, and despite fervent entreaties from his mother, on remaining at home. Since army discipline, which is always apt to seem irrational to the neophyte, was particularly irrational in 1848, and since it is on the whole maintained by respect for authority and fear of consequences, the one-legged Commandant, if he knew anything of his neighbour's son, may well have expected trouble.

And trouble there certainly was, more than once all but sufficient to bring the boy's career as a cadet to a sudden and ignominious conclusion. He was awarded numerous good conduct badges, we are told, but from time to time hot temper and resentment at some apparent injustice were too much for him, and there were scenes after which neither senility nor physical disabilities were needed to account for the exasperation of the elderly Commandant. In particular there was the day when for some reason which Gordon considered inadequate the cadets were forbidden to leave their dining hall. A senior corporal, with arms outstretched, had been posted at the head of the narrow stairway which led up to it and the throng of cadets hung back, irritated but obedient, in the doorway. It was more than Gordon could bear. Thrusting his way to the front, he lowered his head and charged. Butted violently in the stomach the unfortunate representative of authority was precipitated head over heels down the stairway, to disappear through the door at its foot with the splintering crash of glass with which Woolwich was by now all too familiar. The corporal was fortunate enough to escape unhurt, but it is hardly surprising that the aggressor narrowly escaped expulsion.

Despite the good conduct badges, scenes of this tempestuous character were frequent enough for an exasperated instructor to exclaim to Gordon, with that lack of prescience which is not uncommon in school reports, that he would never make an officer. In which opinion Gordon's retort, which was to tear the epaulettes from his own shoulders and fling them at his superior's feet, may for the time being have confirmed him. For one at least of the Woolwich staff Gordon however acquired a respect which lasted all his life. Of Eardley Wilmot he would write to his brother Enderby long afterwards, in October, 1875:

Very sorry Wilmot did not get R.M.A. There are few men I ever saw like him. I know no one who [sic] I ever felt more respect for and think few cadets could muster up courage to tell him a lie. Boys have very sharp eyes and I do not think one cadet, however much they feared him, would have wished him ill. He raised the whole morale of the Academy, made what were likely to become blackguards gentlemen and never before or after has the R.M.A. been as it was in his time. And to put a sunflower, Adye, there instead of him! Too honest, too uncompromising, that is his fault. Now F.E.W. (as it used to be on our paper) never favoured me or anyone. He remembers scenes with your brother and Lord Anglesea and Parker and old Lewis R.E. after one of which he said "If I had been the Govr. I would have put you in the Black Hole." I only remember his justness and uprightness and love of truth which we all may have though [we do?] not always stick to it in our youth.

Towards the end of the four years at Woolwich there was an official inquiry into allegations of bullying and in the course of his evidence a newcomer asserted that Charlie Gordon had struck him on the head with a clothes brush. In all likelihood the charge was true, for although Gordon could never have been a bully, almost to the end of his days he would frequently lose his temper, so that his passage through savage lands was marked by a succession of explosions and belabourings which did nothing to diminish his popularity—"the men like my justice, candour, my outbursts of temper," he would write to his sister from the Sudan—while with colleagues and superiors he was constantly involved in what he described as "fearful rows"; and even friends at home, whose affection had been won by his almost feminine gentleness and consideration, would be astounded from time to time as the vivid blue eyes blazed with incomprehensible wrath over a trifle. The episode of the clothes brush resulted in the boy's losing six months' seniority. It was a severe penalty for what had admittedly not been a severe blow, but the harassed Commandant may have been taking into account previous infractions of discipline, for which, it is said, Gordon was always ready to take more than his fair share of blame. And, in any event, the additional term at Woolwich, since it enabled Gordon to pass into the Engineers instead of the Artillery, before long seemed to him to have been a blessing in disguise.

So far there had been little to suggest that Charles Gordon was destined to differ markedly from the conventionally high-spirited and courageous subalterns of whom so many were now maturing in unconscious preparation for the trenches of the Crimea. To the other-worldly convictions which were to dominate his adult life he seems as yet to have been a stranger. At his mother's knee he had already been taught that every word of the Bible is literally true, and from the discourses of Mr. Capel Molyneux, of Holy Trinity Church, Woolwich, " a well-turned-out person who used to ride in the Row," he had learned that every human event has been inexorably preordained from eternity. And these two doctrines would in due course be incorporated in the highly personal creed which was to become the mainspring of his life. But spiritually he would always be a solitary, and although in his early years often influenced by individuals he was too much of a rebel to take kindly to institutions, and for institutional religion as practised by the Gordon family in his childhood he soon conceived a hearty distaste. The regular church-going, the interminable sermons, for which the only compensation was the curtained pews " where you could have made your toilet and no one would have been any the wiser "—to the end of his life he remembered it all with a shudder. " What husks," he would write, " the Evangelical religion is! " He stoutly refused to be confirmed. For one thing, he was now regarded by the respectabilities of Woolwich as a wild young man; he had no intention of reforming; and to be confirmed, he concluded, would be a " useless sin." Moreover, confirmation meant submission to an institution, husks and all. The religion of the institution did not attract him; he had not yet begun to formulate his own.

3

It was not to be long, however, before that absorbing process, or at any rate the prelude to it, commenced. In June, 1852, Gordon had passed out of Woolwich, a second lieutenant in the Royal

Engineers, leaving the Royal Military Academy with few regrets, little general education, a marked proficiency in surveying and a lifelong horror of examinations. At Chatham, the headquarters of the Corps, to which he was posted for nineteen months, he had been regarded as an intelligent and hard-working subaltern. And then in February, 1854, he was ordered to Pembroke Dock to assist, not for the last time, in the construction of a series of useless forts. " All the men here," he reported, " are sporting moustachios, but their growth is stunted at present." Pembroke, like most small military stations, was full of gossip, of which Gordon, who thought it spiteful, strongly disapproved. Indeed, though he liked his Colonel, and received frequent invitations from the Colonel's wife, he cannot have cared much for his new station, for his correspondence in later life is full of sardonic references to the horrors of English social life— the most frightful discomfort in the desert always seemed to him vastly preferable to an English dinner-party—and his social experience was so limited that his diatribes must have been founded to no small extent upon his memories of Pembroke.

At Pembroke he made friends with " a very religious captain of the 11th of the name of Drew." Drew seems to have been an enthusiast with a bent for evangelism. He kept *The Priceless Diamond* on his mantelpiece and had soon lent it to his new friend, and encouraged him to study *The Remains* of the Reverend R. McCheyne and the *Commentaries* of Scott. The young man responded readily to these advances. Simple and enthusiastic himself, he kindled swiftly at genuine enthusiasm in others and possessed a singularly shrewd eye for make-believe. The creed of Captain Drew and *The Priceless Diamond* may have differed little in essentials from that which he had already encountered, with marked distaste, at Woolwich; only, and this ensured the startling contrast in his reception of it, it was doubly personal in character. Personal both as now involving no formal adherence to an institution, and also in that Drew's beliefs were obviously all-engrossing and whole-hearted, colouring his entire life, while the church-going of the Gordon family—always excepting Augusta, now a spinster of thirty-

three much given to studying pious works in her bedroom—had
seemed rather the conventional, if loyal, acceptance of a formal
social tradition. It was hardly to be expected that Gordon would
be satisfied for ever with the teachings of Captain Drew or even
the *Remains* of the Reverend R. McCheyne. Sooner or later, so
powerful were his idiosyncracies, he was bound to require a religion
of his own, constructed by himself. Meanwhile, however, Drew
had fired a train which would lead in due course to explosions
stranger than he could foresee. Meanwhile, too, this first conversion,
for such it must be reckoned, transformed Gordon's whole outlook.
He felt " much happier and more contented " he reported to
Augusta. As he drove about the countryside with Drew in a gig
even Pembroke was transfigured: " now I would not wish for any
prettier place." It was to Augusta that he confided the change. " I
hope," he wrote, " that I have turned over a new leaf, and I should
like you to give me some hope of being received." Did his parents,
he wondered, " think of eternal things? " Could he do or say
anything which would help them to do so? " Dearest Augusta,"
the letter ended, " pray for me, I beg of you." He received his first
Communion that Easter. But he still refused to be confirmed, and
to the end of his life he never joined a Church.

4

But early that year the war with Russia had broken out, and the
young lieutenant's new interests did not prevent him from growing
increasingly anxious to be posted to the Crimea. How to achieve
his ambition was another, and a formidable, question. The
organisation of the British Army had scarcely altered since Waterloo,
and in October, the month in which the battle of Balaclava was
fought and the siege of Sebastopol commenced, and with British
troops beginning to die like flies, the War Office was devoting close
attention to a change in the full-dress uniform of officers, and
issuing a series of meticulous regulations about gold braid and

scarlet waistcoats. Gordon was profoundly irritated. Not that he was as yet critical of the War Office; he was determined, however, to live within his income and it seemed doubtful whether his recently purchased coat could be altered into the newly prescribed tunic. It is hardly surprising that as autumn drew into winter it became obvious that the nation which was teaching industrial organisation to the world was quite incapable of feeding and clothing twenty thousand of its own soldiers six miles distant from the fleet which supplied them.

The Gordon family had by now moved on to Gibraltar, where General Gordon was in command of the Royal Artillery, but Charles's two elder brothers were already in the Crimea and he grew increasingly restive. Even the society of Captain Drew and his wife, " a very stylish person," did not reconcile him to Pembroke Dock, though she was an ardent admirer of Mr. Capel Molyneux and though he actually reported " her hair tho' luxuriant is rather Auburn; I like her very much "—the only occasion, I believe, in the voluminous correspondence of a lifetime in which he commented on the appearance of a woman. But he was impatient, and he even seems, for the first, and last, time in his career, to have tried the effects of a word in season in an influential ear, writing of his eagerness to see active service to Sir John Burgoyne, an old friend of the family who happened at this time to be Inspector General of Fortifications. When, however, at the end of November the impatiently expected communication from the War Office at length arrived it proved to contain nothing more exciting than orders to proceed immediately to Corfu. The exasperated youth at once concluded that his mother, too, must have been turning her more experienced hand to backstairs influence and dashed off an expostulaion to her at Gibraltar. But although Sir John Burgoyne may have moved slowly—and after all, despite the fourteen years of high command which still awaited him he was already seventy-two—he had, it soon transpired, eventually moved, and four days later the orders for Corfu were superseded. Gordon was to leave for the Crimea without delay. Within forty-eight hours he had presented

himself at the War Office, received his instructions and hurried
down to Portsmouth.

The subaltern who eventually left London for Marseilles on
14th December, 1854, somewhat aggrieved that authority had
refused to prepay his overland passage, must still have seemed, to
himself as well as to others, destined for an orthodox, and in all
likelihood a distinguished, military career. The wild spirits of his
boyhood were apparently firmly under control, he had abundantly
proved his professional competence—no one at Chatham or
Pembroke would have dreamt of prophesying that he would never
make an officer—and if he had experienced a religious conversion
it could not be said that there was anything unconventional, or
even unprofessional, about that. For the evangelical tradition, of
Bible in one hand and sword in the other, was still powerful in the
British Army, as the story of the Indian Mutiny would presently
remind the world, and it was particularly powerful among the
Royal Engineers. Of the profound unorthodoxies, both of creed
and conduct, of which this particular young man was capable there
had at Pembroke been little, if any, evidence. It may be that from
time to time the stylish Mrs. Drew had found cause to raise her
eyebrows at some odd twist of theory or unexpected blaze of
indignation, and it is certain that the local ferryman long remembered the young gentleman who, rather than wait for the ferry,
preferred to wade through the river in his clothes. But on the
whole the episode of Pembroke represents an interlude of professional orthodoxy between the powder-barrel of which the elder
Gordons had been so conscious at Woolwich and the unpredictable
adventures which were so soon to follow.

5

He reached Balaclava on New Year's Day, 1855, in the depth of
the frightful winter whose scandals and tragedies swept away both
the old British Army and its Peninsular traditions. But to the

anxious Gordons in Gibraltar his regular weekly letters can have brought no hint of crisis or even of undue discomfort. He notes " roads bad beyond description " and " officers in every conceivable costume foraging for eatables," and mentioned casually that last night two subalterns were frozen to death; but his one serious complaint is the inaction of the rival armies. '' At present we are at a standstill," " we are doing nothing," " still at a standstill "— week after week throughout the first two months he reiterates the ejaculations of impatience. Of the devoted labours of Miss Nightingale amid the inferno of Scutari there is no evidence that he had so much as heard. Even from the front line trenches, which he reached on 17th January, he reported that he could not be more comfortable in England.

Nor was he deliberately softening the tones of the picture for the sake of his anxious relatives. These were undoubtedly his genuine sentiments. When he wrote " I do not think I was ever in better health, and enjoy the work amazingly " he meant, as usual, precisely what he said. He was irritated by the vivid Press accounts of the sufferings of the troops and the incompetence of their commanders which were now horrifying the public at home, and had led, that January, to the fall of Lord Aberdeen's government, and he frequently warned his parents not to believe newspaper reports of conditions at the front. For the officers, he insists, there are no real hardships, and even the trials of the rank and file are largely their own fault, for they were " like children," quite unable to look after themselves, and in this respect compared most unfavourably with the French, whom he had observed on the voyage out cheerfully fending for themselves under conditions which would speedily have provoked a mutiny in a British regiment. It was not unnatural that he should be critical, since he was wholly indifferent to comfort himself. Moreover, he was a born soldier with a natural genius for warfare now rapidly awakening, and it was by no means only in the dilatoriness of its elderly commanders or the inadequacy of its commissariat that the army of the Crimea was all too obviously in need of reform.

As soon as he reached the trenches Gordon noticed with surprise the readiness of his fellow officers to remain under cover while their men were out on working parties, and of the men, thus left to their own devices, to scamp their work. His own first experience of a petty independent command provided ludicrous evidence of the lowered morale of the army. Ordered to supervise the construction of a line of rifle pits in advance of the foremost trenches, he collected with some difficulty eight men and the requisite complement of picks and shovels, and to protect his working party begged ten sentries from the officer in command of the advanced trench, who complained lugubriously that this was his first tour of duty in the neighbourhood. Disdaining to disclose that he was himself equally inexperienced, Gordon led his little party out into the darkness, only to find that by some oversight some caves on one flank of his projected rifle pits had been evacuated. Since there was now a possibility that they might be sheltering enemy snipers he proceeded, not without some misgivings, to explore them " almost alone." When this eerie reconnaissance was safely over he left two of his sentries on the hill above the caves and took two off with him on a détour, to be posted beneath them. No sooner, however, had the three of them worked their way round to their objective than two rifles cracked in the darkness and bullets struck the ground unpleasantly close at hand. The two sentries whom he had brought with him withdrew in a panic, the working party bolted; and the shots proved to have been fired by his own sentries above the caves, who had thereupon themselves fled incontinently back to the trench, leaving their caps behind them. With considerable difficulty Gordon arrested the flight of the working party, led it back and kept it digging all night, a hundred and fifty yards from a Russian picket. But nothing would induce the sentries to leave their trenches again.

It is hardly surprising that Gordon should soon have acquired the reputation of possessing more knowledge of the enemy's movements than anyone else in the trenches before Sebastopol. Moreover, he had soon come to the conclusion that the readiest method of steadying nervous troops was a display of exceptional coolness by himself. Indeed, it is probable that a picturesque refinement of bravado which he was later to make famous had already suggested itself to him. For there was an occasion when, seeing a group of soldiers who had suffered such heavy casualties that they had not so much as a non-commissioned officer left to command them, he leapt into their trench and then, raising his head above the parapet, deliberately exposed himself to the enemy's fire. But he was not only seeking to hearten the soldiers in that particular trench, he was also performing a private act of faith. For it was already his rooted belief that since he was everywhere and always in the hand of God he must be in no greater physical danger when under heavy fire than when reading a newspaper in barracks. No bullet touched him, and henceforth he never faltered in an article of faith which might have been summarised in words from the Gospel of St. Luke, *Be not afraid, only believe.* Moreover, it had chanced that his only weapon at the time was a light cane; and a few years later the memory of the salutary psychological effects of this somewhat theatrical episode prompted the practice which was to make Gordon's Wand of Victory a legend throughout China.

For the rest, he had, as was only to be expected, several narrow escapes—his diary records, during his second month, " struck by a spent ball," an incident not reported to his parents—he was once slightly wounded and took part in the premature and unsuccessful attack on the Redan, of which he sent a critical account to his mother. " *Privately*," he wrote, " I do not think our troops behaved as they ought to have done; and I believe they say the trenches were too high to get over. Now as the scaling ladders were carried over them this cannot be true." The rigours of the campaign he sustained in perfect health and with unflagging cheerfulness to the end. Indeed, as he frankly admitted, he enjoyed the whole affair thoroughly. Was he not after all steadily discovering his own powers? And not merely the undoubted professional competence of a lieutenant of Engineers; for there were signs that obscurer instincts were awakening. He had realised, he told his parents, that there must always be " something indescribably exciting in war." And when from time to time he would explain how in his opinion some particularly costly reverse might have been avoided by the elderly generals it was always of their timidity that he complained.

Nevertheless, to his companions in the trenches, and indeed to himself, he still appeared a normal Sapper subaltern, now firmly established on the lower rungs of a normal professional career. Certainly he could still cherish normal professional ambitions. He could even explain, in response to anxious inquiries from home, that professionally there was nothing to be gained by " volunteering," and that he certainly did not intend to volunteer. In this instance no doubt he may have been prompted by a pardonable desire to reassure his parents, but this was almost the last occasion on which, coming from him, reassurances of this particular kind could be taken seriously. And there had been an ambiguous sentence in a letter written from Constantinople on his way out to the Crimea. The Duke of Cambridge was in the town, and Gordon reported that he had asked a friend " to mention to the Duke who I was and that I had asked after him." The two had met when Gordon was a child in Corfu, and in all probability, although it is not customary for travelling subalterns to convey informal greetings to royal personages, the ingenuous youth intended no more than a gesture of friendly courtesy. And if recent memories of Sir John Burgoyne's assistance inspired any fleeting visions of further and more august influence, now as then it was assuredly not of promotion that he was thinking.

In short, an unusually daring and, beneath the high spirits, an unusually serious subaltern, but in other respects to all appearances not markedly differing from his fellows. Certainly none of them would have guessed that (as he would confess towards the end of his life) this young man had wished, at fourteen, that he was a eunuch, and had set out for the Crimea hoping to be killed. Young Garnet Wolseley, the future Field Marshal, who formed in the trenches before Sebastopol what was to prove a lifelong admiration for Gordon, had, it is true, already noted that the strangely vivid blue eyes " seemed to court something, while at the same time they searched the inner soul "; but precisely what they courted perhaps not even Gordon himself yet knew. He had not yet consciously begun to frame his strange private theology. And amid the distractions of active service the example of Captain Drew had receded from the forefront of his consciousness. During his journey out from England he was still adding the cautionary " D.V." to the not very hazardous prophecy that his party expected to leave Marseilles next Monday; and three weeks later, newly arrived at Balaclava, he had been careful, when reassuring his parents as to his brother's probable safety, to interject the deprecatory parenthesis " so far as we short-sighted creatures can see." But there are no further reminders from the Crimea of the uncertainty of human calculations, and certainly no signs of the attempt, proposed at Pembroke, to encourage his parents to " think of eternal things." He records with satisfaction that Captain Craigie, killed, " by what is called chance," by a shell-burst, was " a serious man," and that Murray, who fell in the attack on the Redan, was " well prepared." And he deplores the lack of " a good working clergyman." When he reports the death of Lord Raglan, worn out by responsibilities and misfortunes, ten days after the unsuccessful attack on the Redan, he hopes that he, too, was prepared, adding cautiously " but I do not know."

His trench diary (preserved among the Freese papers) is a staccato professional record, of bombardments, trench-raids and the ceaseless drawing of plans. There are one or two references to rain, but none whatever to cold or any sort of discomfort. Casualty totals are faithfully recorded and when he mentions the death of a friend he usually writes of " poor " so-and-so—an epithet which he would have disavowed in later life when the belief that death should be the summit of human ambition had become second nature to him. He records his attendance at a surprising number of funerals and a good many services and church parades, but there are only two entries which betray any preoccupation with religion. The first appears on the 7th/8th April, 1855.

Worked at plan. Rode in afternoon to Inkermann and evening

trenches with Hassard. In spite of salvoes of grape noone touched. Worked very hard at 29 Pr Battery and finished it, working from 8 to ½ past 5. Came up and laid down for two hours, got up, read and partook of the Blessed Communion (God grant it may be beneficial to me and keep me from sin).

And a mysterious entry, undated but probably written on the 1st or 2nd of February, 1856, suggests that he may have been keeping a private record of services attended: " Memo. To ask at Pall Mall about service in trenches on 18th June, 1855, in record of services."

But the principal diversifications of trench routine are an occasional ride, a meeting or meal with one of his brothers, Henry or Enderby, or attendance at an auction of the belongings of a dead comrade. Occasionally an unusually varied day expands the scale of an entry. As on 26th March, 1855:

Rode to Balaklava. Saw Henry and Enderby. Very hot. Races going on. Evening on duty in the trenches. Went down to advance to see work for the night. Captn Hill, 89th, left me to post his sentries. Fired on by Rn picket, struck and left by men. Went out for him after, but found only his coat. Constant alarms. Fired on working party with grape from Redan and shot from Creek.

But only once or twice does a trench episode impress him so vividly that he fills three pages of his pocket diary, and then characteristically there is no mention of himself.

Last night the Rns made a sortie on Right and Left Attacks and French Lines near [?] Took our lines by surprise. Montagu prisoner and 1 sergt and 1 man. 57th driven back after a time with a loss of 10 dead left and 1 wounded prisoner. The officer was killed. Our loss was 6 killed and 10 wounded. They killed a man wounded of the 57th stabbing him in the stomach 15 times. Came as far as No 6 Brigade. . . . On the right they were

led by an Albanian who came over the trench saying Bono
Francese. He killed Captain Brown and was shot himself. 35 £
on his person. Major Gordon was cut off with his party and cut
his way back; he was struck in the arm with a bullet severely.
The Rns got up to our 29prs and had not Col. Tylden been
coming in they would have been taken. He charged them and
drove them out. Our loss was Colonel Kelly, Captn Brown,
Vicars and Lt Jourdan killed and 7 officers wounded. The Rns
left 3 officers and 70 men in our trenches and many more were
taken away by them. . . . The French lost 200 in their attack;
two Zuaves [*sic*] were on the edge of the Mamelon. The Rns
must have suffered fearfully; the officer who led the Attack on
the Left stood on the parapet for some time amid a storm of
bullets; he was at last knocked over. A man of the 57th killed
a Rn who came round the corner by a bayonet in the head. . . .
They took away some of our tools and pulled down some of
our parapet. Ld Raglan and Jones came in the trenches when I
was on duty.

But in general the lengthy letters which he posted so regularly
to his parents were filled with just such detailed accounts of the
fighting and minor incidents of trench life as, in an army which
had not yet invented the military censorship, scores of other young
officers must have been composing. He displays, it is true, a constant
anxiety to spare his family expense, insisting that he needs no money
and that eight pounds a month will cover all his needs, and repeatedly imploring them to spare him the parcels of " comforts "
which it had become fashionable to dispatch to the Crimea. Let
their parcels go to his brothers if they please, comfortable though
he has repeatedly reported them to be, but not to him. Almost his
only reported wants are a new forage cap, a map of the Crimea and
a bottle of Rowland's Odonto, and of these, he reiterates with
urgent underlinings, he must, he positively must, be told the price.

There is a notable absence of self-dramatisation too about these
letters. The fighting he describes with matter-of-fact detachment,

almost as though he were a war correspondent rather than a partici-
pant. The sketches and photographs, which he sends home, he
warns his family sternly are for their private entertainment only,
they are not to be *exhibited*; such comments as he vouchsafes they
must not *publish*. At this time he seldom underlined, and the
explosion into italics, repeated at an interval of less than two months,
marks the gradual growth of an almost morbid dread of notoriety,
counterpart of that profound instinct for quietism, with which in his
divided nature an intermittent but powerful craving for public
action and public applause would wage lifelong conflict.

The siege ended at last in a striking display of pyrotechnics, as
the retreating Russians set fire to the town and blew up their forts
and ammunition dumps. At home some politicians had already
begun to wonder whether in the Crimean war we might not have
backed the wrong horse, but Gordon felt no such misgivings as,
roused from his tent at four in the morning by the sound of the
explosions, he watched the burning town, " a splendid sight," from
the front line trenches. By nature he was far from sensitive to
aesthetic impressions—of Athens he had only reported that it was
" very ugly and dirty," and though he admitted that the Acropolis
was " a beautiful ruin " the interior of Santa Sophia would strike
him merely as vaguely resembling St. Paul's, albeit " more em-
blazoned." But this morning he specially noted the majesty of the
sunrise over the blazing city. It was not of the end of the war that
he was thinking. For himself he was by no means eager for peace.
The British Army after all had yet to redeem its failure before the
Redan and war, he now realised, he could not help enjoying for its
own sake. That war was often horrible, he knew well enough—
that very morning he would find the unburied dead in the trenches of
the Redan a " dreadful sight "—but to the moral problems which to
some it seemed to involve he gave as little thought as to its dangers.
For though his long theological broodings had hardly yet begun he
had not forgotten the teachings of Mr. Molyneux of Woolwich, and
did not doubt that every human event had been ordained by
Providence from the beginning of time. And since both the out-

break of war and every casualty in it had therefore presumably long since been willed by the Almighty there seemed little purpose in concerning himself over either its possible futility or his own fortunes in it.

For a short while Gordon was busy on a survey of the abandoned Russian defences, in the intervals of which he searched the flea-infested litter for "knick-knacks" to send home. After a brief interlude of service with the expedition which captured Kimburn he returned to Sebastopol towards the end of 1855 and spent four months on the systematic destruction of its docks, arsenals and forts. By February, 1856, the Black Sea port had been adequately reduced to ruins, and in the following month the Crimean war officially came to an end. In the shower of decorations and promotions which had already commenced a sapper subaltern in 1856 could expect no share. In accordance with ancient army tradition this manna was reserved for those who, whatever their own qualifications, possessed the one indispensable qualification, seniority. But Gordon was cited in the list of Engineer subalterns who had specially distinguished themselves, and received the French Legion of Honour.

He was not disappointed, for from Whitehall he had expected nothing. In the previous August he had permitted himself a sardonic comment: " I am not ambitious, but what easily earned C.B.'s and majorities there have been in some cases." But in January, as if anxious to make sure that his parents did not mis-understand him, he returned to the subject with one of his still infrequent underlinings: " *remember, I do not think* it is a hard case that we, the subs, do not get anything." " I am not ambitious; " in a few years' time the words would be as unquestionable a state-ment of the simple truth about Gordon's attitude to his profession as any unqualified assertion about a complex character can be, for in a few years' time he would not only be convinced that all worldly ambition is evil but would have ceased to take any interest in the prospect of a conventional army career. At the moment, however, he was at least sufficiently interested in C.B.'s and majorities to comment on them. And during the next two years he would inquire from time to time whether there was any news of the Engineers being divided into civil and military sections, whether a staff corps was to be formed, and whether his parents had observed how, with the relentless lapse of time, his name was " creeping up the list of lieutenants." But no opportunity to join the staff corps offered itself, and even if it had, Gordon would never have allowed himself to be absorbed for long in a conventional career. And as it chanced, his next years were to be spent in a manner which would make a conventional career more improbable than ever.

6

Almost the whole of the next two and a half years he spent in the wilds, helping to survey the new frontiers established by the Peace of Paris. For close on twelve months from May, 1856, he was with Colonel Stanton in Bessarabia. In the previous year the newly completed telegraph line between Constantinople and London had been " thrown open to officers at £1 12s. 6d. per message " and, on his return from Bessarabia, Gordon made use of the strange new device to beg to be released from the forthcoming survey of the Armenian boundary. He received a four-word reply, *Lieutenant Gordon must go*, the confident and peremptory character of which dignitaries of the War Office engaged in correspondence with Gordon in later years, if they chanced upon it in the files, must have regarded with retrospective astonishment and envy.

There followed five months in the Armenian highlands, and then, after an autumn and winter in England, six months in the Caucasus. The scene shifted, but whether in Bessarabia, Armenia or Caucasus the routine seldom varied—the yard by yard examination of a desolate countryside, the camping under the stars, the setting up of trigonometrical pyramids which as often as not the primitive inhabitants would speedily remove, the spectacle of the Turkish Commissioner providing himself with transport by the simple process of summarily commandeering the horses of every caravan he met, the preparation of countless plans, and above all, for the rôle of peacemaker did not come naturally to Gordon, the constant struggle to prevent the Russian and Turkish commissioners from flying at each others' throats. It was a strenuous and often a monotonous life, and though Gordon, as was his custom, scarcely noticed its discomforts, he had not yet thought it necessary to discipline himself into complete indifference to food. A few years later in England he would be making a meal off a stale loaf of bread soaked in a slop-bowl of strong tea with the remark that in half an hour it would make no difference what he had eaten, but in Armenia or the Caucasus he could still occasionally comment on food and drink, on the execrable quality of Russian wine and the remarkable vulgarity of Russian manners. He even sighed for partridge shooting and took a gun in an occasional wolf hunt. But what to some young subalterns might have seemed a major inconvenience of this period of exile, the lack of all civilised society, was to Gordon a positive attraction. Although he noted, as evidence of Russian boorishness, that the Governor of Bessarabia thought he was doing adequate courtesy to the Commissioners by inviting them to tea, and subsequently charging the French delegate six shillings and eightpence for the cards with which they had played whist, he added in parenthesis that he would certainly not have been there himself had there been company present.

It was impossible, however, not to accept when invited to remain to dinner after the official interview at which he handed over the Bessarabian plans to Lord Stratford de Redcliffe, and that autocratic diplomat characteristically observed that he only wished the allies had insisted on seizing the entire province. Nor could he altogether avoid the unwelcome hospitality of the Princes of the Caucasus. It was, however, some consolation to reflect that almost everybody in the Caucasus appeared to be either a Prince or a Princess, and that the Princes were more than ready to accept small gratuities. A visit to the humble and by no means cleanly dwellings of these aristocratic hosts could perhaps hardly be reckoned as a social occasion, particularly since it was always advisable to carry food concealed in one's own pockets. Nevertheless, it was not without some compunction that Gordon reported that his hand was "sticky with shaking hands with so many Princes." And one in particular of the social traditions of the Caucasus caused him repeated embarrassment.

> I am always in fear and trembling lest they should give me anything, as it is necessary to give in return. I, unfortunately, happened to notice a certain letterweight with the Queen on it, and observed that it was like Her Majesty. I was given it on the spot, and with deep regret had to part with my soda-water machine the next day. I admire nothing now, you may be sure.

The lack of feminine society he was far from regretting, for he had already made up his mind that he would never marry. When thrown perforce into social contact with two specimens of the typical English Miss during his return voyage to the Near East in the spring of 1858 he noted the susceptibility to sea-sickness of one and the conventional chatter of the other. She would, he sardonically supposed, "come under the denomination of a very nice, agreeable person;" but it was only too obvious that he and she had no interests whatever in common. As for the ladies of the Caucasus, they were beautiful enough, but their habits were far from dainty, and what with the secret cache of food in one's own pockets, and the constant anxiety not to provoke complications by admiring one's hostess's possessions, it would in any case have been difficult to indulge romantic sentiment. But it was not merely that Gordon found no enchantment in these particular ladies. Women in general, did not attract him; and although with young men the vow of celibacy is often enough an immediate precursor of the wedding bells, to the end of his days Gordon would usually persist in maintaining the curious view that, not only for himself but for most men, marriage is a mistake.

He was equally insensitive to the romantic scenes among which his arduous duties were performed. The wooded banks of the river

Sereth, the Armenian villages with their square, loopholed towers, the carved ceiling of the council chamber in the monastery of Etchmiadzin, the sudden glimpse of the sacred ibis strutting majestic along a ridge of snow, he noted them all, as he noted that he had slid three thousand feet down a steep snow slope on Mount Ararat in less than two minutes, but they did not touch his emotions or stir his curiosity. Even the Armenian church, whose sacred relics positively included a fragment of Noah's Ark, failed to rouse his interest. There would come a time when every detail of the Flood would rouse him to passionate interest, when he would devote days of laborious study to the topography of the Garden of Eden, but just now his mind was not running on theology or the Bible, and his letters home contained only one D.V.

Nevertheless, the sojourn in the wilderness had set its mark upon him. The solitude of these remote borderlands had touched his imagination. Henceforth the mystic in him would always hanker for the lonely places, although the man of action, in perpetual conflict with the mystic, would usually ensure that solitude was not accompanied by leisure for contemplation. Moreover, he had made his first acquaintance with primitive peoples, and had conceived an instant liking for them. The wild Kurdish tribesmen, he noted, " I should not mind trusting at all." And perhaps the strange power which he would exercise over the equally savage peoples whom he was to encounter in many different parts of the world rested in the last resort upon the simple fact that they invariably aroused the same sentiment in him: unlike so many Europeans he did not mind trusting them. His wiry frame seemed impervious to sickness and almost incapable of fatigue. In the autumn of 1857 all the other British officers fell ill for some weeks, but Gordon's health remained as robust as ever. And after the last yard of boundary had been determined, the last princely hand shaken and the last quarrel among his colleagues accommodated, on the eve of returning home he wrote to his parents that " I do not feel at all inclined to settle in England and be employed in any sedentary way." They did not know that he was in correspondence with a Colonel Biddulph, who was in charge of the construction of a telegraph line for the Turkish Government at Baghdad, about an appointment there, but it is unlikely that the warning occasioned them much surprise.

Gordon reached home in good time for the Christmas of 1858. The appointment under Biddulph did not materialise and on 1st April, 1859, he was gazetted captain, and in the following month was appointed adjutant at the headquarters of the Royal Engineers at Chatham, a post generally supposed to mark its occupant out for rapid promotion. His commanding officer wrote to Gordon's father of his delight at the promotion of " that estimable and deserving son of yours. . . . In all the attributes of life he is a first-rate fellow— soldier and son. Long may he be a blessing to you and an ornament to the Service." But though Gordon's professional ambitions were still strong his determination not " to settle in England and be employed in any sedentary way " was a good deal stronger, and a few weeks later he volunteered for active service in the desultory war with China which had just flared up again after the failure of the Chinese to ratify the treaty of Tientsin.

BOOK TWO

WAND OF VICTORY

A<small>T</small> <small>TWENTY-SIX</small>, and indeed throughout his life, Gordon was
slight and wiry. He was five feet nine inches in height, and to
all who met him conveyed an immediate impression of tireless
nervous energy. In conversation among congenial companions he
would pace up and down the room, lighting cigarette after cigarette,
with occasional pauses to emphasise a point by laying his hand on
the arm of a listener, or to eye him searchingly as if to judge whether
he was following the argument with sympathy. On less intimate
occasions his conversation was terse and decisive. "When his mind
was made up on a matter it never seemed to occur to him that there
could be anything more to say about it." His hair was brown and
curly, and he wore a small moustache; the inconspicuous line of
whisker from ear to jaw, which can be seen, for example, in Lady
Abercromby's slightly later drawing of him, now in the National
Portrait Gallery, he did not as yet affect. His jaw was noticeably
square, and the tone of his speaking voice singularly sweet and
gentle. In general, his bearing was modest, if not diffident, and
strangers were apt to take him for a kindly and unassuming civilian.
Indeed at a casual meeting he would have been unlikely to attract
attention or interest, had it not been for his smile, which was
' sweet beyond description "—and for the one feature which none
who met him ever forgot.

Every recorded description of Gordon dwells upon his eyes.
Already in the Crimea Garnet Wolseley had noticed that they

" searched the inner soul." " Light blue and fearless," wrote an officer who served with Gordon in China. Mr. Lilley, who knew him, a few years later, in Gravesend wrote of the

> clear blue eye, which seemed to possess a magical power over all who came within its influence. It read you through and through; it made it impossible for you to tell him anything but the truth. . . . From its glance you knew at once that at any risk he would keep his promise, that you might trust him with anything and everything, and that he would stand by you if all other friends deserted you.

Mr. Stannard, who also knew Gordon at Gravesend, formed a slightly different impression.

> The next moment I was looking into Chinese Gordon's eyes. What eyes they were! Keen and clear, filled with the beauty of holiness, bright with an unnatural brightness, their expression one of settled feverishness, the colour blue-grey as is the sky on a bitter March morning.

Capsune, a Sudanese child, whom Gordon rescued from a slave convoy and had educated in England, gave an account of his first impressions which helps to explain Gordon's extraordinary influence over primitive peoples. " He had eyes very blue," said Capsune, " very bright, and I frightened when I see eyes; I think I finished to-day." And later the child asked the English lady to whose care Gordon had consigned him whether the General's eyes were still blue and could still see through him. He was sure, he added, that Gordon could see in the dark, because " he had the light inside him."

Sir Richard Burton, the explorer of Arabia, wrote, after a meeting with Gordon in 1880:

> I was astonished to find how unlike were all his portraits. No photograph had represented those calm, benevolent blue eyes

and that modest, reserved and even shy expression, blent with simple dignity, which, where he was intimate, changed to the sympathetic frankness of a child's face.

And Sir Gerald Graham, who had been a fellow cadet with Gordon at Woolwich, had served with him in the Crimea and China, and would be almost the last Englishman to see him alive, wrote that

> The force and beauty of Gordon's whole expression came from within, and as it were indicated the man, the steady, truthful gaze of the blue-grey eyes seeming a direct appeal from the upright spirit within.

And yet, the piercing eyes were colour-blind and Gordon could only distinguish one postage stamp from another by means of the numeral printed on it.

But the most vivid picture of this contrast between the un-assuming bearing and the searching and magnetic gaze, as of a lion-tamer turned saint, is contained in the private papers of Mrs. Freese. At her first meeting with Gordon, in the summer of 1867, she would have no idea that he was a remarkable man or had dis-tinguished himself in any way: " yet there was that about his conversation and about his penetrating, yet quiet, calm eye that made me feel at once he was no ordinary man; to me, it was an enigma to harmonise these with his extreme simplicity and almost boyishness of address and his unpretending appearance altogether." And again:

> Almost boyish in his appearance and in *some* of his utterances, yet with an eye and an expression that might have lived 1000 years—I felt he was no ordinary man. But though listening to and watching him all the evening, I was obliged to bid him good night and to let him go feeling that he was an unsolved problem and only hoping he would come soon again that we might unravel him and understand the mystery.

2

It was on 22nd July, 1860, that Gordon set out for the country in which destiny would finally commit him to becoming both lion-tamer and saint. In Paris he saw the sights with Colonel Besson, who had been French Commissioner in Bessarabia—and commented unfavourably on the Louvre. During the sea passage out from Marseilles a young steward, named Kirkham, was accused of theft by a passenger, and Gordon, who was always ready to help those in trouble, and particularly young men or boys in trouble, at once repaid the stolen money and arranged with the captain that Kirkham should become his personal servant during the voyage. Fourteen years later he narrowly missed encountering this man in Cairo. Kirkham, he was told, had been seen drunk in Shepheard's Hotel. He was wearing gorgeous uniform and claimed to be Ambassador and Plenipotentiary of King Johannes of Abyssinia, and to be on his way to London bearing an offer of marriage to Queen Victoria.

At Hongkong, which Gordon reached in the second week of September, he learned of the capture of the Taku forts near Peking, which, a year before, had beaten off an Anglo-French force. " I am rather late for the amusement," he wrote home, adding that this news would doubtless not " vex my mother." On 17th September he landed at Shanghai, and in the basketfuls of recently decapitated human heads suspended from its walls obtained his first glimpse of the nature of Chinese warfare. These were the remains of some of the so-called Taiping rebels who, a month earlier, had been driven from Shanghai by British troops, and it struck Gordon as odd that while, in the neighbourhood of Peking, the Anglo-French force which he was on his way to join was engaged in chastising the Emperor of China, here in Shanghai a British force should have come to his aid by repelling these formidable rebels against imperial authority. That in two and a half years' time he would find himself in supreme command of the army commissioned by the Emperor to crush this same rebellion he could not yet guess. At least, however, he had already realised that the Taipings scarcely deserved the sympathy which in the age of Palmerston and Gladstone the British public was only too ready to lavish upon any rebellion anywhere.

For the present, however, the Taipings were not Gordon's concern. After three days in Shanghai he left for Tientsin, which he reached a few days after the Chinese army had been defeated before Peking by the Anglo-French forces. The brief campaign was virtually at an end. It was the third of our small Chinese wars since the accession of Queen Victoria, and all had been fought for security for British trade, including trade in opium. In 1860 as in 1858 the French were our allies, for though Napoleon III was not much concerned for French trade with China he was anxious to win favour with the Church by protecting French missions, and was never averse to acquiring a little cheap military glory. The retreating Chinese had carried off with them some Allied envoys and refused to give them up. The Allied army, therefore, marched upon the capital, and Gordon, who had moved up with the contingent from Tientsin, to join it, found himself encamped under the walls of Peking on the evening of 6th October. During the interval of negotiation which followed, he seized the chance of visiting the celebrated Summer Palace of the Emperors, so soon to earn a wider notoriety. The palace, whose grounds extended for several square miles and contained more than two hundred summer houses, was a building of great beauty and a treasure-house of exquisite works of art. It was now occupied by French troops, and Gordon, who, as we have seen, was not particularly sensitive to aesthetic impressions, was equally astounded at the magnificence of the palace and the vandalism of the French. " You would scarcely conceive," he wrote,

the magnificence of this residence or the tremendous devastation the French have committed. The throne-room was lined with ebony, carved in a marvellous way. There were huge mirrors of all shapes and kinds, clocks, watches, musical boxes with puppets on them, magnificent china of every description, heaps and heaps of silks of all colours, embroidery, and as much splendour and civilisation as you would see at Windsor; carved ivory screens, large amounts of treasure, etc. The French have smashed everything in the most wanton way. . . . There were carts after carts of silks taken away. . . .

Meanwhile all save four of the prisoners had been surrendered by the Chinese, but it was learnt that these four, all Englishmen, had been tortured to death. The British ambassador, Lord Elgin, thereupon decided to destroy the Summer Palace, in which the worst atrocities had been committed. It was the Chinese ruling caste from which he wished to exact retribution, and the burden of a financial indemnity, the time-honoured alternative, would fall not upon the ruling caste but upon the masses. The palace, moreover, had already been extensively looted by the French before it was destroyed. There was thus a good deal more to be said for Lord Elgin than has usually been allowed for by his critics. It was nevertheless, to say the least of it, an injudicious method of signalising the triumph of Western civilisation; and though Gordon cared little for works of art as such, his conscience pricked him as perforce he played his part in the holocaust. " Owing to the ill-treatment the prisoners experienced at the Summer Palace," he wrote home,

the General ordered it to be destroyed, and stuck up proclamations to say why it was so ordered. We accordingly went out, and, after pillaging it, burned the whole place, destroying in a vandal-like manner most valuable property which would not be replaced for four millions. We got upwards of £48 a-piece prize money before we went out here; and although I have not as much as many, I have done well. Imagine D—— giving sixteen shillings for a string of pearls, which he sold the next day for £500!

The people are civil, but I think the grandees hate us, as they must after what we did to the Palace. You can scarcely imagine the beauty and magnificence of the places we burnt. It made one's heart sore to burn them; in fact, these palaces were so large, and we were so pressed for time, that we could not plunder them carefully. Quantities of gold ornaments were burnt, considered as brass. It was wretchedly demoralising work for an army. Everybody was wild for plunder.

"It was wretchedly demoralising work for any army;" this was the dominant impression left upon his mind; and when he came to command Chinese troops himself he would sternly forbid plunder of any kind.

Six days after this conflagration the treaty of peace was signed, and for eighteen months from November, 1860, Gordon was employed on engineering duties, with the force under General Staveley at Tientsin. General Staveley was his brother-in-law and Gordon noted that, though " you will understand me when I say he is careful of No. 1," I get on very well with him." But it was annoying that his brother-in-law should be his commanding officer, for he soon heard that his brother Henry, almost as a matter of course, had put in a word for him at headquarters. Henry had but obeyed a time-honoured convention, but it was a convention of which Charles Gordon fiercely disapproved. He at once marched off and explained to the disconcerted General that he refused to benefit by backstairs influence. "It is the bother of one's life," he wrote home, " to be trying after the honours of the profession, and it has grown in late years into a regular trade—everyone uses private interest." His motives, no doubt, were mixed. His delicate sense of honour recoiled from personal intrigue; moreover, he had always disliked being praised—he once tore up one of his Crimean sketches after finding his mother proudly displaying it to some friends. And for worldly ambition he already felt something of that mixture of fascination and horror with which a Puritan conscious of a hereditary craving for drink might regard a bottle of whisky. On the whole, he enjoyed himself in Tientsin, for he had a responsible command. "It is a grand thing being one's own master," he wrote, and the words will serve as a key, one of the keys, to his subsequent career.

And there were occasional distractions. Gordon was already concerned for the poor, and at Tientsin he undertook the management of a charitable fund collected for the distressed Chinese of the neighbourhood. Characteristically assuming that the local mandarins would understand and approve the technique of Anglican charity, the sponsors of the fund invited them to select and issue tickets to " the most deserving " of the poor, and when the bewildered grandees not unnaturally declined, themselves fixed a day for a public distribution of cash. On the appointed date three thousand would-be beneficiaries assembled—Gordon spoke of them disapprovingly as " beggars "—and in the crush seven women and a boy were trampled to death. For the rest of his life Gordon's charities were almost invariably private and surreptitious.

3

In the following spring Gordon succumbed to a mild attack of smallpox. He was very seldom unwell, and the unfamiliar experience, or perhaps the enforced leisure, set him thinking seriously again of the religious convictions which had come to him seven years ago at Pembroke, and of which, it was now borne in upon him, he had been too forgetful since. " I hope," he had told Augusta from Pembroke in 1854, " that I have turned over a new leaf," but in 1860 he could write to her of a religiously minded general, " Sir H. Grant is one of yours." In 1862 it was again to Augusta that he confided his new resolve. " I am glad to say," he writes on 15th March, " that this disease has brought me back to my Saviour, and I trust in future to be a better Christian than I have been hitherto. I had a capital friend in the Chaplain, a Mr. Beech, who has been excessively kind." Was this a second conversion? Hardly, for among the Freese papers is a sheet of letter-paper, in Gordon's hand, signed by him and dated 1868, headed " My experience showing the order in which God revealed Himself to me." In it he records sixteen distinct stages in what he evidently regarded as a progressive enlightenment. Only the first three contain any indication of chronology, but at least they make it clear that in 1868 he did not regard the year 1862 as a landmark. It was not till after 1865, he makes it clear, that he was " established; " the crucial conclusion that " His service should be all " would come after his father's death in that year. And this is confirmed by one of the fragmentary notes left by Augusta. Her brother often told her, she says, of the effect on him of his father's painful illness and death—after which he " shut himself up at Gravesend and came out another man." Moreover, it is evident from the Freese correspondence that after becoming " established " he looked back on a period of comparative darkness between his first conversion and his father's death. " My only treasure . . ." he would write in May, 1868, " is greatly enhanced in value to me who lost it for so many years." The smallpox, and the leisure for reflection, doubtless revived vivid memories of the first spiritual ardours of 1854, as well perhaps as " deep depression " at his subsequent backsliding. But he was not " established." And in such of his letters and memoranda as have survived from the two years of incessant fighting which now lay ahead of him, although the letters D.V. begin to reappear, there is no sign, as there would be almost continuously thereafter, of any persistent preoccupation with the mysteries.

4

Towards the end of the following month General Staveley despatched some of the British troops from Tientsin to reinforce the garrison of Shanghai, and Gordon, now recovered, left with them in command of his detachment of Engineers. He reached Shanghai on 3rd May, 1863, and in less than a week was in action against the so-called Taiping rebels. From now on all Gordon's campaigns, whether in Africa or China, would be waged against foes who resembled him in their fanatical devotion to a religious creed, and although the creed of the Taipings was extravagant and macabre in the extreme they may perhaps be said to have possessed the further resemblance that they had fabricated it for themselves. In his youth Hung-sen-Tsuen, their leader, had received some instruction from English and Armenian missionaries. Not long after his failure in a competitive examination for the Civil Service he had founded a religious sect, and proclaimed to his converts that having been caught up to heaven in a trance he had there learned that he was the Younger Brother of Jesus, and had received from God the Father a sword, a seal and a volume of celestial decrees. Thus equipped, he assumed the title of Tien Wang, or Heavenly King, and, proclaiming, like so many despots before and since, the coming reign of the Great Peace or Taiping, proceeded to turn his divine status to political and military ends. A characteristic edict announced that

The Heavenly Father sits on the throne above.

The Heavenly Brother Christ is the next honourable, sitting on the right of the Father, excelled by no man.

By the grace of the Father and Brother we sit on his left. United as one we reign.

Disobey the Heavenly Will and you will be ground to pieces with a pestle.

The last of these assertions at any rate he was soon in a position to substantiate, and the advance of the Taiping hordes was marked by atrocious cruelties. At the capture of Nanking they put to the sword the entire Manchu colony, whose numbers have been reckoned as high as twenty-eight thousand; they burned and plundered indiscriminately and it was their custom to crucify prisoners of war, to pound them to death or to flay them alive. Gordon was always ready to sympathise with the oppressed and he felt strongly as to the sufferings of the peasants. "Words cannot express the horrors these people suffer from the rebels," he wrote, " or the utter desert they have made of this rich province. It is all very well to talk of non-intervention; and I am not particularly sensitive, nor are our soldiers generally so; but certainly we are all impressed with the utter misery and wretchedness of these poor people." The Taipings, however, were indisputably rebels against their legitimate rulers, the Manchu Emperors, and as such Lord Palmerston's government, in which Mr. Gladstone was Chancellor of the Exchequer, was for long disposed to regard them, as Mr. Gladstone would later regard the dervish hordes which devastated the Sudan, with all the benevolence due to a people rightly struggling to be free.

At no time had the resistance of the Imperial forces to the rebels been particularly energetic and of late they had been drawn off to oppose the advance of the allied armies on Peking. Meanwhile, the Taipings had swarmed northward from the south into the rich middle provinces. Nanking, Soochow, and scores of lesser cities had fallen before them, and with the wide delta of the Yang-tze-Kiang and numerous seaports under their control they were now able to purchase arms from British and other foreign traders. As soon as peace had been concluded with the European invaders the Emperor and his advisers were able to direct their not very formidable armies once more against the rebels. Their prospects would have been dubious at best, had not a fortunate accident now brought the Europeans, against whom they had so lately been fighting, to their assistance. For in 1860 the Heavenly King and his hordes were threatening the European trading centre of Shanghai. At the beginning of 1861 the British, who had just completed their own brief campaign against the Emperor, had been able to extort from the rebel chief a promise that for a year at least he would not approach within thirty miles of Shanghai, but before long its leading citizens began to suspect that another attack was imminent. Accordingly, judging their small garrison of French and Indian troops to be inadequate, they had invited an American adventurer, named Ward, to raise and train a force of Chinese, to which, as a stimulus to recruiting, they assigned the optimistic title of The Ever Victorious Army. By December of 1861 the rebels had captured two important towns each about ten miles distant from Shanghai, and the

Heavenly King declined to prolong the year's immunity promised
to Shanghai. By January, 1862, the rebels were within gunshot of
the city. In default of authority from the remote Minister in Peking,
and the still more remote authorities in London, the British Admiral
assumed responsibility for repelling the rebels by force, and some
successful minor operations were conducted by naval detachments,
and later, after General Staveley's arrival in April, by British
troops.

When Gordon reached Shanghai on 3rd May, Kahding, near the
northern limit of the former thirty-mile periphery, had just been
captured, and Staveley's next objective was Tsingpu on its western
boundary. Gordon was in command of the small detachment of
Engineers, and his conduct in the ensuing action made an indelible
impression upon Staveley. Before the attack, the two reconnoitred
the town, which was entirely surrounded by a creek, in a boat, and
Gordon, who had learned in the Crimea that accurate reconnaissance
saves lives, begged to be allowed to land. Not without some misgivings the General gave his permission and was astonished to see
how liberally it was interpreted. " To my dismay," he wrote,

> I saw him gradually going near and nearer, by rushes from
> cover to cover, until he got behind a small outlying pagoda
> within 100 yards of the wall, and here he was quietly making a
> sketch and taking notes. I, in the meantime, was shouting myself
> hoarse in trying to get him back, for not only were the rebels
> firing at him from the walls, but I saw a party stealing round to
> cut him off.

In the subsequent attack which, thanks to this detailed reconnaissance, was a triumphant and almost bloodless success, the crossing
of the moats, and the escalading of the walls by the ladder-parties,
were directed by Gordon with almost unnatural coolness.

This and other successes had all but cleared the thirty-mile radius
when the defeat of an Imperialist army opened the way for a new
advance on Shanghai by the rebels. And on 20th September, Ward,

the commander of the Ever Victorious Army, was mortally wounded. The British Consul thereupon suggested to Staveley that a British officer should succeed him. The General agreed, but did not venture to make any appointment until the approval of the remote authorities in London had been received. And meanwhile Ward's lieutenant, an American adventurer named Burgevine, assumed command. But Burgevine, though courageous, was extravagant, hot-tempered and, as Gordon afterwards said, totally devoid of administrative and military talent; his troops fought bravely but were ill-disciplined and prone to loot; he quarrelled with Li, the new Chinese governor of Kiangsu, and finally, a culminating offence, struck a mandarin. He was dismissed, and the unsolved problem of a British successor assumed a new urgency. The lengthy and precarious process of consulting Whitehall was not yet complete; but by a fortunate accident a letter in which the Minister at Peking had urged that British officers should not be permitted to serve with the Ever Victorious Army encountered a cyclone on its way to the Foreign Office and arrived two months late. In the absence of contrary arguments General Staveley's view was accepted, and on 9th January, 1863, an Order in Council gave permission " for all military officers in Her Majesty's service to enter the service of the said Emperor." On receiving it at the end of February General Staveley informed the War Office that he proposed as soon as he returned to Shanghai to place Brevet-Major Gordon, R.E., in command of what he still described as the Ward Force.

5

Gordon meanwhile had been steadily acquiring the experience which would soon be so invaluable to him. The task of surveying the area round Shanghai, on which he was engaged during December and January, had given him both an unrivalled knowledge of its intricate waterways and a new detestation of the rebels who had devastated it so thoroughly. For two months before

Staveley reached Shanghai and appointed him he had known that
he had been recommended for the ambiguous command and had
been wondering how the news would be received at home. " You
must not think," he had written on 23rd February,

> that I am going to be rash in this matter. I have thought well
> over it and considered that I should not act wisely in refusing
> the same. I wish you to be satisfied that I will not D.V. remain
> out very long and I am sure when you consider all things, you
> will think I have done right.

Mrs. Gordon may have managed to come to the conclusion that he
had done right, but she can hardly have believed that he would
not be rash. Indeed, Gordon himself, to judge by his repeated
protestations, must have felt some doubts as to whether, by his
mother's standards, he would be able to live up to his promise. For
he had almost certainly already resolved to place himself, unarmed,
in the forefront of every engagement, and he may well have
suspected that to Mrs. Gordon, at any rate, rash would appear the
most natural of epithets for such conduct. "... I am afraid you will
be much vexed at my having taken the command of the Sung Kiang
force, and that I am now a mandarin," he was writing on 24th
March. " I will not act rashly, and I trust to be able soon to return
to England. . . . You must not fret on this matter; I think I am
doing a good service. . . . I keep your likeness before me and can
assure my father that I will not be rash."

This was the half-century of Hodson of Hodson's Horse, of the
Lawrences, Rajah Brooke, and *Plain Tales from the Hills*, an age in
which, it almost seemed, any stray detachment of the British Army
could be relied on, should occasion demand, and almost as a matter
of routine, to produce a junior officer capable of pacifying a frontier,
quelling a rebellion or improvising and administering an empire.
Even the British Army, however, in this fabulous era, must be
counted uniquely fortunate, when confronted with the Taiping
rebellion, to have produced Charles Gordon. The task which faced

the young commander—he was just thirty—could hardly have
appeared more formidable. The rebels, flushed with repeated
victories, numerous and well equipped, occupied an area of fourteen
thousand square miles, one of the richest districts in China, full of
walled cities and covered with an intricate network of interlacing
canals, lakes and rivers. The Ever Victorious Army, when he
assumed command of it, numbered between three and four thousand
men, a mixture of ignorant peasants and the riff-raff of Shanghai
officered by a polyglot collection of European adventurers and
desperadoes. The rank and file was long accustomed to loot, the
officers were jealous, quarrelsome and treacherous, and the whole
force was constantly on the verge of mutiny. " You never did see
such a rabble " wrote Gordon, recording his first impressions to a
military friend.

And, as if to make failure doubly certain, Staveley had agreed
that Gordon should be placed under the orders of the Chinese
Governor, Li Hung Chang, that a Chinese officer should serve with
him as joint commander and that he should not go beyond a
thirty-mile radius of Shanghai without previous consultation with
both the French and English authorities. Nevertheless, Gordon had
no doubt that he would succeed. In eighteen months, he told the
Governor, he would have crushed the rebellion. And he was as
good as his word.

Moreover, with the genius of the born commander he turned
the very obstacles which seemed certain to ensure failure into the
chief sources of success. Thanks to his rapid movements and use
of armed steamboats, the devious waterways, which everyone had
assumed would make the defences of the rebels impregnable,
ensured their defeat. He had been infuriated by the slowness of the
Allied generals in the Crimea and attributed most of his own
victories to the speed with which he followed up a preliminary
success. And in the motley ranks of the Ever Victorious Army,
which had been accustomed to the sketchy discipline of the adventurers who had hitherto commanded it, and bitterly resented the
advent of a British regular officer, he instantly established a fear and

admiration which soon developed into superstitious awe. "Within two hours of his arrival," Li Hung Chang noted in his diary,

he was inspecting the troops and giving orders; and I could not but rejoice at the manner in which his commands were obeyed.

Gordon taught his men discipline, but he did not make the mistake of treating them as regulars. He put them into a smart new uniform, it is true, and devised, and procured, a still smarter uniform for his personal bodyguard of three hundred. But save for their uniform, and a discipline inflexible yet adapted to the idiosyncracies of the Ever Victorious, he had deliberately forgotten the lessons of the barrack square when he took over his command, seeming to acquire at once, and by instinct, the highly specialised technique of handling primitive irregular troops. Indeed, the independent command and his rapscallion troops seem to have evoked the wilder strains in his own nature. The Gordon of China was the Gordon who had spent his years at Woolwich amid the tinkle of breaking glass and had torn the epaulettes in fury from his own shoulders, not the methodical map-maker or the punctual correspondent whose letters contained so many promises of caution. Indeed, from time to time there were terrible scenes, when he would face the furious troops alone and quell an incipient mutiny by sheer will-power. If his men hesitated to leave cover during an action he would seize them one by one by the pigtail, drag them into the open and compel them to fire over his own shoulder. For he had realised from the first that personal example was essential, and in the heat of every battle he would invariably be found at the point of greatest danger, a cigar as often as not between his lips, his only weapon a light cane.

His energy was tireless. "Fight—move—fight again," wrote Li Hung Chang ecstatically:

landing his men—planning by night and executing by day—

planning by day and executing by night! He is a glorious fellow!

He would go all day without food, and satisfy his hunger in a few minutes in the middle of the night by sucking a dozen eggs. " For months," wrote an English officer,

> he hardly took his boots or clothes off at night; he would go to his boat and turn into a couple of blankets sewn up in the form of a sack. . . . With all this he invariably looked spruce and tidy, and as smart as if clothes were to be obtained at a few hours' notice.

But Gordon's conduct, like his character, was always full of contrasts. And although it was doubtless the indomitable energy, the occasional ruthlessness and the imperturbable courage of their commander which impressed itself upon his troops, and eventually gave him his unrivalled authority over them, his gentler side was never far to seek. He would shed tears over the sufferings of the wounded, and visit them assiduously in hospital—behaviour which was a startling contrast to the army traditions of the day. He was constantly rescuing derelict Chinese boys from the neighbourhood of his battlefields. Six served as his devoted personal attendants. During the fighting before Quinsan he picked up a small naked Chinese child from the canal bank and continued to hold it in his arms while he directed operations. This child was subsequently educated at Gordon's expense, and by him named Quincey, an Anglicised approximation to Quinsan. The boy, I am informed, lived to be chief of the Chinese detectives in the Hong Kong police force, and later chief of the Shanghai-Nanking railway police. He left a large family, several of whom achieved distinction, and there is still, or was until lately, a well-established colony of Quinceys in Shanghai, very proud of its connection with Gordon.

Again, when a wounded British deserter, captured among the rebels, was brought before him, he cried " Take him down to the river and shoot him," but in a lower voice, inaudible to the troops, he added " Put him in my boat, let the doctor attend him and send him down to Shanghai." A young officer, convicted of betraying Gordon's plans to the enemy, was forgiven on condition that he should lead the next forlorn hope in person. Characteristically, when the opportunity came Gordon had forgotten the sentence and had to be reminded of it by the culprit. Characteristically, too, when the young man duly placed himself at the head of the desperate assault on the stockade of Leeku it was Gordon who was at his side, and into Gordon's arms that he fell dead. Characteristic also was Gordon's only written reference to the incident. " We therefore carried it with a rush. I am sorry to say an officer, *a very good one* ... was killed." And the Ever Victorious Army, which soon learned to take it for granted that in every action its young commander, unarmed and faintly smiling, would be conspicuous wherever the enemy's fire was hottest, doubtless little suspected that as often as not beneath the icy outward calm he was fervently praying to God for victory.

But of all the difficulties with which Gordon now had to contend, his relations with the Chinese governor, his nominal superior, were perhaps, for a man of his temperament, the most exacting. For, all through his life, as he repeatedly confessed in his later letters to Augusta, he was both impatient and hot-tempered. " I like them," he wrote of the Chinese Mandarins, " but they require a great deal of tact, and getting in a rage with their apathy is detrimental, so I put up with it." He did not, however, always put up with it. There would be occasions when the apathy, or worse, of the Chinese authorities proved too much for his never very elastic patience, occasions when he would send in his resignation or even threaten to hand back the cities he had captured to the rebels.

For a while, however, all went surprisingly smoothly. Gordon seldom failed to win the affection and confidence of those who saw much of him, and his modesty was a particularly welcome surprise to the Chinese mandarins. Indeed, Li Lung Chang's innate suspicion of all foreigners did not survive their first meeting. " I hate all these foreigners," he had noted, " but it would not be wise to let them know. It is not the men personally that I dislike, it is their airs of wonderful superiority." But soon after his first meeting with Gordon he was writing:

> It is a direct blessing from Heaven, I believe, the coming of the British Gordon. . . . He is superior in manner and bearing to any of the foreigners I have come into contact with and does not show outwardly that conceit which makes most of them repugnant in my sight. Besides, while he is possessed of a splendid military bearing, he is direct and business-like.

And as their acquaintance ripened into friendship his diary is peppered with eulogies. "What a sight for tired eyes and elixir for a heavy heart it is to see this splendid Englishman fight! . . . If there is anything I admire nearly as much as the superb scholarship of Tseng-kwo-fan, it is the military qualities of this fine officer." And after the capture of Quinsan he declared to Gordon that he was now his brother, worthy to take the place of that other brother whom the rebels had slain. And after numerous fierce recriminations, in the midst indeed of a series of stormy disputes, for all his temporarily nettled feelings Li could still write:

> With his many faults, his pride, his temper, his tongue and his never-ending demand for money, Gordon is a noble man, and in spite of all I have said to him, or about him I will ever think most highly of him.

The never-ending demand for money, it should be noted, was for the troops' pay; for the Chinese authorities found it difficult to accustom themselves to providing punctually for an army which was no longer permitted to loot. As for Gordon himself, he was the last man to demand money. His salary, which had been fixed by Li at £3200 per annum, was reduced at his own request to £1200, and of this he spent four-fifths on medicines and comforts for his men. When Li had had more time to become accustomed both to Gordon's idiosyncracies and to the diplomatic exigencies of his own nominal authority over a youthful commander of genius engaged in conducting guerilla warfare with desperate intensity, he would write in a very different strain: " He has since the beginning of this year consulted me in everything and respectfully obeyed me in everything, and acted in the most harmonious manner with my Generals." When every allowance has been made for the fact that this tribute appeared in a memorial from the Governor to the Emperor of China, it suggests that Gordon could on occasion practise the arts of diplomacy.

6

When Gordon assumed command at Sung Kiang on 26th March, 1863, he found the soldiers of the Ever Victorious Army both resentful at the dismissal of Burgevine, doubtful of their personal prospects under the new regime, and morosely suspicious that a recent defeat at Taitsan had broken the spell of their euphonious title. He at once summoned and addressed the officers. His assurances, and his resolute manner, surprised and impressed them. At least they would see what this new commander was made of. They did not have long to wait. Within five days he had embarked twelve hundred men and all his guns and was steaming off past Shanghai to the relief of Chanzu on the estuary of the Yang-tze, well beyond the prescribed thirty-mile periphery. By 10th April he was back in Sung Kiang after capturing Chanzu almost without bloodshed. The self-confidence of his men had already revived; " my troops," he wrote home, " are in great spirits and would do anything."

Opportunities of testing this prophecy were soon forthcoming. Before the end of April he was moving with a flotilla of gunboats and cargo vessels, three thousand men and the *Hyson* and its 32-pounder, against Taitsan. There were the usual obstructions; but the *Hyson* dragged up the stakes which obstructed the channel and battered down the low bridges which spanned the creeks. By 29th April two of the town's defensive stockades had been captured without much difficulty. The fighting which followed was exceptionally desperate, but in general it set a pattern which was to become familiar—a bombardment of the stockades at the west gate, Gordon leading round detachments to block as many exits from the town as his numbers permitted; Gordon personally reconnoitring the western wall, disembarking his artillery and breaching it with gunfire; Gordon leading the first unsuccessful assault on the breach into a storm of bullets, and after another brief bombardment the second; ten minutes of hand-to-hand fighting in the breach, and then withdrawal and then Gordon leading the third wave, which presses on, wavers, recovers itself and with an impetuous rush bursts through the last defences. And at the end of it all Gordon unhurt, cane still in hand and in the blue eyes an unnatural brilliance.

The Ever Victorious had been surprised and stirred by its new commander's prowess in the field, about which there already seemed to be something of the uncanny, but it was soon to discover that he possessed much rarer military qualities. His next victory was to be a general's battle, not a soldiers'. On 4th May, two days after the capture of Taitsan, he was outside the east gate of the neighbouring town of Quinsan, and there the difficulties inherent in the nature of his command began to reveal themselves. For Ching, the Imperialist general, who had just joined him, was for another immediate, head-on assault, the only type of fighting which he understood. Gordon at once refused. He did not like the look of the eastern wall, and its 18-pounder gun, or of the lofty hill which rose from the centre of the town, and he had no intention of losing an unnecessary man from his little force of three thousand, already so vastly outnumbered by the Taipings. Moreover, the Ever Victorious expected the opportunities to which it had become accustomed under its previous commanders for spending its prize money in Sung Kiang. Gordon, too, had his own reasons for wishing to return to Sung Kiang, and he marched his men back to their base.

There he was proceeding to replenish his ammunition and reorganise his chaotic supplies when his senior officers abruptly resigned in a body. For the regimental commanders, who had been accustomed to feeding their own regiments, and had fed them most incompetently, were enraged at Gordon's appointment of a British officer to control the commissariat. Gordon coolly accepted the resignations and announced that the army would set out for the front at eight o'clock next morning. At eight o'clock, however, only the members of his own bodyguard presented themselves on parade. Gordon immediately arrested and placed in chains a number of non-commissioned officers, and the startled army, thinking better of its incipient mutiny, fell in, ready to march off. Thereupon the majors began to ask to be allowed to withdraw their resignations. Gordon replied that any officer absent at a roll-call half-way to Quinsan would be instantly dismissed. None failed to answer to his name. Such was the equivocal temper in which the small force set out on an almost unbroken series of victories.

On 27th May Gordon rejoined Ching before the east gate of Quinsan but he again declined that naive commander's proposal of a direct assault. For it was apparent that the garrison's only line of retreat lay along the twenty miles of narrow causeway, flanked throughout by canal, which linked Quinsan with Soochow to the west. Accordingly on the 29th Gordon set out in the steamer *Hyson* to reconnoitre the west of the town. On his return he explained to the sulky and bewildered Ching that there could now be no doubt that a direct assault on the east gate would be childish, and on the following day he steamed off again westward with his entire flotilla and about a thousand men. Without much difficulty they reached and occupied Chunyi, on the main canal, eight miles west of Quinsan. Here Gordon sent his own three hundred and fifty to pursue the rebels escaping eastward to Quinsan, left five hundred of Ching's men, who had accompanied him, to hold Chunyi, and himself, with the *Hyson* and several gunboats, set off along the canal westward towards Soochow. Strategy had already won the battle; the rest of the day was a fantastic exploitation of victory.

Threading precariously through countless abandoned sailing boats drifting at random in the canal, the *Hyson*, carrying six Europeans and some thirty Chinese, steamed steadily westward, firing repeatedly on clusters of Taipings escaping along the banks; and emitting from its whistle the eerie ululations which terrified the enemy almost more than its guns. It disembarked six of its crew to hold a large fort hastily evacuated by the rebels four miles nearer Soochow; passed two more abandoned forts and actually took on board a hundred and fifty prisoners. At six in the evening, when less than a mile from Soochow, Gordon reluctantly decided that the time had come to turn back towards Quinsan. It had been an exhilarating day, but the rebels after all might well by now have blocked the canal behind him. There were no misadventures, however, on the return journey; only more exchanges of shots with astonished fugitives, more screams from the steamer's siren, and even another intake of prisoners. As they approached Chunyi once more, cheers and heavy firing could be heard in the distance. Drawing on through the dusk they could see their own gunboats blazing away, and the fort in the village sparkling with musketry. Suddenly, on the bank two hundred yards ahead, a dim mass of humanity became visible. It was the garrison of Quinsan, more than eight thousand strong. As Gordon had foreseen, it was fleeing westward for Soochow. Once again the *Hyson* blew its whistle; the mass on the bank, yelled, wavered and fled; the *Hyson* pursued. Gordon had now about thirty of his own men, and some two hundred prisoners, on board. He could decimate the fleeing masses. What was a Christian commander's duty? The conflicting emotions of that moment of confusion are reflected in the description which Gordon posted home a few days later.

> Matters were in too critical a state to hesitate, as the mass of the rebels, goaded into desperation, would have swept our small force away. We were therefore forced to fire into them, and pursue them towards Quinsan, firing, however, very rarely, and only when the rebels looked as if they would make a stand. . . .

The *Hyson* had fired some eighty or ninety rounds during the day and night; and though humanity might have desired a smaller destruction, it was indispensably necessary to inflict such a blow on the garrison of Soochow as would cause them not to risk another engagement and thus enable us to live in peace during the summer—which it indeed did, for the rebels never came on this road again.

Gordon's own estimate was that in the taking of Quinsan the rebels lost between three and four thousand, killed, drowned or captured, all their arms and most of their boats. His own loss was two killed and five wounded. Meanwhile, Ching had entered the city, unopposed, from the east, still profoundly irritated and still not quite certain that he had not captured Quinsan himself.

7

Gordon soon had to suppress another, and even more dangerous, mutiny. Enraged at his decision to transfer his headquarters from Sung Kiang to Quinsan the artillery refused to parade, and issued a manifesto threatening to blow its officers to pieces. Gordon paraded the N.C.O.'s and inquired who had drawn up the proclamation. When they maintained a sullen silence he announced that unless the name was forthcoming promptly he would have one in five of them shot. A chorus of derisive groans followed. Instantly Gordon seized the loudest groaner, dragged him from the ranks and ordered one of his bodyguard (which was largely composed of youthful captured rebels and was always devotedly loyal) to shoot the man on the spot. His astonished accomplices were then locked up, with the reminder that unless the name was forthcoming within the hour the threat would be carried out. In less than an hour the mutiny was over.

After this incident, however, more than two thousand of the Ever Victorious deserted, whether because they were natives of the Sung Kiang area or because their commander's standards of dis-

cipline were too much for them. Gordon had no difficulty in
replacing them with rebel prisoners captured at Quinsan—" they
went to fight their old friends about a week after they joined me,"
he wrote, " and did pretty well "—but the episode had been trying
and it did not predispose him to equability of temper when a few
days later Ching's men opened fire with rifles and artillery on a
detachment of the Ever Victorious. Brushing aside his colleague's
ingenuous excuses he was only prevented from taking violent
reprisals by the timely intervention of Li Hung Chang's English
secretary. With Li Hung Chang himself, too, there was further
trouble. For that astute Governor was now delaying the payments
due for guns, boats and the monthly wages of the Ever Victorious
Army—perhaps through native indolence, more probably because,
like General Ching, he wished to hurry Gordon into a precipitate
direct assault upon his next objective, Soochow.

Gordon was much harassed too, just now by accusations that
unmentionable atrocities were being committed by the Imperialist
troops from correspondents signing themselves "Justice and
Mercy," " Observer," or " Eye witness," in both the Chinese and
the British Press. The *Friend of China*, which consistently maintained
that the Taipings were deeply religious but much misunderstood
Christians, was particularly venomous. And the charge of atrocities
was endorsed, in a letter to the Foreign Secretary, by no less a
personage than the Bishop of Victoria, in Australia, a critic whose
evident authority was only impaired by his remoteness from any
possible contact with the subject of his strictures. All these accusations were subsequently proved to be false, but charges of this kind
against their representatives overseas have usually been uncritically
welcomed by small but influential sections of the British public, and
in the midst of the more normal distractions of guerilla warfare
Gordon found himself sitting down to write a letter of protest to
the *Shanghai Shipping News*. And all the while he knew only too
well that the safety of his little army, and indeed of Shanghai,
depended upon him alone. " In spite of what you may think about
my saying so," he wrote home,

I am really the only stay of the force, and on my life hangs its existence; and not only that, but now the English garrison at Shanghai is so reduced, there is nothing but this force to keep the rebels out of the thirty miles radius. However, thank God, I am well and not down-hearted, although I feel very anxious at times.

It is not perhaps surprising that Li Hung Chang's failure to provide the money needed for the maintenance of his army, coming in the midst of such an accumulation of annoyances, should have proved temporarily too much for Gordon's patience, so that after numerous fruitless complaints he sent in a formal resignation.

Within two days of despatching his letter he had suppressed, and this time by coolly ignoring it, another mutiny, and captured Kahpu, to the south of his next objective, the great rebel stronghold of Soochow, which the capture of Quinsan already threatened from the east. Two more days and he had captured Wokong, three miles away, and with it four thousand men. Scarcely a shot had been fired in either operation. Yet another four days and the resignation was withdrawn. For Gordon had heard startling news. His predecessor, the American Burgevine, had joined the rebels.

The news reached him on the very evening on which he arrived in Shanghai, full of his intended resignation. He saw at once that there could be no resignation now. The British Consul entreated him at least to sleep the night in Shanghai. But Gordon was in a fever; at midnight he set out on a solitary forty-mile ride back to Quinsan. His thoughts, as he rode through the night along the waterside, revolved round his own immediate difficulties. For unless Gordon was busy solving the problems of God, Man and the Universe, and this was a habit which he had scarcely yet developed, he seldom looked far ahead. And this not only because he already had a profound belief in predestination; besides this, he was wholly indifferent to the customary objectives of personal ambition. Indeed, his complete lack of interest in money, fame or women was one of

G.G.   E the traits in Gordon which made it hardest for his contemporaries to understand him. For some while even Li Hung Chang suspected that he was scheming to become Commander-in-Chief of China, and after it was all over, and Gordon was back in England, an obscure Colonel of Engineers, Garnet Wolseley remarked to him how different the consequences might have been had he been given Gordon's opportunities. " I should have gone there," he said, more than half seriously, " with the intention of wiping out the rebellion and of becoming Emperor of China myself." This was the age of Rajah Brooke and there were precedents for empire-carving by private citizens, but Gordon had no desire to become Emperor of China; indeed, to the end of his life he would take an impish pleasure in the surprise and mortification of potentates and politicians when their most glittering offers were curtly declined. And at the moment he was solely concerned with Burgevine's defection.

For, in part, it had been his own fault. Had he not, despite plentiful rumours, assured the authorities in Shanghai that Burgevine could be trusted, that he himself would be surety for his good behaviour? Had he not done his best to encourage the rebels to make terms, being, as he told his mother, " most anxious to have as little fighting as possible?" And for how long might not the capture of Soochow, and with it the collapse of the whole rebellion, now be delayed by the accession to its defenders, already numbering at least fifty thousand, of the former commander of the Ever Victorious, a number of other Europeans and an armed steamer? That, in fact, Soochow fell three months later would be due in part to Gordon's generalship, but even more perhaps to his character, to the fact that he was the one man in either army whose resolve was indomitable and whose motives were selfless.

His troops had already learned to speak of him with bated breath, and during this August and September his reputation for possessing more than human powers grew fast. It was not so much that after beating off two attempts by the rebels to recapture Kahpu, he took the stronghold of Patachiao, half-way between Soochow and Kahpu, by surprise attack and with the loss of ten killed and forty-nine wounded.[1] What chiefly impressed the Ever Victorious was his seeming invulnerability. When, for example, he was supervising the removal of an arch from the bridge which spanned the water near Patachiao two shots, fired in ignorance by his own men, struck the stone beside him. No sooner had he stepped off the bridge than twenty-six of its arches, among them that on which he had been sitting, crashed into the water close beside the boat which he had just entered. Surprisingly this incident did not move Gordon to comment on Providence, but to one of his rare aesthetic judgments. "I regret it immensely," he wrote home, "as it was unique and very old; in fact a thing to come some distance to see."

Even more uncanny, it seemed to the Ever Victorious, was the spectacle of Gordon before the stockades of Wokong. Seven thousand rebels, under one of their most redoubtable commanders, had advanced from the south upon this town, which lay on the canal about twelve miles south of Soochow and had been captured by Gordon in July. With not much more than five hundred men he had steamed down the canal at night and next morning attacked the sixfold line of stockades behind which the rebels were entrenched. Since General Ching had neglected to obey his orders to destroy the bridges on the Grand Canal, Gordon had been compelled to leave his large steamers behind, and consequently could not turn the enemy's flanks. For once, therefore, it was a soldiers' battle—a bombardment from small gunboats at close quarters and a series of desperate assaults by the infantry. The enemy had seven thousand men behind the stockades and was continually reinforced from the rear; Gordon had his five hundred only, and it was his personal example which decided the issue of the day. As usual he carried a revolver concealed within his tunic, but as usual he did not use it. The only weapon in his hand was the little rattan cane now so well known to his troops as the Wand of Victory. At the

[1] These figures appear in a list in Gordon's hand, found among the Donnelly papers, which gives the exact number of casualties among officers and men in his sixteen chief actions. In all 107 officers and 1458 men were killed or wounded, while 57 officers and 1300 men died of sickness—totals which help to explain the belief of the Ever Victorious in Gordon's supernatural invulnerability.

head of the assault and under the hottest fire he could be seen, to all appearances wholly unconcerned, grasping the cane in one hand and with the other occasionally catching at the sleeve of a waverer and with an imperious gesture pointing him back to the fray. The unconcern was natural enough, since Gordon did not believe that he was in unusual danger. But as usual behind the impassive mask he was fervently praying for victory. And as usual not a bullet touched him. In the eyes of his men there were magic properties in the Wand of Victory. But for Gordon it had by now assumed an almost mystical significance. It was a symbolic reminder of the power of faith.

8

Meanwhile, Burgevine, the American deserter, was contemplating yet another change of allegiance. He was disappointed with his new friends, the Taipings; Gordon had sent a message offering him a safe-conduct if he would give himself up; and three days later there had been a strange interview at the stockades. Burgevine had come ostensibly to discuss his surrender, but at the last moment, in the warmth of Gordon's unexpected friendliness, the old ambitions revived. The adventurer's eyes glittered as he propounded an astonishing suggestion. Why should it not be Gordon this time who changed sides; why should they not join forces and march on the imperial city, Peking? Burgevine, though he prided himself on his shrewdness, was an indifferent judge of character; but even he can hardly have been surprised at the stern reception of this proposal, and he soon agreed to surrender with all his European associates, relying without hesitation on a promise of safe-conduct from the man whom he had just invited to become a traitor. But during the next few days, while Gordon was making the necessary arrangements with the consuls at Shanghai, Burgevine had leisure to brood over his failure. Surely so shrewd a soldier of fortune as he, with a practised eye for the main chance, need not be permanently worsted

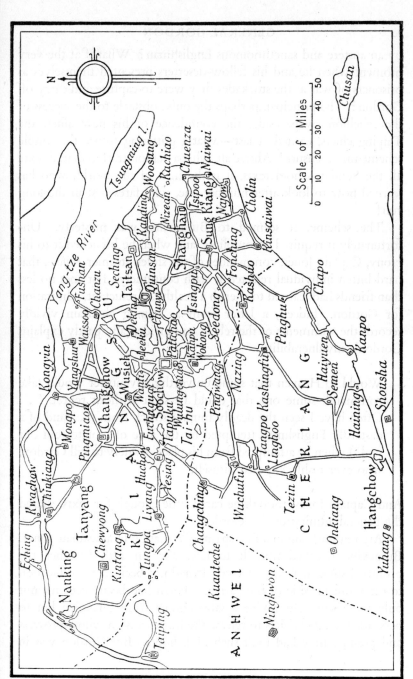

THE CAMPAIGN AGAINST THE TAIPINGS

by an austere and sanctimonious Englishman? What if at the very moment when he and his fellow-deserters presented themselves as prisoners of war at the stockades they were to capture and carry off Gordon? The principal, perhaps the only, obstacle to the success of the rebellion swept aside, the confidence of his new allies, the Taiping chiefs, earned at last—what a glittering future the simple scheme might ensure! Above all, what a demonstration that, despite all the Sunday school texts, it is the man of the world, who has learned how to look after number one, who fares best in the long run!

The scheme, it seemed to Burgevine, was masterly. Unfortunately it required accomplices, and when he broached it to his crony, Captain Jones, commander of the stolen steamer *Kajow*, that hard-bitten individual rejected it with contumely. For foes no less than friends had learned to cherish a healthy, if reluctant, admiration for Gordon. Indeed, a letter from a Taiping chieftain vividly records the sentiments of the rebels, and incidentally partly explains Gordon's invulnerability.

> Would to Heaven that some unworthy adventurer would take command, some one that could be slain without regret. . . . Often have I seen the deadly musket struck from the hand of a dastardly Englishman (tempted by the love of loot to join our ranks) when he attempted from his place of safety to kill Gordon, who ever rashly exposed himself.

And Captain Jones, though he cared little enough for texts, shared the general admiration for Gordon.

After attempting in a first spasm of irritation to assassinate Jones, Burgevine resigned himself to fate, and on 18th October the promised surrender was effected. It had not been easy for Gordon to carry out his side of the bargain. For it had been necessary not only to procure Burgevine a safe-conduct from Shanghai but to persuade the rebel chiefs to release the Europeans on whose prowess and prestige they had built such high hopes. But Gordon was in fairly constant communication with the rebels. Years afterwards he wrote " When in China I used to write to one rebel chief thus ' I know you are not comfortable and if you come to me I will help you.' The fact of this man having had a letter from me used to make the others fear and used thus to produce discord among them." The timely gift of a choice horse to one of the Taipings expedited the negotiations, but in the event Burgevine owed his safety to the very factor which had already wrecked his schemes, the almost superstitious admiration for Gordon which was now almost as widespread among the rebels as in the Ever Victorious Army itself. Burgevine, however, was scarcely the man to draw any moral from this episode. Two years later he broke the promise exacted at the time of his surrender, returned to China and was drowned while crossing a river, whether by accident or, as was widely reported, at the orders of Li Hung Chang.

9

Gordon was now free to concentrate on the encirclement and capture of the chief rebel stronghold, the famous city of Soochow, a long line of grey wall and turret above which a shimmering confusion of pagoda and palace roof peered from the greenery of ancient trees. The fall of Soochow would surely ensure a speedy end to the rebellion, and already Gordon was beginning to look forward to resigning his command. " If I can see a man to take my place," he wrote home in a letter dated 19th October,

> I shall leave this service, my object being gained—namely, to show the public what they doubted, that there were English officers, who could conduct operations as well as mates of ships, and also to rid the neighbourhood of Shanghai of these free-booters.

If Burgevine had not been uppermost in his thoughts at the moment he might have estimated the relative importance of his own motives differently. " I care nothing for a high name," he went on.

> If I had, I should have written far more about the various fights. My hope is that the Chinese Government may feel that they have been fairly treated by me, and learn that we are not all actuated by greed. That they do so now I believe, as they have every confidence in me.

The last two sentences were significant, for as he grew older it would become something like an obsession with Gordon that he must prove to Chinese and Egyptians, to Sudanese and negroes that some Europeans at least could show themselves indifferent to power and wealth.

As for the encirclement of Soochow, it was accomplished with a speed and decision worthy of one who combined a moral fervour profounder than Havelock's with more than Garibaldi's genius for guerilla warfare. His position at Patachiao lay a few miles almost due south of Soochow. Walungchiao, less than two miles to the west of Patachiao, was captured, thanks to a brilliant night detour, without the loss of a man; and a few days later after another deceptive detour he took Leeku, five miles to the north of Soochow; this time, however, a frontal assault, with Gordon, as usual, at its head, was needed before the rebels fled. A week later Wanti, two miles to the west, had fallen to concentrated artillery fire. It remained to cut the line of the Grand Canal, which ran north-west and linked the city with an army of 20,000 rebels forty miles away at Wusieh. The daring theft of one of his two larger gunboats at Shanghai compelled Gordon to abandon his original plans for this enterprise at the eleventh hour. Long before the stolen steamer could reach the rebels, however, he had sailed down the creek from Wanti to the Grand Canal, moved his boats unobserved from creek to canal, outflanked the enemy and captured Fuchuquai without the loss of a man. Save for a narrow bridle-path over the mountains, Soochow was now encircled.

Throughout these rapid and exhausting manoeuvres Gordon was tireless. He never undressed and seldom seemed to sleep. Night or day wherever there was work or danger, he was there, issuing instructions or lending a hand, spruce and alert, a cheroot in his mouth and the Wand of Victory in his hand. Every detail came under his all-seeing eye; he was general, company commander, adjutant and indeed subaltern in himself alone. His orders, even before a major battle, were invariably given by word of mouth. They were brief, lucid and decisive, and he required instant and unquestioning obedience to them. When an over-dainty English regular officer, after a detour to avoid a particularly muddy ditch, reached his destination with Gordon's message he found Gordon already there—and was at once ordered to return to his regiment at Shanghai.

The fall of Soochow was bound to be the crisis of the campaign; Gordon could hardly have foreseen that it was to be a personal crisis also. The success of his negotiations with the Taiping Wangs over the release of Burgevine had encouraged him to hope that Soochow, once encircled, might be taken without further bloodshed. He was to be tragically undeceived. The omens, however, at first seemed favourable. Lar Wang, second in command of the forty thousand rebels in and around the city, was reported to be for capitulation. True, a night assault, undertaken to strengthen the hands of Lar Wang and his party, resulted in Gordon's first and only defeat; and in an attack two days later, during which Lar Wang had promised to surrender the city, there was severe fighting, with Gordon, as usual, in the forefront, before the stockades were taken. Within forty-eight hours, however, negotiations had opened in earnest. Gordon met Lar Wang by night in the cabin of Ching's boat, and soon afterwards came to an understanding with the rebel emissaries. The lives of the Wangs were to be spared and they would hand over the town. Gordon had repeatedly insisted both to Ching and to the Governor, Li Hung Chang, who had now arrived in the Imperialist camp, that the Wangs must be treated with leniency, and he had accepted their ready assurances with all the more confidence since the

Imperialists had behaved admirably after the fall of Chanzu, and by now their camps were full of officers and troops who had from time to time abandoned the rebel cause. On 4th December General Ching received the head of Moh Wang, the recalcitrant commander-in-chief, grim evidence that the party of surrender had obtained the upper hand, and on 5th December the Taiping troops withdrew from the East gate. Only forty-eight days later, thanks to the new telegraph line from Suez, family breakfast parties in England were stirred by a laconic announcement in *The Times* of 22nd January: *Major Gordon captured Soochow on 5th December.*

Gordon, however, was already uneasy. He had prayed for victory and victory had come, but what would be the consequences of victory? After weeks of incessant toil and battle his nerves were taut, and when early that Saturday morning Li Hung Chang refused to give his troops a bonus of two months' pay Gordon retorted indignantly that he would resign if his request were not granted, and that Li could have till three o'clock to reconsider his refusal. He then hurried off into the town. His own men he had halted in strict military formation outside the North gate, but he did not wholly trust Ching's Imperialist troops. To his relief, he found all still quiet in the city, and apparently confident as to his own safety, he proceeded to make his way unaccompanied through streets full of excited rebel soldiers to the house of Lar Wang. Here most of the rebel generals were assembled; they seemed in surprisingly good spirits and assured their unexpected visitor that they were satisfied with the terms which they had made for themselves. Still restless and uneasy, however, Gordon threaded his way on through the turmoil of the city to the mansion of Moh Wang, the murdered commander. Here in a lofty hall, amid overturned chairs, scattered water-lilies, burned-out candles and all the débris of an interrupted feast, he found the headless trunk. Beside it stood a young Englishman, one of his own subalterns, who had chanced this way and had just drawn from the blood-stained robe a packet of letters in Gordon's own hand—letters in which he had guaranteed the lives and property of the citizens of Soochow, if the city surrendered. The subaltern stole away, leaving Gordon, who was deeply moved, standing in profound meditation over the body.

After an unsuccessful attempt to have the corpse buried Gordon made his way back to the walls to await Governor Li's answer. Here before long General Ching arrived, as emissary from the Governor, to entreat Gordon to persuade his men to accept one month's pay as a compromise. Gordon decided swiftly. Night was drawing on; if he was able to announce no settlement before dawn his men were only too likely either to attack the parsimonious Governor or march in to loot the city; for he was well aware that they would greatly have preferred a day's looting to even four months' pay. But there need be no question of endeavouring to persuade them, as Ching had suggested. He would parade them, and order them to accept the unpalatable terms. This he promptly proceeded to do. The men received the news with angry cries and a threat to march on the Governor. Gordon instantly quelled the disturbance, dismissed the parade and posted a guard on the Governor's boat.

Early next morning, 6th December, he marched his men back to Quinsan. He himself at once returned to Soochow. The Wangs, he knew, were about to make their formal surrender to Li, but at the moment he was anxious not so much for the Wangs as for the city. Li had invited him to be present at the ceremony of surrender, but he had declined—perhaps because he feared that his presence would embarrass the defeated Wangs, perhaps because his temper was still ruffled by Li's behaviour on the previous day. In any event, the refusal was to prove a tragic mistake.

Gordon was still troubled by a sense of coming tragedy. He went straight to Lar Wang's house and once more inquired anxiously whether all was well. Again Lar Wang reassured him with every sign of confidence. But Gordon was not altogether satisfied. He was planning, he said, a river expedition to cut out the rebels' steamer, yet he was prepared to remain in Soochow, if Lar Wang had any fears for his own safety or that of the other defeated generals. Perplexed by the insistent solicitude of the mysterious Englishman,

Lar Wang could only shake his head; no, he knew of no reason why Gordon should stay. But Gordon still sensed trouble, and he could not rest. He would go on to the palace of Moh Wang, and see whether Ching had obeyed his instructions to have the corpse buried. As he went, a cavalcade of the Wangs whom he had just quitted passed him, with twenty attendants, riding out for the ceremonial surrender. He was surprised to notice that they were laughing and chattering gaily. At Moh Wang's mansion he found Ching's men about to bury the body. All then, it seemed, was as it should be in the city; he could surely now devote his attention to the river expedition. He turned back accordingly towards the East gate, from which he proposed to walk five miles along the city wall to the South gate, where a boat was awaiting him.

From the wall above the East gate he could survey the city. The sight of a crowd on the river bank near Li's boat, a mile and a half away, was somewhat surprising; but these, he decided, must be casual sightseers, drawn by rumours of the surrender. It was more disturbing when a large force of Imperialist troops from the same direction rushed into the city, yelling and firing their muskets into the air. But soon General Ching himself rode up. And it was obvious that on seeing Gordon, whom he supposed to be already in pursuit of the enemy's steamer, Ching was not only surprised but disconcerted. All Gordon's misgivings revived. It was now after one o'clock, and the surrender must presumably have been concluded. Had the interview gone off satisfactorily, he asked eagerly. Ching replied uncomfortably that the rebel chiefs had never reached the Governor's boat, and when the astonished Gordon, who had so recently seen them lightheartedly setting out thither, began to cross-question him, he involved himself in a tissue of contradictions, evasions and improbabilities, the general purport of which was that Lar Wang had taken alarm and fled.

Gordon announced that in that case he would himself return once more to Lar Wang's house to reassure him. But though he was puzzled his suspicions were not yet fully aroused, and when Ching besought him not to enter the city he was content to ask

Macartney, the young Scottish surgeon who had been Li's secretary, and now held an independent command under the Governor, to go in his stead. He himself set out with Ching to ride along the wall to the South gate. It was a strange journey. From the city could be heard sporadic volleys of musketry, explained by the ingenious Ching as harmless demonstrations intended to frighten a few recalcitrant Cantonese out of the city gates. Occasionally, too, Ching himself, yielding to an irrepressible impulse, would discharge his own rifle into the air. But to Gordon's stream of questions as to Lar Wang not only Ching but Gordon's own interpreter returned obstinately evasive answers. At the South gate Ching rode off, and the interpreter, with a sudden accession of confidence, or veracity, informed Gordon that he thought the General and the Governor did not intend to keep their promises to the Wangs. Upon this Gordon finally abandoned all idea of his river expedition and with the disconsolate interpreter at his side once more rode back into the city.

He soon found that there had been a change for the worse. It would soon be dark, and the streets were full of armed rebels and looting Imperialists. Lar Wang's mansion had already been sacked. Gordon was unarmed and accompanied only by his interpreter, but when a relative of Lar Wang, one Wangshi, besought him to escort Lar Wang's household to his own house and protect it, he did not hesitate. It was a strange and precarious situation for a victorious commander, and when he reached Wangshi's house it became more precarious still, for into the courtyard had crowded several hundred rebel soldiers who immediately barricaded the gates and refused to allow Gordon to leave. It was now pitch dark, he was a prisoner of the enemy he had just defeated, and every now and again plundering bands of Imperialist troops would attempt to force an entry into the courtyard. When Gordon ordered them off they always withdrew; but nothing would persuade the Taiping soldiers to let him go.

Gordon no longer had any doubt but that Li had played him false. Clearly the troops were out of control and the town was being looted; and where, above all, where were the Wangs? As the hours dragged by his anger mounted, and he evolved a desperate plan. He would send for his steamers, seize Li and hold him prisoner until he had handed over the Wangs safe and sound. But how was he to make contact with the steamers? At last, at two in the morning of Monday, the interpreter was permitted to go off, with Gordon's written orders, for the South gate. An hour later one of his escort returned with word that the interpreter had been attacked and wounded by rebels, and that his orders had been torn up. Gordon, who now expected a general massacre, at length succeeded in persuading his captors to allow him to leave. He set out with an escort of rebels, searched in vain for his interpreter and was arrested, and detained for an hour, at the South gate by Imperialists who had failed to recognise him. By now it was five o'clock and, once released, Gordon sent off a message to his steamers and hurried on to the East gate. There he found General Ching.

Gordon's own description of what followed is succinct: " I told him what I thought." In fact, before the embarrassed Ching could stammer more than a few words of explanation or apology Gordon seems to have overwhelmed him with a hurricane of pent-up wrath. This, then, was how he honoured his promise that there should be no looting or disorder! After a few feeble protests that he had only been carrying out the orders of Li, the terrified Ching made off hurriedly into the city, and as soon as he was out of sight and earshot of Gordon sat down and burst into tears. After which he gave expression to his remorse by shooting the first twenty of his own men whom he chanced to encounter. But as to the fate of the Wangs, Ching was guiltily aware, Gordon still knew nothing, and meeting a Major Bailey, an American artillery expert attached to his own headquarters, he succeeded in persuading him to go off to break the news to the terrible Englishman. Even the major, however, when he found Gordon at the stockade impatiently awaiting his steamers, quailed before the blazing blue eyes and cold fury, and in reply to his urgent questions could only suggest that Lar Wang's son was nearby, and could tell him the whole story. The youth was brought and at once, pointing dramatically across the river, declared that there his father and his fellow Wangs had been beheaded.

As he heard the shocking news, Gordon realised that this was what, consciously or unconsciously, he had foreseen ever since the capitulation. For several hours his anger had been mounting; and now for a while he no longer attempted to restrain it. He hastened across the creek to see the grisly relics with his own eyes, snatched up the head of LarWang and, bearing it with him, returned to wait in feverish impatience for his steamers. His anger now bordered upon hysteria. Li and Ching between them—the same thoughts revolved torturingly in his weary brain—had not only betrayed their solemn undertakings to him and to the murdered Wangs; they had involved his personal honour in their own treachery, for if he had not himself countenanced the negotiations by his interview with Lar Wang, Lar Wang would not have surrendered. Moreover, as always, wickedness had been folly. For if faith had been kept, and Soochow and the Wangs had been leniently treated, all the remaining rebel towns would have surrendered without further fighting, and the rebellion would have been at an end. As it was, his months of toil and fighting had been wasted. So at least, in the first revulsion of wrath, he persuaded himself, and it was in such a mood that, long before the steamers had arrived, he decided upon his course of action.

Since the steamers could no longer be used, as he had planned, to prevent the Governor's treachery they should be used to avenge it. He would seize Li, demand his resignation and impeach him before his imperial master on a charge of criminal treachery. If Li refused to resign, then he, Gordon, would hand back to the rebels all the towns he had wrested from them, as some compensation for the crime. It was a wild scheme, but Gordon was in a wild mood. Yet all the while, beneath the turmoil of emotion and the plans for retribution, he was conscious from time to time of promptings towards a very different mood and a very different philosophy. For although the pre-occupations of war had done much to distract him

from that interest in religious problems which had been revived by
the attack of smallpox nearly two years ago, he had not forgotten
Mr. Molyneux's convincing demonstrations that since God is
omnipotent whatever happens must be for the best. Indeed, when
he wrote home a fortnight later he had convinced himself that even
the treacherous murder of the Wangs was no exception to the rule,
and he could recall his conflicting emotions in a mood of comparative detachment.

> You can have little idea of the regret I have for several reasons
> on account of the last affair. In the first place, if faith had been
> kept, there would have been no more fighting, as every town
> would have given in; in the next, we had accomplished the
> suppression of the rebellion with very little loss of life to rebels
> or Imperialists, and not much injury to the inhabitants . . .; in
> the next, if I had not seen Lar Wang, he would not have come
> over; and, in the next, I fear that all my work has been thrown
> away. My only consolation is that everything is for the best.

At last the steamers hove in sight; but, fortunately perhaps, they
had come too late for Gordon's plan. The Governor had already
quitted his boat for the city. Gordon had to be content with leaving
a vitriolic letter, denouncing Li's perfidy and announcing his own
ultimatum. Then, with Lar Wang's son, he sailed back to Quinsan
and flung himself exhausted into his room. Under the bed he had
carefully placed the head of the murdered Wang.

Meanwhile, Macartney was hurrying to Quinsan, as an emissary
from the Governor. For Li had received Gordon's letter. Its contents
he did not know, for, after glancing through the letter, Macartney
had prudently declined to translate it to him. But he knew that
Gordon was beside himself with rage, and he had begged Macartney
to plead with him, incidentally briefing his spokesman with an
exculpatory version of the murder of the Wangs of which all that
can now be said is that it was completely contradicted by the later
account in his own published memoirs, and is no more likely than

the subsequent version to have been true. Macartney reached
Quinsan on his unenviable mission too late for an interview that
night, but before dawn word came that Gordon would see him.
Mounting the stairs, he peered into the twilit room, and could just
descry a dim figure seated sobbing on the edge of the bed. Before
Macartney could speak, Gordon bent swiftly down, seized something from beneath the bedstead and held it aloft, exclaiming
passionately: "Do you see that? Do you see that?" Peering
incredulously in the dim light, Macartney found himself momentarily
at a loss for words, and Gordon cried angrily "It is the head of
the Lar Wang, foully murdered," and thereupon burst once more
into hysterical tears. Realising that the moment was unpropitious
for his mission, Macartney discreetly withdrew.

Some hours later he found himself seated next Gordon at breakfast in a room full of officers and Shanghai merchants. For some
while Gordon was silent. Then he turned and said abruptly: "You
have come on a mission from the Futai.[1] What is it?" To
Macartney's suggestion that a private audience might be more
appropriate Gordon replied, with equal abruptness "There are
only friends here. I have no secrets. Speak out." Seeing that he
had no choice, Macartney took his courage in both hands and
delivered Li's message. He even ventured to point out the incon-
testable fact that were Gordon to carry out his threat of attacking
the Governor he would not merely undo all that he had done in
China, but would only be able to keep his army in being by plunder,
since it would no longer be paid by the Chinese authorities. This
eminently rational advice he concluded with the words "And
how long will that prove successful, and what credit will you get
by it?"

But Gordon would not listen. With an angry stamp of the foot
he ejaculated "I will have none of your tame counsels." And
without more ado he ordered the steamer *Hyson*, and a detachment
of infantry, to prepare to attack the Governor. Thereupon Macartney, declining Gordon's unexpected offer of a passage on the

[1] Governor.

G.G.   F

Hyson, borrowed a horse and galloped off at full speed for Soochow, to warn Li to move his own troops to oppose Gordon. However, Gordon had either already abandoned the idea of attacking the Governor, or else he changed his mind as he steamed towards Soochow. For he contented himself with appearing at Ching's stockade and demanding Lar Wang's body and the release of some members of his family. With these not over-exacting requests Ching readily complied, and Gordon returned to Quinsan. He had perhaps begun to remind himself that even the murder of the Wangs must somehow be for the best.

The events of 6th to 8th December had been lurid enough. Unfortunately, a much more lurid version was to reach London. On 29th January *The Times* published a private letter, written in Hong Kong on 15th December, whose author asserted not only that the Governor, after promising that there should be no bloodshed, had ordered a wholesale massacre of men, women and children, but that thereupon Gordon and a small party of his men had broken in on Li and his mandarins and " fired and loaded and fired again on every mandarin they met." Gordon, he added, was said to have shot thirty-five mandarins with his own hand. Five days later *The Times* own correspondent corrected these fantastic allegations, but it was long before they were wholly obliterated from the public memory. Indeed, later in the same year a clergyman named Worthington presented to the British public a pamphlet, portraying the Taipings as highly civilised religious reformers, and asserting that " Of the 40,000 prisoners who surrendered at Soochow, 32,000 were butchered before the eyes of Major Gordon." As for the *Friend of China*, it made even wilder accusations and stigmatised Gordon's account of the fall of Soochow as a tissue of " mendacity and absurdity." A faint echo of these macabre legends was even to be heard in the hagiographies published after Gordon's death, and writer after writer would assert that he had pursued Li Hung Chang, revolver in hand, intent on executing summary justice—a story which was even revived by W. T. Stead in a celebrated interview published in the *Pall Mall Gazette* in 1884, on the eve of Gordon's final departure for Khartoum.

10

For several weeks, during which no one but he could have held the Ever Victorious together as a disciplined force, Gordon remained inactive at Quinsan, awaiting instructions. To several tentative overtures from Li he had already turned a deaf ear when, on New Year's Day, 1864, there arrived an imposing procession headed by a mandarin and bearing numerous open boxes full of money, and four snake-banners captured from the rebels. Gordon had no doubt as to what should be done with the money, which amounted to no less than ten thousand taels; he ordered it to be returned at once to its senders. The snake-banners presented a somewhat more delicate problem. Two he waved away, for they came from Li, a tainted source; two, since their donor had not been implicated in the treachery at Soochow, he consented to accept. Not long after he had returned to his house, however, the mandarin reappeared, bearing a letter from the Emperor, wrapped in yellow silk. This he reverently deposited between two lighted candles on a table in the hall, and waited expectantly. Gordon read the letter, announcing the imperial gift which he had just rejected, and promptly wrote on the back of it:

> Major Gordon receives the approbation of His Majesty the Emperor with every gratification, but regrets most sincerely that, owing to circumstances which occurred since the capture of Soochow, he is unable to receive any mark of His Majesty the Emperor's recognition, and therefore begs His Majesty to receive his thanks for his intended kindness, and to allow him to decline the same.

He did not add that, Soochow or no Soochow, he would never have consented to accept a gift of money. In due course the *Friend of China* heard of this refusal. It must have been due, it suggested, to the inadequacy of the Emperor's proffered *largesse*.

> We hope that he [Gordon] has stipulated for tens of lacs of rupees. Why should a soldier of fortune not make a fortune? When the major returns to Scotland, will any of his ' canny ' countrymen ask impertinent questions as to the source of the ' siller? ' . . . Dollars cover every defect, and a wealthy soldier can afford to buy the respect which he cannot exact. Let the trade of murder flourish, as it has always done, and let Major Gordon fully enjoy all the wealth that the Manchus can give.

Throughout January Gordon continued to await instructions at Quinsan. Sixteen of his officers had had to be dismissed, but the Ever Victorious was still in being. Then another emissary from Li Hung Chang arrived, in the person of a Mr. Hart, Inspector of Customs at Shanghai. By now Gordon's anger had cooled and he no longer found it so difficult to believe that somehow all must have been for the best. Moreover, Li had paid to the Ever Victorious not only the promised bonus, but handsome compensation for the wounded, and through Hart he now submitted some justification, as well as renewed apologies, for his conduct at Soochow. It was in a much more conciliatory mood, therefore, that Gordon consented to interview the Governor on 1st February, and after Li had promised to announce publicly that responsibility for the execution of the Wangs was his alone, Gordon agreed to take the field again. It was a courageous decision, for though he was still without instructions from his own superiors, he knew that they felt very strongly about the Soochow incident, and that by resuming co-operation with Li he would expose himself to charges of having condoned his behaviour. And not only in Shanghai. At home the House of Commons, as always, contained Members, such as Lord Naes, who sympathised instinctively with rebels anywhere for the sufficient reason that they were rebels, and could be trusted to echo any local criticisms of the reconciliation with Li Hung Chang. Even Lord Palmerston would speak of Gordon as " the unwilling instrument to lure these people into the power of the Futai and . . . of course, so far . . . an instrument to their barbarous execution." However, to the man on the spot the case for renewed action seemed unanswerable. As he wrote to Sir Frederick Bruce in Peking, who thoroughly approved his decision, " I do not apprehend the rebellion will last six months longer if I take the field. It may take six years if I leave."

II

The strategy by which Gordon proposed to finish off the campaign was simple. While Li and the Imperialists blockaded Changchow, he would strike west across the great Taihu lake and so cut the rebel forces in two, and sever communications between their northern and southern bases, Nanking and Hangchow. At first all went smoothly. The all but bloodless capture of Yesing was speedily followed by the capitulation of the more formidable stronghold of Liyang. But at Kintang, where there was severe fighting, Gordon for the first time was wounded. It was only a flesh wound in the leg, and he ignored it until, fainting from loss of blood, he was carried back to his boat. The attack on Kintang had to be abandoned, but as soon as he recovered consciousness Gordon resumed command and ordered the Ever Victorious off on a new offensive. Leaving part of his force to garrison the two captured towns, he set out with four hundred of his own men and six hundred of the captured rebels from Liyang, whom he had already enlisted under his own flag, to recross Lake Taihu and strike westward against rebels reported to be raiding in the coastal area.

He was prostrate in his boat, more than half his thousand men had been fighting against him only a few days earlier, and he was penetrating a district in which there were known to be many thousands of rebels. The manœuvre was very dangerous; in anyone else it would have been the extreme of recklessness, and even with Gordon it failed. For though, as he lay in the boat, the artillery was under his eye he could not keep contact with the infantry, and without Gordon the Ever Victorious could not be expected to live up to its name. The infantry attacked prematurely and were driven back with heavy losses, and reluctantly Gordon decided to withdraw westward and give his wound time to heal.

In less than a week he had recovered and was returning to the attack. Five days later a feint to the south and a pounce from the north had driven the Taiping garrison, ten thousand strong, headlong from Waissoo, his original objective. As the Taipings fled, the long-suffering countryside rose against its defeated oppressors and only a thousand of the fugitives reached Changchow alive. Gordon could not bring himself to pity the victims. Though capable of an almost feminine tenderness, he was fresh from the harrowing scenes of desolation in the neighbourhood of Yesing, where the peasants had been for some while reduced to cannibalism. And thanks to his experiences in China, war for him had already become what it was to remain for the rest of his life, a crusade on behalf of the oppressed. Lord Naes and the Parliamentary critics had not watched men eating human flesh. In a letter to his mother he jotted down his medley of unconsidered impressions and reflections after the pursuit.

I will say this much—the Imperialists did not kill the coolies and boys. The villagers followed up and stripped the fugitives stark naked, so that all over the country there were naked men lying down in the grass. The cruelties these rebels had committed during their raids were frightful; in every village there were from ten to sixty dead, either women—frightfully mutilated— old men, or small children. I do not regret the fate of these rebels. I have no talent for description, but the scenes I have witnessed of misery are something dreadful, and I must say that your wish for me to return with the work incomplete would not be expressed if you saw the state of these poor people. The horrible furtive looks of the wretched inhabitants hovering around one's boat haunts me, and the knowledge of their want of nourishment would sicken anyone. They are like wolves. The dead lie where they fell, and are in some cases trodden quite flat by the passers-by. I hope to get the Shanghai people to assist, but they do not *see* these things, and to read that there are human beings eating human flesh produces less effect than if they saw the corpses from which the flesh is cut. There is one thing I promise you, and that is, that as soon as I can leave this service I will do so; but I will not be led to do what may cause great disasters for the sake of getting out of the dangers, which, in my opinion, are no greater in action than in barracks.

It remained to take Changchow itself, and the rebellion would be crushed; but Changchow was garrisoned by twenty thousand seasoned troops and had defied the besiegers for many weeks. Gordon's arrival, however, at once galvanised the Imperialists into new activity. He himself was tireless as ever, reconnoitring targets, superintending the construction of batteries and bridges and leading the assaults on the breaches. Twice he escaped death as by a miracle, the miracle on which, remembering the Wand of Victory, the Ever Victorious now confidently relied. On the first occasion, with a Major Tapp, he was supervising the building of a gun emplacement by night, well in advance of the main body of his troops, when first one of his own pickets, then some Imperialists in the rear and finally the enemy opened fire on the working party. Major Tapp was killed but Gordon was not touched.

When it came to the final assault the Imperialists wavered under the storm of fire from the breached walls. Li Hung Chang, watching anxiously from a neighbouring hill, saw the Ever Victorious race forward with Gordon at their head, saw Gordon silhouetted for a moment against the skyline, the first to mount the breach. Then Li held his breath, for facing the breach, a mere hundred and fifty yards away, was the rebels' 32-pounder, ready loaded, its muzzle pointing straight at Gordon and its gunner waiting to fire. The victor, it seemed certain, must fall in the moment of victory. There was an agonising moment of suspense and—the gun did not fire. The Taipings had forgotten to keep their powder dry; and Gordon swept on into the town at the head of his troops. The Wand of Victory was in his hand. The Ever Victorious Army had fought its last engagement.

12

For this was the end. The rebellion was crushed. Nanking, it is true, remained to be captured, but that task could safely be left to the Imperialists. The Ever Victorious had done its work, but it was still potentially a dangerous instrument to friends as well as foes; it must be disbanded. So Gordon had decided, on his own responsibility, forestalling the decision of his superiors, and indeed alarming several of them not a little. But then, as he explained in a note to his mother: ". . . on these subjects I act for myself and judge for myself: this I have found to be the best way of getting on "—a principle to which he would adhere steadfastly for the rest of his life. And having decided, he moved with characteristic speed. By the eighteenth of May he was back at Quinsan, by the thirty-first the Ever Victorious had passed into history.

A fortnight later its commander was writing of it with a frankness which he would not previously have permitted himself: " I can say now that a more turbulent set of men who formed the officers have not often been collected together, or a more dangerous lot if they had been headed by one of their own style." None the less, he demanded, and obtained, the most generous grants from the Chinese authorities for his demobilised ruffians. For himself, as always, he was determined to take nothing. He had spent his pay, and more, on comforts for his troops; he had already abruptly refused the Emperor's ten thousand taels; he now, albeit somewhat more ceremoniously, declined an even larger sum. " I know I shall leave China as poor as I entered it," he wrote home, but with the knowledge that, through my weak instrumentality, upwards of eighty to one hundred thousand lives have been spared. I want no further satisfaction than this.

Two gold medals struck in his honour he could not, however, refuse; nor the Order of the Yellow Jacket and the Peacock's Feather, the Chinese equivalents of the Garter and the Bath. And when the inevitable dignitaries arrived with the huge inevitable escort, and, in an atmosphere acrid with the fumes of exploded crackers, unpacked box after box of sumptuous robes and accoutrements the new mandarin was compelled to spend five hours donning a succession of skirts, robes, hats, thumb-rings and necklaces, and only betraying his impatience by an occasional sardonic smile. " Some of the buttons on the mandarin hats," Gordon noted afterwards, " are worth thirty or forty pounds. I am sorry for it, as they cannot afford it over well." In later years, however, he did set some store by the curious wardrobe, and among the Donnelly papers are several pages of notes in his handwriting, in the course of which he enumerates its eight different sets of costumes, and explains that yellow, being the Emperor's colour, is forbidden on pain of death to all his subjects, save the fifty or sixty mandarins of the Yellow Jacket.

With his own hand the Prince Regent of China presented to the British ambassador in Peking a letter in which he dilated upon the extraordinary services rendered by Gordon to China, and besought the British Government to accord him some signal honour. In forwarding this letter to the Foreign Minister the ambassador added an almost equally glowing tribute of his own. " Quite apart from Gordon's skill and courage," he wrote,

> his disinterestedness has elevated our national character in the eyes of the Chinese. Not only has he refused any pecuniary reward, but he has spent more than his pay in contributing to the comfort of the officers who served under him, and in assuaging the distress of the starving population whom he relieved from the yoke of their oppressors.

And, remembering that Earl Russell, being a Whig, if not a Liberal, might well entertain lingering sympathies for the defeated rebels, and would almost certainly not be aware that the Heavenly King's customary modes of punishment were pounding to death and flaying alive, he added a discreetly veiled reminder of their atrocities.

Indeed, the feeling that prompted him to resume operations after the fall of Soochow was one of the purest humanity. He sought to save the people of the districts that had been recovered from a repetition of the misery entailed upon them by this cruel civil war.

The ambassador might, however, have spared himself his pains. The Government, which had recently promoted Gordon to brevet lieutenant-colonel, confined its munificence to bestowing on him some while later a Companionship of the Bath, the traditional reward of its less distinguished civil servants. Perhaps the letters of Prince Kung and the Ambassador had remained unread, like so many more important documents, in some official pigeon-hole; or perhaps the Government could not quite bring itself to forget that Gordon had suppressed a rebellion.

Gordon himself, it must be admitted, however, would do everything possible to encourage its neglect of him, of which he warmly approved. Had he been a man of another stamp he might, like Rajah Brooke, have made himself lord of a province, or, like many an ambitious soldier, have gone home to enjoy the plaudits of society and a swift ascent to high command. But he was Gordon, and from the day when, as a Woolwich cadet, he had torn up and flung into the grate one of his own maps which he found his mother proudly exhibiting to her friends a puritanical aversion to any sort of praise, public recognition or reward had steadily grown upon him. It sprang no doubt from a natural modesty, and a natural indifference to wealth and social prestige, as well as from a sardonic consciousness of the part played by greed and ambition in most successful careers. But it owed something, too, perhaps to an uneasy awareness of the intermittent thirst for action and for power which would so often conflict with the other-worldly quietism which was the deepest vein in his character.

At home, as he could not help knowing, he was already famous; but that was a misfortune whose consequences he would no doubt find means of evading after his return. What concerned him at the moment was to evade the consequences of his fame in China. He had already contrived to slip quietly away from Quinsan, fore-stalling a farewell demonstration projected by the dissolving Ever Victorious. He had declined an invitation to Peking, where he would have been received with all but royal honours. And he had been careful to warn his family, when he sent home his diary of the rebellion, that " I do not want the same published, as I think, if my proceedings sink into oblivion it would be better for everyone." (Later, on finding that his fond family was surreptitiously circulating this journal, he destroyed it.) No account of the rebellion by Gordon now exists, but among the Donnelly papers I found five folio sheets in his handwriting, in which he achieves the remarkable feat of putting together a lucid summary of the fighting without once mentioning his own name.

As for the pæans in the Press, both English and foreign, with their assertions that the very name of Gordon ensured victory, or that twenty million taels would not repay his services to China, it was easy enough to turn a deaf ear to these. And even when the merchants of Shanghai, who but a year before had been angrily denouncing his aggressive tactics, declared in an illuminated address, studded with flowery references to disinterested gallantry and un-deviating self-respect, that his achievements were without a parallel in Chinese history, all that was necessary was the briefest of acknow-ledgments, and the assurance that their handsome letter had given him great satisfaction, that he was deeply impressed with the honour they had paid him and that he had the honour to be theirs obediently C. G. Gordon.

The victorious general, of whom four months ago Robert Hart

had written " the destiny of China is at the present moment in the hands of Gordon," had reverted to the brevet lieutenant-colonel, who for another eight years would remain a regimental captain in his own corps. But he had not quite finished with China, or with great affairs. He must not, he told his mother, " leave things in a mess." He had saved Shanghai, but it must be left permanently secure. A new Chinese army must be trained, the British authorities were agreed as to this. But who was to train it? As to this the authorities could not make up their minds and Gordon decided to do the training himself. For he had realised by now that no official, if there are higher officials in the background, enjoys making a decision, and he wrote home a sardonic commentary which illumines much of his subsequent career:

> I have a box full of all sorts of letters from Lay, Osborne, Sir F. Bruce, Wade, Parkes, Burgevine, and mandarins, of the most contradictory nature, the perusal of which will show you how divided the people out here were upon the line to pursue. No one could get on here but a man who, without offending the swells, takes a separate and decided course; indecision is our bane. A bad plan, in my mind, followed out without wavering, is better than three or four good ones not so dealt with. I mean, of course, if it is seen that the *bad plan* can be improved upon in course of execution, the change should be made; but to wait and wait, as we have been doing, till *some one* comes out, who will settle matters, is merely a waste of time; who this *some one* is no one knows, but there is an indefinable feeling that *some one* is coming, and thence the delay and unwillingness of the authorities to take responsibility.

And so from June to November, with an interlude of five weeks during which he indulged himself in the diversion of completing his ordnance survey of the area, he was busy organising a new Chinese army, of which, he reported, he would have had higher hopes " if the whole country was not corrupt."

But at last the moment came for him to leave. Could he slip away unnoticed? That his arrival in England would be inconspicuous he felt fairly confident; would he not write to his mother on 17th November—it was his last letter from China—" The individual is coming home, but does not wish it known, for it would be a signal for the disbanded to come to Southampton, and although the waits at Christmas are bad, these others are worse." The departure from Sung Kiang, however, presented a more formidable problem. Gordon did his best. On the evening of his departure, after dining as usual in the mess, he rose from the table, bade a casual farewell to the company, as though he was to travel no farther than Shanghai, boarded the famous *Hyson*, hurried to his cabin and shut the door. But he was only partially successful. There had, it is true, been no speeches, but for a mile and a half the *Hyson* steamed past river banks lined with soldiers, flags and lanterns amidst the roar of artillery and a deafening accompaniment of crackers, gongs and horns.

A sharp eye might have discerned a mysterious object bobbing in the wake of the steamer. For Gordon had not forgotten that civilian clothes would be needed on the liner which was to carry him home, and he had ordered a bowler hat and a ready-made suit from Shanghai. But he detested new clothes, and after all, even a new suit may be conspicuous. And accordingly he had stoved in the crown of the hat, and ordered the suit to be tied into a bundle, and thrown into the creek. Here, attached to the side of the *Hyson*, it had lain for some while, and through these turbid waters was now drawn in the vessel's wake, a dim shape glimpsed intermittently in the tremulous spears of mirrored lantern light.

BOOK THREE

APOSTLE OF THE POOR

I N HIS battered bowler hat and artificially aged Shanghai suit
  Gordon reached England in January, 1865, to encounter at first
what seemed a universal conspiracy to expose him to the publicity
which he dreaded. For months the Press had been intermittently
retailing picturesque accounts of his exploits. And now Ministers
and generals invited him to levées and conferences. The man in the
street, whose imagination had been stirred by the Chinese adventures,
much as it would be, a couple of generations later, by the first Atlantic
flyers, eagerly awaited news of him. And his mother, his brother
Henry, even the pious Augusta made it all too plain that they would
have liked to see him making hay while the sun of public and official
favour shone.

Once again he felt himself a solitary in revolt against his environment; " quite fierce " Augusta found him. From his parents' home
in Rockstone Place, Southampton, in which he had at once taken
refuge, he stubbornly declined the official invitations. An offer of
special military employment he declined because it would have
meant promotion over the heads of his friends and contemporaries
of Woolwich days. And before long he had torn up his Chinese
diary, lest it should contribute to the legend which was threatening
to take shape. Even the descriptions of his Chinese experiences
which he occasionally vouchsafed to his family circle would be
abruptly broken off if some member of his audience was indiscreet
enough to display signs of admiration. Social invitations he usually

refused, but here his scrupulous conscience interposed an obstacle. For when invited to dine in London he would decline on the ground that he was about to leave for Southampton, and similarly when the invitation emanated from Southampton he would plead an engagement in London. And then, lest he should have told a lie, he would solemnly proceed to do as he had said, and embark on an otherwise totally unnecessary journey by rail.

In part no doubt this headlong flight from the public eye had been due to a natural puritanism and perhaps also to a consciousness of the faint stirrings of a positive liking for worldly power and public applause, for " boarding the tram of the world," as he called it, with which in later years he would often reproach himself. But in part, too, his quest for seclusion may have been a morbid reaction from the prolonged nervous tension of his solitary command. Only in an occasional letter to one of those who had served under him in China does the tension seem to relax. A note, written on 15th April, 1865, to Moffitt, who had been surgeon with the Ever Victorious and was to marry his sister Helen, displays the old friendliness curiously mingled with the temporary irritability. His journal of the Chinese war had not yet been destroyed and he was still thinking of letting Moffitt use it as the basis for a history of the campaign. After explaining that he has failed to obtain for his friend the promotion which he deserved he goes on:

> I do so long for your return, for I mean D.V. to give you my notes and journal and to let you work over the matter. It is shameful of that old driveller Guy not sending you home direct. . . . I have three months more leave, and then do not know what I shall do. Never think I forget you, you dear old bird, the only fellow who helped me *con amore*. You must come home and I will come over to Belfast. Mayers has gone out to China; he had no money so although a pauper I lent him 100 £.

Gradually, as was inevitable, the world forgot Gordon. The official invitations died away. The newspaper readers found other heroes, so that two decades later, when the name of Chinese Gordon was again in the headlines, many supposed him to be an oriental. During the next twenty years the British Government embarked on minor wars in Abyssinia and in Ashanti, against Zulus, Afghans and Boers, but in none of them did it employ the greatest commander of irregulars in the world. Gordon's contemporary, Wolseley, who had confessed that with Gordon's opportunities he would have been tempted to make himself Emperor of China, rose to be a field marshal and a peer, but Gordon himself was never again given by the War Office an opportunity of displaying his military genius. He longed passionately to join the army which was organised to invade Abyssinia in 1867; indeed, he told his friend, Mrs. Freese, that he had been bitterly disappointed at not being given the command instead of Napier, a general twenty-five years his senior; so disappointed that he shut himself up for two days and " went through something." But since he already believed that whatever is is God's will and necessarily for the best he soon came to accept the War Office's neglect of him without complaint.

2

But though Gordon desired seclusion, and though under the generous regulations of those days he was positively now entitled to two years' leave, he was not likely to be long contented with inaction in the family circle at Southampton. His letters to Major Donnelly during these months contain numerous complaints of his liver—an organ regarded at that time as the mysterious source of numerous physical and mental distempers—and by February he is already hoping to leave England in May. Attendance as A.D.C. (as he put it) on his mother, an affectionate but now a somewhat exacting old lady, occupied much of his time, while as for the social amenities of Southampton they interested him only as a menace to be evaded. From time to time there would be a proposal of new employment from some too helpful friend to be declined, and the note of suppressed exasperation in a disclaimer to Major Donnelly, written in the following year, 21st March, 1866, was probably sharpened by the memory of numerous predecessors.

> I am really very much obliged to you for your kind remembrances and the trouble you have taken about me, but I cannot stand the Paris Exhibn. I do so cordially hate anything of the sort proposed, that I would go anywhere to avoid them [sic]. I am quite aware of the vitiated taste I thus evince, but to seek or in any way go thro' such an ordeal while I have strength to struggle agst it is what I cannot do. So I hope you will take my final resolve (and not be put out) which is, that with many thanks I would rather not go on such a work.

In spite of which he did spend some weeks in Paris in the following year, reporting in April that the Exhibition was only half ready and "in a great mess."

By 1st September he had not only applied to be returned to duty, but had been appointed R.E. officer in command at Gravesend, to superintend the erection of new forts for the defence of the Thames. His conclusion that another fifteen months of furlough would be intolerable had been hastened by more than the tedium of life at Southampton. For it seems clear that it was during these months that he experienced the spiritual crisis which would determine the character of the rest of his life. Not long after his return from China his father died (19th September, 1865), and soon afterwards his brother-in-law. And a memorandum by Gordon among the Freese papers shows that he himself regarded his father's death as a milestone in his spiritual enlightenment. This document, which was written three years later, in 1868, is headed "My experiences showing the order in which God revealed Himself to me." It begins:

1. Ever since I remember, I had a belief that Jesus was the Son of God, and used to have feelings of deep depression on account of my faults at that time.

2. I knew Jesus to be my Saviour, and had assurance but was not
established till I had gone through 14¹years captivity commencing at the Crimean War till 1864.

3. At my father's death I was brought to think how vain the
world was to give satisfaction, but after my brother-in-law's
death, and consequent seclusion at Gosport for a month, God
made me count the cost and conclude that His service should
be *all* and that if *everything* was given up He would abundantly
repay me in this world.

4. After a long dreary struggle (looked back on with horror)
for 8 or 9 months of very earnest work God began to bring
under my body in this way.

5. He gave me first to see that the fruits of the Spirit could be
only had by abiding in Christ or being joined to Him but
how joined was still a mystery.

The remaining entries in this brief spiritual autobiography belong
to a later stage in the story. These first five have taken Gordon well
into his official sojourn at Gravesend; and it was doubtless this
" long, dreary struggle " which he had in mind when his new
friends, the Freeses, whose acquaintance he made in the summer of
1867, asked him playfully what he had found to do before he knew
them; and Mrs. Freese records that " he replied . . . that the days
were dull and long

and that his work at the forts was soon got through, and then
there was nothing to do. ' I used,' said he, ' to walk out to
Chalk in the afternoon and go into the churchyard and think
about my father . . . kick the stones about and walk back again.'

Gordon was to spend nearly two years at Gravesend before he
made the acquaintance of the Freeses. His duties were far from
inspiring. By now he had had a good deal of experience of fortifications, and it did not take him long to perceive that the new forts,

¹ Presumably a slip for " 10."

whose construction he was to supervise, were so sited as to be entirely useless. Since, however, the authorities paid no attention whatever to his representations he had no choice but to continue his day-to-day supervision of the waste of public money on what, though since greatly surpassed, was for those days a gigantic scale. But Gordon did not repine unduly, for he believed, on moral grounds, in the value of hard work to him who did it, no matter what its results. As he would write some years later, when the Sisyphean task at Gravesend was nearing its end:

> The new works are approved of and I expect will be put in hand. This will not give me more work than now, for I could not well have more and it does not signify. Night comes and there is a rest. I do so verily believe in being perfectly employed all the day and evenings to [sic]. This is a world for work, the other for meditation. It is no use discovering spiritual truths in sloth.

And he certainly managed to be " perfectly employed " all day long, though by no means only with official duties. At Fort House, his official residence, his practice was to rise early, take a cold bath and read the Bible before a simple breakfast. By eight o'clock he was on duty. After reading and answering his correspondence he would give instructions for the day's programme in his office and then sally forth to inspect the work in progress on one or other of his fantastic forts. Sometimes he would go on foot, walking with the characteristic rapid gait which, as those who accompanied him were soon apt to complain, was almost a run. Often, however, he would travel by water, and on water as on land he insisted on travelling fast. For the official pair-oared rowing boat he soon substituted a four-oared gig. And whatever the wind or tide he insisted that the Thames watermen at its oars should row as strenuously as if they were on the last stretch of a hotly contested boat-race, so that, spurred on by his repeated " a little faster, boys, a little faster," the four stalwarts would stumble ashore in a pitiable state of exhaustion. And then the slight, wiry figure would dart nimbly about the piles of brick, the earthworks and embrasures, while the queue of junior officers, foremen and contractors, following him as best they could, would marvel at the staccato exhortations with which he would spur on the work: " another five minutes gone, and this not done yet, my men! We shall never have them again."

The midday meal was seldom allowed to interfere with official duties. He usually ate at his office table, the food reposing in a deep drawer, which he would hurriedly close if a caller presented himself. At two his official duties were ended; an occasional call would have to be paid on a fellow officer's family, but in his early days at Greenwich the bulk of the rest of the day was his own. A substantial part of it was devoted to Bible-reading and meditation; he would read a great many newspapers too, numerous religious works, old and new, and occasionally an ancient classic in translation. But, as his subsequent confession to Mrs. Freese showed, at first there were often times when he found himself both melancholy and unemployed. It was only gradually, as he became familiar with his working-class neighbours, and the clergy, missionaries and doctors who worked among them, that he came to devote every spare moment to the round of charity and evangelism which would make of his six years at Gravesend a veritable apostolate to the poor.

3

Since this same period also saw the final crystallisation of Gordon's religious creed, it is doubly fortunate that it should be illumined by the intimate correspondence which he maintained at intervals with his new friend, Mrs. Freese, for the rest of his life, but never more copiously than during the years at Gravesend when he was her near neighbour.

Mr. and Mrs. Freese were then living with their children on modest independent means at Home Mead, Milton-next-Gravesend. They were a religious-minded couple and they first heard of Gordon as an officer who frequently bought tracts and works of devotion at the local depôt of the Religious Tract Society which Mr. Freese had helped to establish. It was not long before he was invited to tea at Home Mead. Mrs. Freese found their visitor both puzzling and impressive, so difficult was it to reconcile his boyish manner with the penetrating eye and the expression " that might have lived a thousand years." The mystery was only solved with Gordon's next visit.

. . . when he was sitting at tea in our room he said something about China which caused me to remark ' Oh! were you ever in China—do tell us something about life there,' and my husband said, ' Did you see anything of the Taiping rebellion when you were there?' ' I should think I did,' he said, ' why it was I who put an end to it '—to which my husband replied, ' You don't mean that,' while I looked at him and wondered for a second or two if it could be possible this young man was bragging—a vice I should not have expected to find in him. Of course presently my husband questioned it out of him and we were both greatly interested at the little he told us. Afterwards we heard more, and then we knew that he was a remarkable man and my puzzle about him was cleared up.

These two visits were the introduction to an intimacy which lasted nearly till Gordon's death. Its basis was the religious fervour which all three shared, and which soon led to other common interests—the sick, the poor and the street urchins of Gravesend, to whom Gordon was soon devoting every spare moment, talks on Genesis, and the leaflets on religious topics which Gordon composed and submitted for Mrs. Freese's criticism. At first he would drop in to Home Mead nearly every day and often twice a day, usually announcing his arrival by a tap of his cane on the window. He presented the Freeses' small son with the key of Fort House garden, which he playfully called Paradise, wrapping it in paper inscribed, with a reminiscence of *Pilgrim's Progress*, " key of the wicket gate."

And for the Freese children the garden, with its lawn and mulberry trees and cannon-crowned ramparts, and its view of the river where the ships swung slowly round as the tide turned, proved near enough to Paradise. Their parents, however, were surprised, when they paid it their first visit, one evening that summer, in search of peace and solitude, to find numbers of aged folk hobbling about the lawn and paths. They, too, it appeared, had been accorded the freedom of Paradise, and the carefully cultivated plots of vegetables and fruit, the Freeses learned, all belonged to various poor neighbours between whom the Colonel had apportioned his garden. Nothing was grown for himself; indeed, he was not particularly interested in flowers, preferring, he explained, the human face divine. Gordon himself, too, the Freese children vaguely associated with Paradise, and for the rest of their lives remembered, as one of them long afterwards recalled, the "indefinable air of mystery and love" which seemed to envelop him. That he was also a hero they had gathered from their parents' conversation, but for them his heroism derived not so much from tales of his achievements in China as from his prowess in childish games and his endearing habit of burying silver coins about the garden, and subsequently directing his young friends to areas in which it would be profitable to dig.

For a while Gordon's orderly was carrying two or three notes a day to the Freeses' house. They were almost all addressed to Mrs. Freese, and doubtless Gordon, who knew so few women, found in her the feminine confidante whom at some time in their lives all men, even misogynists, are said to need. Not unnaturally Mrs. Freese came, long before his death, to venerate Gordon as a hero and a saint, but on Gordon's side at any rate, there was no spark of sentiment in the correspondence; to the end, however intimate their topics, all his letters began 'Dear Mrs. Freese,' and ended 'Yours sincerely.' Though Gordon once told his sister how he regretted not having a son, he had a positive dread of marriage, seeing in it the surrender of that state of solitary independence which his inmost nature craved and which he would seek throughout his professional career, from that first independent command in China to the last lonely scene in Khartoum. It was no doubt that half-conscious dread of the shackles that made him exclaim irritably, when Mrs. Freese urged him to live less frugally and eat more, " Mrs. Freese, I won't stand it. I should not stand that from my own mother."

It was fortunate, therefore, for him that he was sufficiently indifferent to the romantic appeal of the fair sex in general to evade without much difficulty, and indeed almost perhaps without being aware that he was evading them, the advances of the ladies who, even in Gravesend, not infrequently set their caps at him. There was the widow of one of his Chinese officers who, after a few friendly visits from the colonel, inquired, in the then classic formula, what were his intentions—and was informed very simply that he had none. Or the other widow who, presuming upon his bene-volence, would summon him to her side if her chimney smoked, or a minor repair were needed in her house, or even if she was feeling depressed. There was even the invalid beside whose couch he spent many hours, and who had herself moved to lodgings from which she could see her beloved colonel whenever he went in or out of Fort House. And there was Miss Surridge who (Gordon reported to Mrs. Freese in December, 1868)

was plaintive and said think of me at Xmas all alone. I said *I will and wish I was also the same.* She was quite hurt.

But visits to unemployed or invalid ladies were but a drop in the ocean of Gordon's benevolence. For soon Mrs. Freese had intro-duced him to the town missionary, and the town missionary to the abysses of poverty, suffering and ignorance in Gravesend. And from then on almost every waking moment not claimed by military duties, Bible reading, meditation or a visit to the Freeses was devoted to charity and evangelism.

4

This was not the first time that Gordon had been introduced to work among the very poor. He had been sent to Manchester for a month or two that year and had found his way to the City Mission there, and asked to be allowed to accompany a missioner round the slums. He was introduced to a Mr. Wardle with whom he regularly penetrated the neighbourhood of the old Millgate and the Cathedral, then a labyrinth of dark and dangerous alleys, rickety staircases and ruined, disease-haunted garrets. At first, he confessed to Wardle, he was nervous; he had never been afraid, he said, under heavy fire, but the spectacle of his companion warning the vicious and desperate of the consequences of sin gave him pause. But the faith which had turned the rattan cane into a Wand of Victory responded to the unfamiliar challenge. In a well-worn greyish overcoat, whose pockets bulged with tracts, he would sally forth day after day with Wardle or some other missionary, to sit by the bedside of dying prostitute or criminal, or " kneel down for prayer by a broken chair or the corner of a slop-stone, or by the wash-tub." It was from Manchester that he wrote to Augusta on 21st September, 1867:

> Your heart would bleed to see the poor people here, though they say there is no distress such as there was some time ago: they are indeed like sheep having no shepherd. But, thank God, though they look forlorn, they have a watchful and pitying Eye over them. It does so painfully affect me, and I do trust will make me think less of self and more of these poor people. Little idea have the rich of other counties of the scenes in these parts. It does so make me long for that great day when He will come and put all things straight. How long, O Lord, how long!

In Gravesend it was with the street urchins that he began. Boys had always specially attracted him; and because they attracted him he understood them better than he understood women, or indeed men, and was gentler with them. At first he took two or three into his house, fed and clothed them and taught them in the evenings. Others quickly followed, and soon, though he could not house them all, he was keeping a regular night school, evening after evening, with so many pupils that he had had to requisition every room in Fort House for it, and was paying a young man to help him. He taught the boys to write, read and do simple arithmetic, he told them stirring stories of adventure, he expounded the Bible, and in particular he sought to amuse them. At the end of the evening they would all sing a hymn, usually his favourite *A day's march nearer home*. Sometimes there were almost more pupils than he had room for: " there are a lot of boys outside my door like bees before they swarm." Nor did he only teach; he found his boys jobs, usually at sea—flags stuck into a map over his mantelpiece recorded the whereabouts of his protégés' vessels—and he provided them with outfits. Before he left Gravesend he was distributing several hundred suits a year, buying boots by the gross, and sitting up at night mending the boys' clothes with his own hands. " If you have any letters, my address will be Queen's Bench," he scribbled to Mrs. Freese, in humorous allusion to the bankruptcy court (he was referring to the expense of printing his religious tracts, but the outfits of his boys and his gifts and pensions to the old and sick cost him a good deal more).

He spoke of his boys as his Kings or Wangs, a reminiscence, it has been thought, of China, but more probably a reference to their immortal souls—as is suggested by a note to Mrs. Freese in September, 1868. " Great blessings at Perry St: got three rough lads into a room and found they were *kings*! Want more leaflets." " Scuttlers" was another of his generic names for the urchins of Gravesend; and occasionally, in a mood of mingled compassion and sentiment, he would use the more tender " dove."

I have just come back from Tilbury station where there is a Dove ill with scarlet fever, poor little dear; such a nice little fellow.

The little Dove I sent up to see you, Willie Webster, is ill and they think it scarlet fever, so I will not come nigh you for a time. Bob Weston has also got seedy and the Doctor fears the same thing: if it is so, I think I may put off my leave.

His notes are full of references to the Kings and their fortunes and requests for trifling kindnesses from Mrs. Freese: " Do not forget the two seafaring lads, Burgess and Bennett;" " please take a piece of cake to the little R.C. boy who is ill;" " last week Georgie left, I having compounded for his schooling and keep. . . . Bassett left yesterday, a very good place on board ship, £1 per mensem. Next, I have only two boys of the old crew left. Next, I have got a new one till I can get him into Chelsea."

Often a favourite King is sent as bearer of a consignment of tracts or one of the notes which went so often from Fort House to the Freeses—so often for a while in fact that Gordon's orderly complained that half his time was spent carrying notes to Mrs. Freese. A message in April, 1868, is sent " per Kohinoor," Kohinoor being a specially promising King or Scuttler named Styles, who would seem to have gone to sea a week or two later, when a note ends " the bearer little Alex Bowie is a sweet child and has come to succeed Styles who I am glad you saw." But the Kings of Gravesend were a migratory population: a fortnight later, on 6th May, Alex Bowie, " a nice lad," is again recorded as note bearer, and two jocular contrasting sketches of his face, in joy and sorrow, are appended. But that summer Alex, too, has sailed away, and a note ends " P.S. Bowie has left for Sydney. Someone else would not have minded." Somehow, however, instead of reaching Sydney, Alex contrived to get himself involved *en route* in Marshal Prim's rebellion in Spain and returned a hero; and on 31st October, he is carrying three thousand tracts to Mrs. Freese, and Gordon explains " as you wanted to see the lad who went with General Prim I send him up with them."

Gordon's work among the Kings of Gravesend was by no means confined to his own night classes. Soon he was teaching regularly in the local Ragged School, where the lads "hung upon his lips," and visiting their homes, if they had any, or, if they had not, summoning them to Fort House. And wherever he went he was eager to recruit new Kings. "Had a deeply interesting walk yesterday and many adventures with Royalty" (15th August, 1868). The ultimate object of his tireless activities was always, needless to say, conversion, and his schemes for engineering a suitable opening with some elusive street urchin are often reminiscent of Wilberforce elaborately planning a word in season with the Prince Regent.

> Just a line privately to ask you to encourage the visits of little George Parr here, for I want (with His permission) to speak to him about the "*secret*" and I meant to do so to-day, but when I came back I found they had gone. Now I hope you will do this for I want much to do it and it is unnecessary to say to you how important it is.

He would regularly open a conversation with a potential King with the blunt question "Do you believe in Jesus?" and when the boy answered "Yes" would proceed "Then do you know that God lives in you?" and so pass on to expound "the secret." Often he would be haunted by the sense that he was wasting opportunities of evangelism. "If you had been in my state," he writes to Mrs. Freese, "you would not have cared about Kenilworth and Warwick: there were boys running about worth millions and I could not have courage to speak to them."

Outside Gravesend he was still on the look out, but opportunities were apt to be less plentiful, as he ruefully explained when staying with his cousin, Sir William Gordon, in Lanarkshire in the autumn of 1868.

> There is little to be done as far as I can see here in the way of leaflets, for there are so few people to give them to. You may leave them (not always without fear of detection), but there is no one to pick them up. The country is very sparsely occupied,

and the people shun you more than seek you. I would not be the owner of one of these Estates for a great deal and I truly think that better the trials and sorrows of a town for breaking up the fallow ground of the heart than the quiet vegetation with inward corruption of the countryside. I believe there are many Kings (red haired) about but I cannot get at them with facility, as I do not like vexing my old friend, who dislikes tracts very much.

This scattering of tracts, often those which he had composed himself with assistance from Mrs. Freese, had become a habit, designed for the conversion not of Kings only but of his fellow countrymen in general. He would start out on his walks with a pocketful of leaflets, dropping them by the side of a path, or placing them carefully under a stone, on the top bar of a style, in the middle of a narrow track or on some projecting nail in wall or fence. He would even throw tracts and booklets from the window of his train when it took him past men working on the line on his way to London. Astonished subalterns would sometimes follow their colonel's progress across the fields through a telescope, but when tempted to derisive mirth would usually contrive to restrain themselves. Was not this after all Chinese Gordon, and might not these eccentricities even have something to do with his legendary exploits?

The distribution of tracts was by no means confined to the neighbourhood of Gravesend. Mrs. Taylor tells me that her mother, Gordon's cousin, always remembered a walk on which she accompanied him into Weymouth. It was in any case an odd expedition for at this time nothing would persuade Gordon to step on the cracks in the pavement, and his usual rapid gait was diversified by the frequent hops and strides with which he avoided them. And suddenly, seized with a mysterious inspiration, he exclaimed "Wait for me, I must give that man a tract," and rushing after a complete stranger presented him with one of the leaflets which were always carried in his pocket. It is not to be supposed that Gordon found such practical evangelism easy. He had told Mr. Wardle in Manchester that at first he found it far more alarming than to be under heavy fire. Evangelism, however, like the enemy's fire, had to be faced, and in the same spirit. As he bore down with his tract upon the stranger he was assaulting an enemy position and there was an imaginary Wand of Victory under his arm. As he put it to Augusta, " Addresses in vague terms from the pulpits do not arrest attention. It is only by direct attack that attention can be awakened and to do that we must have boldness, not of our own. . . ." For he could always comfort himself with the reflection that it was not the actual words he used but " some invisible influence " which would move his hearers, as it had presided over his battles in China. " This thought makes one happy after having spoken to anyone on this subject; for it matters little what we may say if our spirits are in unison with God, and when we speak for His glory it is not our argument which will convince."

Inevitably some of the young to whom Gordon lent a helping hand subsequently came to grief. There is a story of one boy creeping back to Gordon's door at night after his third failure, a mass of verminous rags, and of Gordon, who had a houseful of reclaimed Kings, leading the prodigal silently to the stable. Here he was left on a pile of clean straw with a hunk of bread and a mug of tea. Punctually at six next morning Gordon returned with soap, towels and clean clothes, ordered the boy to strip and washed him from head to foot in the horse trough. But there is plenty of evidence that more often benevolence was not wasted. A boy who had gone to the Sunday school with the sole object of making himself a nuisance was invited by Gordon to breakfast next morning. After breakfast his host went out with him and bought him a complete outfit of new clothes. They returned to Fort House, where the boy was given a bath and a thorough scrubbing and arrayed in his new clothes. Then Gordon planted him in front of a mirror. " You see a new boy, don't you? " he said. " Well, just as you are new outside, so I want you to be new inside." For some while the boy lived at Fort House. In later life he became a respected and influential town-councillor. After Gordon's death one prosperous citizen called on Sir Henry Gordon and asked to be allowed to subscribe £25 towards a memorial to his brother, to whom he owed all his success. Another recalled how, when he was a neglected King at Gravesend, Gordon had invited him and others daily to dinner and tea, had paid eighteen shillings a week for him and two others to spend six months at the Royal Sea Bathing Infirmary at Margate and subsequently financed his apprenticeship to the sea. And in the 'seventies, with the laconic comment " a nice Dove's letter," Gordon himself passed on to Mrs. Freese another tribute of gratitude.

SIR,
I am at work with Ridley and have been working with him for this last eighteen months so I am as an apprentice at Mr. Holt's and he has told me about you and has let me read your letters in which I was glad to hear you were quite wel.
    Sir . . . I am writing and have not told you who I am. I am that little boy that you teached for a few Sundays at the Mission Room don't you Remember you put our names down in a small book my name is Joseph Eke, and then there was Thomas Brenchley that worked on the railway and when you used to go to London you used to trow out some tracts and Little books. I do remember the time so well I can remember it so well and if it was yesterday. Brenchley is quite well and his wife and child me and Ridley is shopmates and it is very singular that I should come across another scholar of yours. Ridley tells me that you were out in Egypt, I hope this will find you in that sort of climate in the best of health. I go to the Northfleet Chapel now were we have a very good congreation and a very good Minister his name is Mr. Valentine a Scotchman. . . . I am very sorry for Thomas Brenchley for he is going with bad companions and I think he has left the school altogether. They have got those two cards that you gave to the Mission Room one is (God is love) and the other is (Whosoever believeth on Christ the Son of God shall in no wise be cast out but shall have life

everlasting). Something after this is the other card I can remember that about the camp of the Israelites.

I must conclude with my kind love to you and to let you know some of the news of your Old friend at the Mission Room near Northfleet Station.

So remember me to be your Friend

JOSEPH EKE

5

Of all his Gravesend apostolate it was doubtless his activities among the Kings which meant most to Gordon. It even reconciled him to the prospect of a life of comparative inaction: " how far better," he wrote, " to be allowed to be kind to a little Scrub than to govern the greatest kingdoms." His labours among the Kings, however, exhausted but a fraction of his philanthropic and evangelistic zeal. Indeed the Freeses, who had originally introduced him to the town missionary, were at first almost terrified by the daemonic forces they had unleashed. For Gordon seemed to have the energy of ten men. He was for ever visiting the sick. His correspondence is full of references to a paralytic named Carter; he sat with him, sent him books and flowers, devised a gauze frame to protect him from flies and provided him with a daily paper and a small weekly allowance —continued till the man's dying day, long after Gordon himself had left Gravesend. The bedridden Miss Surridge claimed almost as much of his time. Indeed, his whole life was planned in relation to these humble dependents. He postpones a visit to the Ragged School because Miss Surridge wishes to take the Sacrament, and Mrs. Robinson cannot say whether 5.30 p.m. will be a convenient hour. Or he is ready to cancel his own leave because his absence would inconvenience a sick man. " When I come back on the 15 if I ever do, for Richen still lingers on," he writes in October, 1867. And next month he explains that he has abandoned his plan to visit his mother at Southampton for " I went down to Richen after I saw you and could not find it in my heart to leave him, so when you call do not hint at such a thought being entertained."

And in the mean streets of Gravesend, with the assistance of the town missionary, he was always finding new sick beds to visit and new souls to whom to reveal "the secret." On one occasion he discovered a woman alone and apparently *in articulo mortis*. He lighted a fire, made some gruel and fed her with his own hand; and afterwards engaged a nurse and a doctor to attend her until she had recovered. Frequently the dying would send for him rather than for the clergy.

> There is a very beautiful young girl dying to-night, in a few short hours she will glide into a bright balmy land, and see such sights as would pass our understanding. She suffers much poor thing and makes one feel Oh! if I could soften this pang what would I not do. But still it must be true that it is better for her, that she should; otherwise God who loves her so deeply would alter it. (16th May, 1870.)

> After seeing him off to the train at 10.15 p.m. I went to Polly's and saw her off to the Golden City. She left at ten minutes to 12, very happily and beautifully. "What are those bands playing for" she said just before her departure. It was the Harpers with their harps, harping the [?] and the Lamb as she neared the river bank.
>
>   Tune, tune your harps
>   Ye saints in glory
> All is well.   (2nd June, 1870.)

Each day two or three visits to the sick must be fitted into his already overwhelming programme. In Southampton, too, there were Scuttlers, references to whose welfare diversify his correspondence with Augusta, and during Augusta's occasional visits to the Fort House he did his best to interest her in his Gravesend protégés.

Nevertheless, there was much, very much, else, besides the

Gordon by Lady Abercromby

Forts, the Kings and the sick, for which he managed to find time. There were the cement works, at which he conducted a sort of single-handed mission. And there were schools and classes all over Gravesend to be visited from time to time: "I went to Princes St. School, very nice lads *indeed*." He took his school visits and teaching very seriously, and would decline an invitation because "I am engaged at Perry St. and rather like being quiet before the school hour." And then there were Sunday schools to visit on Sunday, and the evening services in a small room in Passenger Court which he frequently attended. He would also spend an hour or two a week at the Workhouse Infirmary, always bringing with him tobacco for the old men and tea for the old women, and usually reading a short passage from the Bible and saying a simple prayer. About the streets of Gravesend he was a familiar spectacle, hastening to the cement works or the Ragged School, or penetrating some obscure alley on his way to a sick bed or in search of the hearth and home of some new-found King. Often he could be seen carrying the unwieldy package of which he had relieved some humble elderly acquaintance encountered on the way. Those who watched him passing on these errands noted a "wonderfully gentle and cheerful expression" on his face. There was "little of military bearing in his carriage" it seemed to them—a view which would have equally surprised the Ever Victorious army and those who had known Gordon only at the Gravesend forts. It is not to be wondered at that at this time passers-by frequently saw roughly scrawled on walls or pavements the legend "God bless the kernel."

His visits to the sick brought him frequently into contact with infection. Although Mrs. Freese now knew only too well that she must not attempt to manage him, she once ventured to remonstrate with him for visiting scarlet-fever patients. His reply is at first sight obscure.

P.S. You speak of the scarlet-fever etc. You do not think the bottom of a coalmine is a nice place to live in though while the collier is there he must do his work and not grumble, or try to leave it. Yet you will not blame him if he would like to have an order passed for him to come up.

He meant that he must not be blamed for running risks, seeing that he regarded death as the greatest of all blessings. All Christians will profess gratitude to the Almighty, in the words of the Anglican Order for the Burial of the Dead, for delivering " this our brother out of the miseries of this sinful world;" but Gordon, one of an extremely small minority, genuinely believed, wholeheartedly and without reservations, that gratitude is in fact due. It was a theme to which he would constantly recur. When his boat fouled a stake in the Thames and sank close in-shore he could not help voicing a regret that the accident had not happened in midstream: " if it had been in the middle I should be at home to-night, in a very bright and happy land . . . and the great comfort of knowing that there could be no further trial." Mrs. Freese thought his point of view morbid, but if she ventured to expostulate he would reply that we are all at school here, " is it very strange if we long for the holidays?" And what he felt with regard to himself, he felt, and sometimes said with engaging frankness, of others.

To be happy here is utterly impossible. We may have praise but no happiness. We must live on the other side of the River death and it is there only that there is rest. . . . This world is at the best only bearable because every day shortens our time in it. Yesterday I was in London seeing a person who had devoted all her means, time and life to visiting the sick etc. She was saying that my sister's marriage might shorten my mother's life . . . as if it was a thing to be lamented about. Either death is the most blessed gift or the most hateful event; there is no mean about the question. Death is the glorious gate of eternity, of glory and of joy unmixed with a taint of sorrow: there is a vast void in us unfilled while here below. Pardon my writing thus, but you agree with me in theory and my hope is that you and I may know it day by day more by experience: therefore if you see any one fading away (which I do not think is my state) envy him or her and say how long how long will I be passed over, when will my time be come? Let this be with patience for we have great works to do, but *be straitened* till the baptism comes. (27th August, 1868.)

Nonetheless, his experience of sick rooms in Gravesend left him with a lifelong horror of a lingering death:

" I have a horror," he wrote, on the last day of 1868, " of a sick chamber. When a poor partridge or hare has been wounded it gets away from its comrades and dies quickly, and that is what I want to do when the time comes, and my course is finished. The watchings, the whisperings etc. around a sick bed are great trials, which I must be spared."

6

There were moments when the poverty, ignorance and disease of mid-Victorian Gravesend moved him to despair. But his compassion for the poor involved no antagonism to the rich. Christ, he remarks, never " took the part of the poor against the rich individually." And sooner or later he was always able to remind himself that whatever is is for the best; a fundamental doctrine which, it seemed to him, was confirmed by the literal interpretation, which was his custom, of many passages in the Bible.

I was reading (he wrote to Augusta) ' The Lord is *good to all.* His tender mercies are *over all His works*'; so He must be good to all the poor shivering wretches, and He must be showing them tender mercies. It is incomprehensible, but must be true: so I comfort myself, as far as my faith will allow me.

Of which a theologian, it must be presumed, would observe that the writer was making insufficient allowance for the presence, and consequences, of sin in a fallen world. But in the long hours of Bible-reading and meditation, early in the morning before official work at the forts began and late at night, when the last King had been interviewed and the last sickroom visited, Gordon had been evolving for himself a doctrine of sin, and of salvation, which was both highly individual and highly unorthodox. He was well aware that the doctrine was his own—*ye need not*, he reminded Augusta, *that any man teach you*—and its unorthodoxy did not trouble him: " I never expect," he wrote, " to find the views God has given me accepted by all: if true, they will prosper, if not, let them perish." But it had become part of his inmost being, and in various shapes it appears and reappears, year after year, in the somewhat impersonal religious discourses which he poured out, not only to Augusta and Mrs. Freese but to numerous friends and acquaintances, from Gravesend, from Galatz, from Mauritius, from Jerusalem and from the Sudan. And though sometimes obscurely expressed, in essence, like everything about Gordon, it was simple.

Man, he believed, consists of two elements, body and spirit, and these are wholly and for ever distinct. The body is altogether evil, and inevitably doomed: God indwells in the spirit, which is, also inevitably, destined for eternal bliss. And this is true, universally and equally, of all men. To take the promises and threats of scripture, as they are usually taken, as addressed to man as a unity, body and soul, can only, he believed, lead to confusion. The threats are addressed to the doomed body; the promises to the soul, which is effectually guarded, by the indwelling of God and the Atonement of Christ, from being corrupted or destroyed. From this simple doctrine strange conclusions follow. In the flesh sin is inevitable; we are powerless to produce good or resist evil; ". . . my earthly shrine is ordained to certain evil works, and my spiritual shrine is ordained to certain good works; . . . neither in one case nor the other can I alter the decree." But if sin is inevitable, it is also, it appears, of no significance. For " whether a man is guilty of the above works " (and he is referring to the formidable list, commencing *Adultery, fornication, uncleanness, lasciviousness*, . . . in Galatians v, 19-21) " or not is immaterial to his ultimate welfare or salvation." And, in fact, we all are guilty: " there is not a being in the earth who is not guilty in God's sight of every one of these works, for with God the thought is the deed." And though all are guilty, all will be saved, for " the evil in each of us is put off at our leaving the stage of this world, as the actor puts off his clothes." God cannot wish any to perish and " who is to stand in His way? "

Sin indeed, it seems, is not only inevitable, universal and of no ultimate significance; it is positively of moral advantage to our souls. For it discloses to us our true state. ". . . if the devil had his way, we should live perfectly moral lives free from malice, etc., etc., and thus be lulled into a state of security. We are *born* corrupt, and if the devil had his way, we should be kept in ignorance of it: our permitted transgressions show us our state." Moreover, Gordon can never forget that all things work together for good. " Every thought that enters our mind is for our good, even those which come from Satan. . . . What a comfort to feel that our temptations and sins are all working for good." But though sin, he maintained, is morally profitable, in that, by disclosing " our true state," it breeds humility, Gordon could not help realising that conscience seems to say otherwise. His solution of the dilemma, if it can be called a solution, was to ignore human standards.

 . . . it is most wonderful what power and strength living for God's view and not man's gives us. I do many things which are wrong and I can truly say that thanks to God I am comforted in all the trouble because I do not conceal them from Him. He is my master and to Him I am alone accountable, and if I own it in my heart that I am culpable I have such comfort that I do not care what my fellow man says.

A strange and, for anyone but Gordon, a dangerous, doctrine. For it followed that there could be no degrees of virtue; it was impossible for one man to be better than another.

We must allow all men come from Adam and are not different one from another in God's sight, however mysterious this may seem. I accept it, and do not consider myself better than any other being breathing.

We are all lepers . . . Adam, Noah, Moses, David, Solomon, Daniel, John the Baptist, Peter, Paul, Herod, eminent divines, bishops, Kings, all are lepers in the flesh: after the flesh you will not inherit. 'Flesh and blood cannot inherit the kingdom of God' (1 Corinthians xv. 50).

But if in the flesh we are all sinners, all equally and all inevitably, in the spirit we are all destined for salvation, all equally and all inevitably. And the doctrine of universal and equal salvation, Gordon realised, would come as even more of a shock to the orthodox than the doctrine of universal and equal wickedness.

'Favouritism' is the cry, 'I cannot tolerate it. If such be the case I would rather not be a Christian. I do not mind the outwardly good being saved, but I cannot tolerate the saving of the outwardly bad. I cannot agree to the fact of a man, who has led an ungodly life all his days, having the same position as myself, who, for many years, at great inconvenience, have attended many prayer-meetings and services and ordinances . . . I ought to be saved for I am better than he.'

Treasured among Mrs. Freese's papers was a pamphlet of sixty-eight pages, in small octavo; *Christ and His Members* by C.G.G., published in 1868. This was one of the compositions which he had so often sent up, by orderly or Scuttler, a few pages at a time, to Mrs. Freese, urging her to read it "carefully, prayerfully and impartially." In it still lies folded a single sheet, printed in bold type, simply summarising the central doctrine—one of those which the Colonel used to distribute on his country walks, or fling from the windows of railway trains. In the pamphlet the doctrine of the indwelling is set forth in all its elaborate mystical and allegorical setting

—the soul the head of the man, the body his heel; man the head of woman, the flesh her body; Christ the head of man, the woman his body; God the head of Christ, and the souls of men His body. It is a strange little work, its style as unexpected as its theme is unusual. For the naïveté and abruptness of Gordon's staccato, unpunctuated letters has vanished, and in its place, despite occasional lapses, there is a dignity, an occasional beauty even, which suggests that, despite his lack of æsthetic sensibility, had he devoted himself to literary composition his familiarity with the Bible might even have given him, as it gave Ruskin, a command of sonorous prose. The following passage, a description of the Antichrist, is characteristic, both of its strength and its weaknesses.

This king of fierce countenance, and understanding dark sentences, who will think to change times and laws, will have power over the treasures of gold and silver, and precious things of this world, and the glory of the things of the earth will be his for three years and a half (a time corresponding to that spent on the earth by the true Christ in humility and suffering); he will make fire descend from heaven to earth, in the sight of men, similar to the visible descent of the Holy Ghost on the day of Pentecost; and he will appear to those who are in the way of perdition, in the strength of Satan, working with all his might with signs and wonders of falsehood; if it were possible he would deceive the very elect or chosen seed. He will be in the glory of the flesh, the very antithesis or contrast of what the true Christ was; for humility, poverty, peace and truth, there will be pride, riches, war and lying; but the Lord will destroy him with the breath of His lips, and by the brightness of His coming, and none shall help him.

Needless to say, no Church had taught Gordon his strange medley of long-pondered beliefs; nor for that matter had he learnt them from heretics. He read, and was much influenced by, *Christ Mystical* by Hall, but in theology, as in strategy, he was all for the independent command. He never joined Church or sect, though in so far as he had any preference it was for the Church of England and English Presbyterianism. " Join no sect," he wrote to Augusta, " though there may be truth in all." At this time he was an occasional communicant at the Presbyterian Church in Gravesend, but did not yet attribute much importance to the Sacraments. To a Roman Catholic dignitary he once said " Do not forget me in your prayers. Catholic and Protestant are but soldiers in different regiments of Christ's army, but it is the same army and we are all marching together." For a while he would join the Freeses every Saturday in reading and discussing the Bible, but soon even this jarred on his individualism and in November, 1868, he wrote to explain that he did not find " meetings " profitable. Too often he could not bring himself to speak his inmost feelings in company: " therefore I set my face against stereotyped meetings as a bondage." The meetings were duly discontinued.

Unaided, he deduced his creed straight from the Bible. The Bible student, he believed, provided that he sincerely attempts to live up to what he learns, needs no teachers. " The secret of reading the Bible is abiding in Him. . . . ' If any man do My will he shall know of My doctrine': ye need no man to teach you: 'I will teach thee and instruct thee in the way thou shalt go. . . .' He, the mighty God, means what He says when He says He will teach us." " Just as much as we live up to the Light we have given us so much the more light shall we receive." In his Bible study, as in his theology and indeed in his daily life, Gordon was determined to do his utmost to ignore the opinions of his fellow men and to rely only upon God. There is a certain arrogance, no doubt, in this solitary approach to the mysteries, this neglect of the accumulated testimony of the saints, prophets and doctors of the church, but it is the arrogance of the Puritan fathers, an arrogance strangely shot with humility.

Gordon believed the whole of the Bible to be directly inspired by the Holy Spirit, and was prepared to accept any dictum in it, irrespective of circumstances or author, as a pronouncement by the

Almighty Himself. Thus he prefaces a quotation of a celebrated passage in Galatians by explaining " God " (not St. Paul) " tells me what are the works of this flesh which profiteth nothing." And he then proceeds to lay it down that " to profit nothing signifies to make no difference, either one way or the other." " Therefore," whether or not a man is guilty of the deadly sins " is immaterial." And if occasionally he is uneasily aware that his creed is leading him into a logical *impasse*, he is content with the comment " such would be the result of these truths, if we followed human reasoning." This was a reflection to which he must often have had recourse, for inevitably in such a creed, so evolved, there was many a logical *cul de sac*. As a lone theologian he believed in a rigid system of pre-destination, in the light of which all human planning must be superfluous, but as a lone commander he did not cease to plan. This contradiction he would explain on occasion by the theory that in practice his fatalism was limited to the past: " I have nothing further to do when the scroll of events is unrolled than to accept them as being for the best. *Before* it is unrolled it is another matter, and you could not say I sit still and let things happen with this belief." Even in relation to the past, however, his fatalism was far from consistent. It did not prevent him from rebuking or punishing servants and subordinates who made mistakes. When a German servant in the Sudan dropped a precious rifle into the river, although in a letter some while later he could comment ". . . as it was ordained to be lost I soon got over it," he would nevertheless administer as severe a rebuke to the erring Teuton as if he had been solely re-sponsible for his own clumsiness. Indeed, Gordon's rebukes could be so awe-inspiring that he sometimes delegated to a colleague the delivery of some reprimand lest the culprit should be completely overcome.

Yet strangely enough the inconsistencies and self-contradictions of Gordon's creed mattered little. Despite them all it *worked*. And not merely because he was prepared in the last resort to ignore the logical *impasse*; to plan when planning, according to his tenets, was irrational; to console himself with the reflection that it was only

irrational in so far as " we followed human reasoning." The strength
of Gordon's creed was not his readiness to turn a blind eye when
it broke down: its strength was the simple fact that the central core
of it was true. For it was in the power of " the secret " that he was
able to become both lion-tamer and saint. If he believed that
"Jesus is the Son of God" God dwelt in him; what more was
needed? From the one tremendous fact all else followed. All life,
down to its most insignificant details, was overshadowed by God,
and God's purposes. " In the dressing-table drawer of my room, left-
side," he writes to Augusta on 15th June, 1867, " I have left my purse
. . . I have not yet seen why I left it, but I am sure it is for some
good thing, perhaps because if I had not done so I should not have
written to you." " I asked Mr. Wyatt, the Catholic Priest," he
writes to Mrs. Freese in September, 1869, " if he knew God lived
in him and he said Yes." Some of Gordon's other beliefs would
doubtless have astounded the Catholic priest, but though he may
have been mildly surprised at the naïvety of this particular question,
he cannot have found it difficult to answer. For " the secret," the
indwelling of the Holy Spirit, was both simple and orthodox.
And it was the mainspring of Gordon's life.

Since, therefore, he had embraced this central truth his heresies
were comparatively of little significance. As William Temple[1]
wrote: " For the Church, commissioned to transmit to all generations the true doctrine which may elicit saving faith, heresy is more
deadly than hypocrisy or even than conscious sin; but for the
individual the one vital matter is personal trust and accepted heresy
in its effect upon his soul may be quite unimportant. There have
been saintly heretics and orthodox worldlings."

Gordon always regretted his belated discovery, the years of
comparative darkness between the first youthful enlightenment at
Pembroke and the fuller revelation at Gravesend: " I have one
jewel given to me and it is my only treasure as it is to many others,
but . . . it is greatly enhanced in value to me who lost it for so many
years." His aim was now a life of union with God, issuing in good

[1] *Readings in St. John's Gospel* (1949), 37, 8.

works. This was the conscious aim of Florence Nightingale also, and years later, when they met, each instantly recognised in the other a kindred spirit.

He never forgot the moment when " the secret " was revealed to him. His account of it is recorded by Mrs. Freese.

> . . . while dressing rather listlessly before dinner his eye fell on an opened Bible on the table and on these words: " Whosoever confesseth that Jesus is the Son of God, God dwelleth in him and he in God." Suddenly it flashed upon him that he had found a jewel of priceless value—he had found what alone could satisfy him, oneness with God: henceforth that was the key to his whole after life and he wondered he had never seen it before. He wondered far more that anyone could read such words and be indifferent to them and he now tried to make them known to as many as he could. . . .

Mrs. Freese herself thought that Gordon read too much into the words of St. John. Mere verbal confession, she warned him, was not enough. When a " little untaught lad " answered " Yes " to the question " Do you believe Jesus is the Son of God ? " Gordon ought not to encourage him to believe that he was necessarily in union with God. But Gordon was adamant. And with him, at any rate, it was a confession not of the lips merely but of the heart. The entries in the brief spiritual autobiography, to which I have already referred, all centre upon " the secret." The next four run as follows:

7.[1] Next He showed me that He was glorified only so far as those fruits were produced.
8. Next that the Holy Ghost produced them.
9. Next the great truth that it was the Holy Ghost *in* me which produced them while myself was dead and incapable of producing anything good.
10. Next that God *in me* gave out faith as the fire gives out heat. . . .

---

[1] There is no number 6 on the sheet.

7

With his fervent self-made creed, his proselytising zeal and his constant contact with the unconverted in slum, sickroom and barracks, it was natural that Gordon should have taken to composing his own evangelistic literature. His notes to Mrs. Freese frequently invoke her assistance: " I send you up two or three pages more, and if you will be in I will D.V. come up for a minute to-day for I want to ask you to look at some notes." He discusses with her a project for having a leaflet translated into Russian, French, German, Italian, Arabic and Spanish—to which, four months later, he adds Danish, Dutch, Portuguese, Greek and Armenian. And a translation into French at least was printed, so that in October, 1870, he was urging Mrs. Freese, who expected to be in the vicinity of the Prince Imperial of France, " please drop a tract near the Prince, it is a gun to give him: leave it in the Park. . . . I have prayed for the Emperor for years and now through you God will perhaps give peace to a poor wearied soul." And there were other distinguished recipients of French tracts. In April, 1871, hearing that a friend with whom he had served in the Crimea had been killed in the Franco-Prussian War, Gordon sent inquiries to the French commander, Marshal McMahon. The opportunity was too good to miss: " I sent him twice ' *Venez a moi*,' etc., and Matt. xi, 29, but not the whole of the tract."

Gordon's philanthropic activities made serious inroads on his pocket as well as his time, and he was often in debt. During the cotton famine at the time of the American Civil War he sold the medal which the Emperor of China had had struck for him, after first erasing the inscription; it fetched £15 for the fund raised to relieve distress in Lancashire. No doubt he remembered the slums of Manchester which he had learned to know in 1867. Parting with the medal had been a wrench, and thereafter " give up your medal " was his way of advising a friend not to set overmuch store by his possessions. And in July, 1874, he reverted to the episode in a letter

to Augusta from Saubat on the Nile: " depend on it," he wrote,
" the wrench is worth it; once over you are case-hardened." He
rebuked Mrs. Freese for wearing a gold watch-chain on the ground
that " it would keep a poor family for a week," and though he
accepted her defence that the thing had been a gift from her husband,
he would never wear a chain himself and seldom his medals—
" having given *all* to God, what am I to keep back? *I see no
limit.*"

Occasionally he was able to make a sacrifice which saved time
as well as money. Thus he had been a keen photographer, but on
New Year's Day, 1867, he was writing to Major Donnelly that he
was anxious to sell his camera for £40: " my reason for parting
with it is that it takes up my time from matters of more import,
and the pursuit is of such an engrossing nature as to grow on me
in a dangerous way for peace and quiet." In order to make time
for his manifold activities he resolutely evaded social and public
engagements. Though he was always ready to teach in a Sunday
school or say a few cheerful words to a sweeps' tea-party or the
aged inmates of the workhouse nothing would persuade him to take
the chair at a public meeting, even on behalf of a good cause. " I
will see your Dr. Knight," he wrote reluctantly to Mrs. Freese, in
April, 1869, " but mean positively to refuse to go on the stage. I
cannot and will not do it. There, that is over." Indeed, he did not
care for good causes. For he had the practical philanthropist's
natural suspicion of platform benevolence and publicly organised
morality. And though his belief that Providence orders all in no
way discouraged his own assaults on ignorance and suffering, when it
was a question of Leagues and Associations of worthy citizens to
promote, or resist, this, that or the other he was apt to remind
himself that human effort is supererogatory. " Like temperance
and other leagues, I do not like them," he told Mrs. Freese. " Let
God work and do not try to work for Him."

For the same reason it did not occur to him that legislation
might improve the social conditions in Gravesend and elsewhere.
It was after all still the era of Laissez Faire Individualism, when with

almost all economists and politicians it was an article of faith that interference by the state could only do harm: Gordon was by natural bent an individualist of individualists, and would have been an individualist even without his predestinarian theology, but it so happened that his theology reinforced his individualism. His contemporary, Shaftesbury, devout Evangelical and, like Gordon, a devoted student of the Bible who could on occasion, like Gordon, practise bibliomancy, was also by temperament an individualist who was profoundly shocked by the sufferings of the poor. Nevertheless, thanks to the opportunities of his public station and his lifelong advocacy of factory, and other, reforms Shaftesbury became unintentionally, and almost unconsciously, one of the first protagonists of the Collectivist doctrines of state interference which were to dominate the present century. Shaftesbury's public and Parliamentary labours touched more lives than did Gordon's lonely apostolate, but less intimately and from a much greater distance.

Mrs. Freese did not altogether approve of Gordon's solitary life. It would be good for him, she thought, and certainly good for them, if he were occasionally to meet some of her other friends. And there could be no question that the unpredictable colonel with the eye "that might have lived a thousand years" would lend distinction to the simple social gatherings at Home Mead. But when, quite early in their friendship, she ventured to admonish Gordon for "cooping himself up," he defended himself very bluntly.

> I have much secular work to do during the day and it is as much as I can do to visit the very few people I do go to in the evenings. I know you and Mr. Freese have every human and many spiritual comforts beyond those of many of our rank of life and therefore though it may be more pleasant there is not any call for me to leave other more important work to spend the immortal hours in desultory converse. If I do that at all it ought to be to my relations who have the first claim on *my time after the flesh*. You will excuse my writing so plainly but it is better that that should be understood. I am sure there is truth in what is said, do not

coop yourself up, but I do not yet see that there is profit in social meetings for me.

Sometimes Gordon's determination to avoid society went further than the refusing of formal invitations. There were occasions when he positively avoided the Freeses themselves. He always left his front door open on principle and one day Mr. and Mrs. Freese walked in unannounced. To their surprise they heard Gordon's footsteps making for the cellar. Not suspecting that the hero could be in flight they made their way to the drawing-room and sat down; but when after ten minutes Gordon had not re-emerged from the cellar they were tactful enough to withdraw.

Fixed social engagements afflicted Gordon with a sense of claustrophobia, and on the rare occasions when he undertook in advance to pay a visit he was as likely as not to break his promise. Occasionally there would be formidable invitations, to a levée or a dinner, which for professional reasons he could not evade; and he was often surprised to find that they proved to be less disagreeable than he had expected. Perhaps he had dreaded them so much that the reality could not match the anticipation; perhaps, when compelled to encounter it he found gaiety and company not without its attractions, and for that very reason avoided it thereafter even more resolutely. "I went to town yesterday in that wet," he writes in December, 1869, "and got back at 12.30 p.m., to dine with Sir M. Stephenson. It was, however, and I will say that of all my forced vagaries, not so bad as I expected. One must go through the daily work and not murmur but the command in China was quiet to my life here." A military levée which he felt compelled to attend in July, 1868, had seemed all the more distasteful in anticipation because it might be regarded as a celebration of the triumphant success of the Abyssinian expedition which he had so vainly, and so self-reproachfully, longed to command. In the previous April, when news of the capture of Magdala had just reached London, he had confessed to Mrs. Freese in a hurried postscript " terribly disturbed by the war tidings, though I was helped. It is (though we may sometimes stumble at it) more important to speak to the 'Scuttlers' than to take Magdala." But the levée, though he could not prevent his thoughts running on Abyssinia, proved not unenjoyable, as he afterwards confessed.

> The event is over and all are a day's march nearer home. Theodore[1] with his upturned face with its glassy eyes staring up into the blue expanse of heaven into which we may trust his bright and glorious soul has entered, is home and Napier fêted and honoured toils on that march to the haven of rest. 'He will not last more' than four or five years was a remark made. It was a glorious sight, 200 officers, the Prince and the Duke, etc., etc.

The forecast as to Napier's demise proved singularly mistaken; created Lord Napier of Magdala that year, and a field marshal fifteen years later, he survived for another twenty-two years.

8

With his equalitarian religious creed, his sympathy for the poor of Gravesend and his complete disregard of convention it was natural that Gordon should often show little patience with the contemporary cult of respectability. It was an age whose besetting sin was arrogance; in which *Punch* depicted the typical *grande dame* haughtily dispensing charity from her carriage and pair, with its liveried coachman and footman. "Bless you, my Lady. May we meet in heaven!" says the curtseying recipient of blankets. "Good gracious!! Drive on Jarvis!!!" ejaculates my Lady in horror. Gordon, who at this time was carrying the bundles of the poor and mending the clothes of his Scuttlers in Gravesend, had no hard words for the rich; but he had the keenest of eyes for sham, and in particular for self-righteousness, and had little respect for Victorian penology. The

---

[1] Emperor of Abyssinia.

General C.E. Gordon. (an hour's sketch taken just before he left for the East. 21ˢᵗ Decᵣ 1882.)

Gordon by E. Clifford
Just before he left for the East in 1882

world, he wrote, permits no extenuation of theft or lies, because
they are offences against itself, but it has no condemnation for
spiritual pride. " Weigh the mother and the son in the Mackays'
case in the sanctuary balances and what would be the result ? . . . I
could condemn a man to death without a twinge and . . . feel that
I was as guilty as he was. *Punish* but let it be with mercy and knowing
we deserve the same fate." He can even sympathise with " our poor
brothers " of the revolutionary Commune in Paris; at least they
have burnt down palaces and not cottages.

It was an age, too, in which even the moderately prosperous
could employ retinues of servants and live in almost complete idleness; whence the prevalence of what an earlier generation had
known as the vapours, a complaint of which Gordon himself always
spoke as ' the doles.' He frequently denounced the doles to Mrs.
Freese, pointing out that they were confined to those with sufficient
spare time to indulge them; " the poor are so much more cheerful
than our class of life "; " you seldom or never hear of the kitchen-
maid or washer-woman having them." His remedy was simple:
" ' take in the washing ' is the great antidote for all our ills."
Gordon himself was not likely to succumb to the doles through
idleness, and his cherished " secret " made for serenity. But the
consciousness of suffering and sin were ever present with him,
and he was often melancholy. He can protest that he is the happiest
of mortals but there is a note of self-exculpation in his voice.

> You must not think I am at [all] disposed to be depressed which
> I am not, thank God. I never lose His presence. Always feel
> cheerful and happy however much I may look otherwise. This
> is a great gift and enables me to go joyfully on. . . . I do not
> think there is so happy a being as I am, perplexed and attacked
> as I am; it seems to be like water on a duck's back.

Yet there were moods in which he could confess that he was by
no means always cheerful. " I read extracts of Lord Byron in
Murray which please me," he wrote in October, 1871, as he was

leaving Gravesend. " He was a melancholy sad man and I am no better. I do not enjoy life and its glories but think too deeply of its realities."

9

Sternly though Gordon disapproved of the doles, he could be long-suffering with its victims. When a hypochondriac friend, who relied on him for consolation, arrived unexpectedly, intent on a lengthy visit, he reported with consternation " *Auto da fé* arrived suddenly and appeared in the garden this morning . . . and is going to stay. I can add no more than a suppressed wish that it was this day fort-night or three weeks." But he did his best for the uninvited guest, and when the three weeks were up, wrote gleefully " Peace reigns here. *Auto da fé!!!* (hurrah!) will leave (hurrah!) on Monday (hurrah!) though I have asked him to stay." Indeed, drawn by his deep inward serenity, the melancholy were apt to seek out Gordon as a moth flies out of the shadows to the lamp. An older namesake of his, Sir William Gordon, who had formed a deep affection and admiration for him in the trenches of the Crimea, and was now commanding in Scotland, came to visit him at Gravesend. (Mrs. Freese, annotating Gordon's letters in later years, was not sure that Sir William was not the Auto da Fé whose departure on a previous occasion had provoked such jubilation.) Sir William was prone to melancholy and when he pressed Gordon to become his A.D.C., the younger man felt constrained, out of sympathy, to accept. But no sooner had he accepted than he was tortured by misgivings and regrets. How could he leave Richen and Carter and Miss Surridge and the Scuttlers? And for Lanarkshire, where, though one might scatter tracts there was nobody to pick them up, where the in-digenous Kings were inaccessible and Sir William disapproved of evangelism? Agonised notes to Mrs. Freese reported the arrival of a letter which he had not had the courage to open. But after a few days of indecision he cast his scruples to the wind and wrote to Sir

William to withdraw his acceptance. "I broke down to-day at
3.30 a.m. and wrote to decline the apt. P.S. The whole business
is now a battle of Waterloo."

A month later, however, he was in Lanarkshire staying with the
general. This was the least that he could do. That the general was
in so melancholy a mood that even this took some doing is suggested
by a letter in which, after reporting that he is just back from a
fifteen-mile walk with Sir William, Gordon adds, " the more one
looks forward to the inheritance [of] the grave the happier one will
be." Not long afterwards he was again with Sir William, who this
time was in so black a mood that Gordon made an excuse for hiding
his host's razors. Sir William's brother, for whom Gordon telegraphed, asked that they should be returned, Gordon complied and
Sir William cut his own throat. The unhappy man lingered for a
week; Gordon was with him to the last, and at his request kissed
him before he died. " Sir William," he wrote, " left for his home
in perfect peace and without pain, and I thank God I would have
nothing altered which has passed." He had resolutely refused his
friend's repeated offers of a substantial legacy, only accepting a silver
teaset which, he said, would serve to pay for his own funeral.
Inevitably, however, he did not retain it long: it soon disappeared,
swallowed up, no doubt, by the demands of his charities. The whole
macabre episode haunted Gordon to the end of his life. Long
afterwards, on 17th July, 1877, during the crisis of a dangerous
expedition against rebels and slave-traders in the Sudan, he dwelt
on it in detail in a letter to Augusta—the mistake which had caused
Sir William's transfer to an inferior post, his mental agony and
gradual lapse into insanity; the winter drizzle and the melancholy
walks of twenty miles a day through the dripping woodlands.

10

Though the Gravesend forts represented little more than routine
to one who was only too well aware that they must inevitably prove

useless, Gravesend itself was engrossing, and Gordon had little time to spare for his wider professional interests. And, in fact, though he cannot yet have realised it, his career as a professional soldier was already behind him. Nor, for that matter, did he bestow much attention at present on public affairs. He read the newspapers, and during the Abyssinian campaign he borrowed the *Illustrated London News* from the Freeses, but soon after the fighting was over he asked that the loan should be discontinued. The routine of the forts and then Bible-reading and meditation, letter writing—he would always be a prolific correspondent—and the Scuttlers, the sick and poor of Gravesend—for the present these were his life, and he was inclined to resent the intrusions of the outer world, whether they came as reminders of past glories or as invitations for the future. The Taiping rebellion and the Ever Victorious army were best forgotten, while as for the future, the secret yearning, of which he could not help being conscious, for a return to the active life surely represented worldly ambition and must therefore be sternly repressed. Sometimes, however, the past intruded unexpectedly. A party of Chinese visitors to England, several of whom had served in the Ever Victorious, discovered his whereabouts and presented themselves in a body at his front door. When it opened they pushed unceremoniously in past the astonished domestic, with excited cries of " Gordon, Gordon, Gordon." Gordon promptly appeared, and the afternoon was spent in the exchange of reminiscences, but when the time came for him to escort his uninvited guests to the station it chanced that they passed a shop window in which Chinese works of art were displayed. Among them was a Yellow Jacket, and Gordon pointed to it, incautiously remarking " I have got that." Instantly, and as one man, his guests knelt down in the London mud to do obeisance—for, after all, the Mandarin of the Yellow Jacket possessed power of life and death. They did not kneel long. Once again they heard the voice which had so often restored discipline when the Ever Victorious was on the verge of open mutiny, and automatically they scrambled to their feet. But as he saw them into their train Gordon must have heaved a sigh of relief.

There was also a letter from Li Hung Chang. After referring to Gordon's work at Gravesend and congratulating him on the marriage of his sister to Dr. Moffitt the writer gave a brief account of the fortunes of various mutual acquaintances and of the further triumphs over insurgents which, thanks to the auspicious halo surrounding his Imperial master, he had himself been enabled to gain. There followed a passage which must have lingered in Gordon's memory.

That peace may long continue I fervently join with you in wishing, but if an appeal to arms should at any time become necessary, I shall whilst taking the precautions enjoined by you in your note, still be inclined to look to you for aid. The flags of the Ever Victorious Army are still in my possession. From time to time I have them unfurled for inspection, and whilst they serve to remind me of old times and doings they also cause my thoughts to wander to you who are so far away.

Save, however, for such rare intrusions the past was effectively buried. The future, however, was more potent. He could but await " the unrolling of the scroll," not seeking to shape his own destiny, but following where he was led. On Easter Sunday, 1871, he was invited by Mr. Gladstone's government to accept the vacant English membership of the Danubian Commission. At first sight it was hardly the sort of post for which his Chinese exploits had marked him out; nevertheless, the Commission had grown out of the boundary delimitation in which he had once taken part, and though officialdom was doubtless wasting the genius of the greatest living commander of irregulars it was at least making him a not ungenerous offer, for the seat on the Commission carried with it a salary of £2000 a year, and some prestige in that ambiguous borderland which lies between soldiering and politics. After some reflection Gordon accepted the offer; it was thus, it seemed, that the scroll was to be unrolled. But he accepted it with a studied lack of enthusiasm, and when, in September, a month before he was to leave, he was summoned to the Foreign Office and received with chilling official indifference he declared that he welcomed this evidence that he was being relegated to the wings of the stage.

> I went to the F. Office and saw Mr. Hammond, the Under Secretary F. Affairs. He was very civil, but knew nothing of my destination and merely expressed a wish to see me, in case of having anything to say before I left. I am glad of this as it shows that the place is not of much interest.

II

Before the end of that September Gordon had left Gravesend for good. Never again would he have a home of his own in England. The second and more arduous stage of his strange career was about to open; but Gravesend, he would have said, had equipped him for it, for there he had found " the secret." Naturally, he did his best to leave unobtrusively, but the coming change of command was known at the forts and inevitably it became known in the back streets of Gravesend. Moreover, there was his furniture to be given away. At first he had promised it all to the Freeses but with increasing frequency as the day of departure approached he would ask apologetically whether Mr. Freese set special store by this table, or that bed—" Mrs. So-and-so would be so glad of it and I thought you wouldn't mind." Mrs. Freese was always ready to waive her claims, but for reasons of sentiment she was anxious for some memento of Fort House and she began to fear that nothing whatever would be left her. Eventually, however, Gordon appeared at her front door one Sunday evening after church bearing in his arms all that remained of his household goods, a drawing-room fender. Of his battle-scarred Taiping flags he had presented several to his favourite school, where once a year for many years to come they would be ceremonially unfurled in memory of ' the Kernel.' There

were no formal leave-takings, but the local newspaper printed a
tribute to the ' exquisite charity ' of one whose departure would ' be
felt by many as a personal calamity.' The parting with the Freeses
Gordon postponed by persuading them to visit Dover from which
he was to leave for Calais. And it was at Dover that he told Mrs.
Freese how thankful he was not to have a wife; the pain of leave-
taking, he said, would be too great, and he would never have taken
a wife with him overseas. At last the day of departure came. Mr.
Freese accompanied Gordon as far as Calais. Mrs. Freese stood on
Dover pier, watching the boat till it, and the figure of Gordon,
waving from the deck, faded out of sight.

12

The parting from the Freeses, and from Gravesend, the nearest
approach to a home he had known for many years, or would ever
know again, had induced in Gordon a melancholy mood, of regret
for the past if not of positive homesickness. Throughout the
Channel crossing he talked to Mr. Freese of their days at Gravesend,
and from Mainz, during the overland journey, he wrote to Mrs.
Freese that there was no place like Britain. Nor did life at Galatz,
on the Danube, which he reached before the end of October, 1871,
prove so engrossing as to obliterate memories of Gravesend. Indeed,
Galatz for Gordon was a sort of epilogue to Gravesend, an epilogue
in a minor key. Like Gravesend Galatz would mean exile from the
world of action, but unlike Gravesend it contained no Kings, no
Freeses and virtually no scope for evangelism or philanthropy. No
sooner had he arrived than, foreseeing what these deprivations
would mean to him, he was seized with a sudden inspiration. Why
should not Mr. Freese, who was in poor health and had lately suffered
some serious financial losses, come out to Galatz, nominally as his
secretary—and bring a Scuttler with him ? He sat down at once to
pen an invitation, painting the potentialities of life on the Danube
in glowing colours.

... I would propose to you to come out here as my Secretary, where you would not have much to do. The Secretary whom Col. Stokes had is going home, and I could offer you for 6 months or a year your keep and house-room and 150 £ a year; this would be about an equivalent for 300 £. You might leave Mrs. Freese and children at Southampton and go home as often as you liked to pay the expense. If you like to come, let me know and come out about middle of December by Vienna, Cracow, Lemberg, Czernowitz. You would be allowed 25 £ for passage here so you would have enough nearly to bring out someone with you. You know after Vienna only nobles, English and fools go 1st class. I was one of the fools. ... You could bring out a Gravesend laddie with you, little Webster, and I could send him home in the spring; or any other *tractable* person you could find. I need not say you would be welcome; would find everything *comme il faut* as far as house is concerned, an Harmonium and horses to ride as much as you like, regular quiet hours with sacrifices of praise every day. Mrs. Freese would find South'ton a nice place and my people know everyone. I think she has tact enough to play the difficult game of keeping in with my family in its various members and would pay my mother plenty of visits and hear a good deal on one text *I do not like.* There is a capital doctor here, and you would be very comfortable; lots of Pickelhaub civilians and Deutsch ladies for to *spriechen* with. ... If you take any laddie out and think Willie Webster is small take Willie or Bill Palmer of Chalk; he has been a gentleman's groom—let him know it is only for three or four months at 3 £ a month with his keep and let him have say from 6 to 8 £ of clothes.

13

But Mr. Freese was not well enough to travel, even first class, and Gordon was left to face the tedium of a Commissioner's life without the solace of a kindred spirit. For the few English in Galatz, he soon discovered, shared none of his own interests; and when they unanimously assured the newcomer that he must do this and would be certain to enjoy that he could but eye them with polite scepticism and register a silent conviction that he would almost certainly do nothing of the kind. Provokingly enough, moreover, he felt a certain responsibility, as English Commissioner, for the behaviour of the English, and this was not always decorous. "We were much bothered by the Waldrons," he wrote to Sir William Goodenough on the 8th of January, " who had rows with every Hotel Keeper at Sarajevo, Bucharest and Galatz. . . . Count Gloria, the Italian Consul, saw Lady Waldron sitting on the stairs of the Grand Hotel at 8 p.m. Her daughter had driven her out of the room. Altogether they, or rather the daughter, behaved very badly. I wrote to Lord Rosslyn about them, as guardedly as I could."

As for the neighbourhood, being semi-civilised it was, Gordon decided, far less interesting than if it had been wholly barbaric; it was, moreover, extremely cold in winter and ravaged by cholera in summer. Nor did the work of the Commission seem likely either to interest, or occupy, him much. It was the counterpart, he wrote to Sir William Goodenough, of a combination of the Thames Conservancy and the Elder Brethren of Trinity House and its efficiency was " not what it ought to be." His predecessor, Colonel Stokes, had kept high state and dominated his colleagues, but Gordon had no wish, he wrote to Donnelly, to " rule in the Commission except with my knowledge." " Stokes," he told Sir William, " was a very solemn ceremonious old thing who thought of nothing but this Commission, in which he ruled as a Despot over all the other Commissioners: if you differed with him, it was at once a personal question, and so at last the other commissioners did not care to get into a personal squabble with him. . . . I was a dreadful thorn in his side, as I could not help showing I did not care a bit for state and differed with him as to allowing the other Commissioners to have a say in all affairs and not only to let them, but to *make* them do so which I have not yet been able to do." Gordon had no liking for the pomps and ceremonies in which his colleagues all delighted. A certain number of official festivities even he could not avoid, but in general life as a Commissioner, it seemed all too clear, would be one of well-paid idleness. He must devise his own occupations.

The town of Galatz itself was far from attractive. As he wrote to Mr. Penman, a Gravesend schoolmaster, on 5th March:

> The place is a large, very ill-found, straggling town. You have mud ankle deep in all the streets, the population cosmopolitan, and numbering many Jews who are an evil-looking lot and who are much disliked. There are lots of Greeks. If you saw the Jews you would certainly wonder that they should have been and are now the chosen people of God, and that our Saviour was of their nation. They are the leeches of the country. The Roumans are a thriftless race, and get into debt to them so that they squeeze the lives out of the people, and living on very little, never spending anything they drain and exhaust the country. One large town here is called the New Jerusalem, from the number of Jews in it.

And so he explored the countryside, noting the comparatively idyllic life of the peasantry, the prevalence of swamps, the ancient battlefields of Turks and Russians and the cunning with which the Russians contrived to control the populace through its priests. But in the Danubian winter walking was almost as perilous as driving. " It is no joke," he told Sir William,

> walking over cracking ice with the view of fish swimming beneath you. The great sobs the ice gives, and the wild wail of wolves makes it cheerful work. Here you may die without any fuss, for there are but few people about. . . . In driving over the ice the horses will get along without breaking the ice, but the carriage goes through and so you dash along, the horses on the ice and wheels of carriage on the bottom. If the horses stop they go in and then it is a fix.

In respect of " spiritual matters," he told Mr. Penman, Galatz meant " complete exile." A service read by the Consul on Sundays and an occasional discussion with an Italian Catholic " who is a nice fellow, but who, of course, must think very differently from us "—this was all it had to offer him.

And so he pored over the Bible, and spent hours in solitary meditation and prayer. He had formed the habit of keeping a long list of those for whom he prayed, and he noted in a letter to Mrs. Freese one curious consequence of his prayers.

> Do you know, my experience is that if you pray for anyone, that person is sure to like you, let him be ever so much agst you at the beginning, at any rate, he will be drawn to you, and eventually his path in life will cross your own. It is even in a worldly way a good investment.

Sometimes, in order to devote himself to these meditations, he had recourse to unconventional methods of shutting out the world. " I had locked myself in," he told Mr. Lilley, " to avoid visitors. An individual tried the door just now but there was no answer." At times he even had recourse to current secular literature, reporting to the Freeses that Martin Tupper's notorious *Proverbial Philosophy*, the fourth and last series of which had just appeared, was a " capital book, and full of wise, deep thoughts," and approving of the " religious allusions " in Longfellow's poems. Charles Kingsley, too, pleased him; for he could never suppress a faint shock of surprise when he came across evidence that others shared the religious beliefs over which he had pondered in solitude. " It is wonderful," he wrote to Augusta, " how he alludes to the same truths. I expect that very many think as we do, if they [? we] knew it."

14

His letters to Mr. Lilley, the Presbyterian Minister at Gravesend, were full of messages to his favourites and inquiries as to their fortunes—" call on Mrs. P. and let me know how they are. Billy's the one I want to hear about;" " I hope that Harry A. is well again; he was a nice laddie and it gives me pleasure to hear of him;" " dear little Arthur, I wish I could see the little wretch." Now he is asking Major Donnelly to befriend a bugler at Dover, now encouraging Mr. Lilley to use his name with any ship captains at Gravesend who may be willing to take boys to sea.

To Mr. Penman he writes, dating his letter 5th March, 1872, " the day of your School treat," that he prays twice daily for the welfare of the school and teachers, and that even among the swamps of the Danube " you see the same careful, loving mothers, the same careless, happy Russian Willie Websters running about as in Gravesend." Typical of many letters which he addressed from Galatz direct to the Kings of Gravesend was one which now hangs, framed, upon the wall of the grandson of its original recipient, Benjamin Niblett, then a boy of eighteen.

MY DEAR BENJAMIN,

I have heard from Mr. Lilley you are at Lee Station, and Mrs. Miller, kind good person, tells me that she has seen you. I dare say that some day you will see me pass your station, perhaps in July, somehow or another. I often speak to a Friend about you and I dare say you hear Him speak in a quiet loving way to you, telling you that He has a bright, happy home where you will not know what sorrow is, that bright and happy land you used to think of. Talk to that Friend in any difficulty and He will help you better than anyone else in this world could. Believe me.   Yours very truly

                                        C. G. GORDON

Nor was it by any means only the youthful Kings of Gravesend who continued to occupy his thoughts. Mr. Lilley frequently recounted the problems of the aged, the destitute and the ne'er-do-wells of his flock, and from Galatz flowed back a steady stream of advice and practical assistance. " He has 25s. a week and no family: less ♀ and more steadiness is what he wants;" " glad to hear of B.; let me know if any money is wanted and I will see what I can do." And the task of finding for " the Old Bird," an aged gardener reputed to sleep his afternoons away in the greenhouse, two reluctant employers prepared to pay ten shillings a week between them for his services involved the new Commissioner in a protracted correspondence, after which a special note of anxiety can be detected in the inquiry " How is the Old Bird and Mrs. W. ? "

15

But it was not easy to be cheerful. The news from home was depressing. His youngest brother died in the first weeks of 1872, leaving a widow and six children under nine virtually destitute. " Which would you wish her to have," Gordon asked Mrs. Freese, " £100,000 in Bank, or the Friend of the widow? We must say the latter." But this did not prevent him from deciding that he must assist her, or from adding to the financial burden of his Gravesend pensions by insuring his life for £2,000 for her benefit.

During this first summer as a Commissioner he was able to leave Galatz for a visit to the neglected British war cemeteries in the Crimea. This, too, was a depressing experience—the Turks were digging up soldiers' bodies to rob them of their rings—but on his way back through Constantinople a chance encounter befell him which was to alter the course of his life. At the British Embassy he found himself in conversation with Nubar Pasha, the Armenian Prime Minister of Ismail, the Khedive of Egypt. The Armenian, ever ready to acquire useful information, inquired whether Gordon knew of an officer of the Royal Engineers qualified to succeed Sir Samuel Baker as Governor of the Equatorial Provinces of the Sudan. And then, struck by the boyish manner and penetrating eye of this unconventional colonel, he went further: would his new acquaintance himself be willing to take service under the Khedive? The task of the Governor, to establish order and suppress slavery in the Sudan, would be a formidable one, but to Gordon just now, as he contrasted it with the inglorious idleness of Galatz, it presented special attractions. Was this the unrolling of the scroll, and such the nature of the task for which first in Gravesend and now in Galatz he had been being prepared? Before they parted, Nubar had gathered that, if the post were offered him, and if the British Government raised no objections, Gordon would accept it.

That December Gordon was back in England for a few weeks' leave. His mother was obviously failing and could hardly bear him out of her sight: " I am in close attendance," he told Mrs. Freese, " very close I may think sometimes; but I fear it must soon come to an end for a time." He rarely left Southampton, but he contrived with his brother, Henry, the Freeses and their children to attend the lying-in-state of the exiled Napoleon III at Camden House that January. For Gordon, who always felt a sympathy for sinners, had for some while taken a fascinated interest in the career of the flamboyant Louis Napoleon, and after the visit to Camden House he asked Mrs. Freese to procure him a photograph of the Empress and of the house itself, and if possible some violets from the graveside. And three days later he could not resist leaving Southampton again. " I was at the funeral " he wrote triumphantly to Mrs. Freese.

I was at the funeral!!! Could not resist it. Came down by 9 a.m. train and left at 11.15 a.m. Do not be vexed at my not coming to you but I had an appt in London and could not spare time ; besides, I don't know why, I felt it much, and wanted to be alone. . . . I think the Emperor was a kind-hearted, unprincipled man, a man who in the respectable world was a bad man, but to whom Our Saviour said, I dare say often, come with me, weary and heavy-laden, and I will give thee rest.

He managed, too, to visit the Freeses at Gravesend one Sunday (though it would be too expensive, he said, to visit the Ragged

School) and told Mrs. Freese that he considered himself shelved at
Galatz. To which Mrs. Freese replied that she believed that like
Moses in the desert he was being prepared in loneliness for some
great work yet to be done.

16

By the third of February he was back in Galatz, having travelled
by way of Berlin, where he had taken off his hat to the Kaiser in
Unter den Linden, and decided that the Germans seemed " a hard
people." Life on the Danube was no more exhilarating than before,
and in letters home he repeatedly complained of his compulsory
idleness. As summer came the usual cholera broke out. From
England came news that his mother was stricken by paralysis. And
the mortality rate among the sea-going Scuttlers of Gravesend was
tragically high. " Martin is married," he wrote to Mrs. Freese
(25th July, 1873). " You remember a white-haired lad. Styles fell
from Masthead and was killed just before marriage. Patrick died of
fever. Marshall and Bennet fell overboard and lie quiet in the deep.
Dawson drowned bathing. Frost has gone home." It was indeed
difficult to be cheerful. And always, an aggravation of all his other
trials, there remained the consciousness that he was shelved. Not
that he was eager, as he had once been, for fighting. Gravesend and
the Secret lay between him and China. And he had seen too much
suffering now to be able lightheartedly to take his share in inflicting
more, even though he could always remind himself that everything,
even cruelty and pain, represents the will of God. He was very
prone to compassion nowadays and when he reported the apparent
sufferings of the sturgeon caught by the Russian fishermen on the
Danube he felt compelled to add " I dare say God softens this to
them also." But although he was no longer so eager for active
service, for action of some sort he did crave. For eight years now
there had been leisure for meditation, and though he had assuredly
not been inactive, there had been no action of the stirring kind which

called forth his special powers. And, perhaps, he told himself reproachfully, as he meditated in solitude or explored the country-side that summer, he also desired public applause, yearning " to board the tram of the world," that tram of which he so vehemently disapproved but which always exercised over him so powerful a fascination.

And recently a rare opportunity to board the tram had presented itself. For during that summer of 1873 an expedition against the King of Ashanti was being prepared. It was not until August that the Cabinet decided to send it, with Sir Garnet Wolseley in command; but it had for some while been generally known that an expedition was probable, and on 24th July the *Daily News* published an article denouncing the system of promotion by purchase in the army and the consequent neglect of the Royal Engineers in general and of Gordon in particular. ". . . in what other way than by crediting it to partiality," demanded the *Daily News*, " can we account for that systematic neglect on the part of the Horse Guards of the high, we might almost say the transcendant, claims of " Chinese Gordon ' ? "

Here the nation, by what may be called a stroke of good fortune, discovered in one of its younger officers such a genius for war and such a power for command as in any other service would have carried the possessor directly onward to the highest posts that a soldier can fill. Never did general in the world's history more successfully raise an army, more admirably train it, more skilfully conduct it from victory to victory. Never, it may well be added, did a hero more modestly and cheerfully lay down his high position. Such a soldier should have been, one well may think, marked out for special favour by those who are placed to watch over the merits as well as the faults of an army. But no; GORDON happened to be an Engineer. In short, he was one of the non-purchase, worse still, of the scientific services. He returned to England to receive a step of brevet rank just too low to qualify him for anything higher than his captain's regimental duties. And it seems to have been the care of the Horse Guards ever since to prevent his again having the chance of the slightest professional advancement. Indeed, when at last selected for a post, it is one of a civil character—well out of the way, as though we had too many such upon our muster-roll to find him a military sphere of action. And so he is left in his remote consulate at Galatz, in the hope apparently, by those who consigned him to it, that his services may be forgotten by his country, as well as lost to its army. And it needs the tremor of an Ashantee war, and the cry of the Press, to call the War Office to the remembrance that we have ready for such needs the best leader of irregulars that the world contains.

If any discouragement were needed to increase Gordon's reluctance to board the tram this would have provided it. He had never tolerated backstairs influence, he had always shunned publicity and here, it seemed, was a combination of the two. He felt bound to apologise. (In this extract, from a letter of 15th November, 1873, I have, for once in a way, retained Gordon's distinctive punctuation.)

The other day I wrote to our Inspector General and said I hope he did not think I felt any way ungrateful for his treatment of me, and that I was afraid he would have been pained at seeing some letters in the papers implying neglect of me. the man who wrote the letters wrote to me the other day, and is sorry I am vexed at the letters being written etc. etc. obliging me to write explanation to him in return. again I wrote to Col. Kerr saying that the R.E. were using my case to push their higher officers. it was ungracious to say on my part and still worse when Kerr told an old friend of mine an R.E. of it and he has written to me about it another explanation for me to him. If I had not written as my thought came, I should have saved this hurting peoples feelings, who meant kindly to me.

On 11th September Wolseley and his men sailed for Africa. On

G.G. K

5th October Gordon was in Southampton on a flying visit, having covered the 1700 miles from Galatz in three and a half days. His mother was obviously nearing her end and she now scarcely recognised the son whom, on his last visit, she had been unwilling to let out of her sight. "I feel so glad of it," he scribbled, in hurried note to the Freeses. Six days later, on 11th October, he was sending them a brief farewell message, adding beneath the signature "Tob. V, 19 to end."

17

On his way back he wrote to Augusta from Berlin that as he passed through Chislehurst "there was a mass of waving handkerchiefs from the upper window of Freese's house. I dropped a letter of adieu on platform as we went past." "You know," he added, "I never care for sights or countries, and so I will say nothing of Berlin: to me all these places are alike." But by "all these places" he meant the cities of civilisation: the waste places of the earth, for which he assuredly did care, were far from being all alike to him.

And life at Galatz, that half-way house between desert and civilisation, remained as unattractive as ever. It was already known there that the Khedive wished Gordon to succeed Sir Samuel Baker in the Sudan, and although as yet there had been no official announcement everyone at Galatz seemed to be angling for invitations to accompany him to Egypt. Moreover, he was continually " wounded by swordfish in the shape of people wanting money," an affliction to which he should have been inured by now. " It is really quite a trial (sent, I believe) and I am such a donkey. I find to pay all my pensions etc. I want 300 £ a year; however the Lord will provide. The only advantage in marriage is to be prevented from these true extravagances."

But in reality, though Gordon would not yet admit it to himself, the appointment to the Sudan was decided. On 8th November, 1873, he wrote to the Adjutant General that he had received a telegram of invitation " a month ago. I have not determined what to do, but the Government have no objection." Throughout October and well into November he continued to behave as though his going were uncertain. "Whether I go to Egypt or not," he writes on 15th November, ". . . and I do not care one way or the other over much." But these last words are the clue to his mood. The truth is that while he was conscious of a great desire to go he also believed that, as a Christian, he ought not to wish for worldly advancement. And hence in a letter of 31st October, while reporting that he has inquired of an insurance company as to the additional premiums required when he goes to Egypt, he writes in the next sentence as though the whole project were still in the air. For his conscience was uneasy: had he left this " unrolling of the scroll " sufficiently in God's hands? And so in a letter to Augusta, dated 9th November, which begins by reporting the appointment of his successor at Galatz, he launches into a general disquisition on the wisdom of leaving all to Providence, a general disquisition which passes insensibly to the particular. Not only ought one to await the unrolling of the scroll but this is in fact what he is doing.

> . . . so it is with men; events will go as He likes. To be happy is to be like a well-broken willing horse, ready for any event. It is hard to accept the position and the only solace is that it is not for long. If I go to Egypt or not is uncertain. I hope He has given me the strength not to care one way or another: twenty years are soon gone and when over, it matters little whether I went or not. When religious people reason with you and say what a deal of good you could do, it is an atheistical saying though they do not mean it. . . . I want to go to Egypt, if I go, free from all ties and engagements to my followers. I want to hurt no one by my policy, and therefore shall try and keep clear of any who might consider that they can claim from me any particular course of action. After a study of Baker's expedition, gathered from his letters in the papers, I think he was guided by a wish to glorify himself.

And with the mention of Baker the tone of the letter changes again, and the writer passes into a revealing reverie on his policy when in charge of the Sudan, with only one belated reversion from 'when' to 'if.' Baker, he says, pushed on recklessly.

My idea would be to get all things ready before going into interior. What is the use of pushing on and then having to come back? I feel quite sure I can do better without Baker; in a month I would know more than he does; whereas if I take him and do not follow his advice he would be vexed. God has allowed slavery to go on for so many years that it cannot be a vital thing to risk life and success for a few months. It is fine to read of its suppression, as Baker writes, but is it the case? Born in the people it needs more than an expedition to eradicate it. Open out the country and it will fall of itself. I am averse to the loss of a single life and *if I go* will endeavour to prevent any happening. . . . I have a Bank, and on that bank I can draw. He is richer than the Khedive and knows more of the country than Baker. I will trust Him to help me out of this and every difficulty.

Eight days later he is still brooding eagerly over the problems of the Sudan, and on the opposition to be expected in England. But he still reminds himself that Providence may have a last-moment disappointment in store for him, and that if that be so he will make no complaints.

They say Khedive gave Baker 20,000 £ on leaving. If I go and he offers me ditto you (and I am responsible to you alone) will not be angry at my refusing it. I feel sure Moffitt says what is right, that Baker will go on the tack that he left because the Khedive would not put down the slave trade. I think that if the country was settled then the Khedive would prevent the slave trade. . . . Your brother has been more or less acted on by sharks who want to come for money. I have told them that if it is in my power to employ them they must belong to A class; viz. A class, those who come for the occupation and interest it may give them, who are content if they are fairly reimbursed their expenses: not the B class who go for the salary and who want to make a good thing of it. My object is to show Khedive and his people that gold and silver idols are not worshipped by all the world. They are very powerful gods but not so powerful as our God. From whom does all the money come from [sic]? From poor miserable creatures who are ground down to produce it. Of course those ideas are outrageous: pillage the Egyptians is still the cry. Did you see *The Times* mentioned an important deputation to Lord Granville recommending him not to recognise the annexation in Upper Egypt unless Khedive agreed to put down slave trade there? Bartle Frere, Kinnaird etc. etc., the root of which I think is in Sir S. Baker. I am quite prepared not to go and should not think it unkind of God. He must know what is best for all. I dare say Baker may have heard I was not going to bind the Khedive by any contract; he might think that Khedive would therefore be able to do what he liked with me, that no contract being made would enable the Khedive to say that Col. G. was not engaged to look after slave trade, that he would do that etc. etc. . . . Poor Khedive, he thought that his generous present would bind up Baker's wounds, but it will not. It is not to be wondered that these people more or less distrust Europeans; in the true crucible we are not better than they are. Agst me will be Baker and his adherents Pce of W . . ., Geographical Society, the anti-Slavery Society and all those men who think they ought to be chosen for the post, and those who naturally think it rather hard for the Khedive to invade and conquer independent tribes. This is a strong body, is it not? If Govt refuses, I shall merely say that " I give his Lordsh. every credit for acting for the best but regret he did not have informed me [sic] such was his intention before he accepted my resig^n of this post, which I had intended, in case of refusal, retaining till March.

But though Gordon was looking forward to difficulties provoked by the sophisticated, at home and in Egypt, it is seldom the sophisticated who move the world. And of the chief difficulties which he was to encounter the source would be a young hermit who after his own fashion was as fanatical and as single-hearted as Gordon himself. Had Gordon known of the existence of the future Mahdi he would scarcely have ventured to hope that his going to the Sudan would not lead to the loss of a single life.

BOOK FOUR

EQUATORIA

ONCE THE decision was taken Gordon, as usual, wasted no time. He was in England, after a brief preliminary visit to Cairo, in December and left for Cairo again on 28th January, 1874. It was a date of conflicting omens, for the twenty-eighth of January was his own forty-first birthday, but on that morning news of Livingstone's lonely death had reached London. The ties which bound Gordon to England were slenderer than ever now: his father and mother and his younger brother, Frederick, were dead, and the ranks of the Gravesend Kings were sadly depleted. Still there were Augusta and Enderby and other members of the family to visit, as well as the Freeses. And at Gravesend he spent some hours with his paralytic pensionary Carter, and called on a number of other worthies, including a Mrs. Dykes and her family: " Miss Dykes," he wrote, " is the nicest girl I ever saw but do not be alarmed; the dead do not marry." His eldest brother, Sir Henry Gordon, once told a friend that when Charlie felt he was becoming too much interested in some lady he would exclaim " I must be off," and within a day or two would have removed himself from the danger zone. But Sir Henry probably overestimated his brother's susceptibility; Charles Gordon had singularly few opportunities of encountering marriageable females and there is no surviving evidence that he was ever seriously attracted by one. Indeed, in his earlier years, to judge from correspondence, he seems to have regarded the marriages of most of his friends and relatives as regrettable mistakes. In course of

time, however, he did come to approve of marriage—for others.
The reasons alleged for the change of mind are not particularly
convincing. " A man who is not married cannot know his faults."
He would write to Watson in 1880:

A man's wife is his faithful looking-glass; she will tell him his
faults. Some men who have sisters may know themselves, but
it is rare. Therefore I say to you (as I have said before) ' Marry! '
Till a man is married he is a selfish fellow however he may wish
not to be so. . . . To me, aged, and having gone through much
trouble, it seems that to marry in this way is the best thing a
man should do, and it is one which I recommend all my friends
to do. You say ' Why do not you follow your own advice? '
I reply ' Because I know myself sufficiently to know I could
make no woman happy.'

There were official interviews also to be fitted in: he saw the
Commander-in-Chief, H.R.H. the Duke of Cambridge, who was
" particularly kind " and begged that Gordon would write to him,
and he dined at Simpson's, where " a conceited puppy " named
Steward, who was to be a thorn in his flesh for some while to come,
talked a lot of rubbish about the Sudan which Gordon suspected to
have been inspired by Baker. There was even an official to see him
off, an infliction which caused him " to forget Hat box and Despatch
box on platform; a thing," he told Augusta, " your brother would
not have done if not forced to be polite." In Paris at his hotel,
appropriately named the *Hotel des Deux Mondes*, he " had a nice
warm bath and felt happy," happy enough to write to Augusta that
he was more certain than ever that " get into what trouble I may,
God will take me out of it."
   That Gordon would get into trouble was always probable, but
the nature of his new command of itself made trouble inevitable.
In 1879 the scramble for Africa was beginning. The travels of
Livingstone, Speke and Stanley had revealed the immemorial secrets
of the Continent, disclosing not only vast potential wealth but the

horrors of cannibalism and the slave trade. Gordon's new province lay immediately north of the area now being partitioned among the Powers, stretching down the Nile from Khartoum, an ill-defined adjunct to the Egyptian Sudan with no fixed boundaries to the still uncharted South. If in the Sudan the Egyptian administration was contemptible, in Equatoria it did not exist. The Sudan itself had had no history until in the second decade of the nineteenth century the Albanian adventurer Mohammed Ali made it an Egyptian possession. But though the Sudan had been easy to conquer, Egypt was quite incapable of governing it. The Khedive's mudirs and beys were incompetent and corrupt; his soldiers cowardly and un-disciplined. And whatever the Khedive might protest to the anti-slavery societies, whatever instructions he might issue to his own officials, he could not help knowing that they encouraged, and profited by, the slave trade.

The trouble to come had not been the only subject of Gordon's musings during his journey; he had also pondered his personal budget. For ironically, although no one cared less for money than Gordon, the formidable dimensions of his private charities had already made money a recurrent anxiety to him, and an anxiety it would remain to the end of his life. When exasperated and exhausted in the desert, he would break off his daydreams of re-signation to calculate the obligations which made it desirable that he should continue to earn enough to give away: " if God wills " (he would write to Mrs. Freese in November, 1875) " I shall have made enough to capitalise the annuity I pay to my brother's widow, which will relieve me of much anxiety." Yet already he had resolutely refused the salary of £10,000 a year, which Baker had received and which the Khedive proposed to pay to him also. £2,000 was all that he would accept. His object, he explained, was " to show the Khedive and his people that gold and silver idols are not worshipped by all the world." In a later letter (of November, 1874) from the desert he wrote, " Do you know that Baker drew 75,000 £ when he left; 40,000 £ was for losses and expenses."

With his modest income, he calculated, he would be able to

meet all his obligations. His outfit was already paid for; he had
left some money behind him in England, and this, with the twelve
hundred pounds which he expected to save out of his first year's
salary, would provide for his pensions and charities. Next year, he
calculated, he would save £1,500, and this would "pay off
Frances," his brother Frederick's widow. It was a comfort that for
two years, as far as he could see, there need be no more worry
about his pensions.

2

He reached Cairo at midnight on 6th February, 1874. In 1874 the
Cairo of the Khedive Ismail was a corrupt and cosmopolitan micro-
cosm of incompetent pashas, rapacious Europeans and suave
ministers ambiguously staving off bankruptcy by borrowing at
thirty-six per cent. Gordon could hardly have found himself in a
more uncongenial society, and his eagerness for the desert and his
lone command increased hourly. His business was with Ministers
who combined the utmost formality with the utmost procrastination, and that he should have got through enough of it to be able
to hurry off from Cairo in a fortnight was evidence, no doubt, of
his own impatience, but even more perhaps of the helpless consternation to which Ismail's pashas were reduced by their fierce and
unpredictable visitor. For Gordon was frank enough, and irascible
enough, to say exactly what he thought and enjoyed " treading on
the corns of the swells," partly because they were swells and partly
because they had no right to have corns. Diplomats in particular
fared ill with him. When Stanton, the British Consul, warned him
not to make an enemy of Nubar, " it was too much, and your
brother replied, in the midst of a circle of guests, that there was
no one living who could do him the slightest injury which he could
feel," adding that he did not care a rap for Nubar or anybody else.
And when Hughes, an Embassy official, admonished him for having
stood up when two Egyptian aides-de-camp left Nubar's salon

" your brother was angelic for a time, and then said, ' Don't bother! ' which, though rude, was effective. However, we are both great friends."

Gordon's very simplicity enabled him to see at once through most forms of pretentiousness. He recorded contemptuously how the cooking in his hotel was not good enough for the Duke and Duchess of Hamilton, how he was pestered by telegrams and letters from that " dreadful donkey " Steward (" I feel sure he drinks "), or how " Duke of This wants steamer—say, £600. Duke of That wants house, etc.," and how the money for such luxuries was ground out of the starving fellaheen.

But there were some varieties of sham which Gordon, whose judgments were rapid and instinctive, did not always detect, for which he even had something of a weakness. Charlatans with a dash of the visionary, or even of the pietist, sometimes attracted him strangely. He had been fascinated by Napoleon the Third, and the Khedive, whom Lord Cromer described as an astute but superficial cynic, attracted him at once. Ismail was an honest fellow, he reported, and genuinely anxious to put down the slave trade. For this favourable opinion there were at least some justifications. Indeed, Moberly Bell, *The Times* correspondent, said that he had never known a man fail to succumb for a while to Ismail's powers of fascination, which were due to an uncanny gift for reading character and adapting himself to the tone and tastes of those with whom he had to deal. Moreover, Gordon's liking for Ismail was reciprocated. " I think Khedive likes me, but no one else, and I do not like them " he wrote; and Ismail soon developed a genuine admiration for his alarming new Governor, whom he described as his ideal of a man. "When that man comes into the room," he would say, " I feel I am with my superior." And this warmth of feeling between the two dissimilars, guarded but lasting, would sometimes stand Gordon in good stead in the arduous days to come.

It is impossible to say as much for another impulsive conclusion at which he arrived on his third day in Cairo. Wishing to emphasise the conciliatory and international character of his coming administration, he had resolved to appoint two native deputies. He remembered how effectively he had been served in China by captured rebels and it at once occurred to him that a captured slave-trader might play the same role in the Sudan. It chanced that Abu Saoud, a notorious, and, it must be added, a villainous, slave trader who had been denounced by Baker, was now serving a sentence in Cairo gaol. Gordon hurried off to interview the prisoner and at once requested that he should be released and appointed to his staff. He knew of course that Abu Saoud's knowledge of the Sudan, and his reputation among the Arabs for successful crime, might prove useful, and he doubtless judged him to be a creature of poor spirit whom he could discipline without difficulty. But Saoud had something of the Khedive's gift for protective colouring, and Gordon was probably influenced almost as much by the prisoner's ready quotations from the Koran as by his own utilitarian calculations. The Khedive was startled, but yielded readily to the unexpected request. The time-honoured principle of setting a thief to catch a thief had its own attractions, and it gained an additional piquancy when sponsored by the apparently simple and Puritanical soldier. But there was a low hum of dismay and disapproval among the Pashas. And this time Gordon's instinct had not served him so well.

The international note had already been struck in Gordon's first appointment to his staff. Romolo Gessi, the former Italian interpreter whom he had met and liked in the Crimea, and who had subsequently served with Garibaldi, had chanced to retire to a sawmill in Rumania within easy reach of Gordon's official residence as British Commissioner. Here the two had struck up a friendship and very soon after Gordon knew that he was to go to Egypt he had invited Gessi to join him. And Gessi had been almost the first person to greet him on his arrival in Cairo. He was, wrote Gordon, " delighted to see me," but of Gessi's wife he did not approve; this, it seemed, was yet further evidence that marriage is almost invariably a mistake; if Gessi had remained on the Danube " he would have fallen lower and lower." In addition to Gessi there were three Englishmen, a Frenchman as interpreter, a volunteer German botanist, two young

German naturalists, who went, oddly enough, as Gordon's personal servants, and two American officers already on the Khedive's payroll. Gordon's selection of his entourage, heterogeneous in character and qualifications as well as nationality, did not prove fortunate. Perhaps too many of them were young; for tropical medicine was in its infancy, and in the climate of the Sudan the sovereign specifics would prove to be prudence and a tough constitution. Perhaps there was too little scope for choice, or perhaps in his impatience to be out of Cairo, and his reliance on first impressions, he did not choose wisely.

Within a few months one Englishman, one American, one German and the French interpreter would be dead and two Englishmen invalided home, while of the two remaining Germans one through sickness and one through fear of sickness would have abandoned the expedition. Only the loyal and indomitable Gessi and Chaillé-Long, the surviving American, would still be active and in Gordon's employ. And, as it was to prove, Chaillé-Long was the most unfortunate choice of all.

It happens that we have an account by this man of the interview at which he was appointed. An uncorroborated statement by Chaillé-Long is not necessarily evidence, for at the best of times he was inaccurate, while whenever he suspected that his own importance was insufficiently recognised by the world at large—and it was seldom that he did not suspect something of the kind—he became incapable of recognising, or speaking, the truth. On this occasion, however, his reception was flattering enough to spare him the compulsion to view it in retrospect through the distorting lens of his own egoism. And though his customary inaccuracy or malevolence may be judged from his description of Gessi as " Gordon's factotum and confidential valet, who had served him thus since the war in the Crimea," there is sufficient verisimilitude about his description of his first meeting with Gordon to make it probable that he was trying to set down what he remembered.

At a midnight supper party, he relates, he unexpectedly received a brief note from Gordon, whom he had never yet met. " Will you come with me to Central Africa?" it ran. "Come and see me at once." Although Chaillé-Long does not say so, he had probably already indicated a wish to join the expedition, for in a passing reference to the appointment Gordon wrote " an American, named Long, a colonel in the Egyptian army, has asked to come with me, and if I can I shall take him." On receipt of the note Chaillé-Long betook himself forthwith to Gordon who greeted him with both hands outstretched. Gordon saw before him an undersized figure with a prominent nose, exaggerated moustache and an expression of mingled petulance and self-satisfaction. The American in turn noted the unmilitary air and " laughing, sympathetic, winsome eyes " of his host, who exclaimed, " How are you, old fellow? Come and take a b. and s. It will help us to talk about Central Africa." On his table was an open Bible as well as the bottle of brandy, which was then not only the beverage with which the English gentleman customarily entertained his friends, but was also regarded by travellers in the East as the most reliable of all prophylactics against tropical fevers—later, indeed, on their way up the Nile, Chaillé-Long reports Gordon as pressing brandy on him expressly for its medicinal properties, " now do take some cognac and don't forget the quinine." Gordon proceeded to explain that the Khedive had told him of Chaillé-Long, and continued brusquely " You are to go with me as Chief of Staff..." To which Chaillé-Long adds, less plausibly, the words " You will command the soldiery. I don't want the bother." For by the time he compiled his reminiscences Chaillé-Long had long since been able to persuade himself that the chief, though unfortunately as yet unrecognised, role in Equatorial Africa had been played by himself, and could comment on his appointment " thus there fell on my young shoulders the triple burden of the staff, the command of the garrison and the command of the expeditions which would extend the frontiers of Egypt." In the light of which, although in the event he did next to no staff work, and neither commanded the garrisons nor extended the frontiers of Egypt, he may well have been tempted to magnify the terms of his commission.

Naturally enough Chaillé-Long was not prepared to accept the point-blank invitation without some further inquiries. When did Gordon propose to start? " Oh, to-morrow night " was the calm reply. That, said Chaillé-Long, clutching, we may suppose, a trifle breathlessly at the familiar world now so rapidly slipping away from him, was out of the question. He would need to purchase an outfit, there were possessions to get rid of and dependents to provide for. " Abandon them all " replied Gordon instantly. As for an outfit, he himself could provide all that was necessary. In proof of which he pulled out a pair of boots and made Chaillé-Long try one on. It fitted to perfection; evidently they need not worry about equipment. They sat on, talking, till four in the morning, by which time Chaillé-Long was completely under his host's spell. That same morning he saw the Khedive, who confirmed his appointment, and added the rider that he would be expected to protect Egyptian interests in Uganda, on which Ismail believed the British to be turning greedy eyes. Gordon no doubt realised that while from his own point of view the appointment of Chaillé-Long, who was already in the Khedive's employ, had the advantage that it would emphasise the international character of the expedition without adding to its cost, in the Khedive's eyes its chief merit was that the American would be well placed for reporting on any British bias in the Governor-General's conduct. To such unofficial surveillance Gordon had no objections; he was already determined while in the Egyptian service to put Egyptian interests first, and Chaillé-Long is no doubt correct in reporting him as having remarked that a British staff officer would have been a nuisance since he might have made trouble with Whitehall.

But Chaillé-Long could not resist adding the usual fantastic embroideries to his account of the Khedive's instructions. Ismail, he declares, explained them by adding that " an expedition is being organised in London under command of a pseudo-American, named Stanley, ostensibly to succour Dr. Livingstone, in reality to plant the British flag in Uganda." As to which it is sufficient to remark that Stanley was now in Ashanti, that no expedition was being

organised in London or elsewhere to succour Livingstone, whose
death had been known for some weeks, and that Stanley's flag when
he flew one, was not British, but American. Later in the letter
which mentions Chaillé-Long's appointment Gordon speaks of " a
good American, a sharp fellow, named Long." His first impressions
were too frequently far from reliable; it may, however, be conceded
that Chaillé-Long was sharp.

Gordon already felt serious misgivings as to the motives of the
Khedive, or rather of his Ministers in general, and of Nubar in
particular. Cairo itself, with its shifty Pashas and absurdly ceremonious court, its dirty streets heavy with the perfume of attar of
roses and incense and resounding with the incessant throb of drums
and twanging of strings and the recurrent ululations of the muezzin's
call to prayer, seemed hopelessly unreal. Was the expedition itself
unreal—no more than a crafty gesture, designed by Nubar to impress
Exeter Hall and the Anti-Slavery Societies? Was the ten thousand
a year, which Nubar had been so anxious that he should accept,
but part of the imposing but disingenuous façade? "I think," he
wrote on 14th February,

> I can see the true motive now of the expedition, and believe it
> to be a sham, to catch the attention of the English people, as
> Baker said; I think the Khedive is quite innocent (or nearly so)
> of it, but Nubar is the chief man. Now what has happened?
> There has been a mutual disappointment. Nubar thought he
> had a rash fellow to deal with, who could be persuaded to cut a
> dash, etc., etc., and found he had one of the Gordon race; this
> latter thought the thing real and found it a sham, and felt like
> a Gordon who has been humbugged.

Nevertheless, he would go forward. Once he was in the desert
the character of his Governorship would depend upon himself, and
not upon Nubar and the Pashas. But until he was clear of Cairo
some concessions to Nubar's appetite for display could not be
avoided. Gordon had proposed to take ship for Suakin, with one

servant, in an ordinary steamer which happened to be sailing from Suez on 18th February, his chosen date. The journey would have been luxury in comparison with what was in store for him, but Nubar was horrified, and insisted that the Governor-General must travel in a special steamer with a retinue of seven servants. And he saw to it that on the 18th Cairo station was thronged with notables to see His Excellency General Colonel Gordon, Governor-General of the Equator, into his special train for Suez. But Nubar's powers of organisation did not extend to the railway itself, and before long the special coach was halted by a derailment on the line, and after a wait of several hours had to be ignominiously attached to the rear of a crowded passenger train. Nor was this the last delay. Near Ismailia three Europeans on horseback signalled the train to stop, and proved to be the famous Count Ferdinand de Lesseps, architect of the Suez Canal, with his niece and another young lady. They had lost their way in the desert and begged for a lift. Gordon left Chaillé-Long and the Khedive's chief equerry, who was escorting him to Suez, to entertain the young French women, and himself plunged into a long discussion with de Lesseps. "He is seventy years of age," he noted; "his wife was confined a few months ago. He is a nice, bright, strong old man."

And so at length, in engineer undress uniform and a fez, "Chinese" Gordon set forth for the land which was to render that earlier soubriquet obsolete. Gessi and the rest of his staff were left behind to assemble the stores and follow in due course. Gordon himself would not wait a day longer. He was accompanied only by Chaillé-Long and an Egyptian A.D.C., a nervous and home-sick young man, who had been bullied by Nubar into joining the expedition, had ventured on impudence with Gordon and been promptly "crushed," and was consequently now almost as terrified of his chief as by the prospect of the Sudan.

3

Gordon could already foresee the essence of the great problems of policy which would unfold when nearly three months later, un-expected and unannounced, he reached the first desolate station in his new province. Despite his Chinese experiences, however, neither he, nor, it may be presumed, his self-confident chief-of-staff, can have foreseen that before long the Governor-General would be improvising rat-traps, mending musical-boxes and sorting stores with his own hands. This grotesque obverse to Governor-General-ship a few weeks in the desert, and a little more experience of native corruption and incompetence, would soon disclose; the stark out-lines of the dilemma inherent in his new command stood out already, however, from any atlas, from the simplest summary of Egyptian history and from his own knowledge of the men in Cairo. His task, it had been made clear enough to him, was twofold: to establish communication with the mysterious Great Lakes to the south, and to suppress the slave trade. The two objectives, it was already clear, were interdependent; how completely interdependent he could not yet foresee.

By 1853 an occasional whiff of grapeshot had enabled the rulers of Egypt almost without opposition to push their outposts a hundred and twenty miles south of Khartoum and overrun Darfur, the desert region to the west of it. Meanwhile European adventurers, some of them Englishmen employing Arab mercenaries, had established a flourishing trade, at first in ivory and then in slaves, throughout Darfur and in the Bahr el Ghazal, beyond the Egyptian outposts of the south. By 1860 the chorus of indignation from Exeter Hall and the anti-slavery societies, and a lively fear of retribution, had induced the Europeans to withdraw. They sold the business to Arabs, the Arabs bribed the Egyptian officials, the slave trade flourished and expanded. In 1872 Sir Samuel Baker, describing a region which he had known eight years earlier could write: " It was then a perfect

garden, thickly populated, and producing all that man could desire.
. . . The scene has changed! All is wilderness. The population has
fled! Not a village is to be seen." By this time the lord of all the
Arab slave dealers, Zebehr, had ceased to pay tribute to the Khedive,
had annihilated his army and was now, in 1874, about to overthrow
the Sultan of Darfur. His slave caravans would thus be presented
with a direct desert route through Darfur, three hundred miles to
the west of Gordon's steamers, patiently patrolling the Nile. It
would be essential now for Gordon to reach the Great Lakes, not
merely in order to satisfy the Khedive or the Royal Geographical
Society, but for the crushing of the slave trade itself. For only a
chain of forts and the opening of the dark interior to legitimate
trade seemed likely to effect that.

Such was the essence of the problem, about to be aggravated
by Zebehr's triumph in Darfur. Zebehr's triumph, however, was
by no means the only aggravation. For there remained at Khartoum
an Egyptian Governor-General of the Sudan, corrupt and incompetent but technically responsible for Darfur. And the finances of
Gordon's Equatorial province were to be lumped in with the budget
of the hopelessly bankrupt Sudan. While as for the Khedive, the
one Egyptian in Cairo whom, up to a point, Gordon trusted, his
motives were even less clear-cut than Gordon supposed. Alarmed
by the rapid growth of Zebehr's power and exasperated by the
denunciations of the slave trade which resounded from Exeter Hall,
he had approved Gordon's appointment in the hope that it would
at least temporarily silence his English critics. Moreover, so long
as he clung to his *damnosa hereditas* there was always the chance that
some unexpected stroke of fortune might mend matters; at least
he was buying time. But that Zebehr could in fact be crushed he
did not seriously hope, still less that the slave trade could be rooted
out. Was not slavery after all a Mahomedan institution of immemorial antiquity? Indeed, a letter among the Bredin papers from
Sir Charles Wilson (as he subsequently became), who was then at
the War Office, realistically sums up the relations between Cairo,
the Khedive and the trade.

The slave trade cry is one got up by Baker to make matters go smooth. No man can in a moment change an institution in an oriental country which has existed for thousands of years, and any reform of that kind must begin at home. As long as there is a demand for slaves in Lower Egypt and Palestine so long will there be a slave trade and all one can hope at present is [to] mitigate its horrors. When the Khedive frees his own slaves I shall believe something is being done, but as long as there are Moslems whose civil and religious code is the Koran there will be slaves.

4

Disembarking at Suakin Gordon mounted his first camel. His prodigies of endurance upon this unamiable beast would soon become a legend in the desert, and the journey to Berber made a fitting prelude to them. The two hundred and fifty miles were covered in three days less than the time allowed for the fastest caravan, more rapidly indeed than they had ever been traversed before, so rapidly that Chaillé-Long, the melancholy A.D.C., the two hundred Egyptian soldiers and even the camels were reduced to the extremities of fatigue. The briefest of pauses and they were steaming up the Nile with Gordon urging the crew to unwonted exertions or wading in the water without his trousers to help haul the vessel off a sandbank. At daybreak four days later they were at Khartoum. From Suakin, Gordon had written home that Chaillé-Long was "a very nice, modest fellow;" the choice of epithets is astonishing. From Khartoum he observed that "self is the best officer to do anything for you." It seems possible that he was already beginning to revise his opinion of his chief of staff.

No premonition of tragedy to come visited him as he stepped ashore at Khartoum; and if it had, the spectacle of Ismail Ayoub Pasha, Governor-General of the Sudan, awaiting him in full-dress uniform, not to speak of a battalion of infantry, a band and an

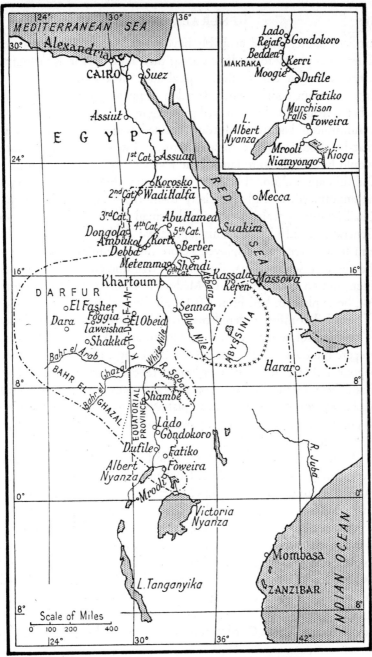

THE SUDAN IN GORDON'S TIME

artillery salute, would probably have proved a sufficient distraction. There was plenty to be done during their nine days in Khartoum— a review and a visit to the hospital and, more embarrassingly, an entertainment from which Gordon slipped unobtrusively away when a troupe of almost naked girls began to dance. And there was a sumptuous banquet. Gordon decided that etiquette demanded that he should make a suitable return. Two hundred notabilities would have to be entertained; he had with him a dozen tin plates and tin cups and no table linen. No matter, dinner must be served, he announced, at eight precisely to-morrow evening. In despair Chaillé-Long appealed to the affable Ismail Ayoub. The Governor-General not only lent him his superlative Turkish chef but leading him to a storehouse, displayed before his incredulous gaze piles of the choicest Sevres china, Bohemian glass, fine cutlery and damask linen, not to speak of bins of Médoc, Burgundy and Champagne. All, he explained, had been left by Sir Samuel Baker, whose ideas of personal comfort differed markedly from those of his successor. A hundred soldiers were set forthwith to unpack these treasures and prepare the feast. Only then did Chaillé-Long and Hassan, the woebegone A.D.C., seek out Gordon to report their triumph. They found him in the kitchen, coat off and sleeves rolled up, busily washing a consignment of cheap plates which he had just contrived to purchase. He had boiled a mass of tapioca and beside him were forty tapioca puddings.

At intervals there would be lengthy arguments with Ismail Ayoub in the course of which Gordon was apt to display a racy informality to which it must have taken the Governor-General some little while to accustom himself. However, it is recorded that when Gordon terminated an over-lengthy interview with a deputation of influential sheikhs and ulemas by exclaiming " Now, old birds, it's time for you to go," the venerable elders retired, after kissing his hand, with deep salaams and in good countenance, and Ayoub Pasha no doubt proved equally adaptable. Argument, however, is perhaps hardly the word for discussions whose outcome was inevitable and which Gordon himself summarised by reporting that

Ayoub, like other Egyptians before him, " tried to cajole one of the Gordon family and . . . was disabused of the idea that it could be done."

As often as not the controversy would centre upon Abu Saoud. All save some of the poor, Gordon found, were horrified when they heard of the slave trader's appointment: " but I am faithful to him, and trust to a higher power to bring me through. Trust in Him with all thy heart and lean not unto thine own understanding: in all thy ways acknowledge Him, and He shall direct thy paths. Either there is a God, or there is none; that is the whole question." Abu Saoud, he still felt sure—more sure than he felt now as to Chaillé-Long—would be most useful; " he is built and made to govern." Gordon himself certainly trusted in God and believed that He overrules all things for the best, and even in Khartoum he contrived to " have quiet times in spite of all the work," waiting for guidance. But often he would be impatient for some speedy solution to an urgent or tiresome problem; and then he would frequently base his decision on the toss of a coin. This, too, he would claim, was a form of waiting upon God, and after all, there is biblical precedent of a kind for it.[1] But neither Gordon nor his theology was logical and sometimes when the fall of the coin did not confirm his own inclinations he would ignore it.

Tossing up about difficult questions relieves me of much anxiety. Two servants who were useless were brought in, and the question whether they went or not decided by a toss in their presence. It went for them once; however, afterwards they were sent away—they exasperated me dreadfully.

One piece of unexpected good news had greeted Gordon at Khartoum. The Sudd, the barrier of dense floating vegetation which had long rendered the Nile impassable below his objective, Gondokoro, had been broken through. Whereas the journey from Khartoum had hitherto taken from eighteen months to two years

[1] Acts i. 26.

he would now be able to reach Gondokoro by steamer in twenty-one days. Prospects seemed brighter, and he issued a " stinging " decree declaring the ivory trade a government monopoly, and in effect establishing martial law, in his province. And then once more a salute of artillery reverberated among the mud houses and he was off again, in a diminutive steamer, on the thousand-mile journey to Gondokoro.

5

Slowly the little vessel breasted the current, chugging at two knots an hour past flat banks lined with gum and tamarisk. There was little outlet for Gordon's demonic energies. He mapped the river, repaired the log which measured the ship's speed, wrote his interminable correspondence, drank boiled water and quinine, suffered the onslaughts of mosquitoes for whose ferocity neither China nor the Danube had prepared him, and observed an occasional native village and the varied fauna on the river banks—basking crocodiles, hippopotami snorting in the shallows, herds of buffaloes and elephants, giraffes nibbling at the tree-tops, storks, pelicans and chattering troops of monkeys. And, needless to say, he read his Bible and meditated on the mysteries of life, and in particular on the mystery inherent in the very existence of some of the tribes glimpsed on the shore, born, it would seem, to perpetual fear and misery. Nevertheless, this was inaction without solitude and he grew increasingly impatient. Chaillé-Long records that on one occasion both Ali, the Arab captain of the steamer *Bordein*, into which they transferred at Fashoda, and Hassan, the homesick A.D.C., came to him, Ali furious and Hassan in tears, and both clamouring to be sent home, Ali because Gordon Pasha had slapped his face and Hassan because Gordon Pasha had called him a baboon, a booby and a baby. And it may well be so, for Gordon's temper was already frayed. His health was good; as in the cold of the Crimea so in the heat of the Sudan, when all around him went down in swathes, he would remain obstinately fit, and from the Sudan as from the Crimea amidst the most frightful discomforts he would regularly report " I have every comfort and am quite well." But he was impatient, and the slow tempo of Africa—the inertia of the Arabs and the ineffectiveness of his staff—perpetually exasperated him.

And he was already disappointed in Chaillé-Long. Indeed, he was even beginning to see through his pretentiousness. On 2nd April he wrote home, in his letter-diary:

> The American is a regular failure. He is so feeble, he can do nothing at all. He lives on what he *has* done, and of course that does not help what has *to be* done now. His object is to prove to me that he is not to blame: another useless thing, for it is not a judgment I have to pronounce, but to get through my work. There are a lot of officers I hate, viz. Capts. " I told him to do it," " I thought you were going to do it," and a host of others of the same class. Their object is self-extenuation and laziness. I hate the reasoning that because the Arabs are slow we must be ditto.

And the entry, three days later, that " ' Feebleness ' was too lazy to come on deck to see the junction " of the White Nile with the Bahr-el-Ghaza doubtless also refers to Chaillé-Long. How could Gordon foresee that seven years later, when he had become an object of world-wide interest, copious selections from his letters would be published under the editorship of Dr. Birkbeck Hill; or that, although the usually cautious doctor would omit the second and shorter of these passages he would imprudently include the former *in extenso*, only substituting for the tell-tale introductory words " the American," a would-be non-committal dash? Charac- teristically Gordon himself would refuse not only to meet, or cor- respond with, the editor, but even to see the proofs of the volume: how could he foresee that Long, well knowing himself to have been the only member of Gordon's staff on the steamer with him during

that first journey to Gondokoro, must instantly recognise the unflattering reference to himself? Or that after this fatal wound to his
self-esteem he would bear an undying grudge against his chief?
It must be admitted that, even if Gordon could have foreseen all
that was to follow, it is unlikely that, scribbling in the heat of the
Bordein, he would have altered a syllable of what he had written.
In any event, the harm was now done: unknowingly he had
ensured his enrolment in the numerous company of those who,
having failed to share Colonel Long's high estimate of himself, must
expect to encounter his sustained malice. And the unlucky Dr. Hill
would even omit the earlier complimentary reference to "a very
nice modest fellow," quoted above.

6

On 16th April, twenty-five days after leaving Khartoum and ten
days later than Gordon had hoped, they reached Gondokoro, the
northernmost of the only two forts which his province as yet
contained. Its population had not even heard of Gordon's appointment as Governor. The prospects could scarcely have seemed more
unpromising. The fort at Gondokoro was held by three hundred
soldiers, the other, at Fatiko, by two hundred, and the soldiers were
Egyptians.

> As for paying taxes or any government existing outside the forts
> it is all nonsense. You cannot go out in safety half a mile—all
> because they have been fighting the poor natives and taking their
> cattle.

But Gordon refused to be discouraged. His letter positively continues: "I apprehend not the least difficulty in the work; the
greatest will be to gain the people's confidence again. They have
been hardly treated." And at this point, in his published version,
Dr. Birkbeck Hill discreetly inserted a row of dots. But Gordon

continued, " and it is extraordinary the intense hatred there is of
Baker." " Your brother is a rock," he wrote a little later, " and
drives the coach with a fierceness which would astonish you as it
does those who do not know him. They are an odd family the
Gordons, proud, etc., etc."

This fierceness was not due only to impatience. It is true that,
having hurried down river so far ahead of his stores, he now found
that he could do nothing without them. But he had also soon
discovered that it was the habit of the authorities at Khartoum to
pay the troops at Gondokoro, such as they were, not in cash but
with intermittent consignments of gin and slave-girls. Gordon at
once decided to return forthwith to Khartoum, in order to have
matters out with Ismail Ayoub, its genial but peccant Governor-
General, and also, since it was becoming clearer every day that
" self is the best officer to do anything for you," to hasten on the
transit of his stores and staff. Before he left he despatched Chaillé-
Long in the opposite direction on an embassy of good-will to the
King of Uganda, from whom presents had recently arrived at Gondokoro. At this juncture this was hardly an appropriate task for a
chief of staff, and least of all for a chief of staff who supposed that
there reposed on his young shoulders " the triple burden of the staff,
the command of the garrison and the command of the expeditions
which would extend the frontiers of Egypt." But Gordon had
already realised that Chaillé-Long would be of little use to him as
a staff officer, and the mission would at least enable him to fulfil
his promise to the Khedive by searching for evidence of British
intrigue in Uganda.

The unlooked for return of the new Governor-General caused
general astonishment at Khartoum. A revolt at Gondokoro seemed
the likeliest explanation, for it was hardly credible that even a mad
Englishman would put himself to the trouble of hurrying down-
river again so soon merely in order to spur on his staff. Ismail Ayoub
himself had at first been inclined to accept Gordon as an amiable
eccentric who would soon shed his idealism in the harsh school of
the desert; but within a few hours of his return he realised that the

very foundations of his own régime were in jeopardy. For Gordon at once charged him with being a party to the substitution of gin and slave-girls for hard cash, brushed aside his unconvincing excuses, told him brusquely that he was lying and extracted from him a boatload of Austrian dollars for his troops. Not content with this, he announced that he would tolerate no interference from Khartoum, that there must be a recognised frontier between the two provinces and that their finances must be kept entirely distinct. The Khedive's approval of these precautions was obtained by telegram from Cairo, and Gordon was off downstream again for Berber. In a letter written *en route* he reported " sharp skirmishing " with Ismail Ayoub, adding not unjustifiably " I think I have crushed him."

In four days he was back at Berber, where his staff had already spent four days unloading stores. He had them off for Khartoum next morning. " The utter helplessness of those about me is lamentable " he wrote. " I have driven them like a herd." He followed himself next day, leaving the Egyptian officials to recover their breath and doubtless to discuss over their coffee for many months to come the astounding spectacle of a Governor-General who checked every list himself and heaved boxes with his own hands. At some time during his second hectic day at Berber, presumably after he had watched his staff's steamers out of sight, Gordon had contrived to write a substantial proportion of his usual prodigious mail. One of the letters now surviving (among the Bredin papers) was to Colonel Goodenough, lately Military Attaché at Vienna. It was very hot and the ink, Gordon complained, was like glue, but in a mood of cool detachment from the turmoil around him he aired his views on the much-needed modernisation of the army. More small-scale manœuvres and much better knowledge of topography, he suggested, were needed. Generals, who are the most ignorant of all, should be required to pass an examination. And he recounts how, knowing that he was about to leave England, he had ventured to embark on the education of one of them, the officer commanding at Chatham, and had presented him with a large-scale

map of his own district, and when he omitted to study it had
administered a frank lecture on his superior's shortcomings. And
then, reverting to the problems of the moment, he adds that as to
slavery he can answer for his own province, but in the Sudan slavery
will flourish until the demand for slaves ceases, in other words until
there is a social revolution throughout Africa. " I have told the
anti-Slavery Socy that their efforts hitherto have only twofold
increased the sufferings of the slaves."

A fortnight later, on 30th May, the first of his four steamers set
out from Khartoum southward for the unknown, and before the
middle of June, having seen them all off, Gordon himself had left
that squalid capital for the second time. There is no record of a
salute of artillery on this occasion. The year was now at its hottest
and for the last three months he had been hurrying up and down
the Nile almost without respite. His own comment, however, was
that life of late had been monotonous. " But," he added, " night
comes regularly, and I have nothing to trouble me."

7

In the years of trial which lay ahead the centre of interest for the
observer of to-day is no longer the deadly climate, the barbarous
lands or the sufferings and destiny of their peoples, but the impact
of all these, and of the varied tribulations which they engendered,
upon the valiant and unworldly soldier who had so rashly committed himself to a hopeless task. For by entering the service of the
Khedive, Gordon had doomed himself to frustration. A soldier of
genius, uniquely qualified to command the loyalty of simple and
warlike peoples, he might have rivalled Clive as a general, or
Warren Hastings as an administrator; but his country had not
chosen to make use of his special talents, nor, it must be admitted,
had he encouraged it to do so. And now on the Nile he was faced
with tasks the very nature of which made it impossible not only
that he should achieve success but even that he should employ his

extraordinary powers to the full. For the aboriginal natives of his province had not yet emerged from the most primitive barbarism, his Arab soldiers were lazy, cowardly and treacherous, and from both he was cut off by the barrier of a language which he did not speak. As for the Egyptian officials, they were mostly both incompetent and corrupt, and his small European staff succumbed rapidly to disease. And so inevitably he spent much of his time in complete mental and spiritual isolation, toiling at the tasks of a junior staff officer, of a storekeeper, of a hospital orderly, even sometimes of a carpenter or a porter. He had never suffered fools or incompetents gladly, but the constant explosions of irritation of which his correspondence at this time provides ample evidence must in large measure have been due to a deep-seated sense of frustration.

He was only too well aware that his temper was failing. " I am quite well but temper very, very short, and it is [a] bad time for those who come across me the wrong way;" " I have given up soft words, if ever I used them, and am now hard and they [the Arab troops] get such *digs*!! " Sometimes he represents that there is an element of policy in his violence: " I am cruel, revengeful, vicious to those under me; a perfect tyrant I am. But you want a tyrant among these people and they take advantage of your kindness, so I mix the two, making frightful examples of perhaps unjust nature for perhaps trifles and letting off culprits in the other direction with no punishment." But when Mrs. Freese, alarmed and perplexed by his reports of his own harshness and irritability, suggested that they must be due to ill-health he brushed the excuse aside: " No, the shortness of temper is evilness, not illness and I fear I am a tyrant at heart." And in a letter to Augusta he suggests that some recent outbursts were caused by the scamping of his prayers: " two hours' sleep and neglect of morning quiet (you know what I mean) was the cause of it."

The truth is that as yet Gordon's religion was scarcely qualified to make him gentle. Its basis was his conviction that whatever happens happens according to the will of God; that in the event, however fantastic or sinister, he was but witnessing the unrolling of the predestined scroll. And although the fatalistic serenity which this belief inspired could arm him against high tragedy it was not proof against petty annoyances. Sometimes, however, he would speak as though it were.

> The intense comfort of no fear, no uneasiness about being ill is very great and more than half the cause of good health, and no comfort is equal to that which he has who has God as his stay, who believes, not in words but in fact, that *all* things are ordained to happen and must happen. He who has this has *already* died and is far from the annoyances of life. I do not say I have attained to this perfect state, but I have it as my great desire.

But to render him less explosive Gordon needed a more deliberate cult of that central Christian virtue which theologians call love—a word which in our language must so unfortunately do duty for several other most dissimilar emotions. And by love he does not seem as yet to have set much store. Indeed, hitherto in all his voluminous letters and memoranda on religious topics the word but seldom appears. Of humility and constancy and courage his religion was already an abundant source, but not yet of the sympathy, gentleness and compassion which are the ingredients, or symptoms, of love. Undoubtedly there was a marked vein of tenderness in his nature. In Gravesend the sick and the poor and, very specially, the Scuttlers, and in China the sufferings of his wounded soldiers and of the Chinese peasants themselves, had evoked in him precisely these qualities. But here there was much less to evoke them. He pitied the negro natives of his province, and when chance offered would care anxiously for some black waif cheerfully abandoned by its relations; indeed, his growing compunction as to the eventual destiny of the negroes would soon colour his whole attitude to his mission. But they did not greatly interest him. " I cannot say," he wrote, " I shall ever take a great interest in the black tribes. They are to me all alike; whether one has a bunch of leaves or a scrap of calico does not make much difference to my mind; they are all black, they shave their heads and they look all alike, male and female." The two diminutive spindle-legged Shillook boys who were with him for a while were a poor substitute for Scuttlers and even with them, owing to the loss of his interpreter, he could not converse. It was only with his staff that there were occasional opportunities of intimate contact and on the whole his staff moved him to exasperation rather than affection.

Seven years later, after a period of solitude and meditation, a new and more tender note finds its way into his reflections. But in this strange new life there was at present little opportunity for meditation, and he sometimes felt that his spiritual life was drying up, and thought regretfully of the Gravesend days. " I could no more give an ' address ' now than I could fly," he would write to Mrs. Freese this summer; and, next autumn, " if I have to come home I hope to search well the scriptures and set myself regularly to study the deeper mysteries in some quiet place." And for the present he seems to have thought of the basic Christian virtue as something of a counsel of perfection.

> You cannot evade it; we are each composed of two beings— one of which we see, which is temporal, which will fulfil certain works in the world; and one unseen, eternal and which is always in conformity with God. One is sometimes uppermost, some- times subdued, but rules in the long run, for it is eternal, while the other is temporal. How else will you explain " This is My commandment, that ye love one another;" this is My *order*. His will or order leaves no option, and must be done: but it is given to our eternal, not our earthly nature, which will not obey and has no part or lot with Him.

And in the long run, he believed, the sins of the earthly are of no account, since all men are also eternal beings, equally sinless and equally destined for bliss.

8

Gordon's first strategic decision had been that a garrison was needed at the junction of the Sobat river with the Nile; for here any slave convoy could be intercepted on its way to Khartoum, whether it came down the Sobat, the Bahr el Ghazal or the Nile itself. On reaching the Sobat accordingly he allowed the rest of his convoy to proceed on its way southward, and himself remained with his two German servants and a small detachment of troops. For he had discovered that his soldiers, who had not yet experienced the discomforts of Gondokoro, regarded Sobat, not without justification, as unhealthy; his presence would perhaps encourage them: " it is much the best way; and one's presence is a host in itself, though I say it." A host in itself—in Equatoria the words would be no picturesque exaggeration but a prosaic statement of fact. But as a commander Gordon had always been too ready to do his subordinates' work, and it was characteristic that he kept not a single member of his staff with him at Sobat. For some while he had thought poorly of their efficiency and he was now beginning to think poorly of their physique, and already suspected that ill health or low spirits would soon render them a positive encumbrance to him. " Day by day I rejoice more," he would soon be writing from Sobat, " amid the discomforts one has to put up with, that I have not more fellows with me, for they would feel the ups and downs very much." Not until he rejoined his staff at Gondokoro, however, would he discover how grimly the reality exceeded his worst fears.

River steamers had been the central feature of Gordon's Chinese campaigns, and they would be the central feature of all his sojourns on the Nile, where he would spend much of his time restlessly awaiting vessels which were weeks, or even months, overdue. At Sobat, a huddle of round straw huts soon flooded out by the tropical summer rains, he was compelled to wait in growing impatience for eight weeks. The delay at least allowed him to concentrate his

G.G.   M daemonic energies on a narrow field: " to do anything," he wrote from Sobat, " there is nothing like beginning on a small scale, and directing your energy, like a squirt, on one particular thing." At the moment he had just constructed " *such* a pair of trousers for one of the blacks." And it at least allowed him to observe the natives of the neighbourhood. It was not an encouraging experience. They were living, he found, at starvation level, not daring to plant more grain lest a surplus should tempt raiders. And, what puzzled Gordon more, they seemed quite destitute of natural affections. A native who, with his wife and two children, had settled close to the station, had imprudently stolen a neighbour's cow and had been detected.

> I happened to go round, and passing the hut saw only one child. " Where was the other?" I asked of the mother. " Oh, it had been given to the man from whom the cow had been stolen." This was said with a cheerful smile by the mother. " But," I said, " are you not sorry?" " Oh, no! we would rather have the cow." " But," said I, " you have eaten the cow, and the pleasure is over." " Oh, but all the same, we would sooner have the cow!" This is perfectly true. The other child of twelve years old, like her parents, did not care a bit. A lamb taken from the flock would bleat, while here you see not the very slightest vestige of feeling. Is it not very odd?

He was constantly succouring derelict blacks, and as constantly having to remind himself that the Almighty not only regarded them as no less significant than Queen Victoria herself but had Himself decreed their sufferings. Nevertheless, it was difficult not to be perplexed by the spectacle. Perhaps, he reflected, the explanation was that there is unhappiness everywhere, perhaps the starving blacks were not more unhappy than the prosperous English middle classes, whose conventional social round and consequent ' doles ' he still frequently remembered with a shudder. Meanwhile, however, the suffering was continually obtruding itself, and the apparent

indifference to it already displayed by some of his staff made one
of his counts against them.

I took a poor old bag-of-bones into my camp a month ago, and
have been feeding her up; but yesterday she was quietly taken
off, and now knows all things. She had her tobacco up to the
last, and died quite quietly. What a change from her misery!
I suppose she filled her place in life as well as Queen Elizabeth.
I dare say you will see—in fact, I feel sure you will see—your
black sister some day, and she will tell you all about it, and how
Infinite Wisdom directed the whole affair. I know this is a
tough morsel to believe, *but it is true.* I prefer life amidst sorrows,
if those sorrows are inevitable, to life spent in inaction. Turn
where you will there are sorrows and troubles. Many a rich
person is as unhappy and miserable as this rag of mortality, and
to them you can minister. This mustard is very badly made
was the remark of one of my staff some time ago, when some
of our brothers were stalking about showing every bone of
their poor bodies.

In contrast with the distressing spectacle of the blacks even the
torrential rain, the defection of one of his two German servants and
the depredations of the innumerable rats, which fought, screamed
and scampered over the mosquito nets all night, were comparatively
insignificant, mere everyday annoyances raising no theological
problems. When the floods came the huts could be moved, and
though perpetual damp was uncomfortable " I prefer it infinitely
to going out to dinner in England." Moreover, with one less
servant he was positively better off, " the best servant I ever had is
myself: he always does what I like;" while as for the rats they
could be captured, one by one, in a home-made trap concocted out
of a pencil, a piece of tin and a dispatch box. And against mere
annoyances, he hoped, at any rate while his provoking staff was
not present to add to them, he was immune: " I am quite well and
am so sustained and supported. The orthodox religion of our

younger days would never bear any great troubles." As for the
interception of slaves at Sobat, ninety-six were discovered beneath
an incoming cargo of ivory, but two days after he had at last left
for Gondokoro a convoy of sixteen hundred was passed through
with the connivance of the Mudir whom he had left in charge—
only to be captured sixty miles farther south by the less venal
Governor of Fashoda.

9

Leaving Sobat at last on 21st August, Gordon steamed as rapidly as
even he could have expected through the now dissolvent Sudd, and
at Shambé, immediately south of it, found Gessi whom he had
ordered some weeks earlier, with Willie Anson, his own nephew,
to establish a station, and teach the natives grain cultivation here.
The energetic Gessi, though lately recovered from a severe attack
of malaria, had made considerable progress: but Willie Anson was
already dead. It was the first of a train of disasters; but the speedy
loss of his own nephew haunted Gordon, and for several weeks his
correspondence was full of regrets that he had allowed so young a
man to join him, and of reminders that he had not wished him to
come. Gessi he insisted on taking on with him to Gondokoro, where
at least, it might be expected, there would be a doctor. Two hours
short of Gondokoro, on 2nd September, he unexpectedly halted " in
order to have one quiet evening before a mass of trouble and bother
and lamentations, etc., which will fall on me when I arrive there."
His reflections during this brief final respite resembled those of a
headmaster on the eve of his first term in an unruly school; and of
the trouble and bother and lamentations which he anticipated the
chief source, he foresaw, was likely to be his own staff. And that
same night he grimly jotted down his plan of campaign: " if the
staff are discontented, they may go; if they stay, they are to give
me their loyal co-operation." He had not foreseen that whether

they stayed or not would too often depend upon factors beyond either their control or his.

But within a few days it became clear that his staff was in dissolution. And precisely a week after his arrival he was describing a situation of which the physical and psychological aspects were almost equally catastrophic.

Such an amount of work with my sick, and no chance of getting them off for a long while, I fear. My place is a complete Hospital. Now I will tell you how we started and what has become of them all. Your brother *well* but a shadow.

> Kemp, engineer, well.
> Gessi well; has had a severe fever.
> His Greek ill, more or less. Result, no work.
> Berndorf,[1] German, who came up on his own acct and now
>   is my servant (ill; covered with boils).
>
> Menges, German servant, sent back ill.
> Russell ill; cannot be moved; invalided.
> Anson died.
> de Witt dead. Amateur like Berndorf.[1]
> Campbell, impostor, but certainly ill. Invalided.
> Linant, " traitor"; very ill, cannot be moved; invalided.
> Long with King Mtesa; have not heard of him for six
>   months.

Of these many should never have come up here if I had had my way about them. Now here they are ill. Linant and Campbell in huts near this, and who are only partially medically attended by one of the best doctors (me) that I know of. Russell is in my tent, a large divan one and wholly under my charge: he is not at all well and has constant attacks of sickness. Add to this all the intrigues about me, a large amount of works of all sorts and

---

[1] So Gordon always spells Bohndorff's name.

preparations to make. Letters of all sorts, the accounts of the dead now all finished and you will see your brother is bothered. . . . Also, I have had the departure of Raouf Bey and all its attendant troubles, letters to Khedive, money letters of Province, accts of officers going away, arrangements for their going down, watchfulness that they take as little plunder as possible (*no end* of trouble about this). Linant and Campbell well enough to be perfect Brigands. Gessi putting off things and forgetting them. No servant, for Berndorf is ill. Things in a dreadful muddle, but all is coming right and I do not feel it a bit; on the contrary it rather amuses me. Campbell and Linant are intensely selfish and have not the slightest consideration for me or anyone. Campbell is not half as bad as he makes out; if you put *your* finger down *your* throat *you* will be sick. I could write you vols. on the various little anecdotes, and how of these two one would try and gain an advantage over the other. It is needless to say that I have treated them handsomely. Linant has cost me a mint of money, but if he had cost me 10 times the amount he would not have been kept by me. As for gratitude, you know, my dear Augusta, that article has long ago left the world. Russell has behaved like a gentleman and I am sorry to part with him. I fear almost he will stay here for good, for he is far from well to-day. I did not give him enough laudanum last night and he did not sleep well. . . .

It was little more than three months since his steamers had left Khartoum. It was melancholy that so many of his few Europeans should have already succumbed, but it was almost equally melancholy that he should at present be able to see so little good in them.

No doubt he had chosen his *entourage* hastily and there had not been many to choose from; moreover, he may well have made too deliberate an attempt to choose according to plan, with an eye on the international aspect of his *entourage*—for there was some truth in his own self-criticism: " I have a wonderful instinct but very bad judgment." But some of the asperity of his criticisms must have been due to physical and nervous strain. Eight days later, he reports that Linant is dead, and that " I am glad that I had made it up with him." But when he goes on to complain that even Gessi, the trusted Gessi, " has no head, forgets everything and procrastinates dreadfully," though one does not doubt that the faithful Italian may have fallen sadly short of Gordon's own exacting standards one finds oneself wondering whether there may not be some connection between this severe verdict and a sentence which follows: " Imagine your brother let in, after all he had said, to paddling about a swamped tent without boots, attending on a sick man all night with more than a chance of the tent coming down bodily." Gordon was a highly conscientious nurse but not so long-suffering as he had been in Gravesend. And his staff did not make good patients. As he complained to Enderby that October,

> As my German is a born idiot it all comes on me, mixing effervescing drinks, medicines, etc. . . . it is always my tent, my bed, my etc. etc., that are given up. However, I do not really care. . . . The odd thing of this illness is the sulkiness of the patient. He will scarcely answer you. It is the same with them all. Will you take some Rum water; no answer. Will you take your medicine; no answer. When my servant, Menges, was ill I gave him such wiggings as moral quinine as did him as much good as the other quinine. No nonsense stood. Take your medicine at once. He had a life of it. It is no use being gentle with them. . . . I cannot do it with the others; I do not like to do it, though I believe if I had with one of them I might humanly speaking have saved him.

There can be no doubt that, taken as a whole, the staff was ill-chosen and unsatisfactory. This, indeed, is indirectly confirmed by the fact that two English subalterns whom Gordon had selected more deliberately than the rest, writing home for them from Cairo, proved a good deal more congenial when they arrived unexpectedly in the late autumn. One of them, a Lieutenant Watson, would soon

be writing home to his mother " I do not wonder at people liking
Gordon. You would if you knew him, I am sure." Lieutenant
Chippindall, who found Gordon's passion for detail a trial, was
more critical. " Really sometimes," he would write,

> I think I shall have a row with Gordon; for though he has such
> a lot of anxiety and worry, he has no right to nag and worry
> you in return for it. Oh! and how he bores me night after
> night about the levels and the distances! I should not mind if
> he would have one good night of it, and settle it; but every
> night to discuss whether Baker's levels are right; whether the
> distance is this or that, what you think; then, if you give an
> opinion to be nailed at once; and your reasons asked and worried
> at, till out of sheer fag you agree to any proposition he likes to
> put forward.

But this, too, was a letter written under strain, and Chippindall
seems not to have realised that all Gordon's plans for an advance
on the Lakes turned upon the strength of the rapids near Dufilé.
And despite his complaints Chippindall, like everyone else, could
not help liking Gordon.

> It would look like desertion to leave Gordon toiling alone out
> here, although he really won't let me do anything. He seems
> always to think that nobody but his blessed self can even screw
> a box lid on. He is a fearful egotist in that way. But he is devilish
> kind to one and really I fear he will almost spoil me for future
> service.

And when he was eventually sent down river, sick, in July, 1875,
he wrote, " I cannot tell you my sorrow at leaving Gordon, for
with all his faults one can't help but love him."

Gordon himself alone remained in unfailing good health. Not
perhaps so wholly unfailing as his home reports suggested, for we
know from another of his letters of at least one attack of severe

internal pains of which he chose to say nothing to his family; yet sufficiently unfailing to leave him perpetually capable of paddling about damp tents, imperiously nursing and prescribing for his patients most of the night, without ceasing to do the work of all of them by day. He had no doubt that his immunity from disease was a by-product of faith. For he believed that as he had walked through the bullets in China unhurt, with the Wand beneath his arm, so here, as long as the Almighty had work for him to do, he was invulnerable; and a few years later he would explain to no less a person than T. H. Huxley how this confidence was itself a pro-phylactic against disease. Huxley, though he became a warm admirer of Gordon's, was a Victorian rationalist and he might have found the reasons for his confidence, had Gordon expounded them, more difficult to understand, but he would recall approvingly his theory of its consequences, and how " I once asked Gordon why he didn't have the African fever. 'Well,' he said, ' you see, fellows think they shall have it, and they do. I didn't think so, and I didn't get it.' " And Gordon reported to Augusta " the intense comfort of no fear, no uneasiness about being ill." Moreover, his faith was armour against bodily ills at another point. The death of many Europeans in eastern climates was due, he once told Sir Richard Burton, to " moral prostration "; that is to say, they were scared of death; whereas " I have no fear of dying in any climate," for he had long looked forward to death as the supreme blessing.

He took precautions, it is true, much as Cromwell kept his powder dry in addition to saying his prayers. Indeed, five days after compiling his melancholy catalogue of invalids, he set off in search of a healthier station, and selected Rejaf, sixteen miles farther south. And he insisted on medical precautions, constantly urging his staff not to forget their mosquito curtains, to bake their *dura* pancakes hard and to take quinine. In medicine he had had no more training than in theology, but even in medicine he was an in-dividualist, and preferred his own theories to the precepts of authority; and the specific of which he was proudest was not so much a prophylactic against tropical disease as his own private version of those comprehensive patent nostrums which were so popular in the last century. " I have been studying medicine a good deal and found out a great thing i.e. that ½ gr. ginger, ½ gr. ipece-cuenha [sic] and 3 grs. of rhubarb make a splendid daily pill, and can be taken without hurt for years or a lifetime."

Abu Saoud, the released slaver, also soon proved to have been an unfortunate choice. This time it was instinct rather than judg-ment which had failed Gordon, but in Cairo, having as yet no experience of the treachery and corruption of which the Arabs of the Nile were capable, he had been misled by the analogy of China, where ex-rebels had so often fought loyally in the ranks of the Ever Victorious. At first, indeed, Gordon had congratulated himself on his choice, attributing to the influence of his reformed chief lieutenant the unexpected friendliness of the local Arabs; but before long Abu Saoud was treating Gordon himself with arrogance and discourtesy and even usurping his functions, mysterious leakages in the store of government ivory had become apparent, and an abortive mutiny was traced to his machinations. As was to be expected, Gordon " opened on him right and left "; he was dis-graced, pardoned, disgraced again and eventually shipped ignomini-ously back to Cairo on a native *nuggar*. Even so there was an inauspicious aftermath to his brief régime when, a few days later, a hostile sheikh surrounded Gordon's tent with a hundred armed tribesmen. Gordon rose, placed his two guns in readiness and ordered them to be gone. The hostile demonstration melted away. It was not the two guns which had cowed them. There were many differences between Arabs and Chinese, but none in the awe with which Gordon could inspire them.

There were no more mutinies. Gordon found the Arabs and Berbers, let alone the negro tribes, less amenable to his personal influence than the Chinese, but they responded after their fashion to the novel experience of a commander who was not merely formidable but just, and for the fierce monotheism of the Mahome-dans, even though it seemed almost completely divorced from a moral code, he, for his part, felt a genuine sympathy and respect.

He compelled his Mahomedan soldiers to construct a mosque and observe, for the first time for many years, their sacred month of Ramadan. He made Friday a holiday and procured them an *ulema*. " Better have more worship than none at all," he said, for worship, though ignorant, was nevertheless worship. To explain the Redemption to them, he decided, was impossible, but he observed with approval the appeals to Allah of a miscreant whom he had just cast into prison and whose daily devotions had not been incompatible with slave-raiding and murder on the grand scale. Even the negro tribes, he believed, as they called upon some dimly imagined deity, were heard by the Almighty. And gradually among the Mahomedans, as they learned that Gordon's faith in Allah was more potent than their own, his fame as a holy man began to rival his reputation as a warrior. A little later he must even have changed his mind as to the possibility of explaining the Redemption. For in a letter of 27th August, 1878 (preserved at the Gordon Boys' Home) he writes, with reference to an unspecified earlier date:

> I assure you, when I asked the black boys (when alone) if they knew God lived in them, they understood me. I used to lead up to it by asking them where they would go when they died; they would point to the earth. Then I would ask them if Allah did not care a bit for them, and they would nod acquiescence. Then I would ask them if He would let them lie in the earth, they would shake their heads; then, whether Allah would take them to Himself, and often with their eyes moist they would say Yes. Then I would tell them to thank Him for any good thing they had, to ask Him to help them when they got into trouble, etc. I never had the opportunity to go much further, but I feel convinced that by leading them up to God thus it would not be difficult to let them understand the Redeemer.

10

On 18th October Chaillé-Long returned unexpectedly from the distant south. He explained to Gordon how, after a month at the court of the King of Uganda, he had made his way back to the southernmost station of the Equatorial Province, discovering a new lake *en route*, and eventually had fought his way almost single handed through a horde of savages. " Long fought his way back," reported Gordon to his brother Enderby (in a letter among the Bredin papers), " past Kaba Rega's frontier station, the same place where Speke was stopped. He and two soldiers who were with him fired 450 cartridges—poor blacks! I *think* it was a masacre or massacre (has it two s or one?)." He had noted approvingly, however, that Chaillé-Long seemed to have been improved by his trying experiences. " I have now only Kemp, the engineer," he told Enderby, " and Long, an American in the Khedive's army, who was very useless before he went to Mtesa, but who now is very useful and active. Nothing like suffering to give a man experience." But Chaillé-Long was not to be useful for long. He was exhausted after his exertions and in four days had departed for Khartoum, undertaking to return in six weeks' time. Before he left, however, an incident had occurred whose grotesque consequences two generations later neither of them could foresee. Gordon recorded it in a letter of 22nd October.

I have been so cross since I wrote to you—and why? The reason is that I was made ill by the utter feebleness of my staff. My friend Kemp came back sick; took possession of me as a servant, and of my things as his; lost his own bed; took mine. I got wet, and a chill; and it was only by a severe course of pills that I am all right again. I have now given orders that all illness is to take place away from me; that the staff are not to come near me except on duty.

Meanwhile, the Khedive was writing urgently that the slave-trade must be stopped, and in reply Gordon was patiently pointing out that since the real culprits were the Khedive's officials and the merchants of Khartoum it would be unreasonable to hang such petty agents as he was able to arrest in Equatoria. But he had begun to wonder whether " a quieter, easy-going, salary-drawing man " might not have suited the Khedive better, and whether he himself might even, by establishing friendly relations with the natives, be rendering them an easier prey to the subsequent depredations of some Arab successor. And in this mood he would ask himself why he had ever accepted service under the Khedive. " The thing slid on little by little," he decided in retrospect.

> Well, I was led into it from perhaps a sort of pity for old [undecipherable] and because I had to live a false sort of life in the Comn. The thing slid on little by little. I felt too independent to serve, with my views, at Malta or in the corps, and perhaps I felt I had in me something that, if God willed, might benefit these lands, for He has given me great energy and health, and some little common sense and I felt vicious at Baker and sorry that our country should be thus represented by him.

And what after all was the alternative to Equatoria? Surrender of his independence and return to " the routine of Engineer duty with all its petty troubles and jealousies." He could, moreover, console himself with the reflection that on the Nile he had achieved detachment, and that for the moment at least " the tram " was no longer a temptation.

> Never shall I forget what I got when I scored out the inscription on the gold medal.[1] Now I have been repaid a million fold! There is now not one thing I value in the world. Its honours—they are false. Its knick-knacks—they are perishable and useless. Whilst I live I value God's blessing—health; and if you have that, as far as this world goes you are rich.

[1] See page 124.

Gordon's object was still to establish a chain of fortified posts throughout his province, in order to bleed the slave trade to death by opening the interior of the country to legitimate commerce. He had already created the first new station at Rejaf, sixteen miles south of Gondokoro; but before moving farther forward he must accumulate supplies at his base, and for supplies he was dependent upon the officials at Khartoum who, needless to say, showed few signs of providing them. Clearly, therefore, he must send one of his own men north to Khartoum to do their work for them. Clearly, also, since his own business was to administer the province, he would need reliable officers to take charge of the advance southward. But how was he to find the men he needed among the scanty remnants of his unsatisfactory staff? Gessi would do for Khartoum, but who was there to lead the southern expedition? It was in mid-November while Gordon was still revolving this problem that Watson and Chippindall so unexpectedly arrived. With them came Ernest Linant, brother of the Linant who had died at Gondokoro and whom Gordon had described as a traitor. The solution of the problem was now obvious. Linant, a person of Gallic address and courtesy, must go to negotiate for commerce with King M'tesa, the others would take charge of the advance towards Lake Albert. Within a fortnight all three newcomers had been sent up to Rejaf to prepare for their departure for the south.

Gordon himself remained behind, increasingly preoccupied with plans for a healthier station than his fever-riddled headquarters at Gondokoro. Eventually he hit upon Lado, on the left bank of the river, not far to the north of Gondokoro. For some weeks he toiled unaided at the task of supervising the move, for the newcomers were at Rejaf and his one remaining servant, the German Bohndorff, had just been invalided south. The mass of detail, the unteachable Arabs and a severe attack of dysentery combined with his complete isolation to make this a period of great strain; " people talk of being dull; why, here I have been alone for nearly three weeks, and never exchange a word beyond a few broken Arabic sayings from morning to night." None the less, he could write

home that he was " glad indeed to escape Xmas festivities in which
you are now rejoicing," and on the last day of 1874 he was able to
leave the ill-fated Gondokoro for ever.

That same day, while still steaming down to Lado, he met the
Khedive coming upstream with two unexpected newcomers on
board. One was Martin Hansal, Austrian Consul at Khartoum, and
the other a young Austrian explorer named Ernst Marno, sent out
by the Austrian Geographical Society. Both intended to join the
explorations in the south. The latter's principal importance for us
is that he has left a painstaking day-to-day account of his sojourn
with Gordon. Hansal, however, soon proved to be in some ways
a good deal less reliable. "Went in to see Hansal, the Austrian
Consul, yesterday at 3 p.m.," Gordon told Augusta; " he was on
his bed, quite incomprehensible either in French or German; discovered at last it was ' cognac '; quite blind with it; capital man
for the Albert Nyanza, would find 60 or 100 lakes for me. . . . Old
Hansal smiled at me most benignantly and kindly with his spectacles
pushed up on his forehead. Not *very well* to-day, effects telling on
him. I never touch any liquor, it is poison to me."

The second week of January saw Chaillé-Long back from Cairo.
He had been absent for nearly twelve weeks instead of the promised
six, and Gordon had commented impatiently on the delay in his
letters home, but by Equatorial standards twelve weeks spent on a
six weeks' journey was almost punctuality. The newcomer brought
news that four hundred soldiers, for whom he had applied in
Khartoum, were on their way up river to reinforce the garrisons; he
did not, however, specify their nationality, and for some while
Gordon, who had learned to his cost the difference between blacks
and Arabs, was on tenterhooks.

Oh, my dear Augusta, for two days I dared not ask Long . . .
whether these troops were Arab or black troops. At last I asked.
They were Arabs!!! Now out of 250 Arabs I brought here, I
should say half were dead and 100 were invalided; so you may
imagine my horror. He did his best, poor Long, but it was

killing for me. . . . This reinforcement was worse than useless—much worse. Out of 150, eighty-four were sick the day after arrival; and now is comparatively the healthy season. If I can only get them up-country before they break down!

Long, sorry to say, has tumbled back into procrastination and forgetfulness, which annoys me. I took the opportunity, when we were in good tempers, to point out to him that we should never be able to get on with one another when near one another. He neglects everything, and, I may say, it is the hunting season, with me for hunter and with nearly everyone else for the hunted. Thank God, I have a splendid memory for business and can thus whip them up well. . . . Long (who for bringing up Arab troops is doomed to take them to Makraka) [is] off in 10 days. It is a good thing to get Long off, for he is a trial to me.

It would be interesting to know more exactly what passed between Gordon and Chaillé-Long when they were not in good tempers. Whatever it was, Chaillé-Long did not forgive it. Moreover, surprisingly enough, Dr. Birkbeck Hill permitted himself to publish the greater part of the above extract from Gordon's correspondence; and though he omitted the last two sentences and Long's name, once again Long cannot have failed to recognise the references to himself since he was the only member of the staff at Lado at this time.

II

On 26th January, 1875, Gordon set out downstream for Sobat, whence reports of trouble had reached him, and it chanced that his arrival there was witnessed by Captain Fred Burnaby, of the Royal Horse Guards. Burnaby was something of a hero-worshipper as well as a traveller himself, but his appearance at Sobat was not due primarily to his own love of adventure or his admiration for Gordon. It was evidence that the British public, which had soon forgotten Gordon after his return from China, was now ready for more news of him—which Burnaby duly supplied in two dispatches to *The Times*. He described the intense excitement as word went round the little station at noon that Gordon's steamer was approaching. Gordon, he explained, was extremely popular owing to his practice of listening to the grievances of the natives, and severely punishing any soldiers who ill-treated them; "his principle in China, as here, has always been that you can get more out of a man by kindness than by any other method." As the *Khedive* anchored:

> The one bugler nearly burst his lungs in ringing out the clear strains of a General's salute, the black captain lowered his sword, and the seventeen men composing the garrison brought their arms to the 'Present,' as a short thickset man, who appeared to be in the picture of health, and was attired in the undress uniform of a Colonel of Engineers, hastened down the ship's side and, approaching the officer and his small force, rapidly inspected the men and their accoutrements.

Immediately after the inspection Gordon took his seat under an awning on the steamer and rapidly transacted the most urgent business of the day. "The number of things he had to settle and arrange," reported Burnaby,

> would have been enough to turn the head of any ordinary mortal, but the Colonel went steadily ahead, giving out one order after another, administering justice to the natives, censuring or praising the officials, ordering punishment here and reward there, all this through an Egyptian interpreter, who gravely rendered every word of Gordon's French into Arabic.

At last when all was over Gordon swallowed a few mouthfuls of food and several cups of strong coffee and, joining Burnaby, proceeded to give him an account of the three expeditions which he was preparing. But he suspected that Burnaby might be a source of unwelcome publicity, and he was not in an expansive mood. Moreover, he had been much annoyed by finding Russell, an original member of the expedition who had been invalided to Cairo, awaiting him at the riverside at Sobat. " I nearly dropped," he told Augusta, " for *Russell* stood there. I could scarcely shake hands with him. I was so angry and your brother gave him his mind pretty freely." For Russell, he explained, was primarily interested in a comfortable job, and two successive letters to Augusta contain detailed calculations as to the various sums of which he had " pillaged the Egyptians " by way of pay and passage money. And so when Burnaby, hearing that Gordon was writing to Russell's father and well aware that the father was an influential member of the staff of *The Times*, urged him to be " more polite," Gordon was obdurate. " I thought of my griefs," he told Augusta, " and had no mercy." And he only consented to give Burnaby a passport into Equatoria after extracting a promise that any future reports he might send to the Press should be confined to descriptions of the country itself and such inanimate objects of interest as he might observe.

12

" Think, think, think is what I am always doing," Gordon had written to Watson before the end of 1874. Often his thoughts circled round " the mystic nature " of the Nile and he would regret not having his Concordance with him, for the Bible surely would throw light upon this ancient mystery. But often, too, just now he meditated an alternative route to the interior of Africa. Why not turn the flank of the Lakes as he had so often turned the flank of the Wangs in China? Why should not the Khedive send men by sea to Mombasa Bay, where a mere four hundred miles of healthy highland marching would separate them from the Lakes and the realm of King M'tesa. Shortly before the end of 1874 he mentioned to Watson this Napoleonic project, which might have added to the possessions of Egypt the territories which are now Kenya and Uganda, and on 21st January, 1875, he reports to his family that he has formally broached it to the Khedive. What is more, within eight months the Khedive had positively dispatched an expedition to Mombasa. The expedition was eventually recalled at the insistence of the British Government; nevertheless, Gordon's conception of a united East Africa opened up from the sea, and even of a railway between Mombasa and the Lakes, had anticipated history by a generation. And in a letter to Augusta written more than four years later, on 20th April, 1879, from the wastes of Darfur, Gordon makes it clear that he had not been responsible for the failure to consult Britain which had foredoomed the project to failure.

> The failure of the Zanzibar expedition was the fault of Nubar, *vide* his letter to me among your papers, in which he scoffs at my warnings to be sure of the good countenance of the British Govt before the expedition left. He says ' I have seen Sir B. Frere and the British Govt would be glad of it '; ' there is no reason for your fears, etc., etc.'

Early in the new year of 1875 the expedition under Linant had set off in the direction of Lake Victoria, that under Chippindall to Lake Albert. Who was to take charge of the south of the province? Not Chaillé-Long, though he returned from the Makraka country in March and, arriving at Rejaf at four in the morning, found Gordon already seated at the door of his tent, cleaning an elephant gun. The usual Bible lay open on the table before him, and the usual bottles of brandy and quinine stood beside it. After proffering both specifics, and stressing the potency of quinine, Gordon explained to Chaillé-Long his conviction, already reported in his letters home, as to their hopeless incompatibility of temper, and suggested that he should return to Cairo with a dispatch for the Khedive elaborating the Mombasa project. Within two days Chaillé-Long had departed. His own eventual version of this final interview would be that Gordon had invited him to become his viceroy, and on his refusal had entrusted him with the letter for the Khedive as a special mark of confidence and esteem. Gordon never saw him again, but his chief part in Gordon's story had yet to be played.

BOOK FIVE

ANATOMY OF A SLANDER

A T CAIRO, which he reached in a state of physical collapse,
Chaillé-Long was warmly received by the Khedive, who was
under the illusion that he had greatly extended the boundaries of
his dominions. After spending a brief sick-leave in Europe he was
placed in command of the expedition to the east coast which Gordon
had recommended. He left Suez on 19th September, but unfortunately the Khedive's sealed orders instructed him to proceed, not to
Mombasa but to the Juba river. He duly occupied Kismayu and
proceeded to wait patiently there for further instructions from
Gordon, but, unlike Mombasa, Kismayu was of no use as a base
for an advance on the Lakes. Meanwhile, moreover, Gordon had
lost interest in the expedition, partly perhaps because towards the
end of 1875 he was temporarily out of heart with Equatoria in
general, and partly because it was becoming clear that an Egyptian
descent upon the east coast, whether at Kismayu or Mombasa,
would not be tolerated by the British Government. And in due
course the Sultan of Zanzibar appealed to Downing Street, Lord
Derby in turn protested to the Khedive and on Christmas day, 1875,
Chaillé-Long received orders to withdraw. To the last his association
with Gordon had been ill-starred.

He did not forget the humiliations of Equatoria or Gordon's
blindness to his outstanding merits. But it was too soon to strike
back, and although the hero of his first book, *Central Africa*, which
appeared in 1876, is unquestionably himself he did not yet venture

on traducing his associates. In 1881, however, appeared Dr. Birkbeck Hill's selection from Gordon's correspondence, *Colonel Gordon
in Central Africa*, and although the editor had omitted a number of
uncomplimentary references to the self-styled chief-of-staff (a title
which Gordon did not use of Chaillé-Long, but which Chaillé-
Long had already assumed) at least two, as we have seen, remained,
imperfectly concealed and wounding enough to embitter him yet
further. And by 1884 Chaillé-Long was ready to begin settling old
scores.

In that year he published, in New York, a book, *The Three
Prophets*, the theme of which was that the religious fanaticism of
three men who had played a leading role in the recent history
of Egypt and the Sudan—Arabi Pasha, the Mahdi and Gordon—
had made them serviceable tools for an unscrupulous British
Government, plotting to steal the Sudan. Much of the substance
of *The Three Prophets* must have been contained in a lecture on
"The three Mahdis—Arabi, Mahomet and Gordon" delivered
by Chaillé-Long in Paris in the spring of this year, of which *The
Times* wrote:

The lecturer attracted a numerous audience in the expectation
of hearing a serious explanation of the Egyptian and Sudan
problem. This expectation was woefully disappointed; for the
lecture was a rambling collection of episodes accompanied by
sarcastic hits at all the personages mentioned. General Gordon is
no hero in M. Chaillé-Long's eyes. Indeed, he, the last Khedive,
Nubar Pasha, Arabi, and the Mahdi are all described as humbugs.
. . . He ridicules Arabi's professions of patriotism, he attributes
General Gordon's success in China to bribery, and he believes
the Mahdi was originally either a slave-dealer or a soldier who
served under himself. He relates anecdotes of most of these
persons, placing them in a ridiculous light. But it is easy to make
game of anybody, and the lecturer did not perhaps notice that a
number of the audience were applying the same process to
himself.

Such a commentary from the leading English newspaper, with its attribution to himself of French civilian rank, cannot have pleased the sensitive colonel. Moreover, his book, *The Three Prophets*, had attracted no attention whatever in England. It contained, however, one passage which was destined to acquire unexpected significance in later years. " In the short intervals of my stay in camp, going or returning from expeditions," he wrote,

> I had occasion to remark the singular habit which Gordon had of retiring to his hut, where he would remain, for days at a time, engaged in the perusal of his ever-present Bible and Prayer Book. When in this retirement, his orders were that he should not be disturbed for any reason of service whatever; *a hatchet and a flag* were placed at his door as a sign that he was unapproachable.

Since Chaillé-Long's sojourns in Gordon's camp had been few and brief, and throughout them all we know Gordon to have been wrestling daylong with the myriad petty details of administration which he could not, or would not, entrust to his subordinates, this picture of prolonged and repeated seclusion at least gave evidence of a vivid imagination in the *soi-disant* chief-of-staff. Its only factual basis would seem to be that Gordon is known on occasion (although not in Equatoria) to have brusquely dismissed a visitor who disturbed him at prayer, and that while Chaillé-Long was with him in October, 1874, as we have seen,[1] after an ailing subordinate had coolly taken possession of his servant and a good deal of his property he gave orders that his staff were only to visit his tent on business. Chaillé-Long's fantasy, however, was admirably adapted to his theme, the religious fanaticism of *The Three Prophets*, and in his eyes it may have had the additional advantage of implying that, with Gordon repeatedly displaying more interest in another world than in his own command, yet heavier responsibilities must have fallen upon the " young shoulders " which already, as he would eventually assert, bore " the triple burden of the staff, the command of the

[1] See page 188.

garrison and the command of the expeditions which would extend the frontiers of Egypt."

But in 1884 Gordon, though cut off in Khartoum, was still alive, and the claims advanced in *The Three Prophets* were comparatively modest. Even so, however, they went unnoticed in England, and twenty-eight years later, as an old man, Chaillé-Long made a last attempt to attract, on this side of the Atlantic, the admiring attention which he was still convinced that he deserved. In 1912 he published *My Life in Four Continents*, and this time he published in England. " All men who have done anything of excellence," he declared in a prefatory note, citing the authority of Benvenuto Cellini, ought to write their autobiographies. And, to make his present objects even clearer, he proceeded to explain that " there was not to my know-ledge until recently a single word in any encyclopaedia in England which noticed my work in Africa. . . . To be precise, there are just five lines, almost furtively written and signed ' F.R.C.,' concealed in an obscure note of the *Encyclopaedia Britannica*, eleventh edition." Worse still, even this note proved to be " a deception calculated to deceive the unwary," by depriving him of the credit which was his due. It is impossible to dissent from the ageing colonel's conclusion that " it does not appear that I am known at all in England." Eng-land's ignorance, however, might yet be dispelled. Unfortunately, so long after the events which he was about, for the second time, to reinterpret, it would not be sufficient merely to give his own exploits the prominence which not even he had yet ventured to assign to them. For by now other reputations were established and, if the author's own eminence was no longer to be unfairly overlooked, would have to be reduced to less disproportionate dimensions. And so in addition to numerous picturesque accounts of his own achieve-ments in Uganda and elsewhere the colonel resolutely represents the explorer, Stanley, as a liar and drunkard, " who may have been affected by overconsumption of manioc when concocting his story "; the valiant Gessi (whose life story, dedicated " to the sainted memory of Gordon Pasha " had been twenty years before the public) as a valet who had earned Gordon's favour by " submitting to being kicked whenever his master's ill-humour required it "; and Gordon himself as advocating the peculation of Government ivory. And to the story of Gordon's prolonged withdrawals in his tent he now added details calculated to leave the most sceptical British reader in no doubt as to the gallantry with which the young chief-of-staff had replaced the absent commander. " A few days after my return to Lado," he wrote,

the camp was attacked in force one night. I had great difficulty in repelling the savage hordes, who, with lighted torches, were endeavouring to turn us out. Gordon was in his hut and gave no sign of coming out. It was during one of the oft-recurring periods when he shut himself up and placed a hatchet and a flag at the door as a sign that he was not to be disturbed, a seclusion which lasted from three to five days. I sent an officer to warn him of our danger but receiving no reply went myself. I entered abruptly and found him seated, very calmly at a table, on which were an open Bible and a bottle of cognac and sherry. I told him of the situation, to which he made abrupt answer ' You are commander of the camp.' Whereupon I hastily turned and left him, but not before I had posted an officer with a half-dozen men specially charged with Gordon's safety. The savages were finally driven away by a vigorous sortie. The next day Gordon entered my tent in the full-dress uniform of the Royal Engineers, and cleanly shaven. He came forward with a quick tripping step as was his habit, and said ' Old fellow, now don't be angry with me. I was very low last night. Come and dine with me. We will have a glorious dinner.'

Chaillé-Long must have penned this tale with considerable relish, and doubtless he did not pause to reflect (although had he reflected he must have known) that should an inquiring reader choose to undertake some comparatively simple investigations he would have no difficulty in exposing it as an impudent, and not even a plausible, figment of the imagination. But no reader did choose.

For *My Life in Four Continents*, like its predecessor, was completely ignored. Chaillé-Long had failed to achieve his grand objective. So far as the English public was concerned, he died, as he had lived, in obscurity. Nor would there be anything to be gained by re-suscitating his egocentric fantasies had they not been already resuscitated by a greater artist than he.

2

In 1918 Lytton Strachey was a frail scholar in intellectual revolt against his social and moral environment during the fourth year of a war of which he bitterly disapproved.

His own literary talent was admirably suited to denigration; it would be entertaining to expose the frailties of war-time idols who could so easily be displayed as far from superhuman, and, better still, as deficient even in some of the pedestrian virtues customarily attributed to them. His targets naturally would be, not the reigning politicians, generals and bishops of the day but their greater proto-types, men and women whose irrational energies and enthusiasms, irrationally admired by earlier generations, had done so much to precipitate the present tragedy.

Gordon, with his boundless energy and apparently inexplicable dogmas, may be said to have selected himself as an Eminent Victorian. And whereas such words as ' martyrdom' and ' tragedy ' had figured lavishly in the titles of the Victorian hagiographers Strachey sardonically selected for his essay a more prosaic title, ' The End of General Gordon.' Gordon's religion he not unnaturally made no attempt to understand; it was manifestly highly irrational, and this was sufficient for his purposes. When, however, he lit upon *My Life in Four Continents* he must have realised that fortune had played into his hands. For oddly enough, despite his contempt for the irrational, the standards by which Strachey judged his historical sources were emotional rather than rational, and he would repeatedly select a passage calculated to present the subject of his investigations in divertingly incongruous guise without investigating its claim to credibility or even, sometimes, its author's manifest self-contradictions. A recent critic has remarked that "Lytton Strachey's account of him [Clough]—the youth who ' thought of nothing but moral good, moral evil, moral influence and moral responsibility,' who lost his faith and ' spent the rest of his existence lamenting that loss, both in prose and verse '—is a vulgar travesty, based obviously on distorted second-hand evidence. It is impossible to believe that he could have read any of that ' prose and verse '. . . ." Much the same way may be said, *mutatis mutandis*, of almost all Strachey's Eminent Victorians, and certainly of his portrait of Gordon.

Although he did not choose to follow Chaillé-Long by representing Gordon as making a habit of kicking Gessi or advocating the misappropriation of government ivory, he readily accepted his story of the macabre episode at Lado. Indeed, he contrived to accept *both* his stories, for although *The Three Prophets* is not mentioned in his bibliography, Strachey's paragraph contains elements from both Chaillé-Long's contradictory versions as well as dexterous adaptations of his own. " But the Holy Bible," he wrote:

> was not his only solace. For now, under the parching African sun, we catch glimpses, for the first time, of Gordon's hand stretching out towards stimulants of a more material quality. For months together, we are told, he would drink nothing but pure water; and then water that was not so pure. In his fits of melancholy, he would shut himself up in his tent for days at a time, with a hatchet and a flag placed at the door to indicate that he was not to be disturbed for any reason whatever; until at last the cloud would lift, the signals would be removed, and the Governor would reappear, brisk and cheerful. During one of these retirements, there was a grave danger of a native attack upon the camp. Colonel Long, the Chief-of-Staff, ventured after some hesitation, to ignore the flag and hatchet, and to enter the forbidden tent. He found Gordon seated at a table, upon which were an open Bible and an open bottle of brandy. Long

explained the circumstances, but could obtain no answer beyond the abrupt words—' You are commander of the camp '—and was obliged to retire, non-plussed, to deal with the situation as best he could. On the following morning, Gordon, cleanly shaven, and in the full-dress uniform of the Royal Engineers, entered Long's tent with his usual tripping step, exclaiming— ' Old fellow, now don't be angry with me. I was very low last night. Let's have a good breakfast—a little b. and s. Do you feel up to it?'

Now in *The Three Prophets* of 1884, the theme of which had been religious fanaticism, Gordon's protracted seclusion is represented as devoted solely to his ' ever-present Bible and Prayer Book.' To these the version of 1912 added ' a bottle of cognac and sherry,' but the epithet ' open ' is applied to the Bible, not, as in Strachey's version, to the bottles and, although Chaillé-Long would perhaps not have been averse to suggesting that the responsibilities which he discharged so triumphantly were increased by the Governor's dipsomania it did not in fact occur to him to do so. For no reader who was familiar with Gordon's repeated recommendation of brandy and quinine as a specific against fever, or had encountered the picture of Gordon, seated in broad daylight before a table on which stood bottles of quinine and brandy, would have interpreted the scene in the tent as a charge of intemperance. And, indeed, it is probable that until Strachey no reader did. And even Strachey, who quietly drops the lighted torches and the vigorous sortie, felt it necessary to substitute " an open bottle of brandy " for the " bottle of cognac and sherry " of his original. And he unobtrusively accommodates the close of the scene to this heightening of colour by adopting the suggestion of a brandy and soda breakfast from *The Three Prophets* in place of the invitation to dinner which figures in *My Life in Four Continents*, the version on which the remainder of his paragraph is based.

3

Had the author of *Eminent Victorians* been a critical historian, or primarily interested in the truth, the numerous falsehoods and inaccuracies which diversify the otherwise tedious pages of *My Life in Four Continents* would certainly have prevented him from accepting Chaillé-Long as an authority. But even without the danger-signals distributed so plentifully throughout the volume at large, a careful examination of this particular passage and its context must soon have convinced him of its worthlessness. For we know Chaillé-Long's movements during his employment under Gordon; there was only one occasion on which the two were long enough in one place together for it to have been possible for him to witness a seclusion of " days at a time " (*The Three Prophets*) or one lasting " from three to five days " (*My Life in Four Continents*). And this (as indeed Chaillé-Long himself makes clear by associating the attack by " savage hordes " with his return to Lado) was the period—of not less than twelve, or more than fifteen, days—immediately after Chaillé-Long had brought up his unwelcome consignment of Arab troops in January, 1875. Gordon was always busy, but during these few days he was even busier than usual. Five hundred native porters had unexpectedly arrived from the south and in addition to these the four hundred and fifty Arab soldiers who had been brought up-river by Long had to be lodged and fed, and a good many of them nursed into the bargain. Moreover, he was arranging, down to the pettiest detail, for the imminent departure of three expeditions. And during these few days he wrote two of his prodigious diary-letters home, in which it was his habit to comment on any unusual incident, however trifling. It is almost inconceivable that he should have omitted to report several days of solitary seclusion in his own tent, and quite inconceivable that he should have said nothing of a night attack by " savage hordes " with lighted torches, only repelled by a vigorous sortie led by the very man whom he describes, in the second of these letters, as having relapsed into procrastination.

Indeed, the mere fact that the apathetic natives of the neighbourhood should have been so suddenly and so mysteriously transformed into savage and murderous hordes would have made news sufficiently startling to fill a letter by itself.

Moreover, by a fortunate chance for the events of this particular fortnight additional evidence is available. For the Austrian Marno was at Lado, and Marno was keeping, with Teutonic attention to detail, a daily diary of events there. Neither in the diary, subsequently published as a book, nor in two long descriptive letters written, during the same fortnight, to the Geographical Society of Vienna, is there the slightest suggestion either of an attack on the camp or of its commander's seclusion.[1] On the contrary there are frequent references to daily discussions with Gordon as to the plans of the coming expedition. It must be presumed that Strachey, having once discovered Chaillé-Long, was content to inquire no further, for had he been aware of Marno even his appetite for irreverence could hardly have induced him to swallow *My Life in Four Continents*.

4

Eminent Victorians had appeared at an opportune moment, coinciding with the moral reaction from the strain and suffering of a war which, it soon became fashionable to suppose, had " settled nothing." By 1919 a disillusioned public was only too ready to smile, with Strachey, at the qualities which it no longer associated with a struggle for victory, but only with misdirected effort and useless sacrifice. And inevitably Strachey was followed by a host of imitators, much less adequately equipped than their prototype for convincing denigration, biographers whose shallow irreverence soon became as tedious as the pompous reticences of the official hagiographies which they outmoded. And while the rival iconoclasts jostled each other about the pedestals of the great Victorians the careless slanders pop-

[1] See Allen, *Gordon and the Sudan,* 87, 88.

ularised by the master spread far and wide. Many, no doubt, angrily rejected the suggestion that Gordon was a secret drinker because such an innuendo seemed incompatible with the man's moral and physical achievements, or simply because they were reluctant to see a great reputation besmirched. But there were many too who accepted it with gusto, as they would have accepted any innuendo against the respectability of the too respectable Victorians. It is unlikely, however, that many either of those who accepted or those who rejected the myth put themselves to the pains of examining the evidence for it. And meanwhile, as was inevitable, it was beginning to be adopted by publicists, naïvely content to accept *Eminent Victorians* as the latest verdict of history. And it is the widespread vulgarisation of the slander during the years between the wars which had made it desirable to expose its baselessness in some detail.

5

Strachey seems to have drawn upon one other authority in this particular piece of denigration, and one only. But although the author this time was more respectable than Chaillé-Long, what he wrote was even more irrelevant. Sir Richard Burton, the traveller, contributed a review of the Khartoum *Journals* shortly after Gordon's death, to the *Academy* of 11th July, 1885. He and Gordon had frequently corresponded, but a painstaking examination by the late Dr. Bernard Allen (whose *Gordon and the Sudan* is indispensable to all students of this subject) has shown that in all probability they only met once and certainly did not meet more than twice. Burton was writing as a celebrated traveller in the East rather than as an intimate of Gordon's.

Burton speaks of Gordon's *Journals* as "lit up with a golden glory: the man is the very soul of honour, the embodiment of what every gentleman should strive to be." Gordon, he says, was "a man whose perfect truthfulness and integrity, whose disinterested spirit . . . made him a phenomenon in the nineteenth century." And he proceeds to comment on what appeared to him to be Gordon's most obvious eccentricity, his belief that he received constant divine guidance in the pettiest, as well as the most important, affairs of life. Hence, Burton suggests, derived the " curious changes of policy and conduct which perplexed his best friends." He instances occasions on which Gordon changed his mind on major issues or important persons, and then he adds: " And so in minor matters; for months he would drink nothing but water, and then prefer, very decidedly, water with whisky." It is obvious that Burton meant exactly what he said, and no more than he said. And no doubt he was correct, although " whisky " is almost certainly a slip for " brandy." In the desert and for months at a time Gordon drank nothing but water and proclaimed the superiority of even " putrid water " to alcohol; and then on returning to Cairo (where Burton met him in 1879) he would for a while, like Burton himself and nine Anglo-Egyptians out of ten, take brandy and water. It is a comment on a minor inconsistency, not a charge of intemperance. Indeed, even had Burton believed that " the embodiment of what every gentleman should strive to be " had in fact been a drunkard it is inconceivable that he should have ventured to make such a charge, or the editor of the *Academy* to print it, in what was virtually an obituary notice, printed six months after Gordon's death and while Victorian England was still resounding with eulogies of the martyred Christian hero.

6

When Strachey's innuendo first became known, and later, after a radio broadcaster's embroidery on it, a few survivors who had known Gordon expressed their indignation in the Press. But those who had been prepared to accept Strachey as an authority were not likely to pay much attention to an expostulation by Slatin Pasha in the *Morning Post*; Slatin Pasha, after all, was almost an Eminent Victorian himself. Even the indignant denials of Watson and

Chippindall, who had lived with Gordon in the inevitable intimacy of the desert, went unregarded.

What after all is remarkable in all this is not that the author of *Eminent Victorians* should have unearthed three ambiguous passages, which he could adapt to discredit Gordon, but that he should not have been able to unearth many more. For Gordon was an eccentric with a particularly strict moral code of his own, of which he made no secret; precisely the kind of person in fact to whom rumour is readiest to impute moral lapses. The sort of man who in the seventeen-eighties was saying that William Wilberforce had married a negress ought surely to have been saying in the eighteen-seventies that Gordon was a dipsomaniac. And had the report of such an assertion once got on to paper, however dubious its origins, not only would Strachey or his imitators have accorded it as much credence as if it had been a statement on oath by the Archbishop of the day, but it would have been next door to impossible to disprove. For it is always difficult to establish a negative; diarists and correspondents seldom note that their contemporaries are *not* thieves and adulterers. Nevertheless Gordon was the sort of man whose whole career may be said to have invited the attentions of the scandalmonger; and that there should have been *sotto voce* scandalmongering of some sort was all but inevitable. After all, a baseless charge of inebriety has been similarly whispered against many famous men—against Kitchener, for example, as he himself recalled when angrily repudiating the slander against Gordon as " a damned lie."

But Dr. Bernard Allen took the trouble to cross-examine anyone he could find who had known Gordon intimately, and could discover no sort of corroboration for the slander. He even investigated the rumours of Cairo clubs, an unsavoury and almost inexhaustible field of research, without encountering anything more solid than an allegation that a member of the Egyptian Turf Club had once been known to remark that " Gordon did himself well." The source of this nebulous assertion was in turn eventually traced to an Arab, who had reported that Gordon's stores, which he helped to pack, included a case of brandy. No Arab, however, was needed to establish the fact that a case of brandy was to be found among Gordon's stores. His letters constantly refer to consignments of cognac. For all African expeditions of this period carried cases of brandy as a matter of routine, and, as will appear, there are plenty of references to brandy in Gordon's correspondence. It is evident that in the desert he regarded it as a specific against fever if taken occasionally and in moderation, but fatal if drunk habitually. Thus writing from the desert in September, 1875, he refers to " my great foe, the liver," and adds " I am sorely tempted with laudanum but resist it for it bites like a serpent. But if any one was addicted to this or spirits there is no doubt he would be a victim to either of them here. It would not necessarily follow he would die, for I have lost many more than Baker did, and his men drank and fought every night and lived through it." And in a letter to Julian Baker, from Abyssinia in 1879 (not more precisely dated) he wrote, " I am low, I will not deny it. No cognac—I am *glad to say*, in the morning, but *regret* it in the *evening*." " I do not touch anything but water " is a constant refrain. And writing to Colonel Charles Harvey on 25th February, 1878, " I do not care much about going to Cairo," he says, " for I drink cognac (which, up here, I never touch from month to month) and then I talk too much." But, despite Sir Richard Burton, there is no inconsistency in being virtually a teetotaller in the desert and behaving like other dinner guests when in Cairo.

After considerable research and correspondence I have myself only been able to discover two fragments of evidence to match Dr. Allen's Cairo clubman. A correspondent informed me that in 1904 when travelling on a liner bound for Yokohama he had encountered a stranger, named Drummond, who told him that Gordon had been a friend of his family's at the time of the Tai Ping rebellion, and used occasionally to stay at his house in Shanghai " and sit up drinking gin all night on his veranda." My correspondent added that Mr. Drummond had not implied that Gordon was a drunkard. I know of no other evidence for these visits, but it is obviously possible that Gordon did visit friends in Shanghai, that he did sit

G.G.   O up all night and that he did drink gin. Again, a distinguished man of letters informed me that, when a young man he had been told by his father, who had not himself known Gordon, that Gordon would not touch alcohol in Mess (this was certainly inaccurate), but that he would indulge at long intervals in a bout of secret drinking. My informant added that he had himself known a man who had completed a brilliant public career without a shadow of disrepute, despite a lifelong addiction to intermittent bouts of secret drinking. It was characteristic, he said, of this man, as of other secret drinkers, that in conversation he always displayed a morbid aversion to any mention of drink or drinking; and it was when I told him something of Gordon's repeated references to brandy—and of the letters to Augusta in which, near the end of his life, he describes in detail his efforts to give up smoking, drinking, and even the reading of newspapers—that my informant declared himself personally convinced that his story must have been inaccurate.

But in the last resort Gordon himself is the most persuasive evidence. For even those who whenever they encounter religion expect to detect hypocrisy can hardly suppose that a man who throughout a life of most exceptional strain and activity preserved such superb physical and mental health was addicted to secret drinking. The American Consul-General in Cairo thus described Gordon in 1876:

> Gordon Pasha is a man of middle height, sparely but strongly built, and giving little indication of the strength, both of sinews and constitution, which has borne him so far unscathed through so many hardships and the African swamps, where the "pestilence walketh at noon-day," and wherein many of his pioneers have laid their bones. Neither in face nor in figure does he carry any traces of his conflict with the treacherous climate, and more treacherous human wild beasts, among whom he had passed the two preceding years. Even his complexion, still comparatively fresh and fair, gave no hint of the kisses of the sun of Central Africa; and his eye was as clear and bright as though he had

just come from promenading on the shady side of Pall Mall.

In East Darfur Gordon would frequently cover a hundred miles on a camel in two days, in districts where the average pace of the creature is normally less than four miles an hour. Camel-riding, as Gordon rode camels, is certainly not compatible with self-indulgence. As for the Sudanese, who regard insobriety with the utmost contempt, they venerated Gordon as something almost more than human; Gordon, said an old man who had once been one of the native captains of his river steamers, " was not a man but a god."

7

It is ironical to reflect that had Lytton Strachey been able to examine Gordon's correspondence he might have found there several passages which, if duly divorced from their context, would have provided a more plausible basis for innuendo. For the truth seems to be that all his life, though in all other respects a natural ascetic, Gordon was a heavy smoker, and from time to time, like most other British colonels of his day, he would, as we have seen, drink brandy. But his conscience was never easy about either habit. And somewhere about the end of 1880, or the beginning of 1881, when staying with Mr. Waller at Twywell in Northamptonshire, he would experience what I have ventured to call his final conversion, abandoning not as yet his positive heresies, but his one great negative unorthodoxy, indifference to the central feature of Christian worship, Holy Communion. Thereafter, as will appear, he mellowed and grew more gentle. Gradually, too, he began to shed his heresies. And partly in order to fit himself to receive the Sacrament, and partly no doubt in consequence of grace derived from it, he set himself at once to achieve the complete asceticism which he had long desired but never achieved. The Sacrament, he told Augusta, was " a weapon for warfare against the flesh," and in particular for warfare against " that immense serpent," " smoking and drinking." And for some while thereafter, as I shall show, his letters would contain references to his private vow to smoke no more than fifteen cigarettes a day, and touch no spirits. Read in their context these passages set the matter in its true proportions. For many years Gordon smoked, and, at intervals, drank spirits, like other men; but when he grew to his full stature he determined to do his best to rid himself of habits which, though natural enough to the average sensual man, were in startling contrast with his otherwise thorough-going asceticism, and had always troubled his conscience.

BOOK SIX

DISENCHANTMENT

FROM THIS spring of 1875 onwards the problem of the great Lakes continued to overshadow Gordon. For by reaching the Lakes he might hope to cut off the slave trade, and incidentally please the Khedive. The Royal Geographical Society, though it officially represented the world-wide interest in the still unsolved enigma of the sources of the Nile, scarcely entered into his calculations, save as a deterrent. For he had a healthy contempt for " geographists " or " Geog^y fellows " as he was apt to call them— " they have no more business to be giving medals to the people than the people have to be giving medals to them "—and he had already resolved that the critical stage of the exploration should be entrusted to Gessi, to Linant, to anyone rather than himself, lest he, too, should earn " the inordinate praise which is given to an explorer " and an extension of the renown which he shunned all the more resolutely because he knew that in his inmost heart he desired it so much. It was a refusal which he was always prepared to rationalise: " I have told Baker that I will not explore the Lake. To be boxed up for a phantasy in a 50-ft. long steamer for a fortnight would be my death. I am not paid for explorations."

For the remainder of his Governorship therefore, although his ultimate object must be to settle the country, Gordon may be thought of less as a Governor than as an explorer in charge of a sparsely equipped and grotesquely ill-manned expedition in hostile and pestilence-stricken lands, in which virtually everything, from pacifying the natives to catching his own sentries asleep at their posts, splicing ropes and checking the screws in the stores, would depend upon him and him alone. In essence his plan of campaign was simple. Slowly, and with infinite difficulty, he established a series of stations, one day's march apart, along the Nile. From Rejaf to Bedden, from Bedden to Kerri, from Kerri to Moogie, to Dufilé, each stage represented weeks of toil. First came the infinity of petty detail to be tackled single-handed. As he wrote to Enderby from Bedden in July:

> You have little idea of the wear and tear of it all. Sometimes I feel quite overwhelmed with the lot of things one has to remember and do. As Burton says of his servant who avoided him like a pestilence, connecting an interview with him with hard labour, so people avoid me, and really I think it is wonderful what a memory God has given me: there are such [a] host of letters, for all things come to you—passages, steamers, Magazines, Powder and Arms, Nuggars; all the petty details, Rows, soldiers, the Khartoum people.

In the neighbourhood of Moogie there were skirmishes, too, and the Frenchman, Linant, who had returned from his successful mission to King M'tesa, was killed with forty of Gordon's least unreliable soldiers. And when at last the *nuggars* were hauled upstream, the tow ropes would part or prove to be mysteriously missing, or a *nuggar* would break loose and whirl down the river, or ground on rock in midstream. And if Gordon himself ceased for a moment to supervise and adjure the eighty satin-skinned blacks who hauled on each boat " each one does what he likes and the utmost confusion is the result."

> Your brother prays the nuggars up as he used to do the troops when they wavered in the breaches in China; but often and often the ropes break, and it has all to be done over again. However, I feel sure that we shall have fully made known to us the mystery

of these matters. Sometimes I think I am punished for some arbitrary act I have been guilty of, for the soldiers have tried me sorely.

But sometimes, too, he would reflect that " the mystic nature of the Nile " might have something to do with these constant mischances, for there must be " some deep and wonderful design in all these trying obstacles." If he had his Concordance with him he might be able to unravel the mystery. It was encouraging, however, that, if there proved to be a cataract a few miles below Dufilé it would be the seventh, and seven (since God rested on the seventh day) was " the mystic number for rest." Alas! when at last Gordon reconnoitred the seventh cataract on foot he heard, for some while before he reached it, " a voice like thunder," and he had no sooner set eyes on it than he realised that no vessel could reach the Lakes without being carried, on the last stage to Dufilé, overland. " IT IS ALL OVER," he wrote in capitals; the *Khedive* would never sail Lake Albert; and he turned wearily to consider the problem of assembling the smaller vessels whose component parts were distributed along the stations downstream. This was in October, 1875. By the end of the year Gessi, with a thousand porters, had transported the sections overland to Dufilé and was beginning to piece them together.

A month after the grand disappointment of the seventh cataract Gordon's mood was such that the characteristically irrational complaints in a letter from the Khedive stung him into dispatching three telegrams of resignation and commencing to pack for departure. Next morning, however, as he rummaged farther in the post bag he found another and more formal communication, from which he learned for the first time how the Khedive had acted upon his advice as to outflanking the Lakes, had dispatched an expedition to Mombasa and actually put Admiral Mc'Killop and three men-of-war under his command. " The letter as far as civility went," wrote Gordon, " was fulsome; he would not let me go—grand career, etc. Now, look here, the man had gone to all this expense, under the impression I would stick to him. I could not, therefore, leave him, so the telegrams . . . were destroyed, and I stay." He made no move, however, to carry out his share of the plan by marching for the river Juba. Two months later he sent Augusta a retrospective *apologia* for his inaction. By occupying the mouth of the Juba river, he explained, the Khedive had selected the wrong objective. " He sent off McKillop and Long to Juba, and told them to wait for me. They will wait a long time, I expect. I am not going to try this with the undisciplined wretched troops I have here; and, though he knows it, he does nothing to help me."

His feeling as to the wretched quality of his subordinates, both Egyptian and Arab, was indeed so strong that it is surprising that it did not drive him to abandon not the Mombasa project only, but the direct advance on the Lakes, and indeed his entire command. For months he scarcely sent a letter home without a bitter complaint of their shortcomings. How vastly inferior were both Arabs and Egyptians to the Chinese! " Cowardly, lying, effeminate brutes these Arabs and Sudanese without any good point about them that I have seen." " The cowardice, moral and physical, of these Arabs is incomprehensible. They were a brave people once and conquered enormous countries and now they are certainly . . . totally devoid of patriotism and you can never rely on a word they say about a disputed point." Even physically he found them poor stuff. " Walk an Arab 10 or 12 miles and if he is not ill the next day I will be astonished." And the Egyptians were no better. " They are the most hopeless set. Continual oppression has made them of such material that you could find no sound principle to work on. Nations have generally some regenerating quality, either a commercial, military, religious or patriotic spirit. These people lack each one of these motive influences." And in the most savage of all these outbursts, written three days after the crowning disappointment at the seventh cataract: " *I hate them!* There! A twopenny-halfpenny nation, for whom it is not worth while to stay a day in these countries. . . . It is the fault of those who persuaded me to come (viz. Rose, Henry's, yours)."

Brussels,
5.1.84

My dear Waller

I hope to be over in a day or two at Southton. The Die is cast. I leave the Army & Go Congo & on 5 Feby. I am glad of it now, & will do my best the King will pay the compensation for loss of my Commission, entire sum his Expenditure has been 600,000 £ up to date, & last year he spent 100,000 £

Part of a letter from Gordon to Mr. Waller, January 1884 before leaving for Khartoum

The only thing I feel sorry
for is the Eating (i e
by Commons) which I shall
miss. Believe me
Yours sincerely
C E Hudson

H.M. very kind. &
considerate.

None the less, these were the people for whom he was to sacrifice his life, and, during its closing scenes, his ever-acuter sense of responsibility for them would develop into compassion and, even at last, its natural consequence, affection. And though in the intimacy of his journal-letters he could express himself frankly as to the defects of those often then described as the subject races he had equally few illusions as to the divine right of the Englishman to rule them. The " Egyptians are beginning not to love the English at all, and we may depend on it they will not put up much longer with our dictation." Indeed, he had already come to the conclusion that as colonial administrators the French were probably our superiors.

> Somehow I think the French are better than our nation for these things. They are more plastic. Germans, viz., official Germans, would, I think, never answer. They are too methodical. We seem between the two, which, I suppose, we are by descent.

And the most he can say for British rule in India is that we are bound to resist attempts to expel us by violence: but " I never have been able to answer the query in what way we would lose if we failed to keep it. I never knew an officer who had been in India who could, or even felt inclined to, speak in favour of its possession."

2

In the province which, as distinct from the secret of the Lakes, he accepted as his primary concern, the effects of a strong hand were becoming evident. Incompetent or dishonest officials had been summarily dismissed: " I make no hesitation, *lettres de cachet* are signed and people are whisked into exile at once with no trial, for trials are mockeries where a man is rich." He had astonished the natives by paying for their ivory and their labour, with the result that he could walk safely, unarmed and alone, where an Egyptian official would have needed a battalion to protect him. And he had begun to enlist Niam Niam warriors, stalwart cannibals from the interior, as a bodyguard, a military precaution which was incidentally also one of his many economies. In 1875 Equatoria, once a perpetual financial strain upon the Khedive, positively contributed £48,000 to his exchequer. It had all been the work of the Governor, as for that matter had been the dusting of white ants off the stores and the manufacture of rocket-cases out of an old pump. And it had been done in the intervals of a prodigious correspondence; "last night just as I was going to bed the letters came—sixty or seventy private letters and a mass of official news!! Oh, dear! I read till two a.m., and am now answering them." To almost all his private correspondents he replied conscientiously, scrawling swiftly but legibly on flimsy unpunctuated sheets, often mottled with rain or perspiration. "Are my stops better?" he asked Augusta in a parenthesis. "I never learnt grammar or dancing!" To Augusta each week went his journal-letter, sometimes twenty sheets long, and occasionally a paragraph on some topic uppermost in his thoughts would be dispatched, identical down to the missing stops, to two or three different recipients.

Lately, however, he had begun to discourage unwelcome correspondents, usually influential persons too prodigal with their advice, by ignoring or snubbing them. Sir Samuel Baker in particular seems to have received a good many rebuffs. "One more letter will collapse him" Gordon writes in January, 1876, and next month he sends a diplomatic warning; "Baker is sure to go to Enderby for explanations why I have desired to cease my correspondence with him, but as Enderby does not know the reason he can easily put him off. He is a snob and I am delighted at having rid myself of such an acquaintance." Next June, however, Sir Samuel was still writing: "a letter from Baker put away and *not* read, a letter from Grant not to be answered; much the best way." Although Gordon held that Baker had claimed much more than he had achieved, one suspects that his chief reason for disapproving of him just now was that he had recently reported, in a letter dated 12th December, 1875, an evening at the Royal Geographical Society at which he had chatted

with Enderby, seen Gordon's latest letter, briefed Burton to " speak
with good taste on the memory of poor Speke," and finally, with
Sir Henry Rawlinson, pronounced a eulogy on Gordon himself.
It can hardly be a coincidence that next month, planning a hermit's
life after his return home, Gordon should have warned Augusta " I
shall refuse all invitations to dine out, and choke off Baker and all
Geog^y fellows and (D.V.) rest a while." And by March there is
quite a catalogue of discarded notables. " Only Eyre remains and
I shall not drop him. Sir H. Rawlinson was never taken up and so
will never be dropped. I never sought Baker, Grant, Sir H. Rawlinson, Frere (Sir B.) or Waller's acquaintance."

But the chokings-off were not permanent; when the barrier of
distance and the trials of Equatoria were no more, Gordon's natural
friendliness would reassert itself. Of Baker, for example, whose
correspondence he had been so persistently discouraging, he would
write several years later that " for eight or ten years he was constantly in my prayers," and Baker would be almost the last person
in England he would go to see before his final departure for Khartoum. Moreover, even Augusta received her share of criticism.
Her letters, he complained, were dull and half a page about Sir
Henry James was excessive. As for the official correspondence it
depended mainly upon his prodigious memory, for the Egyptians
to whom he wrote rarely acknowledged his letters, while his own
secretary was seldom able to find those which he had himself
received.

These incessant clerical and administrative labours in a tropical
climate were varied by occasional long marches and other exhausting
outbursts of physical activity when it was his habit to " accumulate
energy for three or four days, make an extraordinary effort and
finish the work undertaken and then collapse for days." It is not
surprising that, though he was never seriously ill, or ill for long, he
sometimes described to Augusta symptoms which must have seemed
all the more alarming since, though a healthy man, unaccustomed to
illness and devoid of medical knowledge, he was always prepared
to offer a confident, and usually a disquieting, diagnosis. In May,

1875, he had reported " something like a stroke of paralysis," which he attributed to excessive smoking. In October, after an exhausting march and two days without food, it is " an attack of ague—the first I have had since I was 13½ years old at Brighton at Aunt Wellington's." On 3rd January he reports, "great pains in the back," and he has actually been fatigued by a fourteen-mile march. On 16th February there is nose-bleeding; " nearly suffocated last night with the blood. Poor sheath! It is much worn." And a few months later he feels sure that his old enemy, constant smoking, has " more or less affected my heart, yet I will not give it up. It is my only joy. I have not a drop of cognac here." As for cognac, there are repeated complaints that he has had to pay one of his bugbears, Steward, fifty pounds from government funds for sending out brandy which had not been ordered: " I never touch it, what a dreadful man that is!" For all forms of sickness Warburg's Tincture, he was firmly convinced, was a sovereign specific; his letters resound with its praises and he even wrote specially to commend it to the Khedive.

3

But his brief indispositions were probably due, in part at least, to the bouts of depression which with him never lasted long, and in the summer of 1876 he made a spiritual discovery, the importance of which he recognised by referring to it as a " pearl," the title hitherto reserved for his supreme secret, the indwelling of Christ. Two verses in the fifth chapter of the first epistle of St. Peter suddenly burned into his imagination. *Humble yourselves therefore under the mighty hand of God, that he may exalt you in due time: casting all your care upon him; for he careth for you.* Here was the simplest of injunctions, intended, like every injunction in Holy Writ for literal obedience, and henceforth he would obey it. He would hand over his responsibilities, entire, to the Almighty. The resolve brought an immeasurable lightening of the heart—" it is a very great comfort to feel that God will rectify one's defects in this life and make right all mistakes "—and with it his intermittent maladies seemed to vanish. A major victory had been gained over the ego against which he struggled so fiercely all his life. He reported it triumphantly to Augusta in a characteristic passage (10th July, 1875) in which the trifling misquotation of the New Testament—for he carried his favourite passages in his head and did not turn up his references— is not the least characteristic feature.

> Thank God I am quite well, and so happy now I have resigned the government of the Province, and put all the faults on my 'Friend.' He is able to bear them, and will use me as long as He pleases as His mouthpiece and when He has done with me He will put me aside. 'Casting all your cares on him; for he careth for you' had just come to mind. I do not know if you will see this 'pearl' at once, but I consider it a great stride in knowledge of Him. . . . I consider now that I am free from any responsibility about the Province, about my stay or leaving; that He has taken the whole work off my hands and that I am on leave, as it were. What a comfort this is. . . . Since I had the 'pearl' He careth for you, and as it were resigned the rule of the Province I have had much comfort, and if the Francis money has been found I can say *Nunc dimittis* with Simeon.

4

But "the Francis money" was a recurrent anxiety. Though he had never approved his youngest brother's choice of a wife, when she was left virtually destitute with her six young children in 1872 he had resolved to provide for her, and henceforth all his plans for the future were made with one eye on her financial prospects. " I cannot say how long I may be here," he writes to Augusta in August, 1875, " but I think I may clear Frances 2000 £ and something more ere I leave. I am selling my *liver*, I feel, though it is not a cheap purchase." And later in the same month a more elaborate financial calculation is accompanied by some wry reflections on the prospects of the widow and her family:

> I am glad to tell you I have close on 1100 £ here and though I send you only 200 £ now I will send the remainder as soon as I have definitely made up my accounts. You will invest it to pay Francis 2000 £ by bits and bits well bound up. . . . Had I been in England I should have tried to have stopped the marriage for she has a hard-looking jaw which promises a very acidulated old age. Pray put no preventive in [the way of] her marrying again, if there is any chance of such a thing. If I live and can stay out another 6 months, to let her have another 1000 £ of her own, beyond the 2000 £ for the children I would do so if it would make her more marketable.

And in addition to the needs of the unfortunate Francis there was the constant drain of the Gravesend pensioners, so numerous that Gordon could seldom remember how many there were or how much was being paid to them. "I think after this year," he writes in October, 1875, after another reference to Francis's two thousand pounds, "the Gravesend payments might be diminished but I have forgotten what they are." And in the following March "I have written to Miss Browne to ask who the Gravesend pensioners are. The only two I shall keep on are Carter and Clifford and I think you pay their money to Mrs. Waron. I must send a good donation to the Dispensary and to the Ragged School and to Miss Browne's establishment in Gravesend." A note shortly afterwards that "the pensions are £245" presumably represents Miss Browne's reply to his query as to the Gravesend budget. And besides all this there was an allowance for Augusta herself. And not an allowance only; in the summer of 1876 he is buying her a house, and that at a moment when he is in despair over his private accounts. However, the new 'pearl' is not forgotten and bookkeeping is among the cares which he is ready to hand over to the Almighty. Could anyone but Gordon have contrived to pack so much of his private theology,

and so much of his dependence upon literal interpretation of the
S riptures, into a lament over an impromptu balance-sheet?

> I have been, as usual, as ass; spent 980 £ on the Linants and
> 100 £ on Marno, and been careless of my accts to the extent of
> some 920 £. Therefore, out of 5000 £, two and a half years'
> pay, I have sent home £2400, Linant and Marno 1080 £, at
> Khartoum now 500 £, and pitched away in one way or another
> 920 £, and my reflection is that I could certify no one is more
> unfit to have any money than I am, so you may just as well
> oblige your brother and take that blessed house. How the 920 £
> has gone I have not an idea, but gone it has. Someone has got
> it, and that person or persons were destined to get it; it never
> was mine but was lent me, and He who lent has given it to
> someone else and not told me. I have not, I know, spent it on
> merrymaking. As soon as I can you shall have the 500 £ salvage
> from the wreck and then quarterly I will send some home. I
> know it is not altogether right to be so careless, but I think if
> God pleases, He can settle the accounts, and as it were keep my
> books for me. It is a query if it is right to put this on Him, but
> I think if you have a Friend of His might and wisdom you
> cannot too much trust Him, and with His power it is no trouble
> to Him, and therefore the closer your intimacy the better. . . .
> It is ' decided ' that you accept the House as a present from your
> brother.

5

Meanwhile his theology remained unaltered. He was aware that it
was heretical and often spoke whimsically of " the ' unsound '
doctrine." He was aware, too, that it was childlike, and therefore
all the more likely to be true. He summarised it once more for
Augusta from Kerri as based on three main principles—the pre-
existence of the soul; its sinlessness save during its union with the

flesh, from the sins of which it is exculpated by the Atonement; and its inevitable return at death to its natural and pristine sinlessness. To which he might have added that first ' pearl,' the indwelling of Christ, which chiefly influenced his own conduct. For it is by his life, not his theology, that Gordon's religion must be judged, and we have always to remember that (in William Temple's words) " for the individual the one vital matter is personal trust. . . ." And personal trust was the ruling principle of Gordon's life. It was not merely that he had resigned the administration of his Province to God and accepted whatever happened as for the best. He now firmly believed that through daily study of the Bible he received daily guidance: " if a man knows his Bible fairly and then goes forth into the world, God will show him His works." " There have," as Temple says, " been saintly heretics and orthodox worldlings," and Gordon was on the road to becoming a saint. " I ask God," he wrote (29th June, 1875),

> for the following things, viz: 1. Not to be disturbed if the Khedive sent me away to-morrow. 2. Not to be disturbed if he keeps me. 3. Not to have anything of this world come between Him and me; and not to fear death, or to feel regret if it came before I completed what I may think my programme. Thank God, He gives me the most comforting assurance that nothing shall disturb me, or come between Him and me.

When Gordon wrote that " the positive gain in this world by being given these views is immense even in temporal matters " he did not of course mean that he had evolved his theology with the deliberate object of lightening his cares or making himself a more efficient administrator. It was, however, well fitted to rid him of anxieties, and he is sometimes to be found adding touches calculated to render it even more effective in this respect. Thus he genuinely looked forward to death, and his belief in the sinlessness of every soul when released from the body relieved him of all anxieties as to future punishment. Nevertheless, the familiar picture of heaven as an eternity of praise disturbed him; he could not doubt that, if he was to be happy he must be active; there must, he concluded, still be provinces to administer, gigantic tasks still to attempt, in the life hereafter.

He prepared for the final thrust to the Lakes with the half-reluctant conviction that it was God's will that he should not leave Equatoria yet. Nevertheless, nostalgia was growing on him. Half-forgotten figures from the crowded tapestry of Gravesend resume vivid shape in his memory; the Old Bird, Miss Surridge whom once, he recalls with something like astonishment, he used to visit three times a week, and the paralysed Carter, and Mr. Lilley, the Presbyterian Minister. Their troubles, and it is almost always with trouble that he associates them, begin to interest him again. The Old Bird must be kept out of the workhouse; Miss Surridge is doubtless lonely and he really must write to her; Mr. Lilley's financial difficulties are all due to a strong-minded wife, who insists on living above her station and keeping a "huge female servant." The sardonic comments on the horrors of civilisation—the martyr-dom of perpetual dinner invitations and "that dreadful Xmas with its bills and eating"—are sometimes now replaced by wistful re-ferences to its advantages: "I have a sort of feeling that I would like to have no more buffetings in life, no more rows, no more seeing people and grinning like an ape." And even to its material comforts; "I mean to go first-class in the trains and to lie in bed in the morning." A little later indeed he is for once positively anticipating the pleasures of the table, and some respite from the perpetual dry biscuits, broiled meat and macaroni boiled in sugar and water. "I want OYSTERS when I come home, they are good for the brain, with brown bread and lots of them, not a dozen but 4 dozen."

Even now, however, his anticipations of home are constantly interspersed with warnings that he is determined to avoid all social engagements. He will lie in bed till eleven every morning, stroll as far as the docks or the cemetery in the afternoon and evade Russell, whose acquaintance might bring him into contact with the

Prince of Wales, " whom I wish to avoid." To Waller he sends a
very frank warning, directed, through Waller, to geographists and
anti-slave-trade enthusiasts: " Now to avoid giving offence un-
necessarily let me ask you to leave me alone. I want quiet while
at home. I do not want to go and stay or dine out *anywhere* and I
do not want to see either Sir B. F. or Sir H. R. or Grant or any
of the men who worry about Africa." Already he scents threats
to his privacy from afar, for letters and news paragraphs about
him were appearing in the Press, some of them based on his own
private correspondence. Little escaped him in the English newspapers, which he devoured from end to end as soon as they arrived,
but just now he rarely commented on public affairs and it needed
reports of Archbishop Tait's alleged misuse of his patronage to
sting him into an outburst.

> Did you see the Arch Bishop of Canterbury said in House of
> Lords he looked on Episcopal patronage as a *public trust*? Some-
> one routed out how he had dispensed his patronage during
> 2 years. He gave 5000 £ per year in livings to his own relations
> and his wife's and £1500 a year to other outsiders. How a man
> can live after such an exposure I do not know: it would kill a
> smaller man. Nephews, brothers—Mrs. Tait's cousins, etc., etc.,
> they were all put down in the paper. Mrs. Tait's relations had
> the greatest boons given them, showing her influence. A heathen
> nation spite of our profession, with a large amount of idols, gold,
> silver and clay.

On books he spent little time, nor do his references to the
profundities of Martin Tupper say much for his literary perspicacity.
It is only fair to add, however, that from Equatoria he also com-
mends Herodotus and a chapter in Trollope's *The Bertrams*, as well
as commenting unfavourably on the spitefulness of Greville's
Journals.

6

The prospect of applause from " the geographists " had not made him more eager to reach the Lakes and he was equally indifferent to the approval of the anti-slavery societies.

Some philanthropic people write to me about " noble work," " poor blacks," etc. I have, I think, stopped their writing by acknowledging ourselves to be a pillaging horde of brigands, and proposing to them to leave their comfortable homes and come out to their favourite " poor blacks " or to give up their wine and devote the proceeds to sending out *real* missions.

He was certainly not influenced by any desire to emulate or promote the exploits of Stanley, whose long silence was causing anxiety just now. " Did I tell you," he asks (6th September, 1875),

that though I wrote to Stanley a civil note he coolly sends me his packet of letters, the postage of which will cost me 1 £, without a line ? If I did not pay the postage he would say I delayed his letters, and *Daily Telegraph* and *New York Herald* would have abused your brother for doing it for jealousy's sake. Linant gave Stanley my message that he could not pass through the Province with armed men not of the Govt but that I would give him an escort and return his arms afterwards.

As soon as Gessi had begun assembling the smaller boats at Dufilé Gordon set off on an exhausting expedition inland, forty-eight miles to Fatiko and, after a week's pause, seventy-seven miles south again to Foweira. On each journey he averaged sixteen miles a day on foot through jungle grass, scrub and swampland but only reported fatigue and pains in the back. At Foweira he had reached the Nile again, running from Lake Victoria by Lake Kioga to Lake Albert and was well within the territory of Kabarega, King of

Unyoro, sworn enemy of Egypt, in what is now Uganda. That monarch had prudently disappeared into the recesses of his kingdom and Gordon sent troops to occupy two key positions between Lake Albert and Lake Kioga and then himself pushed on to establish a military station in the district of Mrooli, west of the latter. He ended with a forced march of thirty miles, during which he found himself again reflecting on the coming delights, and social pitfalls, of a return to civilisation. At this point, two hundred miles from his base, after dispatching one of his few reliable Arab officers to establish two more stations, one within the territory of King M'tesa of Uganda, he reluctantly turned back on 24th January. A day and a half by canoe to Foweira; a few days there, recovering from sickness due to the hot sun and cold winds in the marshes, a march, much of it at over twenty miles a day, and he was back at Dufilé on 8th February. Gessi and his boats were almost ready. It was still Gessi who was to explore the lakes, for Gordon had not changed his mind; " I wish to give a practical proof of what I think respecting the inordinate praise which is given to an explorer." Gessi, with his prophetic black beard and imperious demeanour, was his ablest subordinate, and after his recent success with the steamer and the two smaller boats Gordon no doubt felt more confidence in him, but he still thought poorly of all his subordinates and as recently as last December had written that " Gessi's brains are all abroad. He cannot fix his attention to anything whatever for his brain cannot contain two directions. He is never wrong, always some excuse." On the seventh of March Gessi was off, with the two smaller boats.

On 29th April Gessi walked into Kerri, where Gordon had been for the last fortnight. He had circumnavigated Lake Albert. The direct connection of the Nile with the lakes was established. The Royal Geographical Society would buzz with excitement. " Nunc dimittis " wrote Gordon to Mrs. Freese. But the cry of relief was premature. For one thing, though he had deliberately arranged that the achievement should be Gessi's, he could not entirely stifle a certain regret that it had not been his own; the old desire to board the tram of the world stirred uneasily. How would he feel, he wondered, if Gessi claimed the whole credit? " I do not think I should care a bit now," he concluded, a trifle doubtfully, " but in old times it would have annoyed me." Some of his letters, he felt bound to admit, had been a trifle boastful; the truth was that he had many natures; " some of my letters are written by one nature, others by the other nature; and so it will be to the end." Talk of two natures, " I have a hundred . . . and they all want to rule."

Moreover, though Gessi had solved one conundrum he had brought back another. For he reported that he had observed, about thirty miles north of the Lake, a large unknown river flowing north-west out of the Nile. Whither did it turn? If it rejoined the Nile might it be an alternative, and perhaps an easier, route between Khartoum and the Lakes? Gordon began to feel that he must find out the truth for himself. When on 17th June Piaggia, another Italian, who had left Gessi's expedition to push towards Lake Victoria, returned with reports of yet another unknown branch of the Nile his mind was made up. He was not surely boarding the tram; these rivers, if they existed, would be vital to his province. Moreover, he had been working on Gessi's reports, and geographists or no geographists his scientific instincts were roused. " It is a terrible stretch of my conscience," he wrote to Enderby, " to force my sketches and Gessi's Lake and River to make them fit. . . . I have rejected Stanley's observns and consequent position of Lake Victoria, adopting Speke's, which fits in much better; (Stanley's come too much to the W and too much to the north)."

On 20th July, 1876, he set out from Dufilé, with the steamer *Nyanza* and two sailing boats. He had had four months of com-parative quiet, the new " pearl," which was to end his worries, had just been discovered. Spiritually and physically he felt a new man, and despite the geographists and their inordinate admiration for explorers he was now determined to map the Nile as far as Lake Victoria himself. A young English volunteer, Lucas, of whom he strongly disapproved, came with him but soon fell ill and had to be left behind. The first stage of their journey, to the shores of Lake

Albert, made it clear that Gessi's tributary of the Nile was a myth. From Lake Albert the steamer took them to the Murchison Falls, but thereafter the Nile was all rapids and the expedition had to struggle on foot through a series of ravines choked by tropical jungle, Gordon surveying the river as he forced his way, by lengthy détours and in pouring rain, through dense undergrowth and creepers. " I am nearly dead," he reported after eighteen miles of it, ". . . but it is done, at any rate, and I am quite sure no one will ever do it again." The geographists seemed very far away. Two more days of fifteen miles each followed; he had several heavy falls and often found himself bound hand and foot by convolvulus or wild vine. " Poor men," he wrote, " it is terrible work for them. . . . I never had such fatigue. . . . What misery! And what for?" Three more days of it and they had struggled into Foweira. Here awaited him the trusted Arab officer who had been sent to establish garrisons in the territory of King M'tesa. Unfortunately he proved to have been no more reliable than the rest when Gordon was out of reach; for, whereas he had recently reported by letter that a garrison of 160 men had been established, at M'tesa's own request, in the royal capital on Lake Victoria, he now disclosed that, so far from having accepted a military occupation, the king was in fact holding Gordon's men as prisoners.

Gordon's first instinct was to push into Uganda with his own handful of troops and compel M'tesa to release his men, but at Mrooli more prudent counsels prevailed. A German who had turned Mahomedan and called himself Emin had recently been appointed medical officer of Equatoria and happened just now to be at M'tesa's court with presents from Gordon. A letter to Emin effected the release of the imprisoned troops, but in it Gordon had proposed to recognise the independence of Uganda and this meant that he would not now be able to survey the ultimate stretch of the Nile, which ran through M'tesa's territories. At least, however, he would survey the river up to Niamyongo, south of Lake Kioga and a mere sixty miles from Lake Victoria. Characteristically he could not help asking himself whether his decision had been partly prompted by his knowledge that it would enable him to return home sooner, lie in bed till eleven every day and eat oysters for lunch. But his conscience was oversensitive, for there can be little doubt that, whatever the geographists might think of it, he was taking the statesmanlike course. Five days' journey, part of it through dense jungle and mosquito-infested marsh, brought them to Niamyongo. There was a native ambush on the way and a spear smashed Gordon's butter tin. He had not been carrying weapons, since his attention was concentrated on defending himself from mosquitoes: "however," he promised himself, "I will carry my revolver to-morrow, though the native will have first shot if he does attack me." On the day after their arrival at Niamyongo, Gordon's farthest south, they turned back for Mrooli, deciding *en route* that Piaggia's Nile tributary, like Gessi's, was a myth.

After a day's rest Gordon turned east for King Kabarega's capital Masindi. He did not move in military formation, and took with him only a small escort of specially unreliable troops, since for some months he had been receiving reports dated from Masindi from an officer he had sent to occupy it. But assertions of this kind from an unsupervised Arab, or Egyptian, officer could not be regarded as evidence, and this personage—"the employé in charge of the troops," as Gordon calls him—had been careful to keep a distance of forty miles between himself and Masindi. When, three days out from Mrooli, Gordon learned the truth he could but push on down a narrow path through high grass with the horns and drums of the invisible enemy sounding on every side. It was an ugly plight and he was conscious of a physical pain in the heart, which would sometimes afterwards recur at moments of extreme peril. But, thanks to the new pearl, his calm remained unruffled; "you never know what you may come on in this land, and never ought to think of the morrow—except that it shall pass as God wills it. People may object, as they like, to what I may say, but nevertheless the faith God has given me is a fountain of support for the present and future, and also for drowning the past." Perhaps it was thanks to the pearl, too, that although four days later Gordon and his men lost their way in the forest " the employé," who had disobeyed orders to march out to meet them, was not punished: " after a fearful row I quieted down and as mercy had been showed me I did the same."

Four weeks later he was admiring the English sparrows at Khartoum. Should he leave the service of the Khedive for ever? " Comfort-of-Body, a very strong gentleman " was decidedly for going home. " Mr. Reason says, What is the use of opening more country to such a government. . . . But Mr. Something (I do not know what) says, Shut your eyes to what may happen in future; leave that to God, and do what you think will open the country thoroughly to both Lakes." He was in an agony of indecision. He had tossed a coin, he could not help remembering, to decide whether he was to come out to Egypt and now, he confessed to Augusta, it seemed likely that a toss would have to decide whether he stayed. But on his way down river he heard circumstantial stories of how the late Minister of Finance, who had been the most powerful man in Egypt when Gordon passed through Cairo in 1874, had just been sent upstream, a lonely prisoner, disgraced and doomed. This surely was an omen, a reminder of what " such a government " could be. Before he reached Cairo he had made up his mind to leave the Egyptian service for ever.

BOOK SEVEN

THE SLAVE TRADE

GORDON REACHED England on Christmas Eve, 1876. He had already changed, or partly changed, his mind. For in Cairo there had been a memorable interview with the Khedive. Each of the strangely dissimilar participants exercised a powerful fascination over the other. It was perhaps natural therefore that when they parted each believed that he had over-persuaded the other. Ismail had pledged himself that the slave trade and the official corruption in the Sudan, which had gone so far to frustrate Gordon's efforts in Equatoria, should be brought to an end. Gordon had said, or at any rate, implied, that in that event he would return. It is evident that it was Ismail who had the better of this exchange. For Gordon was well aware that the Khedive had not the power, and almost certainly had not the will, to end the abuses, while the Khedive knew that Gordon kept his promises, and he was characteristically ready to ignore the fact that this particular promise had been conditional.

It was Christmas Eve and his first day in England, but Gordon detested Christmas festivities. Late that night he scrawled a characteristic note from 7 Cecil Street, off the Strand, to Augusta at Southampton. Clearly he was determined to dispose of his most pressing obligations to friends and relations at the earliest possible moment; as to whether thereafter he either ate oysters or lay in bed till eleven no evidence survives.

I came over to-day from Paris; arrived in town at 7 p.m.;

started at 8 p.m. and went . . . to see Henriques, Lucas' brother-in-law. He was away. I saw his wife, Lucas' sister, a Jewess, yet I talked to her of Jesus and she seemed not to feel it (what a comfort to have Him for a friend). I asked her if she knew God dwelt in her and she said Yes. D.V. to-morrow I shall call on Aunt Amy, then go to Woolwich, finish Henry, Mina, Enderby and Greenshields and scratch them off the visits. D.V. then come back to town and on Thursday finish off the Horse Gds, Foreign Office and War Office, and then D.V. come down to South'ton and scratch off some more people.

No doubt he scratched off other friends too, and though the phrase suggests summary procedure, Gordon never wasted time on trifles and his briefest irruptions were apt to be momentous. Thus we find him writing next June from the frontier of Darfur " Aunt Amy may struggle as she likes. I said to her ' let me put this seed in your heart ' and told her one or two truths which she has not in spite of her previous training been able to stifle. They will sprout, I feel sure ": Aunt Amy had figured on that Christmas Eve list and it seems evident that during his visit to the old lady there had been time for theological controversy, though not apparently for conversion.

He visited the Freeses at Chislehurst too, played with the children and told them stories, and was seen off at the station by the entire family. To the Freeses he had said that he could not and would not return to Africa, and that life there was intolerable. And it was to Mrs. Freese that he wrote on 16th January from Cecil Street, which remained his headquarters, " I am tired, tired and no earthly rest will give me quiet." The diagnosis was exact. No doubt he was tired, but no mere cessation of labours could give his restless spirit quiet. Rest, indeed, was the last state he desired, either here or hereafter, and these few weeks in England were spent in an urgent search for fresh activities. A few days after his return *The Times* had published a glowing tribute to his pacification of Central Africa, and proceeded to suggest that if Gordon were appointed

Governor of Bulgaria, where the great Powers were wrestling with the evergreen problem of the Christian minorities under Turkish misrule, " he would soon make that province as peaceful as an English county." The Foreign Secretary, Lord Derby, seems to have thought something of the suggestion and on 11th January Gordon had had an interview with him, after which he wrote to the British Consul-General in Cairo that he would be unable to return to Egypt. Clearly he did not regard himself as pledged to the Khedive, and while the Bulgarian project faded away—the Powers did not relish the prospect of so unconventional an Englishman, or perhaps of any Englishman, in so important a position—he plunged into plans for an expedition to Zanzibar. Numerous letters on the Zanzibar project passed between him and Waller, who was in touch with Sir William Mackinnon, a shipping magnate whose imagination had been fired by plans for the commercial development of East Africa, and Gordon had got as far as stipulating that he himself should have nothing to do with commerce but should command the troops in the interior and receive a salary of £150 per annum. On 17th January, however, the Khedive, who had now received Gordon's message from the British Consul, sent him a telegram of exhortation and reproof. He referred to " the work which we have begun together " and to their having so recently parted with the words " *Au revoir.*" And he concluded with the challenging words " *je me refuse à croire qu'un gentilhomme comme Gordon veut sous un prétexte quelconque reprendre la parole qu'il m'a donnée.*" Gordon does not seem to have been moved by the invocation of his alleged promise. On the 18th he told Waller that he would refuse the appeal, and on the 19th he still intends to refuse, although his army friends are telling him that the Zanzibar scheme is gross treachery to the Khedive. On the 20th he actually telegraphed a refusal. But on the 21st he has stopped the telegram, having been told that the Duke of Cambridge had said that it was his duty to return to Egypt. The Commander-in-Chief's verdict convinced him that once again the scroll had been unrolled. But on what terms should he return ?

He had consulted his friends, and in particular Colonel Graham,

V.C.,[1] under whom he had served at Sevastopol, and they were unanimous that he ought not to return to Equatoria without control over the Sudan, the headquarters of the slave trade: he must be Governor of the Sudan or nothing. Indeed, without Gordon's knowledge Graham had sought an interview with Lord Derby and explained that it was only on these terms that Gordon was prepared to re-enter the Khedive's service. His friends' advice did but echo the conclusions which Gordon had already reached; and by demanding the Sudan he would in effect be telling the Khedive that without this supreme guarantee his pledges as to the slave trade were worthless. But even so it had come to tossing up. On a postcard dated 21st January he scribbled " After preparation (on return from Woolwich) tossed!! Heads to go, Tail to stay: it fell head!!! C.E.G." The words " after preparation " show that it was only after prayer that Gordon, like the early apostles, resorted to sortilege. Even so, his brothers seem not to have approved of his decision, and he told Waller that there had been " nothing but cutting words from them," and that his whole leave had been one continual misery. On 31st January, 1877, he wrote " I hope to start to-night. I will make a stand at Cairo. . . . The Khedive *ought* to give me Khartoum and I have promised Graham not to go up unless he does do so." But in his heart of hearts he expected the Khedive to refuse.

Ismail, however, could not have been more accommodating. When Gordon reached Cairo and had his second interview " the little fat man looked at me reproachfully and my conscience smote me." Nevertheless " I . . . told him all; and then he gave me the Soudan, and I leave on Saturday morning." Thus simply does he report accession to solitary responsibility for more than a million square miles swarming with savage and hostile peoples, and ravaged by the age-old scourge of the slave trade. To his brief note he added " I go up alone with an infinite Almighty God to direct and guide me, and I am glad to so trust Him as to fear nothing, and, indeed, to feel sure of success." " To fear nothing;" the words were no exaggeration. He had constantly displayed the highest courage but

[1] Lieutenant General Sir Gerald Graham, V.C. (1831-99).

now the most recently discovered pearl, and his childlike acceptance of the scriptural injunction to cast " all your cares on Him," had finally fitted him for the feats of almost superhuman valour and physical endurance which he was about to perform.

2

A fortnight after his interview with the Khedive he had landed at Massowa on the Red Sea coast. Khartoum, his new capital, lay due west. The Sudan, like an irregularly shaped pear roughly bisected by the Nile, lay before him approximately fifteen hundred miles from north to south and, at its widest, a thousand from west to east. West of Khartoum, in the sands of Kordofan and Darfur, lands of the slave dealers, two distinct rebellions smouldered among the fierce Arab horsemen who would one day rally to the Mahdi. To the south-east lay the Abyssinians between whom and Egypt there had lately been war and was not yet peace. And everywhere, whether among the Nubians and Berberines to the north, the primitive negroes to the south or the fanatical tribesmen between the Nile and the Red Sea' poverty and warfare were endemic. Almost lightheartedly Gordon made his plans. He would travel in a vast circle. First along the borders of Abyssinia, where he hoped eventually to pacify both King Johannis and his rebellious lieutenant, Walad-el-Michael. On to Khartoum and a brief sojourn in the seat of government, and thence westward into Kordofan and Darfur to grapple with the slave traders and the rebels; north to the Egyptian frontier and then back far to the south-east for a final reckoning with the Abyssinians; and at last perhaps into the farthest south, through his former province to Lake Victoria.

Save for the voyage back to Equatoria he would have to perform the whole of this prodigious peregrination on the back of a camel. During the next twelve months he planned to ride five thousand miles on camels. Hitherto, though he had broken all records on his first camel journey, he had had little experience of riding the beast.

But now he was to develop a genius for that most difficult and strenuous of exercises, so that his solitary journeys through the vast spaces of the desert soon became legendary, and the peoples of the Sudan, who already marvelled at the courage of a Governor who would ride alone in enemy's country, far outdistancing his escort, marvelled also at the endurance of the rider, and his grace. And as for Gordon, his letters home would contain repeated references to the camel, and above all, to the desert. At first he finds the uneven motion a trial; "pelting along," and he always pelted, "on the camels ought eventually to shake one's organs out of their places." He complains that he has ceased to exist, has become a mere jolting sack of rice and can think no more than a sack. But within three months the camel is "a wonderful creature, and so comfortable with its silent, cushion-like tread." And though at first he finds the camel a cross-grained animal which repels all overtures of friendship, soon, like all skilled riders, he has developed a subtle sympathy with his beast and its idiosyncracies; "the Gordons and the camels are of the same race—[let them] take an idea into their heads, and nothing will take it out."

And almost at once the desert, that breeding-ground of mystics, works its spell. The interminable wastelands have their own message; "it was for this that the Israelites were led through them;" "you learn yourself" in the solitudes. Undoubtedly the years which he spent in the desert, repeatedly in danger and repeatedly at the limit of physical endurance, but always conscious of his dependence upon the Unseen, counted for much in his spiritual growth. A new serenity begins to transform his life. The outbursts of irritation, which had been so frequent in Equatoria, diminish.

As he was setting forth into the unknown he learned that the Khedive had made him a marshal (he was already a marshal in the Chinese Army) and that all the Red Sea coast was included in his command. He was not, he decided, elated by the vast extent of his powers, or, on second thoughts, "only very, very slightly elated," and this, he could honestly say, owing to the confidence which the Khedive evidently felt in him. "I think how many would be weighed down by this immense charge; how they would shrink from accepting it without some other help, for fear of their reputation. But for me I never gave the question a thought. I feel sure of success; for I do not lean on my own understanding and He directs my path." Events to come after all, his failures and successes, each future encounter with negro, Arab or Bedouin—all was already decreed. And from the start he found the trappings of power intolerably irksome—ten men to help him off his camel, his entire escort dismounting whenever he chose to walk, the concentric rings of sentries, most of whom, however, would soon fall asleep, surrounding him every night. It was ironic to reflect that " this is the life of the ambitious and for this men strive and are discontented! "

He visited Keren, the chief town of the territory in dispute between King Johannis and the rebel prince, where the Abyssinians looked " a furtive, pole-cat race," and held his first interview with Walad-el-Michael. Thence by Kassala and, covering 150 miles in two and a half days, to Katarif on the Atbara. All was faithfully reported to Rockstone Avenue, where Augusta must have found much of the chronicle highly disquieting. She was lucky, her brother reminded her, to be living in England and not in the Sudan where, any night, she might have to take to her heels in her chemise. She would do well, he suggested, to remember that " the chemise state," not life as lived in Rockstone Avenue, was man's normal condition.

3

On 4th May, after a camel journey of nearly two months, he entered Khartoum, to be greeted by a vast and enthusiastic concourse. Next day he was ceremoniously installed as Governor-General. He was required to make a speech. It was brief: " With the help of God I will hold the balance level." The swarm of servants in the vast palace on the banks of the Nile were, by Gordon's standards, almost wholly superfluous, not least the eunuch whose duty was to

superintend the Governor-General's *harem*; and his unfavourable
impression of his official residence was only partially alleviated by
the bizarre detail that his predecessor's sister, enraged by the news
of her brother's supersession, had broken most of its windows and
torn the cushions of the divan into ribbons. But these were trifles
and during his brief fifteen days in Khartoum Gordon decreed a
stream of administrative reforms. The use of the kourbash, or whip
of hide, that age-old instrument of torture, was abolished. A box
for the receipt of petitions was set up at the palace gates. Corruption
was at least checked, and the clerks actually brought to the treasury
the lavish bribes paid to them, by time-honoured custom, by
petitioners. (Only for a while, however; before long Gordon discovered that his private secretary, an Arab whom he had trusted
implicitly, had accepted bribes totalling no less than three thousand
pounds.) An obstructive second-in-command was first cowed and
then cashiered. Plans were made for pumping river-water up to
the town.

But the fundamental problem, the slave trade, remained, and
Gordon had no illusions as to the formidable difficulties which
faced him. As a first step, six thousand *bashi-bazouk* frontier guards,
who habitually allowed the slave caravans to pass, must be disbanded, and replaced with trustworthy substitutes, if trustworthy
substitutes were to be found. " Let me ask," wrote Gordon, " who
that had not the Almighty with him could do that? I have the
Almighty with me, and I will do it." There must follow a series of
far-reaching and summary measures, measures decreed by a
Christian which would inevitably impoverish almost every Muss-
ulman in the Sudan. "Who that had not the Almighty with him
would dare to do that? I will do it; for I value my life as naught.
. . . As Solomon asked, I ask wisdom to govern this great people;
and not only will He give it me, but all else besides. And why?
Because I value not the ' all besides.' " Certainly Gordon's spiritual
insight was steadily deepening.

But the crux of the problem was that as long as slave-owning
was permitted the slave trade could not be abolished, and since the

payment of compensation, as in the British Act of 1833, was impossible, slave-owning could not be abolished out of hand but must lapse over a prescribed term of years. Moreover, though Gordon does not seem to have allowed sufficiently for this, the Sudan was but one of the Mahomedan lands in which slavery remained an immemorial and unquestioned social institution. On his arrival in Khartoum Gordon had recommended to the British Consul-General in Cairo a scheme which he had revolved during many hours on camel back. Let it be made compulsory for all slaves to be registered by January the first next, and illegal for any to be registered thereafter. This proposal was at least mainly responsible for the Slave-Trade Convention, signed by Egypt and Great Britain three months later, which prohibited the sale of domestic slaves after seven years in Egypt and twelve in the Sudan. Meanwhile, Gordon could at least strike a blow against the Europeans who settled in the Sudan, owned slaves and paid no taxes. His method was simple: if they declared themselves foreigners he would decree their slaves free, if they claimed to be Egyptians he would tax them heavily. This decree of enfranchisement was seminal; the notion that the days of slavery were numbered had dawned on the Sudan.

But how could he stay in Khartoum? Although he was no longer, as in Equatoria, his own storekeeper and carpenter Gordon would always be his own general. And the trouble in Darfur was coming to a head. In the north there was a revolt against Egyptian officialdom, and 16,000 Egyptian troops were hemmed in in El Fasher. In the south though Zebehr, king of the slave-traders, was no longer in the province, his young son Suleiman, with thousands of armed followers, was threatening to join the rebellion. Gordon set out from Khartoum on 19th May with three hundred men and supreme confidence. He might almost as well have been taking no troops with him, he admitted to Augusta, but after all he " had the Shekinah." He would have no Europeans on his staff; they were too energetic, he said, and too rash. He would have made an exception, had it been possible, in favour of (Sir) Richard Burton. On 21st June he wrote, urging him to accept the Governorship of

G.G.

Q

Darfur. " Now is the time for you to make your indelible mark in the world and in these countries." But Burton declined. " My dear Gordon," he wrote, " You and I are too much alike. I could not serve under you, nor you under me. I do not look upon the Sudan as a lasting thing. I have nothing to depend upon but my salary; and I have a wife, and you have not." Gessi Gordon still refused to re-employ, despite his repeated applications, for Gessi had a family: moreover, latterly he had " got very much too grand," and had been guilty of " peculation." Two months later a furious Gessi was threatening from Cairo the publication of two hundred and fifty of Gordon's letters to him. " It made me laugh," wrote Gordon, " for what interest could anyone have in reading them? . . . Fancy his keeping the letters one by one." It would seem, however, that hardly anyone who received a letter from Gordon ever threw it away.

4

As usual, he moved at top speed. The Egyptian garrison of the frontier outpost of Foggia was spending the day in its usual listless fashion; arms were piled and several of the guard had left their weapons and were drinking at a well, when two distant specks were descried moving rapidly across the vast plain. The officers, aware that the Governor-General was on his way, assumed that his advanced guard would soon become visible and lazily ordered their men to fall in. But before the sentries could get back to their posts or the rest unpile their arms Gordon, on a camel, whose speed by now had begun to astonish even the Arabs, came flying in upon them, in gold-laced marshal's uniform, accompanied by a solitary guide. He had left his escort trailing an hour and a half in the rear. The marshal's uniform was worn as a symbol: for Gordon hoped to quell the northern rebellion without firing a shot, and by sheer personal prestige, partly because he was well aware that the people had every reason for discontent and partly because he had no confidence whatever in his own troops. Soon he was riding, again at unexampled speed, for Taweisha, where he found a tatterdemalion and most unmilitary garrison which had been three years without pay. Scornfully ordering them to be disbanded, he pressed on for Dara with a heterogeneous band now numbering five hundred men, many of them armed with flintlocks and fowling-pieces.

The troops ordered out from Dara to meet him did not come, and it was known that a determined and well-armed enemy number-ing several thousands was in the neighbourhood. If he was attacked there was no hope of escape. Very few Englishmen, Gordon reflected bitterly, had his experience of commanding troops on whom it was impossible to rely. He reflected too how often he had promised himself not to run this kind of risk, and how often, nevertheless, he did so. During the crisis of the march he prayed hard and felt again that physical pain in the heart which he remem-bered on the jungle path near Masindi. And he was vividly reminded of the familiar nightmare in which imminent danger approaches and the dreamer cannot move. However, the moment of peril passed and he reached Dara without mischance, astonishing its garrison no less than that of Foggia. In this neighbourhood he was compelled to attack a threatening tribe, and his coolness in action, and lighting of a cigarette when the fight was at its hottest, astounded a friendly sheikh as it had astounded the Ever Victorious in China. " Never in my life did I see such a thing," said the sheikh two years later to Slatin Pasha; "and then the following day, when he divided the spoil, no one was forgotten, and he kept nothing for himself. He was very tender-hearted about women and children, and never allowed them to be distributed, as is our custom in war; but he fed and clothed them at his own expense, and had them sent to their homes as soon as the war was over." This victory enabled Gordon to relieve El Fasher itself. The northern operations were complete. With a few hundred men, or rather with his own in-domitable spirit, he had relieved sixteen thousand and driven the rebel leader into the mountains. Gordon himself ascribed his successes to " a series of (called by the world) flukes. All the Chinese affairs were flukes, all out here are flukes and I feel an impostor when people praise me. . . . I fear some terrible collapse will show I am the impostor I know I am, and often this makes me wish I was out of this public life and in obscurity."

Gordon had already realised that in the desert he could do nothing to put an end to the slave trade, save by achieving his grand objective, the breaking of the armies of the slave traders. If he freed captured slaves they would perish. Indeed, he was compelled to purchase slaves in order to turn them into the fighting men he needed to put down slavery; and while he was still engaged in a life and death struggle with the great slave-traders he had to turn a blind eye on the activities of the petty slave-merchants who dealt in ones and twos. All this led to protests in the English Press from persons who appeared to suppose that the Governor-General had only to decree the end of slavery for it to disappear. Gordon was accustomed to criticism of this sort from the benevolent but ill-informed and naturally had no thought of altering his policy " for fear of what ill-informed Europe may say." But he could not help resenting it, and a few weeks later he complained to Augusta, who was too ready, he suspected, to sympathise with the critics, in a moving version of the eternal protest of the man of action against the man of words.

I would have given £500 to have had you and the Anti-Slavery Society in Dara during the three days of doubt whether the slave-dealers would fight or not. A bad fort, a cowed garrison and not one who did not tremble. . . . I would have liked to hear what you would all have said then. . . . I do not believe in you all. You say this and that, and you do not do it; you give your money and you have done your duty; you praise one another, etc. I do not wonder at it. God has given you ties and anchors to this earth; you have wives and families. I thank God I have none of them and am free. Now understand me. If it suits me I will buy slaves . . . and I will do what I like, and what God in His mercy may direct me to do about domestic slaves; but I will break the neck of slaver raids even if it costs me my life. I will do this in the light of day and defy your resolutions and your actions. Would my heart be broken if I was ousted from this command? . . . You are only called on at intervals to rely on your God: with me I am obliged continually to do so. I mean by this that you have only great trials, such as the illness of a child, when you feel yourself utterly weak, now and then. I am constantly in anxiety. The body rebels against this constant leaning on God; it is a heavy strain on it; it causes appetite to cease. Find me the man—and I will take him as my help—who utterly despises money, name, glory, honour, one who never wishes to see his home again, one who looks to God as the source of good, and Controller of evil . . . and one who looks on death as a release from misery; and if you cannot find him then leave me alone. To carry myself is enough; I want no other baggage.

And he sent an identically worded protest to Waller. For despite his boast of having choked Waller off he maintained a regular correspondence with this energetic campaigner against the slave trade. Indeed, their friendship remained unbroken to the end despite the fact that almost every letter from Equatoria contained a challenge to the reformers to cease preaching the impossible from Press and platform; "give up your comfortable homes, and, living as the apostles, come out to the Sudan and raise its people from their degradation."

To Gordon disciplining rebel tribesmen eighty-five miles north of Dara came word that young Suleiman, crown prince of the slave-traders, had moved threateningly north from his headquarters at Shakka to within three miles of Dara. It was said, too, that Suleiman proposed to seek Gordon with an offer of submission, and every intention of attacking if he saw the government's forces to be weak. Gordon's response to this news was magnificently characteristic. He knew that Suleiman's forces were formidable and his own worthless. He concluded that his only chance was to cow the slave traders and their army into submission by sheer force of personal authority.

Clearly it was essential that he should reach Dara before it was attacked. Selecting a small escort, he set out on the morning of 31st August. At four in the afternoon of 2nd September he swept into Dara " like a thunderbolt "—alone. He had covered the eighty-five miles in thirty-six hours, leaving his escort far behind. It was some while before the garrison recovered from its astonishment sufficiently to give a salute. News that a governor-general was in the desert danger zone had been astonishing enough; a governor-general without every available soldier massed to protect him passed comprehension.

Suleiman at once sent for permission to visit the Governor-General that evening, but Gordon was determined not to appear to be treating with the general of a hostile army. Whatever the risks, he would remain the Governor-General on a tour of inspection among the lawful subjects of the Khedive. This was undoubtedly an occasion for the Wand of Victory. Accordingly he sent word that he would himself visit Suleiman's camp next morning, went to bed and slept peacefully " forgetting my miseries." At dawn he rose, put on his gold-laced uniform and selecting a small escort of his own brigands rode out to the brigand camp. Young Suleiman met him at the outposts. Gordon had prayed for him, as was his custom before a first encounter with a native chief, thereby establishing, he believed, an invisible link. The youth conducted him through the serried lines of black troops and Arab chieftains. At last he was face to face with the spearhead of the slave-trade; three thousand formidable fighting men, he judged, as he passed coolly along the scowling ranks; " Smart, dapper troops, like antelopes, fierce, unsparing, the terror of Central Africa." At a sign from their chiefs they could have massacred Gordon and his escort and overwhelmed the small unwarlike garrison of Dara. But brigands and brigand-chieftains alike were dumbfounded by his presence among them, alone. The mysterious calm, the air of confident authority seemed to speak of resources of which they knew nothing. Above all, the lion-tamer's imperious eye travelling along their ranks held them nerveless. Not a man stirred. Gordon reached Suleiman's tent safely, and there, after accepting a glass of water, ordered Suleiman and his entourage to report to him at Dara forthwith to receive his orders. He then rode out through the silent, staring lines and returned unscathed to Dara.

He could not tell whether, like lions when the lion-tamer's back is turned, the slave-traders would now attack. But Suleiman and his chieftains duly presented themselves, to sit in a silent gaping circle while Gordon roundly informed them, in broken Arabic eked out by signs, that he knew that they were plotting rebellion and that he intended to disarm them. They went off for consultation and later that day promised submission. But promises, as Gordon had good reason to know, meant little and there followed a period of acute suspense. But although, as Gordon afterwards learned, therehad been prolonged indecision among the brigands, no attack was launched, and on the third day half of them came over to join Gordon, while the remainder, under young Suleiman, set out for Shakka.

But even now Gordon was not content. He resolved to follow Suleiman to the slave-traders' inmost den, and to take with him only four companies of his own troops. " I am running a great risk," he admitted; " but I will trust to God to help me, and the best policy with these people is a bold one." Moreover, he had been attracted by the graceless Suleiman, a good-looking youth of about twenty. " My heart yearns over him," he told Waller, and at first he spoke of him as " poor little chap;" and although he soon substituted " the cub," and reported that a flogging would do him a lot of good, he had not abandoned hope of reforming the young outlaw. At Shakka, to which only one foreigner, an American, had hitherto penetrated, Gordon's personality overawed the slave-traders as completely as at Dara. He insisted that Suleiman should withdraw to the Bahr el Ghazal. The cub was all submission and begged repeatedly to be recognised as chief; he even embraced Gordon's feet, but Gordon did not trust him and " your brother," he told Augusta, " was Augusta-like and was inexorable."

5

During the most critical days in the desert his regular letters to
Augusta had continued not only to report each day's incidents in
detail but to dwell at length upon his theological musings. From
time to time he still tossed a coin, but only when " things are so
balanced that I cannot see my way," and never without a reference
to the first chapter of Acts. His creed had in no way altered; he
even still believed in previous existences of the soul, and when his
brother Enderby complained that several articles of his creed were
contrary to Scripture he was content to reply that it was sufficient
for him that they brought him peace. But it was no doubt owing
to Enderby's criticisms that for some while his letters to Augusta
are fuller than ever of apologies. And in an interesting passage some
months later he traces the origins of his now unshakable belief that
every human soul is destined for eternal salvation.

> Once I did believe that some perished altogether at the end of
> the world—were annihilated, as having no souls. After this, I
> believed that the world was made up of incarnated children of
> God and incarnated children of the evil spirit; and then I came
> to the belief that *the two are one.*

The result of his musings, as always, was added confidence in his
own beliefs, and even a twinge of conscience for his failure to
convert his own family. " I wish I was with you, with Lizzie, who
wants someone to show her the truth, and with Aunt Amy and
Henry and Rose. All these are thirsty souls and I regret (no, I do
not regret, for He will find other means) I cannot be allowed to
point out the fountain." And in his growing serenity he could look
back with amused repugnance on the gloomier aspects of the
religion of his childhood.

I confess I hate the going to church. I shall never go, I expect,

if I ever return home. You know in old times the " *wrestling*,"
as they called it, when they had what they were wrestling for
all the time; it makes me laugh to think of. I never saw such
gaiety. Prayer meetings every night. I saw May toiling up the
" Hill " with such an immense Bible; she would much sooner
have had a hoop. . . . What bondsmen we were!! Do you
remember the Irish famine and Molyneux? It was a sort of
delirium. What fearfully long sermons; always an hour! What
have you done with your religious library? It must have cost
you a mint. . . . One used to mock somewhat at the worshippers
of Baal . . . cutting themselves, but I feel sure they did not cry
louder or wrestle more than the Dissenters of our day.

6

Four weeks after leaving the slave-traders' eyrie Gordon was in
Khartoum. The Anglo-Egyptian Slave Convention had now been
signed, but he knew that outside the great towns it could not be
enforced without a military occupation of the whole country. A
week of intense activity in the capital inevitably included an excess
of official interviews, during which, though Gordon considered that
he displayed the patience of Job, he would sometimes drag an over-
punctilious visitor down on to a seat, or shout at petitioners " till
they forget their missions for fear." " Altogether," he confessed,
" scenes are constant, and cause great amusement to the bystanders."
It might be thought a disadvantage, he admitted in a letter to Sir
Richard Burton, that he knew so little Arabic, but his fatalism
provided an unexpected justification for the deficiency. For his
decisions " are fixed to be thus and thus, whether I have exactly
hit off the circumstances or not."

Soon he was off on a tour of inspection to the north. He reports
that having given up all wine and spirits he sleeps much better, but
is desolated by the misery south of Dongola, where the crops had
failed. On 10th November news of a threat to the Abyssinian

frontier brought him hurriedly back to Khartoum and by mid-December he was in Keren. Walad-el-Michael, the source of the trouble, was in the mountains north of the town with seven thousand armed men. Gordon remembered Suleiman and Shakka and resolved once again to put his head into the lion's jaws. He believed that he still had a task to fulfil in the Sudan and that so long as he had a mission, as in China, he would be divinely protected. Danger was a challenge, not to his courage but to his faith. And so, brushing aside the protests of his advisers at Keren, he made his way, with ten men, over the mountains to the rebel camp. "I do it because I wish to trust in His promises, and I feel sure, however trying it may be (and it is trying to me in a great degree) that I gain in strength and faith by it. If He wills me to fail, so be it." He did not fail. The rebel came to terms and Gordon's only regret, as he returned after a long conference in the mountains, was that at one moment, when it seemed likely that his host intended to hold him prisoner, he had warned him that if he did so retribution would inevitably fall upon him. For by hinting at the long arm of Britain he had shown want of faith. His aim was to trust Providence to the uttermost and he had partially failed.

7

He returned deviously, by Suakim and Berber, for Khartoum, intending to ride on into Darfur to assure himself that the slave caravans were no longer crossing the desert. But before he reached the capital a long telegram from the Khedive urged him to hurry at once to Cairo "to arrange his [the Khedive's] financial affairs." It was an astonishing request, but in his desperation Ismail had persuaded himself that the man who had performed miracles in the desert would perform a miracle in Cairo, and intimidate the Commissioners of Debt as triumphantly as he had overawed the slave-traders. And Gordon, though he cannot have forgotten that he had seldom contrived to master his own private accounts, was prepared to accept the unrolling of the scroll, and was much less alarmed at the thought of conferences on high finance than by the prospect of renewed contact with civilisation: " the idea of dinners in Cairo makes me quail. I do not exaggerate when I say ten minutes per diem is sufficient for all my meals, and there is no greater happiness to me than when they are finished." The thought of " a host of embryo rows " in Cairo was perhaps some consolation. Contact with civilisation came before he reached the capital. At Assuan a polite note from the young Earl and Countess of Aberdeen, who were on a honeymoon tour, expressed the hope that they might have the opportunity of seeing Colonel Gordon on their *diabiyeh*. Gordon at once concluded that his aristocratic compatriots wanted a tow down river and was in two minds whether to accept their invitation. His suspicions were at once confirmed when he boarded the *diabiyeh*. The countess, " a great fat girl," was evidently tired of the Nile. The request for a tow came at once and Gordon replied that he had already guessed the motive of their invitation. Lord Aberdeen made no comment, his countess blushed. Gordon reluctantly agreed to the tow but declined an invitation to dinner. During the journey downstream he reflected with distaste on the Aberdeens' " cool request " and on the butler and lady's maid who accompanied them, and asked himself why his journey should be slowed down by " butterfly people who come for their pleasure and then sicken of it." After five days he ordered the tow-rope to be slipped. " No invite to the Highlands, deer-stalking, etc., etc., with the Earl! " However, he would reach the financiers and the embryo rows all the sooner.

On the journey down there had been time, too, to ponder over Enderby's objection that his doctrine of sin was contrary to Scripture. No doubt, he admitted to Augusta, many passages in Scripture " taken isolated, would be opposed to this view," but she, at least, would " by the Spirit, discern how these passages are to be applied." As for him, he remained convinced that, despite theologians down the ages, sin does not separate man from God, who " is not one whit further from us, or more angry with us when our evil actions show themselves, than when they do not." It was during the journey down, too, that he decided, as a contribution to the national economies which would obviously be necessary, to halve his own salary once more. On his appointment he had at once reduced it from twelve thousand to six thousand pounds a year; now it was to be cut down to three.

At Cairo he was plunged at once into an environment in which slave-traders and the desert solitudes seemed infinitely remote. From the railway station he was driven direct to the palace where the Khedive had kept dinner waiting for an hour and a half. At once Ismail took him aside and requested him to accept the Presidency of the coming Commission of Inquiry into Egyptian finances. Gordon readily agreed and then, still half-dazed and covered with dust, found himself sitting down to a banquet at the Khedive's right hand. The private palace in which he was subsequently lodged, with its blaze of mirrored lights and retinues of gentlemen-in-waiting, did nothing to dispel the impression that he had inadvertently strayed into the *Arabian Nights*. " My people are all dazed and I am ditto," he wrote, " and wish for my camel."

Egypt was hopelessly in debt. Four European Debt Commissioners had been made responsible for collecting interest, at the formidable rate of seven per cent, for the European bond-holders. Then, as for long afterwards, taxes in Egypt were exacted almost exclusively from those who could least afford to pay them; five-sixths of the inadequate resultant revenue was needed for the bond-holders and by now the country was virtually bankrupt, its official salaries unpaid, while a horde of unsecured creditors were clamouring for satisfaction. It was in this desperate situation that the Khedive had agreed to a Commission of Inquiry, but he still objected to its examining the details of national expenditure; moreover, he maintained that the Commissioners of Debt, being interested parties, were not entitled to a seat on it. And already, during their brief conversation before dinner, Gordon had promised Ismail that he, as President, would object to the Commissioners' presence. But the spider's web of the diplomats was soon enmeshing him. There were repeated visits from sceptical Consuls, and interviews with de Lesseps (of whom, despite his frivolous manner and picnics in the desert, Gordon surprisingly noted " I like old Lesseps very much "), with Messers Walker and Pasquali, the Khedive's financial agents, whom Gordon at once instinctively suspected, the former because he parted his hair in the middle and the latter because his name suggested an Italian singer; and with Cherif Pasha, the apathetic Minister of Finance. And almost, it seemed, by chance, in one of the numerous and resplendent ante-chambers of his private palace there was an encounter with Captain Evelyn Baring, the cautious and accomplished young Englishman who was destined to play no inconsiderable part in the story of Egypt and of Gordon. " Pretentious, grand and patronising," was Gordon's verdict; " when oil mixes with water, we will mix together."

His own solution, as always, was simple and direct. Suspension of the next instalment of interest on the debt should be announced at once, and the coming inquiry should dispense with the services of the Commissioners of Debt. But repudiation of debts was less familiar to the last century than to our own. And Baring, though unlikely to ride 3840 miles a year on a camel, and less concerned than Gordon with abstract justice, had had a good deal more experience of politicians and financiers, and above all knew what was practicable, and, even more certainly, what was not. And behind Baring was ranged European diplomacy, the European colony in Egypt and a hundred boardrooms and banks. It became ever clearer to Gordon that he was helpless; his only consolation was that he was avoiding banquets, and the drinking of wine, by regularly retiring to bed at eight o'clock, a practice which must have confirmed official Cairo in its conviction that Ismail had selected a singularly inappropriate champion. As for Ismail, he was under constant pressure; he could not bring himself to accept Gordon's suggestion that he should cut the Gordian knot by suspending the interest payments by decree, relying on the authority of one who in his own country was after all only a Colonel of Engineers to shield him from the wrath of Lord Derby; and by 22nd March he had realised that the miracle-worker of the deserts would work no miracles in Cairo, and yielded. On 30th March Gordon left Cairo " by the ordinary train, paying my own passage." He still believed that he could have solved the financial problem, if the Khedive had had the courage to trust him. The diplomats and the financiers had been too much for him. Nevertheless, when he advised suspension of the bondholders' interest he had been right; and Baring and the rest had been wrong.

8

Gordon left Cairo in low spirits. He no longer trusted the Khedive and he had sent a telegram to Whitehall offering his services in view of " the coming war " with Russia; but there was no reply. On his way back from Cairo he allowed himself a ten weeks' détour through the eastern outskirts of his province. But he was in Khartoum by June and positively spent the next nine months in the capital, toiling at a host of administrative problems, most of which, owing to the nature of the Egyptian Government, were insoluble. At least, however, he succeeded, after invoking the aid of Lord Salisbury, in defeating the Commissioners of Debt who had had the effrontery to assert that the Sudan owed a contribution to the depleted exchequer in Cairo. The Sudan had, in fact, hitherto always been a financial drain on Egypt, and much of Gordon's time was spent on a series of far-reaching economies which rapidly reduced the customary deficit. There were the slave caravans too, and though in July he could report that he had established " a sort of Government of Terror " and that twelve caravans had been captured in two months, even his trusted subordinates were all too apt to connive at the trade. Gordon was ruthless when he detected wrongdoers, however highly placed, but in August when Ibrahim Fauzi, whom he had himself promoted step by step to the Governor-ship of Equatoria, was implicated in the scandal he was driven to another toss of the coin.

I have balanced what to do and at last, after asking God to settle it, have tossed up. If it fell with the Sultan's cypher uppermost I would shoot him. It has just been tossed and it fell uppermost the fatal cypher of the Sultan, so unless He intervenes Fauzi will be shot.

The last sentence is characteristic of Gordon's coin-spinnings, which were not infrequently followed by a reversal of the sentence. And though Fauzi was duly arrested and put in chains he was eventually pardoned, accompanied Gordon on his last journey to Khartoum and was with him to the end.

The Governor-General lived a solitary life in his huge palace. Nor, strangely enough, was he always fully occupied. He rose at seven and the morning would be filled with interviews and correspondence, but from one to four in the afternoon there was often " nothing particular to do " and he would sometimes amuse himself by taking a clock to pieces and putting it together again. After dinner it was only on an average twice a week that " Some Arabs came in or Austrian consul or telegraph supt for 2 hrs." And then he would read and go to bed. Khartoum was full of malaria that year, and Gordon, who suffered from a constant sense of nausea, was once delirious, answering the same imaginary petitions over and over again for two nights. This time even Warburg's Tincture failed him and he ascribed his rapid recovery to Dover's Powders. Moreover, he missed the desert and the " nice thoughts " which the desert bred. Nonetheless, on those who met him at this time he produced, as usual, an impression of irrepressible vitality and cheerfulness. Some members of a party of British missionaries on their way to Uganda have left vivid accounts of their encounter with the Governor-General in his palace. " Of course the guard turned out," wrote one,

and several Kavasses ushered us upstairs, and in a large corridor we saw a table laid for lunch, and a little man in his shirt sleeves walking about. I took him for the butler. On looking through the doors opposite I saw a very splendid divan. . . . But on catching sight of us the ' butler ' rushed up and said, ' How d'ye do? So glad to see you! Excuse shirt sleeves. So hot! Awful long voyage. I'll make a row about it. Are you very angry with me? ' A hearty grasp of the hand to each, a piercing glance of small sharp eyes accompanied this flow of words, spoken in a clear, sharp but pleasant tone of voice. Yes, it is he indeed, the liberator of the slaves, the ruler of a country half as big again as France, the Chinese Gordon!

Another member of the party noted[1] the " steely blue eyes, which looked at you as if you would not dare to ask him a question if he did not wish you to do so," and how Gordon smoked a succession of fat cigarettes rolled for him by his Kavasses and would silently raise two fingers whenever he required a fresh one. Gordon offered to show this visitor his Prayer Book and conducted him to his bedroom, which, in contrast to the splendours of the palace, contained a camp-bed, a chair and little else. The Prayer Book proved to be a thick notebook filled with the names of the people for whom Gordon prayed daily. The Mohamedans, the missionary learned, were quite accustomed to finding that he was at prayer, and would wait patiently until he was ready to see them.

But early in July had come news that in the Bahr el Ghazal young Suleiman had driven out Gordon's Governor and massacred his garrison. It seemed that Gordon should either have been more generous with the cub or more severe. In Khartoum there was evidence, too, that the cub's father, Zebehr, was plotting to raise the chieftains of Darfur. The situation did not seem serious enough to warrant Gordon's leaving Khartoum and its many problems, yet it was clear that a courageous and capable commander would be needed to dispose of the cub. Whom could he send? The only European available was Gessi. Although Gordon had refused to re-employ him, he chanced now to be in Khartoum, planning a journey of exploration of his own up the Sobat river and into the unknown

---

[1] To Dr. Bernard Allen (*Gordon and the Sudan*, 141, 2).

hinterland. And now, with the Bahr el Ghazal ablaze, Gordon forgot that he had found Gessi scatterbrained and arrogant, and had suspected him of peculation, and only remembered his coolness and courage. With great difficulty he prevailed on him to accept the command of an expedition against Suleiman. The event abundantly vindicated his decision. Before long he was writing of Gessi " Ought to have been born in 1560, not 1832. Same disposition as Francis Drake."

From mid-July, 1878, until mid-March, 1879, Gessi, who had collected a force of some 2,400 men, was campaigning in the Bahr el Ghazal. Meanwhile Gordon continued to wrestle with his problems, without support either from Cairo or in Khartoum, for " if you ever, in a moment of *weakness*, ask them anything, they give a sickly smile, and say, ' You know best.' Just as H. H. and Nubar telegraph to me." He had believed for some while that he was suffering from *angina pectoris*, and though the diagnosis was his own, and was almost certainly inaccurate, he complained of frequent rushes of blood to the head when " you think all is over." " I have died suddenly over a hundred times; but in these deaths I have never felt the least doubt of our salvation." He was conscious that his temper was worsening again; or perhaps it was only that his conscience was more sensitive. " I am Henry all over for these rows," he wrote, " and cannot help it. . . . I wish I was more Christ-like, but though I do fight I do not feel rancour, and I try and wish them well and do pray for them." And now he was again toying with the notion of retirement. He had ignored three requests to come to Cairo, where the plight of the Khedive was becoming steadily more desperate, and had warned the British Consul that if he came it would be to resign. A few years' service with the Engineers and he would be able to retire as a major general, with a pension of £450. And when Augusta warned him that he would find England dull he retorted that there would always be work for him among the poor. At Gravesend, he had been told, the Ragged School was defunct. It was to this institution that he had presented his Chinese flags; and though it mattered little what became of

G.G.   R those " rags," he might perhaps revive the school. All these months he had spent in Khartoum, save that on Christmas Eve he had ridden off for a hurried interview with the envoy of the King of Abyssinia at Katarif. Even in 1878, though so much of it was spent in the capital, he had ridden 1,620 miles through the desert on camels.

Though outnumbered and unable to obtain reinforcements or adequate supplies, Gessi contrived by ruse and daring to win several victories over the slave traders' army. But by March, 1879, although young Suleiman's stronghold had been destroyed and he had fled north to Shakka, news had reached Khartoum that he was likely to raise fresh troops there and with them to join forces with the mal-contents under Haroun in north Darfur, who were again in arms against Egypt. Gordon decided to set out at once to Gessi's aid. For days his little force made south-west, riding from half-past three in the morning till ten, and again from three in the afternoon till seven, in scorching heat by day and bitter cold at night, over an endless sandy plain, covered with dead grass and scrub, in which water might be expected approximately once every three days. It was existence at its barest, but Gordon was engaged on his constantly renewed struggle to make it barer still. In his meals he had long since ceased to take any pleasure. " I do not smoke as much and never touch anything but water" he reports, soon after leaving Khartoum. And next month he twice congratulates himself that there is no drink to be had but water, for " cognac is death to the liver, though I like it. I shall have no more for months." Another month and he has " almost entirely given up smoking . . .; if I had gone on with it much longer, I believe my heart would have stopped altogether." But he never managed to give it up entirely.

As they rode through the wastes of Kordofan to Gordon's horror they began constantly to encounter, and capture, slave caravans, the outcome of Suleiman's raids in the Bahr el Ghazal. Each capture, and by mid-June they had taken scores of caravans and close on two thousand slaves, stirred Gordon to anguish at the suffering of the victims and despair at his own helplessness. For the worst he could do to the slave dealers was to have them flogged,

stripped of their belongings, and sent " like Adams into the desert."
And the best he could do for the liberated slaves, who could not
possibly reach their distant homes across the waterless and hostile
desert, was to hand them over to some neighbouring tribe. He was
only too well aware, however, that the protagonists of the Anti-
Slavery Society in their remote and comfortable English homes were
incapable of realising the obstacles which faced him, and from time
to time he sent exasperated protests to Waller; " will you tell Mr.
Sturge from me he is silly to write these things—S,I,L,L,Y, *silly* "
(11th April, 1879). If he could stop the traffic, he told Augusta, he
would gladly be shot that night; it was the thought of the slow
crucifixion of prolonged life in the Sudan which appalled him.

At least, however, he could clear out the lairs of the slave
merchants. " The gate of mercy is shut and locked and the key
lost " he wrote to his friend Watson. And while Gessi doggedly
manœuvred against the gangs in the Bahr el Ghazal to the north,
in southern Darfur Gordon stormed in tireless wrath from one nest
of slave merchants to another. Shakka itself, the central " den of
iniquity," was cleared of its raider gangs. He moved in a daze of
exhaustion. Soon he no longer knew the day of the month, only
that he was so many days from Shakka, and he had ceased trying to
count the skulls of long-dead slaves littering the desert tracks. But
the cub himself, though his main army had been broken up, was
still at large with a considerable remnant of his forces, and towards
the end of June Gordon summoned Gessi to meet him at Taweisha.
For several hours they talked together, alone in Gordon's tent. The
Italian looked much older, Gordon noted, but he was much gratified
at having been made a Pasha and " with my gift—i.e. Soudan gift
—of 2000 £." And he was prepared, with the two hundred and
fifty men he had brought with him, to make a last supreme effort
to capture Suleiman and disperse his forces. Gordon authorised him
to kill the cub—or " the son of Zebehr " as he now usually called
him—if he were captured.

9

As Gordon toiled wearily back towards Khartoum word reached him that, under pressure from Europe, the Khedive Ismail had been deposed. Gordon had for some while feared that this would be the outcome of the financial imbroglio in Cairo, on which he had brooded often as he sped across the desert on the trail of the slave caravans. He considered that D'Israeli (as he called the Prime Minister) had mishandled the whole affair from the start. And he felt considerable sympathy for Ismail, the more so perhaps since he had little regard for Rivers Wilson, Baring and the other financial experts. "The R. Wilsons, Barings, etc.," he had written during an interval of the pursuit, "are a mushroom lot and one would not have to go back to any remote period to find that their family mansions were near the Tower or the Minories, and that the head of the family knew the value of pretty worn apparel." Rivers Wilson indeed had had the coolness to ask Gordon for an explanation of the punishment he had awarded to a certain major, and Gordon had replied sardonically that, although it was doubtless possible that the Khedive, delighted with Wilson's management of Egyptian finances, had appointed him Commander-in-Chief, nevertheless, until official notification of this promotion reached Khartoum the Governor-General could not recognise his authority in military affairs. As for Tewfik, to serve under Tewfik would be much the same as serving under Baring or one of the European Consuls. Before he reached Khartoum he had virtually made up his mind to " give this land my benediction and depart."

His inclination to resign was reinforced by his physical exhaustion. A writer in the *Lancet* of 21st June, 1884,[1] presumably relying on the evidence of the letters contained in Dr. Birkbeck Hill's *Colonel Gordon in Central Africa*, remarked that Gordon's physical endurance in the desert would be difficult enough to understand in a strong man and in one who suffered from *angina pectoris*

---

[1] Quoted by Allen (*Gordon and the Sudan*, 154).

and had lost all appetite for meals was " simply a kind of miracle." Gordon was his own physician as well as his own theologian, and his belief that he suffered from *angina*, like his theories as to the effects of cognac on the liver and smoking on the heart, or his reliance on Warburg's Tincture and Dover's Powders, was without scientific foundation. Nevertheless, the physical endurance of a man who, burdened with immense responsibilities and in such a climate, could ride over 7,500 miles through the deserts in three years was certainly a kind of miracle. And for the moment he was near the end of his tether. It was with a great effort that he struggled back to the capital; " I passed the grave once lately and never thought to see Khartoum," he told Augusta; " I will tell you more of it after a while."

Even in exhaustion, however, he was capable of working harder and riding faster than any member of his entourage. Rudolf Slatin, whom Gordon had just appointed Mudir of south-west Darfur, has recorded a glimpse of him on this painful journey back to Khartoum.

I learnt that Gordon was only four or five hours distant, and was on his way to the Nile. I therefore started off again and in a few hours found him halted under a large tree. He was evidently very tired and exhausted after his long ride, and was suffering from sores on his legs. I had fortunately brought some brandy with me from the stock on board his own steamer, and he was soon sufficiently revived to continue his journey. He asked me to come back with him to Tara el Hadra, to discuss the Darfur situation, and to give me the necessary instructions. . . . We were soon in the saddle, but Gordon shot far ahead of us, and we found it impossible to keep up with his rapid pace. We soon reached Tara el Hadra, where the baggage camels, which had previously been sent on ahead, had already arrived. As the steamers were anchored in midstream, we were rowed out in a boat. I found myself sitting in the stern, next Yusuf Pasha esh Shellali, and, as a drinking-cup was near him and I was thirsty, I begged him to dip it into the river and give me a drink.

Gordon, noticing this, turned to me, smiling, and said in French
' Are you not aware that Yusef Pasha, in spite of his black face,
is very much your senior in rank? You are only the Mudir of
Dara, and you should not have asked him to give you a drink.'
I at once apologised in Arabic to Yusef Pasha. . . .

10

At Khartoum news reached Gordon of Gessi's final victory. By a
supremely daring ruse he had surrounded and surprised Suleiman's
camp with his own scanty forces. The cub had surrendered,
attempted to escape and been shot. " God has been truly good to
me," wrote Gordon on 21st July. " ' Those that honour Me I will
honour.' May I be ground to dust, if He will glorify Himself in me;
but give me a *humble heart*, for then He dwells there in comfort."
It was a Nunc Dimittis to the Sudan, and he added " it pains me
what sufferings my poor Khedive Ismail has had to go through."
Eight days later he left for Cairo. Those who had seen most of his
administration in the Sudan knew best what the Sudan was losing.
Messedaglia, an Italian serving in Northern Darfur, wrote[1] that, in
addition to the " sublime self-sacrifice " of his ten expeditions into
the desert: " It is he who gives directions and conducts inquiries,
he who watches and takes care to see that his orders were carried
out, he who probes conspiracies to the bottom, he who judges and
decides, he, in fact, who does everything, sees everything, thinks of
everything with an unparalleled economy of means." For the
natives of the Sudan, Gordon's departure was the disappearance of a
semi-divine being. The moral ascendancy which he had established
throughout the Sudan had been due to what seemed to them superhuman courage and endurance, to the mesmeric powers of the blue
eyes, and not least to his incomprehensible indifference to women
and money. In later years Rivers Wilson recalled that he had
travelled with a Roman Catholic Bishop who was on his way from

---

[1] Quoted by Allen, (*Gordon and the Sudan*, 163, 4).

Khartoum to Rome. To his surprise the prelate expressed the
warmest admiration for Gordon and when asked to what he
attributed his extraordinary influence over the Sudanese replied
simply "his chastity."

At Cairo, which he reached on 23rd August, Gordon had
several interviews with the new Khedive, Tewfik, and found, to
his surprise, that he liked him. "Well, a miracle had happened.
Here was a man with the talent, energy and (?) assurance of the
'Incurable,' with a quality the latter did not possess, i.e. honesty.
It was really quite astounding; he was not profuse at all; in fact,
to this day he has paid me not one single compliment." He informed
the Khedive that he proposed to go to Abyssinia, to "settle with
Johannis," whose generals were threatening an attack on the
Egyptian frontier, after which he would resign and return home.
At this Tewfik was obviously relieved, for Gordon's enemies in
Cairo were numerous. The Europeans objected to his support of
Ismail, and the Egyptians to his crusade against the slave-trade; and
between them they had concocted a rumour that he was plotting
to make himself independent Sultan of the Sudan. But that, Gordon
told Augusta, "would not suit our family."

II

He would dearly have liked to return home forthwith, for he was
very weary; however conscience told him that he owed the
Khedive one more service; "I cannot think of leaving Egypt
exposed to her enemies." And as, after delivering a theological
homily to some Protestant missionaries from Sweden, he set out
from the Red Sea Coast along a track whose difficulties presaged
what was to come, it struck him as an odd coincidence that by all
accounts the King of Abyssinia was, like himself, a religious fanatic.
And perhaps only a religious fanatic could have endured the three
months which followed. For he was now suffering from boils,
brought on by prickly heat, as well as from what he describes as

palpitations of the heart. It was in this physical plight that he toiled along almost impassable mountain tracks and over almost insurmountable summits; slept night after night in the open, even changing his clothes, before a state interview, in a rainstorm under the open sky; submitted to insults and arrests; endured grotesque and protracted interviews with Johannis's general, Aloula, and then, a terrible month farther on, with the King of Kings himself, a madman whose habit it was to cut off the noses of those of his subjects who took snuff and the lips of those who smoked, and who is described by Gordon as " of the strictest sect of the Pharisees— drunk every night, at dawn he is up reading the Psalms." There were several critical moments; one of them at this conference with Johannis when he found a chair placed for him far from the King's throne and to the left, and before speaking a word carried the chair close to the King's right hand. The King had asked " Do you know that I may kill you for this?" and Gordon had replied " I do not fear death." After which the interview proceeded smoothly. But at last, although Cairo buzzed with rumours that he had perished, he re-emerged at Massawa on the Red Sea Coast.

Thanks to the vacillations of the demented Johannis the diplomatic results of the arduous adventure were inconclusive, and it is remarkable chiefly for the astonishing equanimity with which Gordon had supported his trials. No more do the once-familiar outbursts of exasperation pepper his journal, and the most provoking *contretemps* are greeted with tolerant and humorous detachment. He had been travelling with a mere handful of companions and no doubt it was a relief no longer to feel responsible for a vast province and a host of subordinates, but much of his serenity must be attributed to his steady growth in spiritual stature. Already his theological novitiate at Gravesend seemed to belong to another life, and from a riverside half-way between Aloula and Johannis he could write " You make me laugh when you talk of the book I wrote, and Mrs. Freese's corrections. I remember the whole affair so well but the phase has long gone by. I would not go through it again for a great deal."

12

On 2nd January, 1880, Gordon was in Cairo, letting it be known that he was about to quit Egypt for good. This time Tewfik endeavoured to persuade him to change his mind, but he would not listen. The briefest of Gordon's transits, however, could be relied on to stir official Cairo to its depths. There were several stormy scenes with authorities, including Baring, who, being preoccupied with high finance and the bondholders' dividends, displayed insufficient interest in the suppression of the slave trade. Moreover, Gordon's private idiosyncracies were as unpredictable as his public activities. Sir Edward Malet (as he was to become), who had succeeded Vivian as British Consul, has recorded how the legendary newcomer called on him and broke off a discussion of the affairs of the Sudan to take a small filigree silver box from his pocket and present it to his host. Unfortunately Malet, too, had his idiosyncracies and one of them was a lifelong practice of refusing all gifts; and since Gordon continued with disconcerting earnestness to press the box upon him the embarrassed consul had recourse to the suggestion that he should pay for it, not unnaturally supposing that this would close the incident. To his surprise, however, Gordon readily agreed, explained that the box was worth three pounds and accepted three English sovereigns forthwith. The cordiality of the interview was not diminished by this transaction and as Gordon left Malet ventured to invite him to dinner next day. Gordon excused himself on the plea that dinners were not in his line, and the consul was consequently all the more surprised when, as his guests were about to sit down to table on the following evening, His Excellency Gordon Pasha was announced. The unexpected guest, whose advent made the company thirteen, airily explained that he had changed his mind.

A few mornings later the consul received a much greater shock. For Gordon called upon him again, this time to announce that he intended to challenge Nubar Pasha to a duel. The unhappy Malet was aghast. It was astounding enough that a man of Gordon's character and position should contemplate a duel, but it was even more astounding that he should coolly inform Her Majesty's representative in Cairo of his intentions. There could be no doubt, however, of Gordon's seriousness. In company the previous evening Nubar, it seemed, had let fall some disparaging remarks as to Malet's predecessor, Vivian, and " Vivian," said Gordon, " is a C.B. and I am a C.B. too. I will not permit anyone to speak in such a way of a man who belongs to the same order of knighthood as I do. Nubar Pasha shall apologise to me or fight." The astonished consul was conscious of a fantastic sense of having been transported to the middle ages: as in a dream he recalled the speech of Talbot in Shakespeare's Henry II:

> *When first this order was ordained, my Lords,*
> *Knights of the Garter were of noble birth,*
> *Valiant and virtuous, full of haughty courage. . . .*

In vain he pointed out that Vivian had been a public official and that officials must expect criticism; Gordon was inflexible, and it was with the utmost difficulty that in due course Malet contrived to extract an apology from Nubar and avert the threatened scandal.

One other interview of some note there was before Gordon sailed for home. He actually consulted a doctor in Alexandria. This gentleman diagnosed nervous exhaustion and " alteration of the blood," and recommended several months of complete rest, " with no business or political excitement." It was hardly a prescription which Gordon was likely to take very seriously.

BOOK EIGHT

THE FINAL CONVERSION

GORDON SAILED from Alexandria on 10th January, 1880, with the disheartening knowledge that Raouf Pasha, whom he had himself twice dismissed from subordinate Governorships, was to succeed him as Governor-General. And so the old régime of the Pashas would return to the Sudan and his own work would be undone. All through the first day of the voyage he paced the deck alone, wrapped in melancholy speculation. But a distinguished French fellow-traveller, M. Reinach, had been observing him with lively interest and before long succeeded in engaging him in conversation. Gordon, he soon decided, was the most entertaining companion he had ever chanced upon; he was enchanted by his voluble jumble of English and French and by the startling contrast, amid the torrent of his ideas, between those which seemed born of profound wisdom and experience and those which suggested sometimes the simplicity of a child and sometimes the fantasies of a disordered brain. But Gordon, as so often, was being prophetic and amid much else he held forth at length upon the desirability of an Entente Cordiale; indeed, a month later he was scribbling a hurried note to Reinach from the United Service Club, to report that " the chief mountebank, Lord Salisbury, is ill " and that he himself was submitting his ideas as to Anglo-French relations to the Foreign Office.

At Naples he insisted that his new friend should accompany him to lunch with the exiled Khedive near Mount Vesuvius, and listened

with the utmost sympathy to Ismail's laments over the past. Afterwards the cultured Frenchman noted with surprise his companion's
complete indifference to his surroundings; he talked continually of
Ismail and the Sudan, but of the streets of Naples, the ruins of
Pompeii and Vesuvius smoking beneath the snow he seemed totally
unconscious. And though persuaded to go to the Opera House to
see *La Juive* he left after an hour and a half. At Rome it was the
same; he went, half reluctantly, to St. Peter's and found it unimpressive. His only other recorded comment on the Eternal City
was that he could not bring himself to visit the Vatican Museum.

2

By 2nd February he was writing to the Freeses from Southampton,
and two days later he visited them. In the midst of shaking hands
with the family, clustered excitedly about him, he broke off and
said suddenly to Mrs. Freese, " Yes, you were right; they could
not know Christ." He was referring, she realised, to one of his
letters from Khartoum in which he had argued that since the
Sudanese knew God they were virtually Christians. The Freeses
thought that Gordon looked thinner and older, and, by permission,
he smoked a great deal; but he was in high spirits and kept the
children spellbound with tales of the Sudan. In Southampton, too,
he smoked constantly, as he talked theology in Augusta's kitchen,
the only room in which that severe lady seems to have permitted
smoking. Once again he was in hiding from the great world, so
much so that when visitors were announced as he played with his
elder brother's two small daughters in Kensington he crawled under
the dining-room table.

But he was still waging his long guerilla warfare with officialdom,
and a tremor must have passed through Whitehall at the knowledge
that he was actually in London and that any day might bring a
personal call from one whom it had found sufficiently disconcerting
when he was in the heart of the Sudan. Officialdom could only

trust that the well-tried policy of evasion and inactivity would wear down even the fiercest onsets. And when Lady Burton wrote to inquire whether he could help her husband, who was having his own troubles with the Foreign Office, Gordon was compelled to reply:

You write to an orb which is setting, or rather is set. I have no power to aid your husband in any way. I went to F.O. to-day and, as you know, Lord Hammond is very ill. Well, the people there were afraid of me, for I have written hard things to them, and though they knew all they would say nought. I said 'Who is the personification of F.O.?' They said 'Currie is;' I saw Currie, but he tried to evade my question, *i.e.* 'Would F.O. do anything to prevent the Sudan falling into chaos?' It was no use. I cornered him, and then he said 'I am merely a clerk to register letters coming in and going out.' So then I gave it up and marvelled. I must say I was surprised to see such a thing, a great Government like ours governed by men who dare not call their souls their own. Lord Hammond rules them with a rod of iron. If your husband would understand that F.O. is at present Lord Hammond, and he is ill, he would see that I can do nothing. I have written letters to F.O. that would raise a corpse; it is no good. I have threatened to go to the French Government about the Sudan; it is no good.

As usual, he was resolutely repelling the advances of the numerous hostesses who had heard that the man whom somebody had called "the uncrowned king" was in London. But, as usual, there were some functions which could not be avoided, and on 17th February he might have been seen at the Prince of Wales' levée in St. James' Palace. He surveyed the four royal brothers, the aged Lord Beaconsfield and the assembled notables quizzically; " a mass of glitter," he wrote to Mrs. Freese next morning, " to be worms in 30 yrs. time." Nevertheless, when a lord-in-waiting announced him as *Captain* Gordon, the old enemy whom he dubbed

Agag, the spirit of worldly ambition, gave clear signs that he had
not yet been hewn in pieces. And then the Prince of Wales, as he
shook hands, murmured an invitation to lunch next Sunday. Here
was a temptation for Agag indeed, for Gordon had already recorded
his desire to avoid the Prince, and it is possible that it is to the
sequel to this invitation that a story told to Dr. Bernard Allen[1] by
one of Gordon's nephews relates. The Prince, it appears, sent a
formal invitation to dinner, which Gordon declined, whereupon
an equerry set off post-haste to his lodgings in Sackville Street.
" But you cannot refuse the Prince " he protested. " Why not? "
replied Gordon. " I refused King Johannis . . . and he might have
cut off my head for refusing. I am sure H.R.H. will not do that."
" Well, then, let me say you are ill." " But I am not ill." " Give
me *some* reason then," pleaded the equerry, " that I can give the
Prince." " Very well, then," said Gordon, " tell him I always go
to bed at half-past nine." After which the Prince of Wales, who
had a sense of humour, substituted an invitation to an informal
lunch on the following Sunday, which was accepted. To this meal
the Prince also invited his kinsman, the Duke of Cambridge, Commander-in-Chief, who remembered Gordon as a child at Corfu
and had taken an admiring interest in his career. Both royal
personages pressed him as to the reasons for his wish to resign his
commission, of which they had heard. Even if he had wished to,
Gordon would have found it difficult to explain his state of mind
to such an audience, and he contented himself by replying that he
wished for rest. Whereupon the Duke exclaimed " Take a year's
leave then, or more," and roundly declared that he would not accept
resignation. During this conversation the Princess of Wales and her
daughters entered the room, in order to " shake hands with Colonel
Gordon."

[1] *Gordon and the Sudan,* pp. 167, 8. Boulger, *Life of Gordon,* 1896, p. 208, puts the incident
a few weeks later.

3

On the 29th of February Gordon left London for Lausanne. He wanted privacy as well as rest. For the lion-hunters of society had pursued him inexorably, and the Press, as well as his private correspondence, had been full of suggestions, most of them highly unsuitable, as to his future employment. His own head was still full of Zanzibar and he had had a talk of two hours with Sir William Mackinnon. On his way he paused in Brussels. Vivian, on whose behalf he had recently threatened to fight a duel, was now Minister at the court of King Leopold, and Gordon found that he liked him better than when he had met him as spokesman of the financial interests in Cairo. More significantly, he had a conference with King Leopold, who was already anxious to persuade Gordon to enter his service and crush the slave trade in the Congo. The occasion, like so many of Gordon's interviews with the great, had its bizarre aspects. "I arrived here yesterday at 6 p.m.," he wrote on 2nd March, 1880,

> and found my baggage had not come on when I got to the hotel. . . . I found I was *detected*, and a huge card of H.M. awaited me, inviting to dinner at 6.30 p.m. It was then 6.20 p.m. I wrote my excuses, telling the truth, then I waited. It is now 9.30 p.m., and no baggage. King has just sent to say he will receive me at 11 a.m. I am obliged to say I cannot come if my baggage does not arrive. . . . Horrors, it is now 10.20 a.m., and no baggage! . . . Remember, too, I have to dress, shave, etc., etc. 10.30 a.m.—no baggage!!! It is getting painful; H.M. will be furious. 10.48 a.m.—no baggage! . . . 12.30 p.m. Got enclosed note from palace, and went to see the King. . . . He was very civil, and I stayed with him for one and a half hours. He is quite at sea with his expedition (Congo) and I have to try to get him out of it.

A few days later an English clergyman, the Revd. R. H. Barnes, vicar of Heavitree, near Exeter, who was staying at the Hotel Faucon, Lausanne, for his health with a party of friends, was noticing an Englishman who always took his meals in a corner of the dining-room with a young boy. The two seemed to know nobody and to be wholly engrossed in each other's company. The Englishman's face interested Mr. Barnes. Deeply furrowed, it suggested powers of grave and practical thought, and he noticed specially the "delicately expressive blue eyes." Before long the unknown Englishman suggested that he should accompany the vicar on a walk suited to an invalid. He did so, and they talked at length of serious subjects. Mr. Barnes, however, was still ignorant of his companion's name, and even when, some days later, he learned it it did not enter his head that this could be the celebrated Chinese Gordon. And then one day his new acquaintance took him to his room, and Mr. Barnes noticed some strange-looking documents lying on the table. His companion explained that they were death warrants. "Death warrants?" gasped the startled clergyman. "Who are you?" And so he learned that this was indeed Chinese Gordon and that his last act as Governor-General of the Sudan would be to sign the Arabic documents, of which, since they conveyed his formal resignation, he had spoken as death warrants. It transpired further that he was planning to pay visits of inspection to some Swiss schools in the interests of his brother Enderby's sons, one of whom, his godson, Charlie, was his present companion.

By the twenty-sixth Gordon had sent the Enderby Gordons critical comments on several schools, as well as on Charlie's diet and Lord Beaconsfield's administration, had advised them, if they had doubts about Neville, "to toss up with reverence," and was now about to take Charlie to Paris and thence return him to his parents. From Paris he sent detailed advice about the boy's journey, the general tenor of which was that the less he was looked after the better. And on 1st April he wrote long letters to Charlie, who had just departed, and to Charlie's mother. He told Charlie that though he had sometimes found him trying he missed him very much,

asked for his prayers—" just a few words from your heart, even as
you go downstairs "—and urged him to write a letter of thanks to
Mrs. Vivian, adding " make your mother pay the postage." To
his sister-in-law he sent a characteristic mixture of advice and
autobiography.

> I never pretended to Charlie I was a paragon. It would be no
> good, for he is too quick; and I also wanted him to see it is
> nothing to acknowledge one's human failings. So you need not
> fret yourself to keep up appearance, for you will be sure to fail
> under such microscopes. I want C. to understand that in even
> a worldly point of view it is worth while being civil to outsiders
> (to one's own relations it does not matter so much). I have been
> far more helped by little people than by great. I take much
> more pains to *answer letters from*, and to help (if this is in my
> power) the *small* than I would the great. From this I consider
> I owe any success in the world. I would refuse a dinner with a
> king to give pleasure in taking tea with my old housekeeper.
> Let C. read this letter; it will do him good. Tell him when in
> trouble to read his *Scripture Promises*; they meet all soul's
> diseases. . . . The only hint I can give you is to make C. keep his
> room in order, not to leave his clothes littered about.

While in Paris Gordon handed a memorandum on the Sudan to
the British Ambassador, for dispatch to the Foreign Office. As usual,
it was prescient (Disraeli had described a memorandum of Gordon's
on the Near East as the work of a madman, but many of its proposals
were eventually carried out) and, as usual, it could not be mistaken
for the work of anyone but Gordon, if only owing to its concluding
sentence, which ran " Anyhow, it matters little; a few years hence
a piece of ground six feet by two will contain all that remains of
ambassadors, ministers and your obedient humble servant, C. G.
Gordon."

G.G.   S

4

Returned to England, Gordon moved from Sackville Street to Chelsea and continued to wonder what he should do next. He had begun to visit the sick again, and in particular a Miss Wylde, who was suffering from an incurable disease. " I do not want a good place," he wrote to Mrs. Freese on 21st April, " I want a place of danger and exposure, and I feel I would seek it in the hospitals if I cannot find it elsewhere."

His thoughts had doubtless been turned to the hospitals by Florence Nightingale. Miss Nightingale, who was now sixty, had, as Dr. Jowett of Balliol had recently told her, become a myth in her own lifetime. Earlier that month Gordon had written to ask her to help his cousin, Mrs. Hawthorn, to persuade the War Office to investigate the ill-treatment of patients by orderlies in military hospitals. He came to see her, they discussed religion and found that their experiences had been remarkably similar. Both had thought out their theology unaided, both were aiming at a life of union with God, issuing in practical good works. Miss Nightingale failed to convince the War Office that Mrs. Hawthorn had a case, but a friendship quickly sprang up between her and Gordon. He came to see her frequently during these few weeks. On the day after he had told Mrs. Freese that he might seek danger in the hospitals he was writing to Miss Nightingale " I gained the hearts of my soldiers (who would do anything for me) not by my justice, etc., but by looking after them when sick and continually visiting the Hospitals." He called several times, too, this April on Lady Burton in Upper Montagu Street. On one occasion he inquired whether she knew the origin of the Union Jack, and when she confessed her ignorance he sat down cross-legged on the hearth-rug with scissors and paper and cut out several specimens. That night Lady Burton pasted one of them in her journal.

Inevitably, too, while Gordon was in London there were encounters with some of those with whom he had dealt most fiercely by letter or telegram while in the Sudan, and as usual they found that his wrath was not enduring. Rivers Wilson, who last year had been Finance Minister at Cairo and had incautiously ventured to criticise Gordon's treatment of an errant major in the Sudan, was now in retirement under temporary official disfavour, and one morning he left a card on Gordon. Next morning Gordon called on him and explained that he wished to apologise for the rudeness of his telegrams. They had not met before and Wilson at once took to " the strange little unpretending man," and added, like everyone else who met Gordon for the first time, a comment on his eyes " like blue diamonds." A day or two later Lord Salisbury questioned him about Gordon, and Wilson replied that he quite realised that for the Foreign Office Gordon was officially " impossible," but that for exceptionally difficult tasks in uncivilised countries he was ideally fitted. " If you told him to capture Cetewayo, for instance, he would get to Africa, mount on a pony with a stick in his hand and ask the nearest way to Cetewayo's kraal, and when he got there he would get down and have a talk with him." Lord Salisbury, however, was a cautious man and it is doubtful whether he was convinced. In any case, his days at the Foreign Office were numbered, for this April Lord Beaconsfield's administration fell.

5

For Gordon the consequences were immediate. At the end of April he was walking with his brother, Henry, and as they reached his brother's front door in Elm Park Road, a hansom cab pulled up beside them. Gordon walked on, but in a moment his brother called him back and begged him to speak to the gentleman who had hurriedly descended from the cab. It was Sir Bruce Seton, who had been sent by the Marquis of Ripon, the newly appointed Viceroy of India, to invite Gordon to go out with him as his private secretary. The offer of so eminently unsuitable a post, and Gordon's prompt acceptance of it, constitute one of the most mysterious episodes in his career. He, if not Lord Ripon, must have known that it would require precisely the qualities which he did not possess, tact, social orthodoxy, self-effacement and a diplomatic readiness to say one thing and mean another. All that can be said is that Lord Beaconsfield had just been defeated at the general election and that Mr. Gladstone and the Liberals had assumed office with the usual millenary hopes. It was as an apostle of reform that Lord Ripon was to sail for India in a fortnight's time, and in a moment of over-hasty optimism it seems to have been assumed that to associate with his mission a practical idealist, at once so celebrated and so remote from party politics, would insure it the appropriate aura of moral prestige and emphasise the intention to inaugurate a new era. The Liberal ministers were probably right about the prestige; indeed the philanthropic and literary Lord Houghton disconcerted Lord Ripon by implying, as he tendered his congratulations, that Gordon's appointment as secretary was more significant than his own as Viceroy. But if this was indeed an early essay in the art of what we now call public relations it was foredoomed from the outset. The men who calculated on exploiting Gordon's reputation had not had the advantage of reading his letters from the Sudan, but even so it is astonishing that they should have envisaged him of all men as submitting contentedly to an endless vista of official dinners.

As for Gordon it can be said that he, too, had rejoiced at the " glorious " overthrow of Lord Beaconsfield and his " proud military-feeling ministry," and believed for a while that there was to be a new régime in India. Moreover, both Augusta and his brother, Henry, who had never wholly reconciled themselves to his abandoning an orthodox career, had urged him to accept. He had not been employed by the Tories and in official circles he was generally considered to be mad; if the Liberals were ready to use him he should not reject the opportunity. It was with considerable misgivings that he agreed, and almost at once he realised that he had made a mistake. Within three days he was writing to Mrs. Freese that he wanted her prayers, not her congratulations. It was not merely that, as he told his family, he would now be a satellite instead of a comet; reflection had convinced him that he could expect to make no headway against the vested interests of official-dom. Even before he sailed, Lord Ripon was startled by an indica-tion of what might be to come. At the new Viceroy's farewell dinner party in Carlton Gardens Gordon astonished his host and fellow-guests by insisting on eating every course from the same plate. To whispered expostulations he replied airily "We shall have to rough it out in India, you know, so I may as well begin now." Even Gordon can hardly have expected Lord Ripon, a Whig nobleman, with a patriarchal beard and a monocle, or for that matter any Viceroy, to find himself compelled to rough it in India, and his embarrassing gesture, so far from being a deliberate pre-paration for hardship was no doubt an instinctive protest against the lack of it. An hour before he drove to Charing Cross on 14th May he wrote to Halliday Macartney, whose memories of Gordon raging over the severed head of Lar Wang can hardly have prepared him for the news of the secretaryship, "I am afraid that I have decided in haste, to repent at leisure."

As the Vice-regal party passed through Egypt it fell to the British Consul to accompany it from Alexandria to Suez. In the course of the rail journey Gordon invited him into an empty com-partment and asked whether he remembered the filigree box. Malet had been wrong to refuse it, he said; he had intended to give him a fine suit of armour, had the lesser gift not been declined. Would he accept a present now? And he drew out a small discoloured ivory pocket knife, on which were scratched the initials C.C. Colin Campbell, Lord Clyde, he explained, had carried it with him throughout the Indian Mutiny; would Malet accept it? When the Consul, finally flinging his principles to the wind, replied that he would accept it with the greatest possible pleasure Gordon exclaimed, with an audible sigh of relief. "Ah! Now I am satisfied; you have got something from me." In later years, as he reflected on this curious incident, Sir Edward Malet could only conclude that Gordon had supposed that the gift would exercise a "magnetic influence " on him. When asked whether it had in fact done so, he hesitated and then admitted that times without number he had gazed at the pocket knife and the filigree box, and never without thinking of Gordon; perhaps a mysterious link had indeed been established between them. As for Gordon, when, on the eve of his last fatal journey to Khartoum, he acknowledged Malet's letter of good wishes he told him that he had prayed for him for many years.

During the journey, Lord Ripon afterwards told his wife, Gordon had done admirable work and had established " the most delightful relations " with all his colleagues, including the Viceroy's Jesuit chaplain, Father Keir. But as their ship entered Bombay harbour on 28th May Gordon himself was writing to Augusta that he will never be able to " curb " himself sufficiently to remain in government service and that he expects to resign in late September or early October. This soon proved to be an underestimate; he resigned five days later, on 2nd June. The immediate occasion was characteristic. Lord William Beresford had asked him to acknow- ledge an address presented to the Viceroy at Bombay, and to say that Lord Ripon had read it with interest and would reply in due course. Gordon retorted that Lord William knew perfectly well that Lord Ripon had not read the address and would never reply to it, and that as for himself he was not prepared to be responsible for this kind of letter and intended to resign. And he handed Lord William a letter of resignation. Gordon's old friend, Sir Andrew Clarke, had travelled to India with the Viceroy, and as soon as dinner was over Lord Ripon hurried him off to his room to discuss the delicate problem of the communiqué which would be needed to announce the resignation. For Gordon after all was to be a symbol of Lord Ripon's intention to be a reforming Viceroy, and his speedy withdrawal would need some explanation. Together they drafted a form of words, and Clarke took it to Gordon, only to find that, though much distressed, he was not prepared to com- promise. They parted in the small hours, apparently without having reached an agreement; but at six in the morning Clarke returned, and found Gordon " altogether in a better mood." After this second conference Gordon went off gaily, to find Lord Ripon chipping an egg at breakfast, and inform him that he had news which, so far from spoiling his meal, would " only make him laugh." He proceeded to explain his decision, declaring that his position had been that of head spy and a living crucifixion. Lord Ripon replied that he was doing right, and they parted on the most amicable terms. Gordon then returned to Clarke and dashed off an official letter in which, Clarke considered, he took too much blame on himself. But Gordon would not allow a word to be changed. " A grand, honest fellow " was Clarke's final verdict on the episode.

The speedy resignation had not of course been due only to the necessity of writing an over-diplomatic letter. Gordon held strong views as to the excessive payments to British and European officials in the East, views which he had repeatedly emphasised by drastically reducing his own salary, and he had already realised on the outward voyage that there was no hope of Lord Ripon's initiating reforms of this nature. Only two days earlier he had written to Florence Nightingale that among British officials in India " the element of all government is absent, i.e. the putting of the governors into the skin of the governed." And soon he would be telling Augusta that " the way Europeans live there is absurd in its luxury; they seem so utterly effeminate and not to have an idea beyond the rupee . . . All the salaries are too high by half above rank of captain. It is a house of charity for a lot of idle, useless fellows." Moreover, the Viceroy had rejected his advice that Yakub Khan, the ex-Amir of Afghanistan, who had been charged with responsibility for the murder of the British Minister and his staff in Kabul, should be reinstated, preferably by Lord Ripon with three thousand cavalry, but, failing Lord Ripon, by himself. And thus it came about that Gordon, who had insisted on repaying the whole of the expenses which Lord Ripon had incurred in bringing him out, was left completely penniless and at a loss where to go, and what to do, next.

5

But not for long. His resignation was announced in the London newspapers of 4th June; on the 6th he received a telegram from Sir Robert Hart, Inspector General of the Imperial Customs in Peking: " I am directed to invite you here. Please come and see for yourself. The opportunity of doing really useful work on a large scale ought not to be lost. Work, position, conditions can all be arranged with yourself here to your satisfaction. . . ." Within forty-eight hours Gordon had replied " Inform Hart Gordon will leave for Shanghai first available opportunity. As for conditions Gordon indifferent." At the moment he had only a small sum of money borrowed in Bombay (he had declined a handsome gift politely proffered by an admirer), and he did not know even whether the British Government would approve his going to China. But he knew that China was on the verge of war with Russia, he supposed, mistakenly as it proved, that the invitation had been inspired by his friend, Li Hung Chang, and he did not doubt that he was faced with another unrolling of the scroll. He promptly wired to the Horse Guards: " Obtain me leave until end of the year; am invited to China; will not involve Government." The last four words must have struck a familiar chill into many hearts at the War Office, and still more in the Foreign Office. For the Russian Government and the Russian Press were already showing signs of alarm at the news of Gordon's intentions, and who in Whitehall could venture to reassure them with any confidence? A brusque exchange of telegrams between London and Bombay terminated in a flat official embargo. " Reasons insufficient; your going to China is not approved." Rarely indeed in their dealings with Gordon had the authorities ventured to substitute decisive action for the evasive tactics which had usually served them so well, and now that they had at last been compelled to do so it proved, as might have been expected, a complete failure. Without further ado Gordon embarked upon a cargo boat for China. Now more than ever, as he set out on his ill-defined mission, penniless, officially disowned and ignorant as to his own status, he seemed to be assuming the character of a knight-errant. Nevertheless, as he left Bombay he took the statesman-like precaution of issuing a public statement in which he made it clear that his chief aim would be to persuade the Chinese not to go to war with Russia. Possibly the authorities in Whitehall found this reassuring; more probably their courage failed them; whatever the reason, they capitulated, and at Ceylon Gordon found another telegram awaiting him: " Leave granted on your engaging to take no military service in China."

There were no other passengers on the cargo boat and during a sea-passage of three weeks even Gordon was compelled to rest. They reached Hong-Kong on 3rd July and almost the first person to greet him was Quincy, whom he had rescued, a naked waif, from the battlefield at Quinsan, now " a first-rate young fellow " with a wife and three children. At Shanghai he met many former acquaintances and several of the boys of his bodyguard, now moon-faced adults. Lar Wang's son, the handsome youth who had first broken to him the news of his father's murder, was now a mandarin " like an ox." All this was melancholy, but, worse still, Gordon was beginning to see dimly into the complex of intrigues in which China was involved. At the outset it was disquieting to discover that whoever had inspired Sir Robert Hart's invitation to him it was not, as he had optimistically assumed, Li Hung Chang, and that it might have been one of several persons actuated by more sinister motives. For it appeared that several foreign Powers were endeavouring to induce Li, who was the chief advocate of peace with Russia, to march on Pekin, overthrow the young Emperor and the war party, and establish a government of his own. And it even seemed possible that the true author of the invitation, whoever he might be, had hoped that the former commander of the Ever Victorious would ensure victory for Li's army by placing himself at its head. Gordon had spoken the simple truth when he said in Bombay that his object would be to prevent war, and it now appeared that at its simplest his task would be threefold; to persuade Li not to rebel against Pekin, to persuade Pekin not to go to war with Russia, and to keep himself out of any fighting there might be. He hastened at once to Li Hung Chang at Tientsin.

Li, unlike his other former friends, had changed little in appearance and greeted Gordon warmly. But he was undoubtedly being urged into high treason by foreign diplomats, and soon one of them roundly proposed to Gordon that he should take command of Li's army, march on Pekin and depose the Emperor. Gordon thought it best not to take this suggestion seriously, and he laughed it off with the reply that though he was equal to a good deal of filibustering, this was too much even for him. But he realised that in a situation which might develop both swiftly and unforeseeably he could not rely on keeping his promise to the War Office, and accordingly he telegraphed to the Horse Guards that he could not desert China in its present crisis, that he wished to be free to act as he thought fit, and that he therefore begged to resign his commission. For a while he stayed on at Tientsin, constantly in conference with Li and constantly using his still potent influence to induce that astute but undecided statesman not to listen to the counsellors of violence. Before long it became evident that Li had been convinced, and Gordon decided that it was now his duty to go to Pekin to persuade the court to abandon any thought of war with Russia. It was a somewhat hazardous enterprise, for the hotheads, he realised, might assassinate him before he could convince the court, but in a curious way he felt responsible not only for China, but for Li. " Li Hung Chang," he wrote, " is a noble fellow, and worth giving one's life for; but he must not rebel and lose his good name. It is a sort of general election which is going on, where heads are in gage."

In Pekin the British Minister, whether in anxiety as to Gordon's safety or because he had been instructed to see that he did not transgress diplomatic etiquette, ordered him to stay in the British Legation and pay no visits without official permission. Sir Thomas Wade was an estimable citizen and an accomplished Chinese scholar but he was not likely to succeed where the entire War Office had so repeatedly failed, and keep Gordon in order. As might have been expected, Gordon ignored his instructions and did not once cross the threshold of the Legation. But he had several conferences with the Grand Council and it is unlikely that the assembled mandarins ever forgot the experience. Gordon began by explaining in detail that they were much too weak to go to war. And to emphasise his argument and the sombre character of their prospects, he said that if war should come and they were prepared to destroy the suburbs of Pekin and remove Emperor and court to a distant place of safety he would consent to help them, but not otherwise. When the outraged notables protested that the Taku forts were impregnable he laughed scornfully and assured them, with all the authority of one who had captured countless Chinese forts, that they could easily be taken from the rear. When, feebly but obstinately, they still argued, his language became so undiplomatic that the interpreter was seized with panic and refused to translate such derogatory epithets applied to such august dignitaries. Whereupon Gordon snatched up a dictionary, rapidly turned its pages, placed his finger firmly on the Chinese word for "idiocy" and thrust it successively under the startled eyes of each member of the Council. At last he wrote out terms of peace under five heads and left them.

Not content with this, he prepared two memorandums for the Council, one an outline plan, brief but lucid, for the regeneration of China, the other—which, coming from Gordon, could hardly have been more authoritative—an exposition of the advantages, for Chinese troops, of guerilla warfare. Yet a third, which ran to fifty-two articles, and which he wrote " as a Chinaman for the Chinese," he had presented to Li Hung Chang. From Pekin he returned for a while to Li's headquarters at Tientsin but soon found that, his object there having been already achieved, he was *de trop*. He accordingly decided to quit China, and by 16th August he was at Shanghai and about to leave for Aden. In six weeks he had played a decisive part in preventing both a rebellion by Li Hung Chang and a war between China and Russia; nevertheless, he was in a melancholy mood, for the future was once more obscure. It was at this moment that he was handed another telegram from the War

Office. "Leave cancelled. Resignation not accepted. Return England forthwith;" it was certainly a spirited renewal of the offensive. "It did not produce a twitter in me" wrote Gordon. "I died long ago, and it will not make any difference to me. W.O. cannot trust me and I am prepared to follow the unrolling of the scroll."

7

But as the steamer bore him towards Aden it was all too clear that there had as yet been no unrolling. He revolved once again the advantages of attacking the slave trade from Zanzibar, he remembered King Leopold and his overtures as to the Congo, he even thought of Australia and, since Rajah Brooke's second-in-command happened to be on board, he was momentarily tempted by the possibilities of Borneo. It was evident, he wrote to Augusta, that he had lived his life out before it was finished. As to one resolution only he was quite clear; he would leave England for good, if possible by December. And he sent her more of the familiar calculations as to family pensions—a hundred more for Freddy's girl, perhaps a hundred for Herbert—and warned her that he would have to resign from both his clubs and lodge on the Embankment.

From Aden he dispatched a reproachful message to the Horse Guards: "You might have trusted me. My passage from China was taken days before the arrival of your telegram which states 'leave cancelled.' Do you insist on rescinding the same?" It was almost as if a lion tamer was complaining of having been bitten by a sheep. The authorities were not only moved to compunction by this unexpected appeal but acted with exceptional rapidity, for next day Gordon received a message granting him six months' leave. Sir William Mackinnon had offered him a free passage from Aden on any vessel of the British India Steam Navigation Company to Zanzibar or any other quarter of the globe, and it was probably the lessening of tension with Whitehall which finally decided him to

take the more conventional course and return home. Before the end
of October he was once more smoking in the kitchen of 5 Rockstone
Place, Southampton.

It was evident at once that his old enemy Agag, and the temptation to hail the tram of the world, had assumed a more formidable
guise than ever. For whatever might be thought of him in official
circles, the public, which had not suffered from his idiosyncrasies,
had taken him to its heart as a romantic Christian knight-errant, and
Press as well as society was speedily on his trail. And of the two he
found the Press a good deal harder to resist. Almost as soon as he
reached Southampton came a proposal from Gibson Bowles that
his portrait should be included in the famous series of *Vanity Fair*
cartoons. Gordon's first instinct was to refuse, and on 25th October
he replied "*I do not like* to be put before the world in any way.
Kindly do not put it down to pride, my refusal." But Bowles was
insistent and three days later Gordon is prepared to compromise.
Perhaps after all, so long as he did not seek notoriety himself, his
conscience would leave him in peace. "I will write to you as a
friend," he began a letter to Bowles,

> for I confess to a liking to [sic] *Vanity Fair, Truth* and *The World*.
> They keep people in order, who could not be touched in any
> other way. With respect to the likeness, pray do what you think
> fit. Had I come to you, then *many* of *my so-called* friends would
> have given me acidulated remarks and said I had pushed myself
> forward. I can assure you I get very nasty little remarks some-
> times, and thence I avoid as far as lays in my power giving ground
> for them. It appears that in society if one poses as a personage
> one gets abused; if one avoids society one gets the same. It
> makes little difference to me, for I am a strong believer in man
> not having any free will.

Even so the citadel did not fall at once, and it is not until 13th
December that he promises that Augusta will send Pelligrini
(" Ape," the *Vanity Fair* cartoonist) a photograph. Early in January

there was a first sitting. Like everyone else, Pelligrini was at once struck by his subject's most remarkable physical feature; " he laughed at your brother; he says ' He is all eyes;' and *I* know it, and *you* know it." At a second visit Gordon spent two hours expounding " the great truths " to the cartoonist. Perhaps he was all the more determined not to neglect such opportunities because he was still not quite certain whether the cartoon might not represent a victory for Agag after all.

The cartoon, which was far from flattering, appeared in the issue of 19th February. As usual, it was accompanied by a short word-portrait which, commencing with the challenging words " Chinese Gordon is the most notable of living Englishmen," contrived to summarise his career with surprising accuracy. The brief character-sketch with which it concluded is interesting evidence that unofficial London, at any rate, had begun to realise that in its horror of eccentricity officialdom was wasting a man of genius.

Colonel Gordon is the most conscientious simple-minded and honest of men. He has a complete contempt for money, and after having again and again rejected opportunities of becoming rich beyond the dreams of avarice, he remains a poor man with nothing in the world but his sword and his honour. The official mind, being incapable of understanding this, regards it as a sign of madness. And as it is found that besides being utterly without greed he is also entirely without vanity or self-assertion, he is set down by the officials as being " cracky " and unsafe to employ in comparison with such great men as Lord Chelmsford,[1] Sir Garnet Wolseley, and Sir George Colley.[2] He is very modest and very gentle, yet full of enthusiasm for what he holds to be right. This enthusiasm often leads him to interfere in matters which he does not understand, and to make in haste statements he has to correct at leisure. But he is a fine, noble, knightly gentleman, such as is found but once in many generations.

[1] Defeated by the Zulus at Isandhlwana, 1879.
[2] Defeated and killed by the Boers at Majuba Hill a week after this issue of *Vanity Fair*.

The problem of Agag presented itself even more perplexingly in the selection of Gordon's letters from the Sudan, which Dr. Birkbeck Hill, soon to be celebrated as editor of Boswell's *Johnson*, was now busily preparing for the Press. During the previous summer Gordon had agreed that his letters from the Sudan should be entrusted to Dr. Hill. The concession was surprising, but its value was not a little diminished by the stipulation that the writer would neither see nor correspond with the editor, and would read neither manuscript nor proofs. Dr. Hill, insisted Gordon, must assume sole responsibility and do his work as though the writer of the letters were already dead. And he added that he himself must not be praised, and that nobody else must be abused. A final proviso, that his Arab secretary, Berzati Bey, should receive special eulogy it was comparatively simple to satisfy and Dr. Hill duly included a lengthy footnote and a somewhat unimpressive photograph of " the black imp." But though he set manfully to work, the editor naturally found that under so many restrictions his task was far from easy, and now that the hero of his book was within reach he was tempted to consult him at least on problems of fact. The request caused Gordon much uneasiness. " How can a dead man supervise a book ? " he asked plaintively. And once again a compromise was reached. Gordon prepared a map for the volume; and he even cleared up difficulties of detail, but here his brother, Henry, acted as go-between so that Dr. Hill was able to announce, in his Preface, that he had " neither seen nor corresponded with the man whose Memoir I have sketched." And it was Sir Henry Gordon who read the proofs.

Before long there were even voluntary contacts with the Press. In the first half of November Gordon visited Pembroke; the old ferryman was still there and remembered his impatiently wading through the river, but almost everyone he had known when he was a subaltern at Pembroke seemed to be dead, and the fact that after so many perils he himself was still alive seemed to him to confirm his belief that God still had purposes for him to serve. By 13th November he was in Ireland; and in Bantry and Glengariff he meditated on the age-old grievances of that distressful island. Gordon had never yet admitted that a problem was insoluble, and fresh from wrestling with the far more deeply-rooted abuses of the Sudan he was soon prepared to prescribe a panacea for Ireland. On 30th November he wrote at length to his friend Colonel Donnelly.[1] He denounced the complete lack of sympathy between the landlords and their tenants, asserted that in eleven counties, which he named, the Irish were " living on the verge of starvation in places in which we would not keep our cattle " and that their condition was " worse than that of any people in the world," and proceeded to outline an ambitious scheme for the expropriation of the land-owners at a cost of eighty million pounds. From one who had so lately been studying slavery in the Bahr el Ghazal such assertions were startling. His letter was a private one, but Colonel Donnelly felt that it was too important to remain so and on 3rd December it appeared in *The Times*.

Any pronouncement from Chinese Gordon was news, and the letter provoked a fusillade of leading articles. *The Freeman's Journal* of Dublin pointed out ecstatically that " one of the most remarkable men of our own or any time " had arrived at substantially the same conclusions as the Irish Land League. The *Pall Mall Gazette* suggested that the real importance of the letter was that it must awaken the English people to the magnitude and urgency of their responsibilities. *The Times* described it temperately as " a strong illustration of the heroic method of dealing with Ireland." The *Standard* remarked cautiously that " Colonel Gordon, having for the moment abandoned his Chinese and Egyptian friends, has turned his attention to Ireland, and in a letter published this morning gives the experience of a superficial glance at the disquieted island."

Thus far his contributions to the Press had been more or less involuntary, but his first inhibitions had now been broken down, and in February he sent to *The Times* a long letter advocating the evacuation of Kandahar, which must have been welcome to the Liberal ministers, who were anxious to evacuate but were receiving

---

[1] The draft, with many corrections, is among the Donnelly papers.

little support from the military authorities. A month later, prompted by recent British reverses, he contributed to the *Army and Navy Gazette* an article on irregular warfare which must have incensed the War Office yet further. On this subject Gordon was beyond dispute the greatest living authority, and, indeed, perhaps the greatest authority of all time, and paragraph after paragraph of his article reads to-day like the most lucid of prescriptions for avoiding the disasters of the Boer War of 1899. But staff officers instinctively discounted a denunciation from Gordon of " the routine and red-tape inseparable from regular armies," wryly recalling his own repeated floutings of military convention. For the Horse Guards had now finally classified Gordon as an irresponsible eccentric; it had not occurred to them that eccentricity, like insanity (and some potentates would go so far as to suggest discreetly that Gordon was " not clothed in the rightest of minds ") is to genius near allied; or that one of the attributes of genius is to see farther than ordinary folk.

8

Early in December Gordon went to stay with Mr. Waller and his family at Twywell Rectory, near Thrapston in Northamptonshire. Waller was one of the correspondents whom, when in Equatoria, he had announced his intention of " dropping," but he had continued to write to him at intervals and the friendship had, in fact, never been interrupted. Before the end of the year he found that " there is a *little* wish to show me off and I have escaped with difficulty dinners and long consequent drives," and he moved into lodgings nearby. But he continued to visit the Rectory, for he enjoyed playing with its four children and he was involved in lengthy arguments with the Rector. Indeed, the visit to Twywell seems to mark a new stage, we may perhaps say the final stage, in Gordon's spiritual development. For Mr. Waller, who had formerly ventured to argue with Gordon about slavery, was now arguing with him,

G.G.   T

on securer premises, about theology. Gordon soon complained to Augusta that his host was "wrapped up in Church dogmas," but he could not bring himself to break off the discussions, and insensibly they produced in him a far-reaching effect. In his positive unorthodoxies, fatalism, the transmigration of souls, the predestination of every human being for heaven, he remained for the time being unshaken. But one great negative unorthodoxy he now abandoned, his indifference to the central feature of Christian worship, Holy Communion. He had already been moving tentatively in this direction, but it seems to have been at Twywell that he experienced what, in view of its memorable subsequent effects, may be described as his final conversion.

His new beliefs, once accepted, were embraced with characteristic wholeheartedness, and he expounded them at length in a remarkable letter of 9th February, 1881, in which Mrs. Freese, who had not infrequently questioned his heresies, almost seems herself to be being taken to task for unorthodoxy. "It may be (which I question)," he began, "that you need not attend to the last wish of our dying Saviour, and it may be that the Lord's death is not to be shown forth by the way He ordained, but these are not the thoughts of His people. . . . The Apostles put the greatest stress on it, it was the rule to administer it on the Lord's day and the Primitive Christians communicated every day. I cannot see when once our eyes are open to a simple command of our Lord that we should be justified in disobeying it, and there was a direct wish expressed." And he continued, in a passage which is evidently in part autobiographical:

To a worthy receiver, one who is ready to abnegate all to God and his neighbour, who regrets his past sins and earnestly desires to lead a pure life, who acknowledges his entire dependence on his Saviour for all things, that little piece of bread, that sip of wine when taken into his body is to that Body the flesh of Christ and the blood of Christ, to all intents as if his body and blood were the *body and blood of Christ* as far as all the effects and benefits and power which the latter have. The very fact of its being such a simple act—foolish to man, wisdom to God—shows some remarkable mystery. . . . It is my believe that Christ will save a non-communicant, but that non-communicant will never attain the subjection of his body unless through the obedience to his Lord's last wish. Consequently, as the soul and body are at variance he will never have peace. The Lord's supper is His Levée. It is there He embraces man and offers Himself to be embraced by man. . . . I have no time to write more. Only remember that I have never thought much of the Communion till lately and never saw its great import. It is the tree of Life. . . .

For the rest of his stay in England, and indeed for the rest of his life, his letters contain constant references to the Communion. " I have had many Comns, and have a good many in prospect up to Easter Monday" (13th April); " Revelling in Comns " (15th April); " The Comn is a deadly weapon against envy, malice and all uncharitableness; it is a love philtre for one's enemies " (6th May). It is noticeable that henceforth Gordon becomes more gentle; the diminished by outbursts of fierce irritation, which had already been the discovery of his last " pearl," now disappear. And more startling consequences were soon to follow.

9

On 4th January he moved to Thames Ditton, and on 10th January to London, where at first he stayed at 8 Victoria Grove, Gloucester Road. He was now planning to take up work in the East End, and went to interview a clergyman at Shoeburyness, to whom he had thoughts of attaching himself as an amateur assistant; after meeting the clergyman's wife, however, ("a fine strapping woman," he reported ruefully to Waller, " who would eat Mrs. Waller on toast ") he decided that this was no place for him. He visited Gravesend and met a number of old friends, including George Parr, formerly one of his favourite Scuttlers, the Old Bird and his pensioner Carter; (Miss Surridge had recently died.) From this expedition he returned " minus £12 10s." and conscious that he had promised a philanthropic lady that when Carter died his pension should be transferred to another beneficiary. To a Gravesend schoolmaster he wrote shortly afterwards that he had been daily " in spirit with you and others I knew there wherever I have been," but that he could not pay another visit at present; the last one had been too expensive. At this time he was writing a number of essays on religious subjects, and sending them to Augusta—not to Mrs. Freese, who had pained him by saying that a pamphlet, *Take, Eat*, which he had just composed, taught transubstantiation. The indomitable Aunt Amy was still prepared to maintain that his views were unorthodox, and she had to face another encounter with her formidable nephew which seems to have left the old lady speechless, but unconvinced: " I crushed Aunt Amy for saying we were unsound, but she may resume it. She had not a word to say."

And in addition to his theological essays and letters to *The Times* he was pouring out his usual stream of correspondence. Many of his letters dealt with public affairs, and were characterised by the piercing simplicity which exposes the heart of a complex problem. And when he found a congenial listener he would hold forth by the hour, and whether on religion or foreign politics always with the same childlike yet penetrating candour. There is a glimpse of him just now visiting Brett, the future Viscount Esher, who as secretary to Lord Hartington, the Secretary for India, had formed a lasting friendship with Gordon at the time of the Ripon imbroglio. Gordon, Brett tells us, would often come to his house in Tilney Street, " a queer figure with a loose muffler round his throat and a hat—by no means a good one—tilted back on his head; the eternal cigarette between his lips. He was of small stature—very small, like so many great men—and of spare figure. He would have passed unnoticed anywhere, except for his eyes. . . ." In the library at Tilney Street Gordon would lounge for hours at a time, leaning against the mantelpiece or walking up and down, and talking of

the Sudan, of China, of the Empire, of sea-power or our relations
with France, while his host listened, enthralled; for " his talk was as
fresh as a spring morning, full of humour and his language as simple
as the book of Genesis." His unconventional visitor, it seemed to the
younger man, " literally walked with God, and if it were not dis-
respectful, one might say arm in arm with God." And he listened
eagerly to Gordon's advice on practical affairs, whether he was
urging him to gather a small band of contemporaries about him,
shun society and spend the Parliamentary recesses in acquiring first-
hand knowledge of Europe and the Empire, or warning him not
to believe either military or civil authorities in India when they
talked about impossibilities. He had not the least doubt, he told
Gordon one day, after reading the official papers, that it was he who
had been responsible for China's keeping the peace.

      In Victoria Grove Gordon was soon complaining that he was
" so hunted " and before the end of February he took flight to 114
Beaufort Street, Chelsea. But not before he had perforce made
several incursions into high society. There was a dinner party at the
Duke of Sutherland's, which he had accepted after three refusals and
at which " nothing was discussed." And there was a small dinner
with the fabulous Baroness Burdett-Coutts among whose far-
ranging interests were several which amply justified an invitation
to Gordon, and his acceptance of it. Born in 1814, the daughter of
Sir Francis Burdett, the Radical, and heiress of Thomas Coutts, the
millionaire banker, for more than forty years she had been entertaining British and foreign celebrities and had counted among her
intimate friends Wellington, Gladstone, Disraeli, Dickens, Napoleon
III and members of the royal family. While taking an active part
in the management of her bank she had endowed bishoprics and
built schools and churches, she had long sent an annual instalment
of Irish emigrants to Canada, had introduced sewing and cookery
into the elementary schools and revived the fishing industry of
Cork. But many of her benefactions were of a nature to appeal even
more directly to Gordon. For she had subsidised the Ragged School
Union, the shoeblack brigades and training ships for poor boys; she

had instituted and supported a sewing-school for women in Spital-fields, assisted Spitalfields weavers to emigrate, founded the Flower Girls' Brigade, and set up a youth club in Shoreditch; she had been a pioneer of model tenements in Bethnal Green and of something like a garden city at Highgate, and she was a passionate supporter of the societies for the prevention of cruelty to both children and animals. And now, a few weeks ago, she had astonished the world by announcing her engagement to a young man named Ashmead-Bartlett, less than half her own age, and London was full of ill-natured gossip.

Not many days after this very dinner party there would be a wedding so sudden that invitations reached the guests while they were still in bed on the morning of the ceremony. In spite of which, and in spite of the fact that the Baroness's income was said to be £300,000 per annum, Gordon may well have felt that at the table of the philanthropic Baroness he would not be straying too far outside his own world. Moreover, the brief account of the occasion which he sent Augusta shows not merely that he enjoyed it, as he frequently enjoyed social functions when once he had brought himself to attend them, but that, like Wilberforce, he made it a practice, when in society, to seek opportunity for a word in season on serious subjects.

Just back from Burdett-Coutts. I went to Eyres[1] at 7 and went on at 8 to Coutts. Lady Keppel and daughter in room and Sir H. Keppel.[2] Then in came Baroness and Ashmead-Bartlett; a nice old thing; A. B. a young man of 28. Sorrow for their suffering in my heart. Then came Sir H. Green and wife and Duke of Sutherland[3] and Mr. Greenwood[4] of St. James's Gazette and Sir Henry[5] and Miss Parkes. Dinner 13 (as table

[1] " Governor Eyre " (1815-1901) Governor of Jamaica and hero (or villain) of the *cause celebre* as to his ruthless suppression of a native rebellion, 1865-6.
[2] Admiral of the Fleet Sir Henry Keppel, G.C.B. (1809-1904).
[3] The third duke (1828-92).
[4] Frederick Greenwood (1830-1909) founder and editor of the *Pall Mall Gazette*, which he left for the newly-founded Conservative *St. James's Gazette* in 1880.
[5] Sir Harry Parkes, diplomatist distinguished in the Far East (1828-85).

[sc. plan] enclosed). Got away at 1 a.m. . . . . I spoke what words
Christ my Saviour gave me to B. Coutts and Lady Keppel.
The Baroness took to Gordon, and he to the Baroness. We have
seen that he attached a special significance to inanimate links with
his friends, and when he left England he asked her for a memento,
something which she had habitually used. She gave him a letter-
case which had long lain on her table and it is said that he carried
it about with him to the last.

10

His future was still obscure. Florence Nightingale was urging him
to return to India, but this the government would not have permitted, nor, Gordon told her, could he bring himself to " accept
the shibboleth of the Indian or Colonial middle classes. To me they
are utterly wrong in the government of the subject races; they
know nothing of the hearts of these people." And he added
despairingly: " I consider my life's work done, that I can never . . .
seek employment where one's voice must be stilled to one particular
note—therefore, I say it is done. . . . I cannot visit the sick in London;
it is too expensive. I can do so in Syria, and where the sick are there
is our Lord. My dear Miss Nightingale, what am I to do? " But
subconsciously he was moving towards a decision.

For though there were occasional assaults by Agag, one specially
noted by Gordon as a result of a letter from the Prince of Wales'
equerry, for some while self-humiliation and withdrawal from the
world had seemed increasingly desirable. Already he had decided
never again to write to the Press. " Yesterday afternoon at 4.30
p.m.," he reported on 28th March, " Agag died very happily. He
was a nice fellow but too insidious. I promised Watson not to
write any more to any papers about *anything*; so that is over."
And it was in this mood, and on the spur of the moment, that he
made his decision. As late as 21st April he was still planning to
leave for Syria on 2nd May. But then he chanced to encounter

Colonel Sir Howard Elphinstone, V.C., at the War Office, lamenting his approaching relegation to the remote and unpopular command of the Royal Engineers in Mauritius. Without a moment's hesitation Gordon told him to dismiss his troubles: "I will go for you. Mauritius is as good for me as anywhere else." And the substitution was duly effected, Gordon's only stipulation being that he should not receive the customary payment, of about £680, for an exchange.

He left England for Mauritius early in May and on his way spent the best part of three weeks in Havre. It was at Havre that news reached him that Gessi, worn out by his privations in the swamps of the Bahr el Ghazal, had died at Aden. " Gessi! Gessi! Gessi!" he wrote. " How I warned him to leave with me! When at Toashia [Taweisha] how I said 'Whether you like it or not, or whether I like it, your life is bound up with mine.' He knew your brother to the depths. . . . Gessi is at rest, and he knew, I think, the truth, for I had often talked to him and have for years and years prayed for him." And at Havre as he meditated sadly on past and future it seemed to him that despite his voluntary exile he had not yet cut himself off sufficiently from the world. For though he could tell Augusta that, not without a struggle, he now rejoiced at " having cast off the cords, except the one with you, which bound me to England," it was borne in upon him that he should have broken with the army too. For the army " is as it were the medal, and *it must be given up.*"

It was in this mood of stern self-criticism that he wrote, on 17th May, his most revealing reference to his latest spiritual discovery, and that its full consequences began to unfold. " I go not to the Table for salvation or in fear. I go because the antidote to the poison in my flesh is there. . . . I feel you are inevitably bound to realise this great weapon for warfare agst the flesh." And now in his efforts to prepare himself worthily for the Sacrament, and in consequence also no doubt of the grace derived from it, he set himself doggedly to achieve the complete self-mastery which he had so long desired. Despite all his intermittent struggles he still smoked heavily and often drank spirits. On the following day he wrote to Augusta that " ever since the realisation of the sacrament I have been turned upside down; the process dates from the time I was at Twywell." He has been exploring his heart and " I may say that I never could have thought so many holes and corners would have been searched out as have been." He describes how he has realised the unworthiness of all the achievements, in the Sudan and China, with which he had been most content. And he goes on: " Then came the smoking and drinking in which former [sic] I enjoyed. I have to-day smitten that immense serpent, a yellow-brindled one, and for six months no spirits at all and only 15 cigarettes a day. Terrible work with that snake. However, there is the pledge for six months, with trust for strength to keep it, written down in my Diary." The pledge, as will appear, would entail an anxious struggle.

Before he left Havre he saw Sarah Bernhardt arrive from America; she was standing on the poop of her ship, wearing a tri-colour flag. " To my mind," was Gordon's odd comment, " Colley and Sarah are on a par;" General Sir George Colley had been defeated and killed at Majuba in the previous February. On 24th June Gordon reached Mauritius and, though he at once had an interesting conversation with the bishop, and lent him a copy of *Eucharistia*, he was not favourably impressed by the island. Its military standards were low (the worst he could wish his country's enemies, he told Mrs. Freese, was that theirs might be no higher), and an apprehensive first survey of its society suggested that the few congenial officers, " married and tied up to their wives," would be inaccessible, that the garden parties for archery and lawn tennis must be avoided like the plague and that there would be no one with whom to explore " the great truths." Later he would discover one exception with whom an occasional brief conversation on " deep things " was possible, and he would much enjoy an occasional country expedition with a party of younger officers, himself setting out in the battered top hat and old morning-coat of the *Vanity Fair* cartoon and organising the route, and precautions against chills, as carefully as if on active service. But in general, he led, as he had intended to lead, a solitary life on the island, and in solitude the consequences of his latest spiritual discovery continued to unfold.

II

He went regularly to Holy Communion. His conscience, he found, grew steadily more sensitive. And he stoutly maintained the struggle to mortify the flesh. From time to time he reported to Augusta on his vow to drink no spirits and to cut down his cigarettes. On 8th August he has banned sherry too, and is thinking of giving up claret. On Christmas day he wrote at length:

> Had an early Communion and took up a sacrifice, one of the children of Anak. You know 18th May I had sentence, no spirits till 18th Nov., six months. That past, I had about 10 days, then passed another sentence of 6 months but it did not do. I was always open to attack on that flank and kept on praying for strength against it. . . . So to-day I have given it up altogether and mean D.V. to take no wine at all. Next Sunday is another Comn, and if God wills I hope to offer up another victim, but am not sure what. It will be with respect to smoking. I do this because I think anything is cheap to give up if one can have more communion with God. He needs it not but indulgence is a thing which clogs the way of one's walk. . . .

On 2nd January, 1882, he mentions that all is going well with the vow, and adds: " I reason (He reasons in me) that if one's body is His temple one must not put things in it that make one carnal." Next day he reports that he has almost completely given up wine also, " a great blessing ", and on 20th January that " spirits are knocked on the head altogether to my great gain. I think they are a deadly poison to the soul," and on 6th March that he is " so glad God gave me freedom from that bondage."

All this will assume its true proportions when seen as one facet of a comprehensive determination to grow in grace, which derived from the widening of his spiritual horizon at Twywell and was his continual preoccupation throughout his residence in Mauritius. Thus long before the end of 1881 he was contemplating another, and equally arduous, sacrifice. In a long letter to Mrs. Freese on 11th November he emphasises the claims of asceticism: " Subdue the flesh and you will see Him now. I can now quite enter into the feelings of those ascetics." The cause of their own comparative spiritual poverty, he suggests, is " not feeding on the word of God." And he goes on " As long as we prefer the Paper of to-day to the Bible things are wrong with us, yet I greet the Paper with greater joy than my Bible." The English newspapers had always been a passion with Gordon when in exile; he could not restrain himself from devouring them eagerly from end to end as soon as they arrived, and now for some while he shrank from sacrificing them. But by the beginning of March he had made up his mind. " I have come to a conclusion," he wrote to Augusta; " may God give me strength to keep it! *Stop all the newspapers* and utilise the subscription, as far as it has not run out, in getting any papers you may like for Lizzie, etc." Newspapers, he explains, feed his passion for proclaiming his own opinions. His craving for politics is a disease and must be stifled.

He had been partly moved to sever this long-cherished link with the world by the wholly new conception of the Scriptures at which he arrived in Mauritius. Hitherto, he had thought of the Bible as a sacred historical book from which indeed the deepest truths might be learned, but indirectly, as it were, by the exercise of the reader's powers of reasoning. Now it had come to him that the Scriptures are still " alive," *oratio recta* not *oratio obliqua*, the direct voice of God. He wrote a paper, *Oracles*, on the theme that all through the ages, like the ancient Greeks and Romans, men had believed it possible to question God, and to receive answers. He argued, with numerous references to the Old Testament, that, like the ancient Greeks and Romans, the ancient Hebrews had preserved a sacred place in which, through their high priest, they could seek oracles from on high. Surely God must be as ready to give instruction and guidance to-day? His voice, he concludes, is incarnate in the Scriptures; here (in the words of the Coronation service) are the lively oracles of to-day. To the casual the Bible is but a book, to the spiritual " it is alive and makes alive." And on 24th November he thus describes what now became his constant practice:

> My belief is that whenever we are in doubt about anything, we should place the matter before God in prayer, then take the Bible wherever we may be reading, and having our attention fixed on the subject of our prayer seek to get the answer, and take it in just the same way as if we heard God's voice.

12

His solitary life allowed scope for spiritual growth, but it also allowed time for other diversions, and naturally, being Gordon, he evolved some bizarre theories. On a visit to the Seychelles he encountered the Coco de Mer, the giant nut which takes seven years to ripen on a palm which needs a century to mature and is to be found nowhere else in the world. Sir Compton Mackenzie has said[1] of the ravine in which the mighty palms are most plentiful " I cannot hope to evoke the mystery of that ravine. . . . I never had such a conviction of man's immortal destiny." And Gordon convinced himself that the Coco de Mer was the forbidden fruit of the Garden of Eden. He also argued elaborately, drafting plans and maps and calculating water-levels, that Eden itself must lie close at hand, beneath the Indian Ocean. He sent Augusta an account of the successive stages of this twin revelation, an astonishing medley of coincidence, chance association and irrational deduction. A good deal more unexpectedly, through Colonel Donnelly, he sent repeated messages on the subject to the great T. H. Huxley. Whatever Huxley, who was to become President of the Royal Society next

[1] *The Listener*, March 2, 1950.

year, may have thought of Gordon's theories, there can be no doubt that, like almost everyone who encountered him, he admired Gordon. They had met and talked several times at Colonel Donnelly's and from Mauritius Gordon wrote: "I enjoyed Huxley's conversation very much. I wish he could believe with me that we leave this petty earth for spheres of immense power and intelligence." And after Gordon's death Huxley sent a message of sympathy to Donnelly. "Poor fellow!" he wrote:

> I wonder if he has entered upon the "larger sphere of action" which he told me was reserved for him in case of such a trifling accident as death. Of all the people whom I have met with in my life, he and Darwin are the two in whom I have found something bigger than ordinary humanity—an unrivalled simplicity and directness of purpose—a sublime unselfishness.

There was time too, to ponder over more practical topics, and particularly over sea-power and the Empire, a subject which had long fascinated him. For Brett and others he wrote papers criticising recent developments in Egypt, advocating coaling stations in the Indian Ocean and urging the superiority of the Cape to the Suez Canal as a route to the East. Moreover, his penetrating eye had soon perceived that a garrison of four hundred in Mauritius could not hope to defend an island five times the size of the Isle of Wight, and that, as at Gravesend, his military duties were wholly irrational. It would be much more sensible, he told Brett, to equip the forts adequately and hold them with a garrison of two hundred. He wrote memoranda on the Mauritius forts which were doubtless received in Whitehall with the same indifference as had been his complaints of the Gravesend defences. "Sometimes," he told Augusta, "ambition makes me think 'What a waste of time to be out here!'; but it soon ceases to disturb me, and I am glad I have no anchors." He preached occasionally, too, to the Chinese coolies on the in-dwelling of God. And there were still pensioners and dependents to be remembered. From Mauritius he paid the debts of his nephew Herbert in Havre, sending £90 for this purpose and corresponding at length with Mr. Mason, an Englishman in business there, who was to disburse another £40 and see that Herbert received £2 a week for a year from Gordon " to avoid his giving any more trouble to my brothers and sisters." And all this while, needless to say, he attended meticulously to his military duties, drawing up lengthy reports on the inadequate forts and ruthlessly disturbing the traditional inertia of the garrison. When he left, the colonel who temporarily succeeded him wrote to Augusta that he had lost " the most thorough officer I have ever served under, and a most kind friend."

13

In the spring of 1882 Gordon was promoted Major General and informed that he was to be relieved on 6th April. On the second of April he received an urgent invitation from the Government of Cape Colony. While he was at Lausanne in the spring of 1880 he had been offered, and had declined, the command of the Colonial forces at the Cape at a salary of £1,500 a year, and a year later on 7th April, 1881, while still hesitating as to his future, he had sent a private wire to Cape Town, offering his services " for two years at £700 per annum to assist in terminating war and administrating Basutoland." To this telegram the authorities in Cape Town had vouchsafed no reply. Since then, however, a desultory war with the Basutos, which had commenced in 1880, had dragged on for another year and it seems to have occurred to them that the former commander of the Ever Victorious was the man to bring it to an end. They had accordingly obtained permission from the Colonial Secretary to invite Gordon to renew his offer, and now urged him to come at once. It almost seemed that wherever white governments were in trouble with native peoples they would send for Gordon. Two days after receiving the invitation he embarked for the Cape on a sailing vessel of 300 tons. He supposed that he had been sent for, not as Chinese Gordon to conquer the Basutos, but as the ruler of the Sudan to pacify them, for he detested war and knew that he possessed what some described as a mesmeric power over primitive peoples and he himself called the faculty of getting into their skins.

He was not disillusioned at once. He reached Cape Town after a month's agonising sea-sickness on 3rd May, and on 13th May he could still tell Mr. Waller that he found the government very considerate towards the Basutos, and that he hoped " by God's active help to obtain Balm and heal their stripes." Even, however, if Mr. Merriman's government, which had invited him, had been thinking in terms of balm for the Basutos, which is doubtful, the government of Mr. Scanlen, which succeeded it, was less inclined to heal stripes than to inflict them. Moreover, Gordon astonished and perplexed official Cape Town from the outset. Dinner with the Governor on the day after he landed had been a chapter of minor accidents. Perhaps they were due to Gordon's customary discomfort in society, perhaps to the jaundice which threatened him, but, as he ruefully reported to Augusta, " I dined with Sir Hercules Robinson, trod on Lady Robinson's train going into dinner, called her *Lady Barker* on going away—a person she hates—and spoke evil of several people in Hong Kong and elsewhere who had been kind to me." Then his insistence on accepting no more than £880 of the modest salary of £1,200 offered him had made headlines in the Cape Town Press. And already there were disquieting signs that the sympathies of the unpredictable visitor were with the natives. He had sought out Cetewayo, the Zulu King who had been sent to Cape Town after his defeat at Ulundi in 1880, had told him that he had prayed for him regularly since the battle of Isandhlwana and presented him with an ivory-headed stick. A few days later, and still little more than three weeks after his landing, he had drawn up a memorandum setting forth the numerous breaches of its treaty obligations to the Basuto of which the home government had been guilty and pro- posing that a Basuto assembly should immediately be summoned, and permitted, without supervision, or interference by British officials, to voice the grievances of the people. Mr. Scanlen was horrified. He passed the memorandum to the Colonial Secretary, Lord Kimberley, who promptly replied that it was none of his business, whereupon Mr. Scanlen decided that it should be none of his either.

Since Gordon had also accepted the post of Commandant General much of his five and a half months in South Africa was spent in drawing up proposals for the reorganisation of the troops as well as for the pacification of the Basuto. He enjoyed the attempt to cut through the military red tape, for, as he told Colonel Donnelly, " I do hate in my soul our complicated system with which we are so complacently satisfied." All these documents were full of penetrating common sense; indeed, his final memorandum on the Basuto[1] became in due course the basis of the eventual reconstruction of their country; but all were ignored, for the time being and to the utmost of their ability, by Mr. Scanlen and his colleagues. Their predecessors, not they, had brought this crusading genius to Africa, and, in any event, they could only mistrust a general who, besides proposing to do away with circumlocution and formality in the army, openly declared that he would not fight the Basuto, and seemed more interested in their grievances than their misdoings.

As for Gordon, he was tirelessly active and not unhappy. Despite every distraction he still wrote occasional theological disquisitions, and attended Holy Communion whenever possible. And he believed that he was making slow but perceptible spiritual progress. " I solemnly believe," he wrote to Mrs. Freese,

that constant Communions do give great strength, for when I am in the voyages I am cut off from them and am as carnal as ever I was. My place is one . . . of ill-natured criticism of others, evil-speaking, back-biting which to me seems mean and despicable. Yet with all this God gives me to feel the actual personality of Our Lord even as I would that of any other man. Of God's friendship I am assured. He gives me the faculty of being in His presence in Christ without effort, without much

[1] Cape Government Papers G 6-83, page 10.

thinking or exertion. Why then am I not better? Constant inward prayer, not once an hour but always, constant sense of His in-dwelling in whatever one does is what I need. Yet I can say truly certainly not a couple of hours pass without my addressing Him and truly I may say I do desire to leave this world, also that I am willing *all* should be higher than me.

He had taken warmly to Colonel Ffolliott, the secretary to whom he had compelled the government to allot a third of his own salary. There were long conversations on Gordon's various " pearls ", and soon he could report that his secretary " receives the truth," though, as was not surprising, he had not yet " reached the point of looking on death as life." It was one facet of Gordon's heroism that he had long since shaken off the inhibitions which had once made it as painful to him as to most men to speak naturally and openly of his religion, so that informal, and almost unconscious, evangelism was now habitual with him. But with Ffolliott there had naturally been inhibitions, military as well as psychological, to overcome: " Ffolliott used to call me ' Sir,' " wrote Gordon. " I said 1/- fine each time. He soon ran up a bill of 15/-, but now having lost his respect I never can get a ' Sir ' out of him."

Now that he was in Africa Gordon recalled that Dutch was one of the languages into which the leaflets which he had composed at Gravesend with Mrs. Freese had been translated, and he asked Augusta to send him out a consignment. They arrived as he was about to go north to the Free State, and he wrote on 12th August that " as in the auld time long ago I shall be dropping them near the Boer farms and along roads. What hundreds I did give away; how I used to run miles, if I saw a Scuttler watching crows in a field! . . . Send me the whole lot out unless you want them; I mean of all languages; it is the loveliest leaflet I ever saw, and it looks fresh now."

But a sinister climax to the Cape Government's growing disapproval of his unconventional methods and undisguised sympathy for the natives was at hand. By arrangement with the

Secretary for Native Affairs, a Mr. Sauer, he went to visit Masupha, a recalcitrant Basuto chieftain. Sauer knew, for Gordon had told him, that if he visited Masupha he could not afterwards take part in hostilities against him; yet while Gordon, alone save for three companions, was a guest, at the mercy of the formidable and suspicious chief, Sauer deliberately induced another Basuto chieftain to attack the camp. The enraged Masupha at once suspected treachery and Gordon would have been butchered forthwith had it not been for his obvious indignation at the news of the attack and the awe which Masupha had already conceived for him. Once again, as when he faced Suleiman's slave-hunters alone or emerged unscathed from among the Taiping rebels on the day of the murder of the Wangs in Soochow, he owed his safety to what F. S. Oliver has called that "strange, mesmeric influence, quite inexplicable in scientific terms" which he exercised over primitive peoples.[1] Despite his enemies in high places Gordon had hoped much from his lonely interview in the Basuto camp and had even offered to remain for two years as a magistrate in Masupha's territory, but the treachery of Sauer had effectually prevented him from coming to terms, and he at once decided to resign. In the course of his farewell to the Cape Government he wrote:

> I state, therefore, that it is to me impossible to act against natives who I believe are being treated unjustly by the defective Government of the Transkei. The Secretary for Native Affairs has admitted certain of these abuses, but it needs more than that admission to satisfy my conscience.

14

There had been another aspect of Gordon's visit to Basutoland,

[1] Attempts have been made by South African writers to explain away the apparently treacherous conduct of Sauer. See especially Tylden, *The Rise of the Basuto* (Cape Town, 1950), page 180 and the Cape Government publication G, 6-83 (1883), page 31. I do not doubt, however, that the account given above is substantially correct in view of Gordon's own comments quoted in Boulger, *Life of Gordon*, 248, 9.

even more memorable than his narrow escape from death. For there he chanced to meet Cecil Rhodes, who was serving as a member of a Commission on the claims for compensation by loyal Basutos. Characteristic, indeed, of the British Empire was this chance encounter in so remote and barbarous a region between these two strangely contrasting personalities, each in his own highly individual fashion the epitome of forces deep-seated in the England of the Victorian age. The man who, though only twenty-nine, had already founded the De Beers Mining Company, and dreamed of the world supremacy of the Anglo-Saxons, moved no doubt in a world remote from Gordon's, and yet the two had traits and sympathies in common. For Rhodes like Gordon was an altruist, and though he spent himself on seeking wealth he did not seek it for himself; like Gordon he was a lonely man, absorbed in his own gigantic dreams, and like Gordon he was in some ways as simple as a child. He possessed too a shrewdness, piercing like Gordon's yet vastly more practical since it was not perpetually in conflict with a theocentric impulse. The two talked long together, and each conceived for the other a fascinated respect which he never forgot. It was Rhodes, twenty years the younger, who warned Gordon not to speak to the Basutos as if he were their overlord, and Gordon, with all his memories of the dictatorship of the Sudan, who next day meekly told Rhodes that he had taken his advice, adding " I did it because it was the right thing, but it was hard, very hard." It was Rhodes, too, who, venturing on to more questionable ground, assured Gordon that he had been foolish to refuse the Chinese Emperor's proffer of wealth, since without wealth no great achievement was possible. And when they parted Gordon begged Rhodes to stay and work with him in Basutoland; " I never met a man so strong for his own opinion," he said; " you think your wishes are always right." And no doubt in those solitary unrecorded interchanges Rhodes had unburdened himself of his crude boyish religion, as well as his visions of far practical horizons.

But Gordon, too, was " strong for his own opinion," and in the realm of the spirit he was a master where Rhodes was a tiro.

And though Rhodes, who had already entered Cape politics, could not accept Gordon's offer, it is clear that he never forgot their conversation, which must have recalled to him his boyhood in the vicarage at Bishop's Stortford, and the days when he himself had thought of becoming a parson. One more invitation from Gordon was to reach him—a telegram on the eve of the last journey to Khartoum, and this, too, he was compelled to refuse. But when news reached him of the final tragedy he repeated over and over again " I am sorry I was not with him! I am sorry I was not with him! "

Moreover, among the voluminous unpublished notes compiled for the Rhodes Trust by Mr. E. A. Maund, a member of Rhodes's entourage, there is an illuminating account of a conversation shortly after the fall of Khartoum. Rhodes was much moved on hearing that Maund, who had lived near Augusta in Southampton, knew Gordon well. " Oh! you knew Chinese Gordon? " he said. " He had a wonderful power with natives. . . . You knew him! " " It is curious," he continued, in words which recall Gordon's own comment on the speaker's obstinate convictions, " but somehow he exercised a strange influence on me. He united spiritual ideas or sentiment with tremendous activity, and had such a belief in his own way of doing things as to amount to obstinacy. He was a ready listener but self-willed to a degree. We got on, however, capitally together, for we both believed in moral suasion rather than force in dealing with native chiefs." And he went on in a pensive monologue, as if talking to himself, to recall the two invitations which he had been compelled to refuse, and to expatiate on Gordon as a man of both theory and action. It became evident that he knew a great deal about his doings in the Sudan and on the Nile and, moreover, that he had been at once puzzled and fascinated by the spectacle of a man capable, like himself, of ruthless and heroic action yet, unlike himself, contemptuous of wealth and dominated by profound religious conviction. He plied Maund with questions. Was Gordon a fanatic, a fatalist? Maund recounted what he knew of Gordon's independence of churches and creeds and said that he prayed five times a day, facing Jerusalem. He recounted, too, he recalls, " how Gordon in his cheery, waggish way would sometimes greet me . . . with a slap on the shoulder and ' Well, how is the Tabby? ' " and asked if he had ever so greeted Rhodes. " No," said Rhodes, laughing, " what did he mean? " Maund explained the reference to the tabernacle and to Gordon's theories as to the indwelling of God. Rhodes did not smile. " Extraordinary man " he muttered to himself. " And yet so practical. I should think he alone understood himself . . . a fanatical enigma."

And then, his speculation still playing on Gordon's faith, and his own abandonment of his early beliefs under the impact of Winwood Reade, Darwin and Gibbon, he observed that he supposed Gordon must have known something of modern science— of Newton, the limitless universe, the solar spectrum? Yes, Maund assured him, Gordon had often talked of science, and was convinced that modern discoveries " in no way contradicted religions but only confounded priestcraft." And the strange duologue ended with Maund venturing " You must remember Gordon was a soldier-saint, and you will acknowledge you are not quite soldier or saint." But frequently during the next ten years, when he chanced to be alone with Maund, Rhodes would revert to the subject in terms which made it plain that he was still pondering on Gordon against the background of the vicarage at Bishop's Stortford.

15

Gordon sailed for England on 14th October. After paying for his passage he was once more virtually penniless, for he had been unaware that under a new regulation, published while he was in Mauritius, his British army pay would be discontinued while he was in South Africa. Nor had he any clear notion as to his future. His life, as he frequently remarked, was ended, yet he must do something. Sir William Mackinnon had been writing, and telegraphing, to him at intervals since July to urge him to assume command in the Congo for King Leopold—with numerous assurances that His Majesty's only object was to do good and that God's blessing would undoubtedly rest upon the enterprise. But for the moment relief at being " free of all this turmoil " was Gordon's principal emotion. " There will be another fearful row " he had told Augusta shortly before he left. " These things have not moved me at all. I thought more of a Scuttler who shed tears when I spoke to him of God's living in him than I have of all this affair. We are a pig-headed race, the Gordons. . . . The Cape Govt are conies. . . . What a queer life mine has been, with these fearful rows continually occurring! They will amuse you, I hope." He still felt that he was called to a contemplative life rather than to further action. There had been moments in South Africa when he regretted having stopped his supply of newspapers, and during June he was reading *Public Opinion* and *The Weekly Times*, but by now he was out of touch even with the course of events in Egypt. All that he could say was that God would decide whether he should go to the Congo, and that if he did not he would seek solitude in the Holy Land. And from his ship, the *Kinfauns Castle*, he wrote to ask Augusta in which of the Southampton churches the Communion was most regularly celebrated.

He remained in England only from 7th November to 28th December, and most of this time he spent at Southampton with Augusta, who was unwell. Sir William Mackinnon continued to press the East African venture on him, but, apart from his increasing desire to escape into solitude, there was an apparently insurmountable political obstacle to service under King Leopold. For a number of expeditions of various nationalities were already in East Africa, and Gordon, who foresaw the inevitable conflicts which must ensue, had for some while insisted that Leopold must obtain permission to use an international flag. Leopold had no desire for an international flag, but a great desire for Gordon, and he now suggested that if only he would enter his service they would "examine the question together" and would no doubt in time solve it. More truthfully he went on to explain that although at the moment there was no mission for Gordon, he desired " to take you from this moment as my counsellor. You can name your own terms." And, reverting to the disingenuous, he concluded with the assertion that " the cause which I hope to make succeed in Africa is that for which you have already done so much." Gordon was undoubtedly relieved that the international flag stood between him and the King of the Belgians. The scroll had not unrolled. He would go to Jerusalem.

Meanwhile, for a few weeks he remained at Rockstone Place, carrying on his usual prodigious correspondence. One of his letters went to Capsune, the small negro boy whom he had rescued from the slavers and who was now with a Miss Felkin, in England. " Ever since you met me . . ." he wrote, " every day have I prayed for you —in Abyssinia, India, China, Mauritius and Cape; always every day I have remembered that poor little chap who stood under trees and told me of the slave traders. This is the look of the place [he added a sketch]. God brought us together never to be separate. My dear little fellow, pray for me and you will give me more than all the millions of the earth."

BOOK NINE

WITHDRAWAL

ON 16TH JANUARY, 1883, Gordon reached Jaffa and on the 17th he was at Jerusalem. He was to spend almost the whole of this year in Palestine. He had long dreamed of withdrawal from the world. For some while now he had been coming to think " quiet " necessary to the development of his true self, and had spoken of it with increasing wistfulness, often referring ruefully to the ambition, " back-biting " and other failings to which, save in his too rare moments of peace, he was prone to give way. Alone in the Holy Land, without responsibilities, forgetting the world, surely he would find quiet, and with it the steady growth in grace of which he had glimpsed the possibility when his visit to the Wallers at Twywell two years ago had opened new spiritual horizons. So he hoped; but as one studies the voluminous and often eccentric speculations which he poured out during his self-imposed exile it is impossible to resist the conclusion that he did not find peace, not, at any rate, the peace which he sought, and that he did not find it because he was not yet fitted for it. Nor was it merely that this deliberate withdrawal proved to be but a brief interlude, itself prologue to the final tragedy in which the man who had savagely repressed his passion for politics, and dreamed of taking refuge from the world, would return to become the plaything of politicians and the central figure on a brightly lit stage watched breathlessly by all mankind. Of death itself he had long thought as a mere transference to larger spheres of action, and now Palestine, though it could not bring him wider responsibilities, proved but a field for activities of a novel kind but almost as engrossing as those which he had abandoned. Many of the qualities of the mystic Gordon possessed, but the injunction to " be still " was more than he could obey.

Usually, it is true, his gaze was steadily averted from the world which he almost believed himself to have finally renounced, and in particular from the Sudan, over which the storm clouds were now swiftly darkening. Only occasionally did some chance encounter provide evidence that his interest in world affairs was imperfectly anaesthetised. We have an account from two sources of an un-expected visit which he paid to Lawrence Oliphant, who was then living at Haifa, at the foot of Mount Carmel. The French, rendered doubly suspicious by the recent British occupation of Egypt, had not been able to believe that Gordon's interest in Biblical sites was not a cloak for more sinister activities, instigated by the British secret service. He was constantly shadowed, and on one occasion, in order to exhaust his follower, pressed on so far from Jerusalem that he spent the night at Nablous and pushed on next day to Haifa. To Oliphant he held forth at length on Egypt, and Valentine Chirol, who chanced to be staying with Oliphant, records an after-dinner conversation which Gordon began by declaring that the only hope for China was to clear out every foreigner, and ended with the equally categorical assertion that only a foreign occupation could save it. After Gordon had left the room Oliphant remarked that this was a man after his own heart " for he is not afraid of con-tradicting himself and whatever he says always rings true." But despite these excursions into politics what struck Oliphant most was the other-worldliness of his guest, his humility and his " underlying meekness." He noted his prayer-lists, and how, after using strong language about " a very high personage," he added hurriedly, " I pray for him regularly." " The most Christ-like man I ever knew " was his eventual verdict.

Gordon had found a house three miles from Jerusalem at Ain Karim, surrounded by barren hills and " solitary enough." Before long he was writing to Mr. Waller " You must find me something to do." But the request was superfluous. He had already launched himself on pursuits capable of keeping him busy for much longer than the year he would spend in Palestine. He was alone and unemployed, he was in the Holy Land and he had his Bible. The consequence might have been foreseen. He plunged into an intricate series of investigations and speculations, in which topography, Old Testament history, Biblical exegesis and theology were inextricably intermingled. His writings during these twelve months, if collected, would fill several stout tomes. One slender volume, *Reflections in Palestine*, would be published during the siege of Khartoum, when the world was greedy for any ray of light on Gordon; it must have mystified his admirers not a little. With Augusta, and with his brother Henry, he maintained a prodigious correspondence, excerpts from which have been printed. Nor were these by any means the only correspondents to whom he communicated his conclusions. To Mr. Barnes alone he wrote forty-seven letters from Palestine; most of them were lengthy and one contained seven thousand words. "I deluge a poor old German, Mr. Schick, with these papers and plans," he wrote to Mr. Barnes; Dr. Schick was an architect, and an authority on Biblical archaeology, who was working in Jerusalem; three hundred pages of Gordon's correspondence with him are still extant.

2

At first his energies seemed likely to be focused upon topographical problems. Where was the true site of the Crucifixion, of the Garden of Eden, of the various Gibeons mentioned in the Bible? What was the authentic boundary between Benjamin and Juda? All this required not only many journeys about the environs of Jerusalem, but continual searches in Bible and Concordance, together with much of what may perhaps be called the inspired guesswork which had played a considerable part in the growth of his personal theology. Seldom can an investigator have been further removed, by temperament and training, from the world, and

methods, of scholarship. The miniature library which he had
brought out with him was soon discarded; he would trust entirely,
he decided, to Bible and Concordance; "it is much more satisfactory to be given God's truths than to find them out with great
labour from books." And even the Bible, he was convinced, was
mainly allegorical, in the sense that it contained an inner meaning
so that the actual text was often but "a sheath or vehicle for the
incorruptible word." And this inner meaning he sometimes seemed
to grasp without being able to explain, even to himself, the grounds
for his conclusions: "one sees it instinctively," he said, "but not
with power of expression." Naturally, therefore, Gordon's processes
of reasoning are frequently as obscure as when, in Mauritius, he was
identifying the Coco de Mer with the forbidden fruit.

> I am working this out (but cannot yet see it), that our life is the
> Bible history, and that Our Lord's life was the same. If it is
> good for me it may become clear, for I feel sure it is so. It
> would be nice if we could see where we are and get warned for
> our future guidance; say one was at Jacob, then one would be
> prepared for Egypt and brick-making.

The Holy Spirit, he believed, would guard him from over-fanciful
interpretations of Scripture.

He was a skilled map-maker, and topography had always
fascinated him. But the topography of the Holy Land was doubly
fascinating, for at every turn he found himself confirming Old
Testament prophecies or disposing of the long-established theories
of Biblical commentators. There are plenty of passages in his letters
which irresistibly remind one of all those middle-aged officers of
the Royal Engineers who during the world wars devoted their spare
time to foretelling the date of the armistice or the fall of Jerusalem
by calculations based upon the Book of Daniel or the number of
the Beast.

A, B, C, D is a raised platform; now between g and f is only thirty yards, so, if the Temple was to the west of the rock (as it must be, if the rock is the altar of burnt offering), the Holy of Holies must be now *trodden on*, as prophesied in Daniel viii, 13, by people walking between *h* and *g*.

But with Gordon topography, like everything else, was bound to merge insensibly into theology. The contour of a mountain, the contiguity of two sites at once present a spiritual significance. The more sacred of the two hills on which Jerusalem is built suggests the shape of a victim laid upon an altar; it is a hieroglyphic, Gordon concludes, of Christ and His Church. The valley of Tophet, so near to the Dead Sea, is surely " a type of the world, close to Gehenna."

And it was largely out of such shadowy indications and analogies that he now constructed his theological and historical theories, and not least the strange cosmogony, in the course of which he recounted in detail how earth was once encased in a vast cocoon of waters, in which the devil with his hosts sought refuge after his fall; how creation was thus " an invasion of Satan's Kingdom, the calling up of a dead world out of the grave of waters;" how earth is enclosed in a hollow globe, the firmament, on which rests the throne of God, immediately above its counterpart, the altar of burnt offering in the temple of the earthly Jerusalem, which was the shadow of God's dwelling-place; how man, created to drive Satan out of the kingdom he had usurped, was moulded out of the clay of the Potter's Field, close to the Rock (or Golgotha), and placed in a garden eastward of the Rock (and precisely localised by Gordon); how the devil emerged from his watery hemisphere, persuaded man to eat of the forbidden fruit, and regained a foothold in his lost dominion; how consequently every man born thereafter has carried the devil's taint in his body; how the flood thus became a necessity and earth was again a waste, the devil's waters, and Satan himself had his seat upon the Rock, now once more submerged; how when the waters subsided and Noah emerged from the Ark his first sacrifice was offered on the Rock. on which Abraham also would sacrifice Isaac and our

Lord would be crucified; how the perpetual battle between man
and the devil must end at last with the devil ignominiously imprisoned in the hollow centre of the globe which he has sought to
rule, and the waters, his peculiar dominion, will disappear into the
ground, by way of what is now the Dead Sea; and how at last the
spiritual city will descend to earth upon the exact spot where
Jerusalem now stands.

Such is a bald and fragmentary outline of one of Gordon's
excursions into the remotest past and future. It is not surprising
that during the siege of Khartoum, W. H. Mallock should have
concluded a painstaking study of it in the *Fortnightly Review* with
a comment on the strangeness of the reflection that such were the
views of a man upon whose fate now depended the destiny of nations
and the future of English politics. Yet they are entirely characteristic
of its author, and not least in their combination of extravagant fancy
with prosaic detail. Thus when the voice of God first fell on earth
at the creation, Gordon tells us, the devil fled to that point of the
hemisphere of darkness farthest from the throne of God, which he
particularises as " over lat. 31° 47′ S long. 144° 45′ W, close to
Bass Isle, south of Otaheite, not far from Pitcairn's Isle, where the
mutineers of the *Bounty* settled." And he adds, as corroborative
evidence, that if a line were passed through Jerusalem and the centre
of the globe " this axis would present the northern hemisphere as
nearly all land while the southern hemisphere would be nearly all
water. . . In Revelations and Daniel the beasts (evil powers) came
out of the sea." Extravagant fancy and prosaic detail, certainly; yet
at times extravagant fancy rises into the realm of poetic imagination,
and the simple staccato language of his normal correspondence takes
on a novel dignity and rhythm, full of echoes of Biblical prose.

Oh! thou afflicted and torn by the tempest, great shall be thy
peace. Thy holy ones will not see corruption. They leave a
land in which they are strangers and sojourners and have no
abiding cities but live in frail tents (in the day the drought pursues
them, and by night the frost), for a city in which there are many

mansions, eternal in the heavens. A crown of glory are they, and a royal diadem in the hand of their King. Before ever a star was made, He loved them with an everlasting love, a love knowing no ending and having no beginning.

3

Naturally, as rumours of how Gordon was spending his time in the Holy Land began to reach London, there was much shrugging of shoulders in Whitehall. No further confirmation surely was needed of what authority already knew; there might be an odd streak of genius in the man, but all too clearly he was not quite sane. And yet, as always when Gordon was apparently at his most eccentric, a solid foundation of common sense underlay even his most exuberant unorthodoxies. By the beginning of July he had moved from Ain Karim to Jaffa, largely because, now that he had satisfactorily settled the sites of Golgotha, Tophet and Zion, there was little more to do at Jerusalem; moreover, at Haifa he had met a missionary who had promised to find him work at his mission in Jaffa and who, though the two naturally soon differed on theology, subsequently said that he learned more of the life of the spirit fom Gordon than from any man he ever met. And although most of his acquaintances on hearing of his speculations naturally dismissed them as but another of his amiable eccentricities, the most important of them have in fact been taken very seriously by many learned persons, have provoked a voluminous literature and even led to the foundation of a society enthusiastically supported by scholars, artists, men of affairs and dignitaries of the Church.

Gordon was not quite the first to maintain that the Skull Hill, a cliff just outside the city wall of Jerusalem and bearing a remarkable resemblance to a human skull, was the true site of the crucifixion; at least four writers before Gordon, among them Renan in his *Vie de Jésus*, had championed the theory. But it was the knowledge that it had been endorsed by Gordon which first gained it wide accept-

ance in Britain and North America, and since his day an impressive
sequence of scientific and literary authorities[1] has accepted what is
now commonly known as "Gordon's Calvary." Moreover,
Gordon was the first to assert that an ancient tomb in a garden
adjacent to the Skull Hill was in all probability the veritable sepulchre
in which Our Lord was laid after the crucifixion. It was a spot to
which, while in Jerusalem, he had frequently resorted for prayer
and meditation. This contention, too, has provoked a considerable
literature, including a sceptical report to the Palestine Exploration
Fund by the learned Dr. Schick himself. No such striking consensus
of experts endorsed "Gordon's Tomb" as had accepted "Gordon's
Calvary." In a sense, however, his thesis as to the Tomb produced
even more remarkable results. For in 1893 the Tomb, with the
enclosure in which it lies, was purchased by public subscription,
with the active support of Benson, then Archbishop of Canterbury,
Randall Davidson, Bishop of Rochester, who would in due course
succeed him, and numerous other bishops, as well as scholars, writers
and notabilities in impressive variety. And to this day the Garden
Tomb Association continues to ensure that Gordon's Tomb shall
be "kept sacred as a quiet spot, and preserved on the one hand
from desecration and on the other hand from superstitious uses."
It had been yet another battle with tradition and Gordon had by
no means had the worst of it. It is probable that the renown of
Gordon's Calvary and Gordon's Tomb, could he have foreseen it,
would have pleased him better than the renown of Khartoum.

4

With the spiritual results of his exile, however, he was increasingly
dissatisfied. "I am trying the experiment of giving up all hindrances
to a holy life," he told Augusta, "and though rid of those hindrances
(which were pleasures to me) I am yet empty of any increase of

---

[1] It includes Sir J. W. Dawson, Director of the Canadian Geological Survey, Professor
Hull, F.R.S., Sir Henry Rider Haggard, the novelist, and Lawrence Oliphant.

spiritual joy." But perhaps he had hoped for too much. He had striven to give up the world and to mortify the flesh, and these sacrifices had doubtless brought a growth in grace, of which indeed his own dissatisfaction with his spiritual condition was itself evidence. Yet, often though he quoted it, he had not contrived to obey the injunction " Be still; let go." Do what he would, he still yearned for activity. It must not, he told himself, be public activity—he sternly repressed the itch to send Lord Dufferin his " ideas on Egypt "—but to activity of some sort he must soon return. " You know I do not like idleness; I want to get to a place where I can find sick people to visit, feeling sure that is the necessary work for me; I think He will direct me, so I seek no advice elsewhere."

Nevertheless, a spiritual balance sheet of his Palestine exile, if it could be struck, would contain some significant entries on the credit side. For one thing, there is evidence that he was abandoning his central heresies. Hitherto he had persisted stoutly in his belief that every human action is predetermined and that every human soul, whatever its earthly record, is destined for eternal bliss, and the protests of the orthodox had left him entirely unmoved. But on 9th October he writes to Mr. Barnes: " I had the heresy of no free will and no eternal punishment. I have come back to the fold and wish I had never said or written a word against either." And on 29th September: " I will now say I do not venture to enter on the question of universal salvation, and I am sorry I ever transgressed in giving an opinion." There is a humility about these recantations which had been somewhat conspicuously lacking in Gordon's private theology hitherto, and is even more striking than the recantations themselves. It is tantalising that this long, and un-expected, step towards orthodoxy should have come just as our information as to his theological speculations is about to dry up; but perhaps it is more important that in his personal creed, in which he had in truth always been self-assertive, he was now becoming self-distrustful, for the change is a familiar and unmistakable symptom of that spiritual growth whose absence he was so ready to lament.

He was growing more sensitive too; or rather, for he had always been sensitive, the range of his sensibility was extending. He recorded that spring how he came to resolve never to shoot again. His servant had brought him a hen partridge, captured on its nest, " such beautiful bright eyes and red bill;" the bird's wings were tied, and as Gordon took it to cut the string it fluttered and died. " I felt it very much, and do still, though I am accustomed to death and think it no loss. However, that day the gun was doomed." It seems likely that, disappointed though he undoubtedly was with the spiritual fruits of exile, he was nevertheless obscurely aware that there had been a pregnant change. And it was perhaps in some such moment of recognition that he sent Mr. Barnes from Jaffa the most revealing of his brief spiritual autobiographies:

I wished I was a eunuch at 14. I went to Crimea, hoping without having a hand in it to be killed. I survived and lived, but not wishing to be too closely acquainted with God, nor yet to leave Him. I used to pray as my men went up the breaches in China for their success; thank Him if they succeeded; never wanted to know Him any closer. Swung as a pendulum in wide sweeps. Came home from China, saw my father die. Saw if Jesus did really die He must have died for some greater result than that seen in the Christian world. Went to every sect, found no good. Slaved at prayer; up in November at 4 a.m.; and one night at Ranger's House something broke in my heart, a palpable feeling, and I knew God lived in me—which I have never lost.

5

It was not, strictly speaking, an idle life. Normally, " having plenty of time," he rose at seven, read and prayed till eleven or twelve, worked at his Biblical researches till four, rode along the sandy shore, walking his horse on the return journey, and read and wrote again until ten or eleven. And his Bible studies were occasionally

diversified with attempts to learn the elements of astronomy, and
with the preparation of an elaborate project for the digging of a canal
from Haifa to the head of the Gulf of Akabah on the Red Sea. On
at least one occasion he invited all the British and American residents
of Jaffa to his hotel for Bible-reading and prayer. And it is recorded
that, hearing from a Mr. Friedlander of the arrival of some destitute
Jewish immigrants, he hurried back to his room, unpacked his
portmanteau, and hastening back to Mr. Friedlander's drawing-
room, deposited a large bundle of clothes and a sum of money on
the table. His correspondence, too, as always, was prodigious. And
by no means all of it dealt with Biblical archaeology. He still distributed characteristic *obiter dicta* among his friends. To Donnelly,
whom three years before he had actually urged to marry, he wrote
from Jaffa: " I like all men, even *cats*. Women are fearful, yet most
valuable. I dare say they think us ditto. I fear susceptibilities or
I would say more."

But though it was hardly an idle life it was too idle to last.
Mackinnon had begun to press on him renewed proposals from
King Leopold, who was now anxious that he should accept a salary
forthwith, as a kind of retaining fee. Gordon declined the retaining
fee, but when, on 15th October, he received a telegram from
Mackinnon claiming him for the Congo, he telegraphed to the War
Office for permission to accept. On the 24th the War Office
dispatched its reply, " The Secretary of State has declined to sanction
your employment on the Congo." But the adverse fate, which so
constantly brooded over the War Office's dealings with Gordon,
decreed that some Levantine clerk should transmit its telegram in
a variant form, " Secretary of State decides to sangdon your
employment on Congo." Once again, it appeared, the scroll was
being unrolled, but this time Gordon had misgivings. He could
not, however, forget his promise to Leopold; " there is no help for
it," he told his brother. " I must go to the Congo, unless anything
I do not see turns up." By 17th November he had been undeceived
as to the wording of the War Office telegram.[1] Not only, it
appeared, would Whitehall not employ him, it would not allow

anyone else to do so. However, " has declined " in place of
" decides " only meant that in order to serve under Leopold he
would have to resign his commission, and he did not alter his
decision to return home in December. But he had begun to think
of the Congo as a road to a speedy death rather than worldly
advancement, a notion which he conveyed to Mr. Waller in an
elaborate periphrasis:

> I have a nice house, with garden and no worries, in the horizon,
> and if by the keeping of my promise [sc. to Leopold] I would
> get a free and speedy passage to it . . . I would be very glad; and
> it seems that the Congo is the route which is quickest to it, if,
> as I think, I am called there. Of course this will not be to your
> ideas, who have so many anchors out in your wife and chicks.

Early in December he embarked at Jaffa in a sailing vessel for
Port Said. Storms drove the ship into Haifa, where he stayed for
six days with Lawrence Oliphant, who did his best to persuade him
to abandon the Congo and offer his services in the Sudan. But
Gordon merely replied that he was in honour bound to Leopold,
and that in any case neither the Foreign Office nor the War Office
would ever willingly employ him again. Still cherishing this well-
founded belief he reached Brussels on New Year's day, 1884.

---

[1] His brother was wrong (*Events in the Life of Charles George Gordon*, page 290) in saying
that he only learned of the mistake on reaching Brussels.

BOOK TEN

DEUS EX MACHINA

IN BRUSSELS matters were soon arranged. On the day after his arrival Gordon saw the King and promised to go to the Congo next month. He would cross to England, resign his commission and return to Leopold. Leopold would compensate him for the loss of his army pension. It all seemed very simple. That same day he wrote to Mackinnon and his brother Henry asking them to arrange for the commuting of his pension. Henry must make his will for him too—and there were twenty-eight nephews and nieces to be remembered. Henry must arrange everything, in fact, so that he himself need only post his resignation; for he declined to come to town " to be asked this or that; why this, why that? . . . Discuss matters I will not. This is a thoroughly selfish letter." He presented Leopold with a model of the Rock of Jerusalem, visited Malet at the British Legation, ordered several copies of a photograph of himself taken by a Brussels photographer in 1880, and wrote to H. M. Stanley, who had been at work in the Congo since 1878, to make it plain that he had no desire to supplant him:

> . . . I will serve willingly with and under you, and I hope you will stay on, and we will God helping kill the slave traders in their haunts; for if we act together in the countries where they hunt, and make treaties with the chiefs, we can prevent their raids and truly stop the slave trade. . . . No such efficacious means of cutting at the root of slave trade ever was presented as that

which God has, I trust, opened out to us through the kind disinterestedness of His Majesty.

All, it seemed, was settled. He would not see the Sudan again. To Donnelly he wrote "I have weighed the affair and there is no other option. Egypt is hopeless. Nothing can stem the career of 'Nemesis' who has only taken her preliminary canter in London." And to the Secretary of the Anti-Slavery Society, on 5th January, he sent a memorandum to the general effect that the chief hope of crushing the slave trade was now to strike a blow at its sources in the Congo area, and that " now that General Gordon is going out as second in command to Stanley " a fatal blow to the slave hunters might be expected. The memorandum might be published, but anonymously, and " above all things, put in no gilt for me; you can do so for King Leopold and Stanley." And it must not appear before 7th January, when he proposed to send his resignation to the War Office. On 7th January he landed in England and at 11 p.m. that night posted his letter to the War Office from near Augusta's house in Rockstone Place, Southampton. But news of his plans had already leaked out, and on 5th January *The Times* had contained a leader on " Gordon and the Congo," regretting the prospective loss to the Queen's army of " one of its brightest ornaments." This was embarrassing enough, since the War Office had expressly refused to permit Gordon to go to the Congo at all. But though Lord Hartington wrote to Lord Granville that it was awkward, and what were they to do, the awkwardness was soon forgotten, swept away in the storm of Press, publicity and public excitement which, within a few days and for very different reasons, would begin to beat about Gordon, with ever increasing intensity, for the remainder of his life.

2

On 8th January, less than **twenty-four** hours after Gordon had posted his letter of resignation to the War Office, a short, slight, bearded man of eager aspect rang the bell of Augusta's house in Rockstone Place. "Can I see General Gordon?" he demanded, when the door was opened. "I am General Gordon" was the reply. Nothing daunted, the stranger explained that he was W. T. Stead, editor of the *Pall Mall Gazette*, and that he had hurried down from London to seek Gordon's views on the crisis in the Sudan. Recalling Agag and the tram of the world, and his own resolve to seek obscurity and keep silence, Gordon replied that he would say nothing about the Sudan. But he had admitted Stead into the house, introduced him to his friend, Captain Brocklehurst, and seated him on Augusta's leopard-skin-covered couch. And Stead was not easily turned from a purpose on which he had set his heart. Moreover, each man was soon conscious of a liking and admiration for the other. For Stead came of a religious Nonconformist stock, and when, not long before, he took over his new editorship he had vowed that he would use it to promote the spread of the Kingdom of God on earth. In Gordon he had recognised one of the most valiant of all champions of the Kingdom, and he was prepared to enlist among his most devoted admirers. Moreover, he had a persuasive case to plead. Only yesterday he had written a leading article in which he reluctantly accepted as inevitable the British Government's decision, unofficially rumoured in Cairo, that Egypt must evacuate Khartoum, and with it the entire Sudan. Would not Gordon give him, the *Pall Mall Gazette* and, above all, the world, the benefit of his unique knowledge of the Sudan, and comment on this news? Gordon was horrified by what he heard, and by its probable consequences to his "poor Sudanese;" his last scruples vanished and he proceeded with the utmost animation to unburden himself of a torrent of facts and arguments. Had he realised that Gladstone's government had indeed finally made up its mind about evacuation he would probably have held his peace; not, needless to say, out of consideration for the government, but because it was an article of his creed that when the scroll had unrolled it was impious to question the event.

For two hours Gordon talked and Stead listened. And then Stead hurried back to London with a sheaf of notes and the little copy of *The Imitation of Christ* which Gordon had pressed on him as he said good-bye. Next day, 9th January, the front page of the *Pall Mall Gazette* carried a leading article, headed " Chinese Gordon for the Sudan," in which Stead insisted that in Gordon's opinion evacuation meant massacre, and urged that the government must reverse its policy, and that Gordon himself should be sent out " to assume absolute control of the territory, to treat with the Mahdi, to relieve the garrisons, and to do what he can to save what can be saved from the wreck of the Sudan." Next day *The Times*, and every important newspaper in the country, reproduced the greater part of the interview. A shudder, as at impending doom, ran through the nation. Gordon, and only Gordon, reiterated the Press in chorus, could avert disaster; and Gordon must go to Khartoum.

Gordon had been for some while out of touch with British newspapers, and, in any case, had no wish to return to the Sudan or attract public attention. Nevertheless, had he been planning a sensational reappearance, as *deus ex machina*, on the centre of the world stage he could hardly have timed his return to England more opportunely. For four and a half years of cumulative disaster in the Sudan had at long last driven Gladstone's reluctant Ministry to abandon its thesis that disaster in the Sudan was none of its concern. And very soon now, compelled by popular agitation to take action of some sort, it would be urgently seeking some means of acting which would combine the least possible risk with the greatest possible satisfaction to an impatient and apprehensive public.

3

In the Sudan in May, 1881, while Gordon was on his way to Mauritius, an obscure *fakir*, of Dongolese birth, had suddenly declared that he was the Mahdi, the Expected One, and would victoriously restore the faith of Islam. By August he had announced a coming Holy War. By September a chain of untoward events had compelled Mr. Gladstone, the protagonist of peace and retrenchment, to crush Arabi Pasha's rebellion in Egypt at the battle of Tel-el-Kebir. Britain thereby became the solitary European power behind the Khedive's throne; nevertheless, Ministers continued to believe that they had no responsibility in the Sudan. And for a little while longer it was possible to remain in happy ignorance of the forces gathering in its remote recesses. But on 17th January, 1883, the day on which Gordon reached Jerusalem, the Mahdi captured El Obeid, the capital of the province of Kordofan. The British Government, however, continued to insist that it could accept no responsibility for what happened in the Sudan. Not only indeed did it decline to do anything, it declined to advise the Khedive and his bewildered Pashas what they should do. Thereupon the Khedive proceeded to prepare an expeditionary force under the command of a retired British officer, Colonel Hicks. Mr. Gladstone's government disassociated itself punctiliously from the appointment and made it clear that no serving British officer would be permitted to join Hicks's force. So rigorous was its aloofness that, although it had itself already been warned by Lord Dufferin that Egypt would be prudent to abandon part of the Sudan and concentrate on defending Khartoum and the Nile, it scrupulously refrained from passing on this advice to the Khedive or Colonel Hicks. Not without reason Baring, who had returned to Cairo as British Agent in the previous September, described the government's abnegation of responsibility as wholly illusory, " a mere phantasm of the diplomatic and parliamentary mind." Indeed, had Ministers been less eager to evade responsibility now, they might have been spared the much more alarming responsibilities which were to befall them in the near future. For in due course the ill-starred Hicks advanced into the wilds of Kordofan, where he and his entire army were surrounded and slaughtered by the Mahdi's dervishes. When news of the disaster reached Cairo, on 22nd November, Gordon was in Jaffa and had already determined to go to the Congo.

The fate of Hicks's army horrified the British public. Suddenly the shadow of the Sudan fell menacingly across the political scene, which it was to darken for many months to come. More than one phantasm of the Parliamentary mind had dissolved abruptly on that 22nd November. It seemed scarcely credible now that only thirteen days before, Mr. Gladstone had announced, at the Lord Mayor's banquet, that Britain was about to evacuate Egypt. The question now was how could the Mahdi's victorious dervishes be kept out of Khartoum, or for that matter out of Cairo? Even before the news of the disaster reached London the government had tacitly abandoned its illusion of complete detachment by instructing Baring, on 20th November, to advise the Khedive to abandon the Sudan " within certain limits." But within what limits, and how? For soon alarming telegrams were reporting that Khartoum could not be held. Her Majesty's Ministers had still got no further than declaring that "the Egyptian Government must rely upon their own resources." But they were only too well aware that the resources of the Egyptian Government were negligible.

4

And now in the ear of one uneasy Minister after another there began to be whispered the quiet, inevitable suggestion, Why not Gordon? The first hint had come in a dispatch from Lord Dufferin, towards the end of 1882. But Sir Edward Malet, who was then Consul General in Cairo, reported that the Egyptian Government did not favour the proposal; and to British Ministers Gordon was still an unpredictable eccentric who had recently fallen foul of the government at the Cape. The crisis did not yet call for such desperate measures. But a year later, on the very morning on which an incredulous public was reading the news of Hicks's fate in its morning newspapers, a certain colonel, who had served under Gordon in China, wrote a hurried letter to Gordon's old friend, Sir Andrew Clarke. There was one man, and only one, he said,

competent to tackle the problem of the Sudan—" Charlie Gordon."
Sir Andrew promptly sent the letter on to the Chancellor of the
Exchequer, Erskine Childers. "My advice would be," he wrote
in a covering note, " to place the whole affair without reserve in
Gordon's hands. If the Mahdi is a prophet, Gordon, in the Sudan,
is a greater."

"Place the whole affair in Gordon's hands;" for a harassed
Minister these were indeed tempting words. Childers sent the
suggestion on to the Foreign Secretary, Lord Granville. And on
this occasion at least Lord Granville did not delay. On the very
next day he wrote to the Prime Minister: "Do you see any
objection to using Gordon in some way? He has an immense name
in Egypt—he is popular at home. . . . He has a small bee in his
bonnet. If you do not object, I could consult Baring by telegraph."
The suggestion was beginning to take shape. Gordon had immense
prestige in Egypt—Lord Granville should have written " the
Sudan "—and he was popular at home. A government pressed to
do something, and with no clear notion what it ought to do, might
surely do worse than employ Gordon " in some way." The very
vagueness of the proposal made it attractive. For in a sense Gordon
was a programme in himself. In 1880 the Liberal Government had
sent him to India with Lord Ripon, largely because his reputation
for idealism was one means of announcing to the world that Lord
Ripon was to be a reforming Viceroy. If it were now to use him
" in some way" in the Sudan, was it not conceivable that his
prestige might in some mysterious manner overawe the Mahdi and
his dervishes? And even if it should not, Gordon after all had a
great reputation at home too; and it might at least be hoped that
the mere announcement that Gordon was to go to the Sudan would
solve a political problem even more urgent than the threat from
the Mahdi, by allaying the growing anger and impatience of the
British public. The more Granville thought of it, the more attractive
seemed the proposal to send out the solitary, heroic figure, cane in
hand, into the maelstrom of the Sudan. It would be easy, it would
be infinitely cheaper than sending a military expedition, it would

silence the clamour of the critics, and it would shift responsibility
to one pair of shoulders. Mr. Gladstone's reply was favourable, and
on 1st December Granville telegraphed to Baring. Would General
Charles Gordon be of any use to Baring or the Egyptian Government, " and if so, in what capacity? "

The suggestion was tentative and vague, but it had been made.
But Baring received it coldly. He still thought it prudent to leave
" the whole responsibility of the Sudan affairs " to the Khedive
and his Ministers. Eight days later, however, he had changed his
mind. The Egyptians, he now said, must be instructed what to do.
And two days after that, on 12th December, the members of the
Khedive's Council placed themselves " absolutely in the hands of
Her Majesty's government." Unfortunately, Her Majesty's govern-
ment was rent by internal dissension over a projected Reform Bill.
Threats of resignation flew backwards and forwards across the table
in Downing Street, while outside public clamour for a policy in the
Sudan grew more vociferous. Ministers, says Lord Morley, who
was their ardent supporter, quailed. More than ever, recourse to
Gordon assumed the attractions of a panacea. Between 13th
December and 4th January there was a brisk exchange of dispatches
and telegrams with Baring, the upshot of which was that at last the
British Government had issued an unequivocal command: the
whole of the Sudan must be evacuated. It had not, however, as yet
suggested how evacuation was to be effected.

Baring had already got as far as remarking, in a dispatch of 22nd
December, that it would be necessary " to send an officer of high
authority to Khartoum with full powers to withdraw all the
garrisons in the Sudan and to make the best arrangements possible
for the future government of the country." But he had mentioned
no names. And the Cabinet, despite Granville's previous inquiry
about Gordon, had not commented on his suggestion. On 9th
January the *Pall Mall Gazette* published Stead's interview with
Gordon. On 10th January Granville wired again to ask Baring
whether Gordon would be useful in Egypt, and on the 11th Baring
again replied that he thought not.

It is not surprising that the *Pall Mall Gazette* interview should have caused general alarm. The Cabinet, which knew very little about the Sudan, had decreed evacuation, and here was Gordon, who knew a great deal about it, asserting first that evacuation, save of Darfur and Kordofan, would be folly—it would endanger Egypt and set all Arabia and Syria in a ferment—and secondly that it was impracticable. How, he asked, were six thousand men to be moved from Khartoum? Would the Mahdi supply them with camels? They certainly would be stripped of everything they possessed, and they would almost certainly be massacred. Far better to defend Khartoum at all hazards. And even if the government intended evacuation it ought never to have announced the intention, which was a mere invitation to the Sudanese to desert *en masse* to the Mahdi. The interview contained a number of suggestions, one of which was that Sir Samuel Baker should be sent out as Governor-General, and made it clear that Gordon did not consider the Mahdi to be particularly formidable. On 11th December, within forty-eight hours of its publication, the Cabinet must have realised that, as the *Pall Mall Gazette* put it, " there is a storm brewing over the question of Khartoum of which Ministers will do well to take heed betimes." The country, it said, heard with indignation that the ablest living leader of irregular troops was no longer in the service of the Queen. On the same day the *Morning Advertiser* warned the government that if disaster overtook the fugitives from Khartoum " there would be an outburst of indignation from the civilised world." And next morning it added, more explicitly, that " all England has been looking for the employment of General Gordon in the present crisis."

Queen Victoria had not needed these admonitions. On 10th January she sent Granville an admonitory note, the opening words of which might have served to introduce any of the numerous communications as to the Sudan which she would address to her Ministers during the coming months. " The Queen," she said, " is very anxious about Egypt. Half measures and indecision will not do," And she pointed out that Baring's requests for an answer to his inquiry, of 22nd December, as to the employment of English officers had been ignored. In reply Lord Granville protested that he had twice asked Baring " whether Chinese Gordon would be of any use." And three days later, on the 15th, he was writing to Sir Henry Ponsonby, the Queen's secretary, to explain that, despite an assertion in *The Times* that Gordon had resigned his commission and would leave for the Congo in a fortnight, he had, in fact, not been " turned out of the army." " I have inquired (now for the 4th time)," he added piteously, " whether he could be utilised in Egypt." And he ventured on a brief character sketch, doubtless intended to strike a discreet note of warning: " he is a genius, and of a splendid character. It is a great pity that there should be some eccentricity."

But by this time Whitehall itself had begun to move. On 9th January, the day on which the *Pall Mall Gazette* interview was published, Gordon had scribbled to his brother, Henry, " Flight is only refuge," and next day, the 10th, he did flee, to Mr. Barnes's vicarage at Heavitree near Exeter. It was natural that he should associate Barnes, with whom he had so lately been corresponding voluminously on his Biblical and theological speculations in Palestine, with escape from the world. At Heavitree, on 11th January, for the last time in his life, he attended Holy Communion. On that day, too, he called on Temple, Bishop of Exeter, and went to Sandford Orleigh to visit Sir Samuel Baker. As Baker and Barnes and he were being driven between Newton Abbot and Sandford Orleigh Baker urged that if the government invited him to go back to the Sudan as Governor-General he should accept. Gordon said nothing, but Barnes noticed that his eyes flashed and an eager expression crossed his face. And Gordon must have noticed that he was observed, for late that night, after the vicar had gone to bed, he came to his room. " You saw me to-day? " he asked. " You mean in the carriage? " replied Barnes shrewdly. " Yes," said Gordon. " You saw *me*; that was *myself*; the self I want to get rid of." Next morning, 12th January, while Granville was phrasing his first Sudanese apologia to the Queen, Gordon travelled back to

London. He still meant to go to the Congo; indeed he reminded Sir Andrew Clarke, in a letter from Southampton that same day, that he had given his word to Leopold and resigned his commission; " so there is an end of that." On the day on which Gordon left Heavitree, however, a telegram from the Adjutant General, Lord Wolseley, was delivered at the vicarage. Forwarded to Rockstone place, it reached Gordon on Sunday, the 13th. It requested him to visit Wolseley at the War Office.

5

Gordon of course knew when he presented himself at the War Office at 2 p.m. on the 15th, that the resignation of his commission would not be the chief topic of conversation. He could not, however, know that on the previous day Granville had sent Gladstone, who was at Hawarden, a telegram couched in the vague and tentative phraseology of which he was a master: " If Gordon says he believes he could by his personal influence excite the tribes to escort the Khartoum garrison and inhabitants to Suakim, a little pressure on Baring might be advisable." Since *The Times* had announced that morning, the 14th, that the new Egyptian Minister for War was to go to Khartoum and superintend the evacuation of the Sudan, the mission which Granville now half-proposed for Gordon was comparatively modest, and possessed the supreme attraction of committing the British Government to little or nothing. Nevertheless, it was a proposal to ask Gordon for action, not advice; and Mr. Gladstone approved it.

From the moment, however, when Wolseley greeted his visitor at the War Office on that fatal Tuesday afternoon there gradually developed in the minds of all the chief Ministers so complex a confusion that eventually none of them, and least of all the Prime Minister himself, knew what Gordon had in fact been instructed to do. On this occasion neither of the two Ministers present at the War Office, Lord Hartington, the Secretary for War, and Lord

Granville, thought it necessary to see, or speak to, Gordon himself, though Granville sent him " a civil message." Gordon's own hasty summary of his visit was " got W.O. at 2 p.m. Saw Stokes (very kind) and then Wolseley. W. was with Lords Granville and Hartington from 2 till 5 p.m., I waiting. Lord G. sent me a civil message." As for Wolseley, he had at once told Gordon that the authorities had decided to withdraw their ban on his serving in the Congo and that accordingly he need not resign his commission. There might, however, be tasks to be performed for his own country first. Would Gordon be prepared " to go to Suakim to inquire into the condition of affairs in the Sudan?" Unlike Granville, he had suggested inquiry not action. The first seeds of a upas tree of misunderstanding had been sown.

Gordon received the suggestion favourably and, at Wolseley's request, promptly jotted down, under eight heads, some rough notes as to the proposed investigation. They commenced unequivocally " To proceed to Suakim and report on military situation of Sudan and return." And they included the characteristic proviso " Government not indebted beyond passage money and £3 per diem travelling expenses." The conflict between Wolseley's proposal and Gordon's notes on the one hand and Granville's inquiry of Gladstone on the other seems not to have struck the Foreign Office officials, who dispatched a telegram to Cairo that night. Gordon, it informed Baring, was ready to go to Suakim " on the understanding that the only object of his mission is to report on the military situation in the Sudan, after which he would return and his engagement towards Her Majesty's Government would cease. He would take his instructions from you. . . ." The last seven words, it is true, might conceivably one day open the door to much wider possibilities. But for the moment all seemed smoother sailing than the government could have hoped. A brief personal note from Granville to Baring contained the usual timid medley of hints and doubts, but betrayed the chief reason for ministerial satisfaction. " He might be of use in informing you and us of the situation. It would be popular at home but there may be countervailing objections." " It would be popular at home! " For the moment the Foreign Secretary felt that he could congratulate himself. A mission of inquiry to Suakim would cost the government almost nothing and would commit it to almost nothing. In spite of which Ministers would be able to claim that they had taken the one step likely to allay the growing public agitation; they had called in Gordon.

After leaving the War Office Gordon wrote his name in the callers' book at the Prince of Wales's and the Duke of Cambridge's and made a round of farewell visits—on Sir Andrew Clarke, General Eyre, Sir Lintorn Simmons and the indomitable Aunt Amy, still not wholly converted. He then dined with his brother Henry, signed his will and went on to Colonel Donnelly and Captain Brocklehurst. Returning to his hotel at 11.30 p.m. he found Mr. Waller of Twywell, and with him and Brocklehurst, who had followed him, sat up talking till two in the morning. At six he rose and by ten he was in the train for Dover, " very glad and very happy to have ended quietly that chapter." " Do not mention it," he warned Augusta, " but there is just the chance I may have to go to Sudan for 2 months and then go to Congo; but I shall not go as Govr Genl, only as military officer to report on affairs."

Throughout the rail journey from London to Dover Gordon was expounding to Mr. Waller and Captain Brocklehurst, who were travelling with him, his theories as to the Temple of Jerusalem, illustrating them with sketch after sketch, the last barely completed as they drew into Dover. But while the train had been steaming through Kent, in Cairo a slightly bewildered Baring had dispatched two telegrams which between them ensured that Gordon would go to the Sudan and that the confusion as to what he was meant to do there would be permanent. For by the morning of 16th January Baring knew that the Egyptian War Minister had declined to go to Khartoum to supervise the lengthy and dangerous task of evacuation, on the not unreasonable grounds that the British authorities insisted on proclaiming in advance the intention to abandon the town.

Thus unexpectedly bereft of all means of carrying out the policy of evacuation Baring decided to forget his previous objections to the employment of British officers, and at 10.30 a.m. he dispatched a telegram in which he invited the British Government to " send out at once a qualified British officer to go to Khartoum with full powers, civil and military, to conduct the retreat." Not many minutes, however, after the Agent-General had crossed this Rubicon he received the telegram which the Foreign Office had dispatched on the previous evening on the strength of Gordon's interview with Wolseley, and found that it proposed, not executive action at Khartoum but a brief inquiry at Suakim. It was no doubt irritating to find himself offered a one-man commission of inquiry a few minutes after he had asked for a commander in the field, but Baring did not pause long for reflection. Three-quarters of an hour after the dispatch of his first telegram he had sent another. Commencing with a reference to " your telegram (No. 28A) of yesterday " its opening words, " General Gordon would be the best man," suggest that Baring was accepting Granville's proposal of Gordon as an adviser. What follows, however, made it clear that he was proposing something very different.

. . . General Gordon would be the best man if he will pledge himself to carry out the policy of withdrawal from Sudan as soon as possible, consistently with saving life. He must also fully understand that he must take his instructions from the British Representative in Egypt and report to him. . . . I would rather have him than anyone else, provided there is a perfectly clear understanding with him as to what his position is to be and what line of policy he is to carry out. . . .

Here is no question of a mere report on the military situation. Baring was now proposing that Gordon should be offered the immensely vague and immensely dangerous task of somehow evacuating Khartoum, an operation for which nobody had attempted to prepare any plans and which, the Egyptian War Minister had calculated, it

G.G.   Y would take from seven months to a year to complete. But the new and larger plan had at the outset been inextricably involved with the modest original proposal.

Even if the British Cabinet had wished to disentangle the two projects, and to accept the additional risk of defining its own wishes precisely, it scarcely allowed itself time to do so. As soon as Baring's telegram, accepting Gordon, was received it was decided to summon all the Cabinet Ministers who happened to be in London, to recall Gordon and conclude the whole affair. It is possible that the fact that a majority of the Cabinet, and in particular the Prime Minister himself, were out of reach may have encouraged Granville and Hartington to act quickly. Wolseley's telegram reached Gordon in Brussels at two o'clock in the afternoon of the 17th, the day after his arrival; " come back to London by the evening train." Gordon dashed off a note to Augusta (" I am not the least moved by all this. I will not take Govr Genl Sudan. I will only report on situation "), saw King Leopold, who was " furious," at three and caught the eight o'clock train. He reached London at six on the morning of the 18th and was taken by the faithful Brocklehurst to Knightsbridge Barracks. " Washed and went Wolseley. He said Ministers would see me at 3 p.m. I went back to Bks and reposed. At 12.30 W. came for me."

6

Besides Granville and Hartington only two Ministers—Sir Charles Dilke, President of the Local Government Board, and the Earl of Northbrook, First Lord of the Admiralty—were present at the War Office and it is impossible to resist the conclusion that it was their conduct on this momentous occasion which made the eventual tragedy inevitable. It has to be remembered at the outset that in their eyes it was not a momentous occasion. Even in the early summer, though Gordon would by then have been for several weeks besieged in Khartoum, his fate would only receive a few minutes' perfunctory consideration at the close of Cabinet meetings. And at the moment the four Ministers were chiefly concerned to reach some decision which would end the Press agitation for Gordon, and leave the Cabinet free to concentrate upon its dissensions over the Reform Bill. None of them, and indeed none of their colleagues, knew anything to speak of about the Sudan or the true nature of the danger there, but they did know that Gordon had incautiously made it plain that he did not consider the Mahdi to be particularly formidable, and whatever misgivings they might have as to Gordon's other opinions this was a view which they were very ready to accept. Moreover, they were only too well aware that their absent but formidable chief was most anxious that if Gordon were to be used his powers should be severely restricted, and that in approving Granville's telegram of the 15th, with its offer to Baring of Gordon's services, the Prime Minister had insisted that if Gordon " reports what should be done, he should not be the judge *who* should do it, nor ought he to commit us on that point by advice officially given. It would be extremely difficult after sending him to reject such advice, and it should, therefore, I think, be made clear that he is not our agent for the purpose of advising on that point." The precise meaning of the closing words of this admonition was certainly far from obvious, but at least it was clear that Mr. Gladstone was determined that his government should be committed to nothing. If Gordon went out he should go only to bring back advice, and the advice need not be taken. Whether such a mission, if its conditions were disclosed, would satisfy the Press and the public was another question. Nevertheless, despite Mr. Gladstone's insistence on a mission so restricted in scope, the fact remained that even he had approved Granville's earlier proposal to send Gordon to Suakim to exert his personal influence over the tribes. And now Ministers had been summoned to act on a telegram from Baring which proposed explicitly that Gordon should " carry out the policy of withdrawal from Sudan." Even for clear heads and stout hearts, even if the whole Cabinet had been present, with the Sudan as the only item on its agenda, it would have been a perplexing situation.

Gordon's own account, or rather his accounts, in three separate letters, of what happened are perfectly explicit. To Mr. Barnes he wrote:

> W. came for me and took me to the Ministers. He went in and talked to the Ministers and came back and said " H.M.G. want you to understand this Government are determined to evacuate the Sudan, for they will not guarantee future government. Will you go and do it? " I said " Yes." He said " Go in." I went in and saw them. They said " Did Wolseley tell you our ideas? " I said " Yes; he said you will not guarantee future government of Sudan and you wish me to go and evacuate it? " They said " Yes," and it was over. . . .[1]

To which it need only be added that while Gordon waited in Lord Hartington's ante-room for Wolseley's return the spectacle of a private secretary writing at a desk there reminded him vividly of his own experiences with Lord Ripon, and he could not resist asking him " Do *you* ever tell a lie? " Unfortunately, Wolseley returned before the bewildered official, for all his familiarity with Parliamentary questions, could frame an appropriate reply.

It is altogether clear that Gordon understood that he was to have executive powers, and that he had been commissioned to " carry out the policy of withdrawal," precisely as Baring had proposed. When, however, we enter the half-lit world of official instructions and Ministers' notes all clarity disappears. The official instructions to Gordon[2] (incorrectly stated by Lord Morley, in his *Life of Gladstone*, to have been drafted by Gordon himself) are a mere rendering into slightly more pompous official verbiage of the original version still extant in Granville's own handwriting.[3] Apart from indulging the age-long preference of the civil service for using as many words as possible—Gordon was to " pay especial consideration to the

---

[1] *Charles George Gordon* by the Rev. F. H. Barnes, 102, 3 (corrected).
[2] Blue Book. See Appendix to Morley's *Life of Gladstone.*
[3] Public Record Office Papers, F.O. 78, No. 3696, quoted in Allen, *Gordon in the Sudan* 231, 2.

question of the steps that may usefully be taken "—the instructions
only depart from Granville's draft in requiring Gordon to proceed
to Egypt instead of Suakim. And Granville's draft was an obvious
attempt to conflate the proposal contained in the notes which
Gordon had written for Wolseley, that he should merely " report
on the military situation," with Baring's request that he should
" carry out the policy of withdrawal from the Sudan as soon as
possible." And like Granville's draft the official instructions contrive
this conflation by commencing with Gordon's own words " report
. . . on the military situation," and discreetly introducing authority
for the extensive and dangerous executive powers which Baring
had demanded under the cloak of one apparently innocuous
sentence: " You will consider yourself authorised and instructed
to perform such other duties as the Egyptian Government may
desire to entrust to you, and as may be communicated to you by
Sir E. Baring." This was an ingenious expedient indeed. In the
event the words might prove to mean nothing—or everything.
But the four Ministers were taking no risks; they had at any rate
covered themselves. If executive powers were eventually conferred
on Gordon, it would be the Egyptian Government, through Baring,
which conferred them. And the British Cabinet could always say
that, so far as it was concerned, it had sent him out to report. With
equal accuracy, it is true, it could, if need be, claim that it had
authorised him to take action; but at the moment, as the four
Ministers surveyed future possibilities, and remembered Mr. Gladstone's admonitions, they must have considered it unlikely that they
would wish to say anything of the sort. Mr. Gladstone wanted
Gordon to advise, without committing anybody to taking his
advice, and to the Premier they could, and would, represent that
they had in no way transgressed his wishes. Baring on the other
hand, wanted Gordon to take command of the retreat from the
Sudan, and they did not hesitate to make it clear to him, too, that
his demands were being satisfied. Indeed, in a covering telegram
to Baring Granville actually expanded the words " other duties "

in the official instructions by adding " beyond those specified in my dispatch."

Where there is duplicity, even subconscious duplicity, there is usually confusion, and the mental confusion of the four Ministers after their interview was undeniable. Dilke, who arrived late at the meeting, was apparently convinced that they had instructed Gordon to report, and no more; " we decided," he wrote,[1] " that he should go to Suakim" (not Egypt) " to collect information and report on the situation in the Sudan. This was the sole decision taken." Lord Northbrook, on the other hand, wrote, more accurately, to Baring that " the upshot of the meeting " had been that Gordon was " to report on the best way of withdrawing garrisons, settling the country, and to perform such other duties as may be entrusted to him by the Khedive's Government through you." What mattered, however, much more than the mutual contradictions of Dilke and Northbrook was Hartington's report to Gladstone.[2] And Hartington omitted any reference whatever to performing " other duties," or to executive action of any kind. He enclosed the notes which Gordon had prepared on the 15th, when his mission was still envisaged by all concerned as purely advisory, and explained that " the enclosed notes, written by himself, sketch the terms on which he would be willing to go." Of the subsequent transformation of the whole project brought about by Baring's telegram of the 16th, and the interview with Gordon on the 18th, he said nothing whatever. And the rest of his brief report to the Prime Minister was peppered with phrases indicating that the Cabinet had asked for nothing but advice: " He was unable to indicate the nature of the advice which he would give. . . . He might recommend. . . . Or he might not recommend. . . . He would give no opinion without seeing state of affairs on the spot."

Had Lord Hartington been an unknown suspect in the dock, charged with some petty fraud, can it be doubted that the contrast between the official instructions and his account of them must have

---

[1] *Life of Sir Charles Dilke*, Gwynn and Tuckwell, ii, 29, 30.
[2] *Life of Spencer Compton, 8th Duke of Devonshire* by B. H. Holland, i, 418.

been sufficient to convict him? We know him to have been an honourable man, but even so the best that can be said for him is that he must have reassured himself by reflecting, most optimistically, that the instruction to " perform other duties " might conceivably never be implemented, and that if and when Gordon did assume executive powers they would technically have been entrusted to him by the Egyptian Government. Since, however, Hartington knew well enough that the Egyptian Government would only confer these powers when instructed to do so by Baring, and that Baring could only issue such instructions with the express permission of the British Cabinet, even this defence is threadbare in the extreme.

And so it was that Mr. Gladstone, who duly telegraphed his approval next day, came to suppose that Gordon had been sent out solely as an adviser—and (since he had himself stipulated at the outset that his advice need not be taken) a suspect adviser at that. From this illusion the Prime Minister never contrived wholly to free himself. He must very soon, it is true, have realised that the mission would inevitably involve action; indeed, four days after Gordon's departure the Prime Minister offered no objections to a proposal that he should be made Governor-General of the Sudan or to the drafts of proclamations which he proposed to issue. But he would remain acquiescent only so long as Gordon's avowed object was the evacuation of the Sudan: as soon as circumstances made evacuation impracticable Mr. Gladstone's indignation at the reversal of his policy would be intensified by the ineradicable impression that from the outset Gordon had overstepped his instructions. Mr. Gladstone was seventy-four years old, and he did not change his mind readily. His view of the tragedy to come would be persistently coloured by a resentful sense that an erratic soldier had recklessly involved an unoffending government in a sea of unnecessary troubles. There is some evidence that, after it was all over, he realised that Hartington had been the fount and origin of much of the misunderstanding and prejudice which bedevilled the government's conduct of affairs in the Sudan. Lord Rendel, an intimate companion and fervent admirer of the Prime Minister, records[1] that in his own opinion Hartington should have shouldered more of the blame. Gladstone himself, he admits, never said this much, but on one occasion, when Rendel ventured to remark to him that Hartington " with all his virility had no chivalry ", it was noticeable that the Prime Minister did not dissent.

For the moment, however, the Cabinet had triumphantly achieved its immediate object. For the Press received the news of Gordon's mission with a pæan of approbation. The comment in every major newspaper was studded with such phrases as " relief and satisfaction " and " universal outburst of approval." And it was everywhere assumed that Gordon had gone, not to report and advise, but to effect " the pacification of the Sudan." For the moment nobody paused to reflect that he had been sent to tame the victorious Mahdi, to withdraw fifteen thousand souls from Khartoum and to pacify the Sudan, armed only with his personal influence, his Wand of Victory and unlimited drafts upon the empty treasury of Cairo.

The Queen, however, was already full of forebodings. Unlike the Prime Minister, she had been informed accurately, by Granville, as to the terms of Gordon's mission,[2] but she was by now convinced that in its handling of the crisis in the Sudan Gladstone's government, which had already been so dilatory, would be dilatory to the end. Writing to Sir Evelyn Wood of Gordon's departure she permitted herself to be frank.[3]

> Why this was *not* done long ago and why the right thing is never done till it is absolutely extorted from those who are in authority, is inexplicable to the Queen. Over and over again she has urged by letter and by cypher that energetic measures were necessary; but *not* till the whole country became alarmed —and she flatters herself also, in deference to her very strong pressure—was anything done.

[1] The Personal Papers of Lord Rendel, 43.
[2] The Letters of Queen Victoria, Second Series, iii, 473.
[3] The Letters of Queen Victoria, Second Series, iii, 474.

7

Characteristically it had taken the government eight weeks to reach its decision but, characteristically, too, it did not take Gordon eight hours to act upon it. He left by the eight o'clock boat-train that night, without kit of any kind. Before he left he found time to telegraph to Mr. Barnes " if He goes with me all is well," and to scribble a postcard to Augusta, instructing her to send models of the Rock of Jerusalem to Brocklehurst and the King of the Belgians; time, too, to pay a last visit to Reginald Brett, and pace the nursery in his worn overcoat and muffler with the baby in his arms. He was in the highest spirits; all his cares, said his brother, Henry, seemed to have disappeared. And why should he not be cheerful? He must have known that, failing some divine interposition, he was being dispatched on a forlorn hope, but he believed in divine interpositions. Moreover, if the Almighty did not choose to intervene, it was highly probable that he would be killed, and to death he had eagerly looked forward ever since, as a subaltern, he set out for the Crimea.

The authorities in general, however, did not believe in divine interpositions; they, too, must have suspected that the chances of Gordon's returning from his mission were small, and some of them may already that evening have been feeling some compunction at the price which he might be called upon to pay in order that by yielding to popular clamour the Cabinet might temporarily escape from an awkward situation. Indeed, it may well have been some such uneasiness which prompted so remarkable a galaxy of dignitaries to present themselves at Charing Cross to wish Gordon farewell. Lord Granville bought his ticket, Lord Wolseley carried his one small handbag up the platform and H.R.H. the Duke of Cambridge opened his carriage door for him. But no ceremony in which Gordon was a central figure could be expected to pass off without surprises. At the last moment one of his nephews hurried up, breathless, with his uniform in a metal case. And as the train was about to move Wolseley discovered, to his consternation, that Gordon, as usual, had not thought of money and had only a few shillings with him. Hurriedly he searched his own pockets and handed over his watch and chain and all his loose cash. And then having watched the train draw out of the lighted station into the darkness beyond, the great men turned away and were escorted by respectful officials to their waiting carriages.

BOOK ELEVEN

THE POLITICIANS

I. Prologue to Tragedy

As GORDON travelled across France and Italy with his companion, Colonel Stewart, a lean, ascetic cavalry officer, he drafted a succession of proposals for Lord Granville. On the Mediterranean he wrote to Augusta " if people ask after me, tell them they can greatly help me with their prayers, not for my earthly success, but that my mission may be for the glory of our dear Lord, the welfare of the poor and wretched, and, for me, what He wills, but above all, for a humble heart." And for Baring he prepared a memorandum in which he explained that he would carry out the evacuation, without fighting, if possible. Should he, however, " be unable to fulfil all their expectations," he would " hope that Her Majesty's Government will give me their support." He trusted, in other words, that he would be able to discharge his prodigious task with no human aid beyond his reputation and his Wand of Victory, but should he find himself in serious difficulties he assumed that the government would not abandon him. Under all the circumstances it was a modest assumption.

Gordon had intended to travel by way of Suakim, avoiding Cairo altogether. At Port Said, however, he received a telegram from Lord Granville, urging him to go to Cairo to confer with Baring. His old friend, Sir Gerald Graham, sent a note from Cairo to the same effect, urging him to " throw over all personal feeling, if you have any, and act like yourself with straightforward directness."[1]

[1] Sir G. Graham, *Life, Letters and Diaries*, ed. R. H. Vetch, 253.

And Sir Evelyn Wood, with Colonel Watson,[1] who had served
under Gordon in the Sudan in the old days, was waiting at the
docks, with a cordial autograph letter from Baring, to persuade
him to accept the invitation. Somewhat reluctantly he agreed. It is
characteristic of the confusion and prejudice into which Ministers
so soon fell, and of their success in persuading themselves that at
every stage Gordon jettisoned his own plans, that Lord Edmond
Fitzmaurice, who was at this time Parliamentary Under-Secretary
for Foreign Affairs, should subsequently have asserted, in his *Life of
Earl Granville*,[2] that the change of route was solely due to Gordon's
whim. The traveller arrived in Cairo on 24th January—in a special
train, but without luggage or a servant. Graham, who met him,
thought him greyer, but strong, well and in high spirits.

Next morning there were friendly conferences with the Khedive,
Nubar Pasha and Baring. It was optimistically agreed that Gordon
was to evacuate the whole of the Sudan, without the use of force
and without loss of life, and he was provided with two *firmans* from
the Khedive, one appointing him Governor-General, and the other
announcing that he was sent to evacuate the country and establish
an organised government. Baring was of course merely exercising
the authority conferred on him by the government—to instruct
Gordon to " perform such other duties as . . . may be communicated
to you by Sir E. Baring." He duly informed the Cabinet of what
had now been agreed and the Cabinet in due course intimated its
approval; but Ministers had already contrived to forget their blank
cheque for executive action, and a month later, when their nerves
were tauter, they could not resist sending Baring a retrospective
reproof, in which they spoke of these instructions as having
" virtually altered General Gordon's mission from one of advice
to that of executing or at least directing the evacuation not only of
Khartoum but of the whole Sudan." Lord Morley[3], too, refers to
" this vast alteration," and Lord Edmond Fitzmaurice to Gordon's
mission having been altered, at the conference with Nubar and

[1] Letter to his sister (unpublished), January 25, 1884.
[2] *Life of Earl Granville*, ii, 383.
[3] *Life of Gladstone*, iii, 153.

Baring, " from one of a merely advisory character into an executive commission."[1] Baring, defending himself many years later, attributed the expansion of Gordon's powers to Gordon himself. This was of course true, in the limited sense that the plans now agreed on had mostly been proposed by Gordon, but false in its implicit acceptance of the suggestion that they involved an extension of authority beyond the terms of the original instructions. And it is this quite baseless suggestion, of an unauthorised discrepancy between the London instructions and those now improvised in Cairo, which firmly embedded itself in the comments of subsequent writers.

2

That night there was a great dinner party at the Residency. Gordon, as usual, had done his best to evade it, pleading that he had no dress clothes, but he was firmly assured that dress clothes could be borrowed for him and he was forced to yield. Another twenty-four hours, after all, and he would be beyond the reach of dinner invitations for ever. All the dignitaries present at the banquet were most cordial to him; perhaps, like the Cabinet Ministers on the platform at Charing Cross, they were visited by some sense of compunction, as they thought of the solitary journey into the unknown. Nubar Pasha, with whom Gordon's relations had once been so acrimonious, actually embraced him; "Nubar embraced me on both shoulders," Gordon wrote to Augusta from Korosko a week later. "What a terrible thing!" Next day he sought out the Residency housekeeper with the dress clothes over his arm, and requested her to sell them and send the proceeds of the sale to the Boys' Club at Gravesend. But when the embarrassed woman pointed out that the clothes had been borrowed he took the reminder in good part and directed her to return the outfit to the lender with his thanks.

[1] *Life of Earl Granville*, ii, 383.

That evening Gordon was to set out for the desert; he would
have been in Cairo only forty-eight hours, forty-eight hours, as it
seemed to him, too long. And already the unfavourable omens
were accumulating. On the previous day there had been a chance
meeting whose immediate consequences might have warned a more
cautious, or a more worldly, man than Gordon that even the modest
degree of official support on which he counted was unlikely to be
forthcoming. At the Prime Minister's house he had unexpectedly
encountered Zebehr Pasha, former lord of the slave-hunters, who
was sentenced to death in Khartoum in 1879, but had been reprieved
after Gordon's departure and had been living for six years in Cairo.
Although Gordon had had Zebehr court-martialled as a rebel, and
had authorised the execution of his son, the "cub" Suleiman, he
was now visited by one of his sudden intuitions—a "mystic feeling"
he called it, which can hardly have been due to the prepossessing
appearance of Zebehr, whose face, according to Graham, resembled
"a death's head tenanted by a demon." Baring had already agreed
that a confederation of petty sultans was the likeliest form of substitute government to succeed Egyptian authority in the Sudan:
here, evidently, in this powerful and much-dreaded chieftain, was
the instrument of destiny by which the federation might be established. At Gordon's request a meeting was arranged on the afternoon
of his last day in Cairo. Zebehr declined to shake hands with him
and denounced him bitterly for his own misfortunes and the
execution of Suleiman. Gordon hotly recalled the crimes of both
father and son, and the interview degenerated into a wrangle as to
the authenticity of a letter which had supplied the principal evidence
against Zebehr. At the end of it Baring was convinced that Zebehr
was too hostile to be allowed to work with Gordon. In this view
he was supported not only by Nubar but by Stewart and Watson,
and he must have known, too, that Mr. Gladstone's government,
which had a more than wholesome respect for the political influence
of the anti-slavery societies, would be in the last degree unlikely to
approve of the promotion of an ex-slaver. To "mystic feelings"
Baring attached no importance whatever. He was the epitome of

common sense, and on grounds of common sense the case against Zebehr was unanswerable.

Nevertheless, it would have been more prudent, as well as more generous, to accede to Gordon's request that he should be permitted to take Zebehr with him—the first since Baring's note to Port Said had assured him that he could " rely on my most cordial support and assistance." Granted that the proposal was dangerous, a leap in the dark, granted that it was founded upon an irrational intuition, yet was not Gordon's whole mission a leap in the dark, " an expedition perhaps as hazardous," it has been said, " as any man in this world ever undertook? " Was not the only possible justification for sending him out, alone and unsupported, to pacify a province and tame hostile armies, the forlorn hope that his mysterious power over primitive peoples, his immense prestige, his strange ability, proved both in China and the Sudan, to turn rebels and criminals into loyal soldiers, and above all, the man himself, unorthodoxies, intuitions and all, would somehow achieve a miracle? And since the authorities were not giving Gordon an army, was not the only hope, for them and him, to give him his head? If they wanted caution they should not have called in Gordon, and now that they had called him in caution should have been forgotten. It was folly to hope to have it both ways; to send out a solitary man of genius, and then forbid him to exercise his genius.

At Sir Evelyn Wood's that evening, the evening of Gordon's last day in Cairo, his friends found him silent and preoccupied; yet earlier that day he had written to Augusta " I feel quite happy, for I say, If God is with me, who can or will be hurtful to me? " His reserve may have been partly due to lack of sympathy with his host, whom he found " wrapped up in things of this world," but already the refusal of his first request had cast an ominous shadow over his departure. Indeed, the whole company was conscious of a sense of unease, and Gordon, who disappeared for a few minutes to visit the sleeping children upstairs, afterwards wrote to Mr. Barnes that this incident, and a similar escape to the nurseries during Baring's dinner party, had been the only pleasant incidents during his stay in

Cairo. He left by rail at about ten o'clock. " May He be glorified,"
he had written to Augusta that morning, " the world and the
people of the Sudan be blessed, and may I be the dust under His
feet."

3

When he left Cairo, on 26th January, Gordon had precisely a year
to live, and throughout those twelve months, though he would
never know it, he would be the most celebrated personage in the
world. In every civilised country the public waited in fascinated
suspense for news of the lonely figure speeding on its perilous
journey towards a perilous goal. The English were traditionally
mad, and foreign spectators of the slowly unfolding tragedy were
at first undecided whether to marvel most at the seeming madness
of a government which had dispatched a solitary general on a task
which to all appearances it would need a civil service and a couple
of armies to accomplish, or at the apparently insane self-confidence
of the man who had accepted so fantastic a commission. But as in
every country the Press poured out romantic accounts of Gordon's
spectacular achievements and fanatical faith the world began to ask
itself whether, though his success would undoubtedly be a miracle,
a miracle might not conceivably be vouchsafed.

" *I am not* (thanks to God) *moved* even a little." So Gordon
wrote during his second day in Cairo; it was a phrase which, with
slight variations, had already appeared in several of his letters since
his mission was announced. And perhaps the sovereign service
which, first in London and then in Cairo, he had so far rendered
had been to reassure wavering politicians and a bewildered public
by the mere spectacle of the serene confidence with which he
accepted his unparalleled responsibilities. Indeed, the spectacle had
been too reassuring, for the simple reason that few of the spectators
recognised its origins, and thus attributed too much importance to
Gordon's underestimate of the Mahdi and too little to his child-like

Sketches of the Temple at Jerusalem drawn by Gordon in January 1884

trust in an overruling Providence and his sublime indifference to his own fate. And now he felt it necessary to extend the stabilising influence of his personality yet further afield. Before leaving Cairo he had telegraphed to Khartoum " Do not be panic-stricken. You are men not women. I am coming."

For the first five days of the journey, by rail to Assiut and thence by steamer to Korosko, Gordon and Stewart were accompanied by Graham and his A.D.C. Gordon's friendship with Graham went back to the Crimea, and Stewart, too, was congenial. This time there would be none of the constant dissatisfaction with his European entourage which had haunted him during his previous missions to Equatoria and the Sudan. As for Graham, he watched Gordon and his changing moods with melancholy intentness, almost as if he were in the presence of a man condemned to death. He noted his frequent talk of the Holy Places and the Coco de Mer, his plans for the Sudan, and particularly his plans for the handing over the negro provinces of Equatoria and Bahr el Ghazal, south of Khartoum, to the King of the Belgians, to be administered by Gordon himself after he had evacuated Khartoum, so that the supply of negro slaves could be cut off at its source. He noted his occasional irritability, and the charm of his more frequent genial moods, and how he would jest in execrable Arabic with his Egyptian aide-de-camp (who addressed him as " father "). He noted how after a night during which all but he had slept he was the freshest of the party next morning. He marvelled at the patience with which he would listen to the interminable compliments of the Arab visitors who presented themselves *en route*, and wrote in his diary " you can see his kindness shining in his face when the natives crowd round him, kissing his hand." Graham judged that Gordon was troubled in mind, although entirely unconcerned for his own safety. And, indeed, this uneasiness is discernible in the brief letters which Gordon wrote from the steamer; for although he assured Augusta that he was as safe in the Sudan as at Southampton (and to believe so was of the essence of his religion) and that he was confident all would be well, unexpected phrases such as " altogether things are very bad " suggest that he was reassuring himself almost as much as his sister. And on the 28th a casual observation that this was his fifty-first birthday is immediately followed by the confession "somehow nothing that I could tell you would be very cheering." He was, however, much cheered, he wrote more than once, by the knowledge that many were praying for him.

The plan for a confederation of petty sultans after the withdrawal of Egyptian authority had already been clouded by the ban on Zebehr, and during the journey to Korosko it was further prejudiced by the unprepossessing behaviour of a negro Emir who had been extricated from comfortable obscurity in Cairo and packed off in a bemedalled but ill-fitting uniform, to be restored by Gordon to his ancestral authority in Darfur. Nobody had foreseen that this unpractised potentate would be attended by several brothers, twenty wives and numerous female attendants, that he would endeavour, with signal unsuccess, to commandeer the only saloon on the steamer and thereafter drink heavily throughout the voyage. From Korosko, on 31st January, Gordon scribbled an ominously significant note: ". . . think things have been greatly exaggerated. Have no fear of Mahdi's advance. God willing, I hope for a satisfactory solution. Mahdi nephew of my old guide." He was still thinking of the Mahdi as a mere composite figurehead, the product, like Arabi, of nationalism and, like Zebehr, of the slave raiders. The discovery that the prophet was the nephew of his own former guide, sprung from the unwarlike riverine tribes, seemed to endorse his unflattering estimate. He was still underestimating the dangers ahead. A religious fanatic himself, he had not yet realised that what faced him now was religious fanaticism.

At Korosko Gordon must set out across nearly three hundred miles of nearly waterless Nubian desert. Graham walked beside his camel for a while, the Arab escort riding ahead. "At last I left him, saying 'Good-bye' and 'God bless you.'" Graham never forgot the spot in which they parted, a wild landscape of barren hills divided by black ravines—like so many openings to the pit, he could not help thinking, where any who entered must leave hope behind.

He waved farewell, then climbed the highest hill and through his glasses watched the small caravan winding along a sandy valley beyond. He hoped, as long as he could see them, that Gordon would turn so that he might wave to him once more, but he rode on without a sign until he rounded the dark side of the hills, and was seen no more.

4

By 8th February Gordon was at Abu Hamed, and could still report that " I hope D.V. to get all settled in a few weeks."[1] At Abu Hamed a fresh camel bolted with him and he feared a fall, which, he explained, the superstitious Arabs would have taken as an evil omen. He added that he himself deduced from the incident " that God will bless my efforts, but that it will not be to my glory "— which presumably was not an omen. Every stage of Gordon's journey was now being reported in the world Press. The general expectation seems to have been that he would not reach Khartoum. *The Times* of 11th February, which announced his safe arrival at Abu Hamed, warned the government in a leading article (and just now it was an exceptional issue of *The Times* which contained no leading article on Gordon) that it would be lucky if within the next few days it found itself having to consider how Gordon could be helped to hold (not, be it noted, to evacuate) Khartoum, and not " the situation which would have to be faced if he should fail in reaching his destination." In the same issue the Madrid correspondent reported the profound sensation in Spain occasioned by a rumour that Gordon had been captured.

On the 11th he was at Berber. When the news reached Paris *The Times* correspondent telegraphed that " no idea can be given . . . of the deep impression made here by his cool and courageous march." It was at Berber that he informed a council of notables of

[1] Miss Gordon's treatment of this sentence (*Letters of General Gordon to his sister*, 376) is a good example of the free hand she always permitted herself as editor. She renders it " I hope all will be settled in six months, D.V."

the coming Egyptian withdrawal from the Sudan. It was a rash step, for he had himself pointed out, in Stead's interview, that as soon as evacuation was publicly announced "every man will go over to the Mahdi." Moreover, when the notables reminded him that the Anglo-Egyptian Convention of 1877 had provided that domestic slavery in the Sudan should come to an end in 1889, and asked whether the Convention would hold good after the withdrawal of Egypt, he answered that it would not. The reply was self-evident common sense, a simple statement of fact, but it, too, up to a point, was rash, for he must have known that there were plenty of politicians and philanthropists at home who would always refuse to admit the existence of an unpleasant fact, and would duly denounce him for having condoned slavery. When, however, his first proclamation at Khartoum confirmed his realistic attitude and there were questions in both Houses, *The Times* manfully supported him, pointing out that the choice was between sacrificing the scattered garrisons and tolerating slavery for the time being.

As, bearing Gordon, the *Tewfikieh* steamed away from Berber the populace in its thousands lined the banks, weeping, shouting and waving. The reception at Khartoum, on 18th February, was even more tumultuous. As "father" they had hailed him at Berber and as "father" he was greeted at Khartoum by the thousands who pressed forward to kiss his hand or embrace his feet. No sooner had he arrived than he ordered the official tax records and the official *Kourbashes* to be burned on one gigantic pyre in front of the palace. The prison doors were opened, the council of notables was summoned. "I come without soldiers," he told the crowds, "but with God on my side, to redress the evils of the Sudan. I will not fight with any weapons but justice. There shall be no more Bashi Bazouks."[1] All that night Khartoum was loud with rejoicings and ablaze with lights. "Not a bad day's work" commented Moberly Bell of *The Times.*

[1] Irregular troops (in every sense of the word), whether Turkish, Arab or Egyptian.

5

Meanwhile, however, the government, confused and timid, had jettisoned and rejettisoned its own policy. On 25th February Herbert Gladstone, himself a junior member of his father's administration, had declared at the Albert Hall, in a speech amply reported in *The Times*, that " the Government would do all they could to enable those garrisons to retreat safely or to get away from the places they held. The Government would bear that responsibility without resigning it to others." Nothing could have been clearer or more explicit, and nothing could have been clearer or more explicit than the words of Mr. Gladstone himself in the House on 12th February; Gordon, he said, had gone out " for the double purpose of evacuating the country by extricating the Egyptian garrisons and reconstituting it by giving back to those Sultans their ancestral powers." No suggestion here of a merely advisory mission! Gordon was in the Sudan to evacuate the garrisons on behalf of the British Government, which acknowledged sole responsibility for the task. The Prime Minister had even accepted Gordon's proposal of a federation of petty sultans and announced it as his own policy. A week later, however, on 19th February, Ministers had changed their minds once more. It was the last day of a debate on a formal vote of censure on the Egyptian policy of the government. When the debate opened Ministers had seemed to be in jeopardy, but news of Gordon's triumphal entry into Khartoum had just reached England, suspense, which had been mounting steadily since he left Cairo, was ended and the country was in festal mood. Ministers were now assured of victory in the lobbies; Gordon had served their immediate purpose. Lord Hartington summed up for the government. " I contend," he said, " that we are not responsible for the rescue or relief of the garrisons either in the Western or the Southern or the Eastern Sudan."[1] Gordon, he explained, had merely been sent out to oblige the Egyptian Government, and it was the Egyptian

[1] Hansard, February 19, 1884 (col. 1441).

Government (although the British Government had compelled it to instal Ministers who would carry out the British Government's policy, and although it was receiving daily instructions from Baring) which bore the sole responsibility. Despite all appearances to the contrary, Britain was *not* intervening in the Sudan.

This statement, surprising enough in its abrupt contradiction of recent and equally categorical Ministerial declarations, was yet more surprising in its contradiction of universally known facts. For the government, whose declared policy was peaceful evacuation, had already, against Gordon's advice, sent a British army into the Sudan. On 5th February it was known that a force of Egyptian gendarmerie, under General Baker, sent to relieve two beleaguered Egyptian garrisons on the Red Sea, had been cut to pieces by the rebels. The British Press, almost with one voice, denounced the iniquity of permitting a massacre of the helpless Egyptians, and ominous analogies with the Bulgarian atrocities began to appear in Liberal journals. *The Times* reported an official in English service in Cairo as exclaiming " Thank God, I am not an Englishman." Faint-hearted as ever in face of a determined Press campaign, Ministers quailed again. Instinctively they turned to the solitary figure now hastening across the desert between Korosko and Abu Hamed; was he not after all nominally Governor-General of the entire Sudan and was not the Red Sea littoral part of that province? They would consult Gordon. Did the news of Baker's defeat, they telegraphed, affect his decision to go to Khartoum? Above all, could he make any helpful suggestions as to the beleaguered garrisons? Gordon, who clearly understood that his mission was to be peaceful so long as that was humanly possible, replied firmly that it would be highly discreditable to recall him, and that an assembly of notables should be summoned to Khartoum. But the government was hard pressed; its military advisers were urging that a British force should be sent to Suakim, which was threatened by Baker's defeat. Not without embarrassment, for traditionally military intervention was anathema to Mr. Gladstone and the Liberals, Ministers telegraphed again; what did Gordon think of the proposal? Gordon replied that he would much prefer rumours of British intervention to intervention itself. But then came news that one of the Egyptian garrisons had been cut to pieces, the debate on the vote of censure was beginning, Ministers were increasingly uncomfortable, and at a hastily summoned Cabinet they decided, despite Mr. Gladstone's objections, to send four thousand British troops to relieve the surviving garrison and protect Suakim. Often afterwards as the confused tragedy unfolded they would complain that Gordon had committed them, in defiance of his instructions, to the use of force; but, in fact, they had themselves drawn the sword little more than a fortnight after Gordon left Cairo, against his wishes and while he still believed that force would not be necessary. This was indeed intervention in the Sudan, more thorough-going than, even a week before, any Minister could have imagined. Hartington's defence of it was characteristic of the Cabinet. The Red Sea area, he admitted, as the debate on the vote of censure moved to its triumphant conclusion, was technically part of the Sudan; for practical purposes, however it could be regarded as entirely distinct; Britain, once more the logic was inexorable, had *not* intervened in the Sudan.

6

As soon as he could escape from the jubilant crowds Gordon sat down in the comparative quiet of the palace to put on paper his proposals for the future. It was his practice always to write down a plan as soon as he had formed it, though he was well aware that he might be compelled to substitute a new plan to-morrow. And now, as when he was serving under the old Khedive, he faithfully dispatched all his successive projects to the authorities. Graham had thought that the habit was due to the fundamental impatience of a man of action, and also to the humility of this particular man of action—who desired what should be known or done to be known or done at once, and cared everything for the task in hand, and nothing for what the authorities thought of him. Gordon himself defended it on the ground that in a swiftly changing situation his superiors were entitled to know everything that was in his mind. In any event, Baring and the Cabinet, who were not accustomed to such frank and frequent communications, undoubtedly found them both alarming and confusing. And their alarm and confusion was vastly increased by the simple fact that Gordon's messages, some of which travelled to Cairo and on to London by post and some by telegraph, reached them without chronological order or logical sequence. Moreover, as if to endorse and perpetuate the confusion, the official Blue Books which were hurried out from time to time printed Gordon's dispatches not in the order in which they were sent, nor under subject headings, but simply under the dates on which they had happened to reach London. Only when Dr. Allen[1] took the trouble to examine the dispatches in due chronological order, and in relation to the circumstances in which they were written, did their coherence and fundamental common sense become apparent.

Meanwhile, as they puzzled over the staccato and often contradictory communications, couched in language so different from that to which the memoranda of civil servants had accustomed them, Ministers had some excuse for telling each other that they had sent a wild man to Khartoum, and were entitled to wash their hands of him. And, though Gordon could not guess it as he sat down in the sudden quiet of his room in the palace on that February day, this was precisely what they would do. The memoirs and biographies of the politicians responsible for his fate protest constantly to high heaven that he was unpredictable and uncontrollable and that accordingly they must not be held responsible for his fate. " I thought, and still think," wrote Sir Charles Dilke, " that Gordon had lost his senses, as he had done on former critical occasions in his life."[2] To Sir Charles Dilke himself, however, even exculpations founded on Gordon's behaviour were superfluous: of Gordon's mere setting out from Egypt he would write " here ended our

[1] *Gordon and the Sudan.*
[2] Gwynn and Tuckwell, *Life of Sir Charles Dilke,* ii, 35.

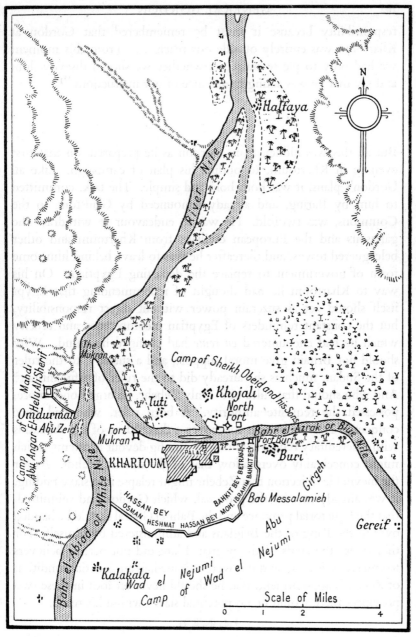

KHARTOUM AND ITS ENVIRONS

responsibility because it must be remembered that Gordon at Khartoum was entirely outside our reach. . . . From this moment we had only to please ourselves whether we should disavow him and say that he was acting in defiance of our instructions."[1]

7

But all this was hidden from Gordon as he prepared, on that first evening in Khartoum, to outline his plan of campaign. Like all Gordon's plans, it was both bold and simple. The task, committed to him by Baring, and already announced by Gladstone to the Commons, was twofold. He was to endeavour to withdraw the garrisons and the European civilians from Khartoum and other beleaguered towns, and thereafter he was to leave behind him some form of government to replace the departing Egyptians. On his way to Khartoum he had thought of recommending that Egypt itself should act as suzerain power without direct responsibility, but the constant reminders of Egyptian incompetence and cruelty which he had encountered *en route* had changed his mind. Why should not Britain give moral support, and a subsidy, to the ruler of the Sudan, much as she already did to the ruler of Afghanistan? And who should that ruler be? Only Zebehr, he urged once more, possessed the requisite authority. A born ruler, who had once conquered Darfur, he was moreover a descendant of the Abbasids with a hereditary religious authority among devout Moslems which might conceivably overshadow that of the upstart Mahdi. As for the inevitable objection that Zebehr might relapse into slave raiding, it was already met by the proposal, which Gordon had submitted, that the Equatorial province and the Bahr el Ghazal should be handed over to the King of the Belgians and administered by himself. For these were the lands of the negro; Islam did not permit believers to enslave believers; and if it were enjoined, as an essential condition of Zebehr's appointment, that he should never set foot in these two provinces there would be no potential slaves within his reach.

[1] id., ib., ii, 34.

It was a bold scheme. But the situation was desperate, and the remedy, though bold, was far from desperate. It convinced Graham, who saw that the only alternative was anarchy under a " many-headed Zebehrdom" of the unregenerate kind. It convinced Stewart; " Zebehr is the only man," he told Baring. It even convinced Baring; " I believe Zebehr," he told the British Government, " to be the only possible man." And it convinced Moberly Bell of *The Times*. " Make up your mind," he advised the government, " to sacrifice your prejudice or Gordon. You have put him in the lion's mouth and he is shrewd enough to see the only way out of it. He is too brave to tell you that the refusal of Zebehr is Gordon's death-warrant—unless you send an army instead." But none of these gentlemen had to count votes or forecast divisions, and the plea did not convince the Cabinet. On 26th February Granville's answer reached Khartoum. There were, he said, the gravest objections to the naming of Gordon's successor by the government, and he disclosed their nature. " The public opinion of this country," he explained, " would not tolerate the appointment of Zebehr Pasha." This verdict Gordon at first accepted as final, an unrolling of the scroll; but it was not final, for Baring himself would reopen the struggle to persuade the British Government to authorise the action which might well have saved both Gordon and the Sudan; he would even venture on an admonition of such stark frankness and common sense as to leave it unique in his official correspondence. " It is for Her Majesty's Government to judge of the importance to be attached to public opinion in England," he telegraphed on 28th February,

but I venture to think that any attempt to settle Egyptian questions by the light of English popular opinion is sure to be productive of harm, and in this, as in other cases, it would be preferable to follow the advice of responsible authorities on the spot.[1]

[1] cf. Lord Cromer *Modern Egypt*, i, 497-98.

The Queen, in whom common sense often approached genius, was usually for the man on the spot, and she instinctively sided with Baring and Gordon. " This is very important," she wrote to Sir Henry Ponsonby, " and Sir E. Baring certainly speaks out very strongly." And in an uncontrollable eruption of italics and capitals she continued:

Pray cypher that I trust the *good and permanent tranquillity of Egypt* will be *looked* at and thought of—and *not public opinion* HERE which is fickle and changeable. . . . Sir E. Baring is evidently *not* pleased at what the Queen *must* call the miserable, weak and " too late action of the government."[1]

But by then Ministers were facing one of the recurrent dilemmas of Parliamentary government; public opinion, though uninstructed, was inflamed and menacing; inevitably it mattered more to them than the opinions, or the fate, of the men on the spot.

8

Moreover, before Ministers finally rejected the urgent request of the man they had dispatched on the forlornest of forlorn hopes, and the reiterated advice of their own official representative, the gulf of misunderstanding between them and Gordon had widened. He had at once begun to evacuate Khartoum. Women and children were sent down river, and he had dispatched a characteristic telegram to Nubar, asking that he should " send a kind-hearted man to meet them." The Egyptian troops were separated from the Sudanese and sent across the river to Omdurman to await transport by steamer to Berber. Not a few of the notables of the town were alarmed by these measures, and protested that the Egyptian soldiers might yet be needed, but Gordon had caused a text in Arabic, " God rules the heart of men," to be set up over his state chair, and would point to

---

[1] Letters of Queen Victoria, Second Series, iii, 480.

it when his visitors showed signs of timidity. He had already sent the Mahdi an offer of peace. For a short while it seemed that by mere personal ascendancy he would achieve the impossible.

Meanwhile, however, General Graham was sailing down the Red Sea with four thousand men, sent by the British Government to attack the very tribes whom it expected Gordon to pacify. And soon news began to reach Khartoum that the whole of the surrounding country was in revolt. The Council of Notables resolved that troops must be sent out in response to the appeals for help from loyalists. In fact, all that was sent was a steamer, with Stewart on board, which confined its activities to distributing proclamations of peace; but unfortunately Gordon sent Baring a telegram on 26th February, in which he carelessly used the words " expedition starts at once to attack rebels in vicinity." Unfortunately, too, when Baring transmitted it to London he omitted to transmit other telegrams in which Gordon had spoken of " paper warfare " and had made it clear that he was steadily evacuating Khartoum. Ministers were thunderstruck. So Gordon was already resorting to violence! Unaware that he had in fact not fired a shot, unaware, too, as yet, that, under their orders, Graham was about to slaughter some thousands of Arabs at El Teb and Tamaii, they told themselves that their orders were being flouted by the man whom they had never fully trusted and had nevertheless commissioned to work a miracle for them.

Nor was this all. Gordon had already on 26th February issued an Arabic proclamation, in the course of which he declared that British troops were on their way, and would soon be at Khartoum. The actual phrase was coined by an Arab translator, but the notion that British troops would soon be nearing Khartoum was a legitimate speculation. For Graham's victories could only darken the prospects of Khartoum unless and until British troops appeared upon the Nile. Berber was the unmistakable key-point for the evacuation of refugees either by way of Abu Hamed or the coast to Suakim, and it was only two hundred and fifty miles from Suakim. Moreover, in England it had been widely assumed that Graham's army would be used to succour Khartoum and " it is some satisfaction," *The Times* had declared on 16th February, in one of its stream of leading articles on Gordon and Khartoum, " that the British force now on its way to Suakim is . . . more powerful than is likely to be needed for the immediate purpose of the relief of Tokar, and, therefore, if General Gordon should, on his arrival in Khartoum, find it necessary to call for further assistance, it will be possible to render it without unnecessary delay." But there were more self-contradictions in the Cabinet's policy than Gordon, or *The Times*, had yet imagined. It had, in fact, no intention of sending troops to the Nile. An angry Press campaign (and an angry meeting in the Guildhall with the Lord Mayor in the chair) had induced it to send troops to Suakim, but in the absence, as yet, of a Press campaign for directing them to Khartoum, it saw no reason to send them any farther. And Ministers would continue to believe that, though they had fought a pitched battle with the Mahdi's levies in the east, it would be a dangerous and unwarrantable act of aggression to send a few hundred British troops to keep open the indispensable river route by which alone Gordon could accomplish the task they had entrusted to him. They had willed the end, but declined to will the means. And so Gordon's assertion had deepened the mistrust of the Cabinet: Dilke called it " an amazing lie."[1]

"Gordon had frightened us out of our senses,"[2] Dilke noted at the time of the rash reference to attacking the rebels. And worse, much worse, was to come. For on that same fateful 26th February Gordon dispatched yet another lengthy telegram acknowledging Granville's refusal of his request for Zebehr, and it contained phrases which finally convinced the Cabinet that their envoy had flung caution to the winds—and Dilke that they were dealing " with a wild man under the influence of Central Africa which acts upon the sanest man like strong drink."[3] And the suave Lord Rendel, Mr. Gladstone's intimate, was doubtless echoing the Prime Minister's opinions when he pronounced that Gordon's long experience of

[1] Gwynn and Tuckwell, *Life of Sir Charles Dilke*, ii, 40.
[2] id., ib., ii, 40.
[3] id., ib., ii, 41.

savage lands had made him " useless for civilised work." For the
tragedy was not only that Gladstone and his colleagues did not
understand the Sudan or Gordon's dispatches, but that they did not
understand Gordon. Accustomed to a slow sequence of verbose
but cautious minutes from well-disciplined civil servants and conventional generals, they were first bewildered and then shocked by
a hail of communications lacking all chronological order, full of
informal interjections, parentheses and admonitions, and presenting
a daily, and sometimes almost an hourly, picture of the reactions of
a heroic, eccentric and other-worldly genius to a situation which
they themselves did not begin to understand.

> " You must remember," ran the fateful telegram, "that, when
> evacuation is carried out, Mahdi will come down here and,
> by agents, will not let Egypt be quiet. Of course my duty is
> evacuation and the best I can for establishing a quiet govern-
> ment. The first I hope to accomplish. The second is a difficult
> task and concerns Egypt more than me. If Egypt is to be
> quiet, Mahdi must be smashed up. Mahdi is most unpopular,
> and with care and time could be smashed. Remember that,
> once Khartoum belongs to Mahdi, the task will be far more
> difficult; yet you will, for safety of Egypt, execute it. If you
> decide on smashing Mahdi, then send up another £100,000
> and send up 200 Indian troops to Wadi Halfa. . . . I repeat that
> evacuation is possible, but you will feel the effect in Egypt, and
> will be forced to enter into a far more serious affair in order to
> guard Egypt. At present it would be comparatively easy to
> destroy Mahdi."

" Mahdi must be smashed up! " Once again Ministers were
frightened out of their senses. For they immediately assumed, and
a score of biographies and memoirs have perpetuated the assumption,
that Gordon was announcing his own intention to attack. "Gordon,"
wrote Dilke, " having heard that Zebehr was refused, telegraphed
his policy of smashing up the Mahdi, which, however, he seemed

inclined to attempt with a most inadequate force."[1] Once Gordon was in Khartoum, wrote Sir William Harcourt, he was "seized with the idea of smashing the Mahdi." Gordon "soon wrote," says the biographer of Lord Granville, "that . . . the Mahdi must be smashed up, and he determined with characteristic energy to do it himself."[2] Yet the briefest examination of the telegram is sufficient to show that, on the contrary, Gordon was not announcing his own decision but asking for the government's, with the warning that if the Mahdi was not suppressed now, he would have to be suppressed, with much greater effort and peril, later on. The telegram was a telegram of advice, and events to come, from the fall of Khartoum to the battle of Omdurman, would justify every syllable of it.

There were, it is true, some excuses for the men in Westminster. For Gordon's telegram had reached them a mere twenty-four hours after his bewildering reference to attacking the rebels. Moreover, Baring, who seemed fated to exacerbate the misunderstandings between Gordon and the Cabinet, had forwarded with Gordon's latest telegram a message of his own in which he inaccurately summarised an earlier proposal from Khartoum and represented Gordon as having asked that three thousand " black troops " should be retained in the Sudan. Gordon had, in fact, made the eminently reasonable suggestion that to assist Zebehr in maintaining order after his own departure—Granville's first veto on Zebehr had not then reached him—three thousand " Sudanese troops "[3] should be retained in the Sudan. Ministers, however, at once irrationally assumed that the " black troops " of Baring's garbled version were to be Egyptians, the very men whom Gordon had been commissioned to withdraw, and was in fact withdrawing, and that with them he proposed forthwith to attack the Mahdi. " 3000 black Egyptian troops," noted Dilke, were to be the " most inadequate force " with which Gordon contemplated " smashing up the Mahdi."

[1] Gwynn and Tuckwell, *Life of Sir Charles Dilke*, ii, 40.
[2] Lord E. Fitzmaurice, *Life of Lord Granville*, ii, 385.
[3] B. M. Allen, *Gordon and the Sudan*, 287.

The last photograph of Gordon

9

By now accordingly, the last day of February, the stage was already set for tragedy. In London Ministers, all too ignorant of the realities of the Sudan, grotesquely misinterpreting what they knew and now deeply suspicious of their envoy, were ready to turn a deaf ear to the demands which Baring was renewing for the appointment of Zebehr. In Cairo Baring, conceivably in order to concentrate upon Zebehr, was withholding for four days the telegrams from Khartoum which, if they had been allowed to reach the Cabinet, would at least have made it clear that Gordon was planning evacuation, not an attack upon the Mahdi. And alone in his palace—for Stewart and Power were reconnoitring the White Nile—Gordon was calculating, down to the last biscuit, the provisions required by the refugees he was evacuating, and telling Augusta that the prayers of others were all he had to lean on, that he would never read a newspaper again and that the peculiar physical pain, " which comes from excessive anxiety," and which he had first noted on the jungle path in Equatoria, would return at times when he contemplated the possible fate of the populace for which he was responsible. Meanwhile, he sent Baring a prophetic warning that, if he was not to be allowed Zebehr, evacuation could never be completed without some attempt to overawe the rebels by a show of force on the frontier of the Sudan. He asked for two hundred British troops at Wadi Halfa, and that some Indian Mussulmen should be moved from Suakim to Berber. It would have been difficult to make a more modest request of the most powerful government in the world, whose prestige in every capital was now irrevocably involved in the fate of the Sudan. But Gordon had not much hope that it would be granted. " I maintain firmly policy of eventual evacuation," he telegraphed on 1st March:

but I tell you plainly it is impossible to get Cairo employés out of Khartoum unless the government helps in the way I have

G.G.   2 A

told you. You refuse Zebehr, and are quite right (may be) to
do so, but it is the only chance. It is scarcely worth while saying
more on the subject. I will do my best to carry out my instructions, but I feel a conviction I shall be caught in Khartoum.

And now the struggle over Zebehr, which Baring had courage-
ously renewed, approached its climax. On 5th March a dispatch
from Frank Power in *The Times* drew the attention of the public
to the possibility of the appointment. On the same day the Cabinet
met and sent Baring a temporising reply, to the effect that Ministers
saw "no reason at present to change their impressions about
Zebehr." A commission of inquiry, traditional expedient of the
harassed Minister eager to postpone an awkward decision, was out
of the question, but the Cabinet hit upon the most hopeful available
substitute by attaching to its half-hearted refusal a request that a
detailed report on every garrison should be dispatched to them by
post. But the fortnight's respite, which they might reasonably have
expected, was not allowed them. The Press was in a ferment over
Zebehr. On 10th March an interview with Gordon, telegraphed
by Frank Power, appeared in *The Times*: only Zebehr, Gordon
had said, could ensure the safety of Khartoum, and Graham should
send two squadrons of cavalry to Berber. And on the 10th, in the
Commons, W. E. Forster, the Liberal Member for Bradford, paid
a resounding tribute to Gordon's character and genius, but fulmi-
nated menacingly against the appointment of a slave trader.

The Cabinet met again next day. It did not know that three
days earlier Gordon had warned Baring, in a series of brief telegrams,
that Khartoum was about to be besieged, for Baring had forwarded
these crucial messages by post instead of telegraph. But it did know
that the Liberal Press was furious at the suggestion of Zebehr, that
the anti-slavery societies were on the warpath and the House hostile.
In short, as Lord Granville explained apologetically to the Queen,
who had urged the Cabinet to accede to Gordon's request, if Zebehr
were sent "the public opinion of this country, however unreasonable, would be violently excited." That for the Cabinet at least no

question of principle was involved he made clear in a characteristically disingenuous concluding sentence: the government's refusal, he explained, " does not altogether shut the door to the future consideration of Zebehr being used." But the argument from public opinion was conclusive. For the British public was in one of its self-righteous and irrational moods: better, far better, that anarchy and slave-raiding should persist in the Sudan than that they should come to an end under a ruler who had himself been a slave-raider. After the political auspices had been taken only one Minister was prepared to support the nomination of Zebehr, and though that one Minister was Mr. Gladstone, he was ill, in bed. The Queen was horrified at the Cabinet's decision. " Parliament should be *told* the truth," she protested to Sir Henry Ponsonby, " and how Gordon has again and again told them what to do, and that they have refused." And to the unhappy Granville she telegraphed one of those penetrating sentences whose sheer common sense and good feeling crystallised the essentials of a complex situation in which the subtle Gladstone and the timid Granville were equally at sea: " having placed entire confidence in Gordon, have you now decided to throw over his advice and that of Baring and risk loss of all the garrisons ? "

Once again the Cabinet had quailed. It is probable that, public opinion being what it was, no government could have sent Zebehr to the Sudan and survived. But this government had done nothing to enlighten public opinion. And the charge against Ministers is heavier, far heavier, than this. For they had sent Gordon on a mission of incalculable difficulty and danger in the forlorn hope that his prestige and his intuitions would somehow avail to pacify the Sudan. Yet they now committed themselves to an all-embracing refusal to accept his advice; for the telegram which announced their final decision not to send Zebehr, announced also their refusal to send troops to Berber. Gordon was thus to be denied both the only means of saving Khartoum, and the only means of effecting the evacuation. Ministers had lost confidence in their envoy and they were accordingly in honour bound to recall him. But their fear of public opinion, which had compelled them to refuse Zebehr, forbade them to recall Gordon. For the journals which had been loudest in repudiating Zebehr had been foremost in demanding that Gordon should become a sort of permanent Rajah of the Sudan. And so the government left him to his fate. In retrospect one of its members, Lord Selborne, would confess[1] that to employ a knight-errant on so hazardous a mission " without giving him more or less of a free hand, or to judge his action under circumstances of difficulty by rules of red tape and routine was an offence against the fitness of things," an offence, however, which Lord Selborne and his colleagues would repeatedly commit. The telegram in which Ministers conveyed their final twofold rejection of Gordon's advice ended ironically with the information that his appointment would be prolonged for any reasonable period which he might need to carry out the evacuation which they had just rendered impracticable.

But Gordon never saw the telegram. For on the following day, 12th March, the Mahdi's hordes descended upon the Nile. The siege of Khartoum had commenced. From this moment until the last week of July only one communication from Baring or the government reached Gordon. Occasionally messages from Gordon, precariously smuggled through the enemy's lines, would reach the outer world, and at first Ministers were perplexed to find that they contained no reference to their own missives, for it had apparently not yet occurred to them that one characteristic of a siege is that it interrupts communications. It was not long, however, before they hit upon a satisfactory explanation. " General Gordon had the messages but did not choose to answer them."[2] This further evidence of Gordon's insubordination strengthened, if that were necessary, their conviction that they could not be held responsible for what happened to him. Indeed, it is significant that Ministers, who had already found so many impressive justifications for leaving Gordon to his fate, should have continued to produce additional justifications

[1] *Memorials, Personal and Political*, ii, 138.
[2] Lord Edmond Fitzmaurice, *Life of Lord Granville*, ii, 392.

in such rapid succession. One of the most remarkable accretions to
this growing armoury came from Lord Granville, although Lord
Granville already believed that Gordon had assumed vast and unforeseen executive powers, had adopted an unauthorised policy of his
own and was setting out, without an army, to " smash the Mahdi "
—and that " the government was thereby relieved of responsibility."[1]
Gordon, after all, could be said to have volunteered for a dangerous
mission, or at least to have instantly accepted the Cabinet's suggestion that he should undertake it; and from this Lord Granville
was able to draw a cogent analogy. "When a number of men
volunteer for a forlorn hope," he told the House of Lords on 27th
February, ". . . there is no obligation in honour on the commander
of the army to risk any more lives in saving that forlorn hope."

[1] Lord Edmond Fitzmaurice, *Life of Lord Granville*, ii, 386.

BOOK TWELVE

THE POLITICIANS

II. Tragedy

AND SO Gordon embarked alone upon the last and greatest of his lonely enterprises. For few if any in all the history of war are the episodes in which the moral power of a solitary individual has achieved so much. Solitary, for although until 9th September Stewart and Power were with him, from the first Gordon, and Gordon alone, was, in and by himself alone, the defence of Khartoum. Without a staff he was the high command, and without an administration he was the civil government. And with the mysterious power which he had always exercised over primitive peoples he inspired confidence into the terrified populace, and discipline and courage into the raw volunteer levies of negro slaves which he began to raise—for the Egyptian troops, as usual, were utterly unreliable and before March was out a thousand of them had been put to panic-stricken flight by a handful of Arabs. From a palace which before a month was up would be under constant rifle fire he planned the building of the ramparts and visited them nightly, armed the steamers and ordered their sallies, supervised the issue of every ounce of food, told the *ulemas* what to preach and the Notables what to believe, designed and issued paper money, manufactured and issued decorations, punished crime and judged civil disputes. And, above all, he nursed the morale of the bewildered population. For he knew that a blind confidence in " the father and saviour of the Sudan " was its only stay, and that if ever a stray underling about the Palace, or the throng of Arabs patiently waiting at its outer gates to kiss his feet or hold up their children for him to heal by a touch, should catch a despondent glance or a doubtful word the whole city would at once be plunged into despair.

And so despite the doubts which beset him as the full indifference of the government to the fate of Khartoum became slowly apparent, despite labours and anxiety which reached the limit of human endurance, he must always preserve an air of calm and smiling confidence. Even at the beginning of March, Power had observed the effects on Gordon of this unceasing nervous tension, but only owing to the accident that he occupied a neighbouring room. "One day of his work and bother would kill another man" he wrote home. "Yet he is so cheerful at breakfast, lunch and dinner; but I know he suffers fearfully from low spirits. I hear him walking up and down his room all night (it is next to mine). It is only his great piety carries him through." Gordon himself had long since been familiar with the task of animating an army, or a province, with a spirit beyond its normal compass and knew all too well what it demanded. "For my part," he would write in his Khartoum *Journal*,

I am always frightened, and very much so. I fear the future of all engagements. It is not the fear of death, that is past, thank God; but I fear defeat and its consequences. I do not believe a bit in the calm, unmoved man. I think it is only that he does not show it outwardly. Thence I conclude no commander of forces ought to live closely in relation with his subordinates, who watch him like lynxes, for there is no contagion equal to that of fear. I have been rendered furious, when, from anxiety, I could not eat, [and] I would find those at same table were in like manner affected.

But his spiritual growth of the last few years had prepared Gordon for the terrible months to come. It is clear that the new gentleness and serenity did not desert him. "Gordon is a most lovable character," wrote Power, "quiet, mild, gentle and strong;

he is so humble too." Not all these epithets would have been selected by his European staff in the old days in Equatoria. " He has found me badly up in Thomas à Kempis which he reads every day," continued Power to his mother, " and has given me an *Imitation of Christ*. He is, I believe, the greatest and best man of this century. He asks me who I am writing to, and when I say ' to you,' he says he hopes you will some day give him a cup of tea, and like him. No one could help it. I stay on here to the end. I'll stop while he stays."[1] Such was the impression which Gordon made upon his closest observer in Khartoum, at the time when Sir Charles Dilke, in London, was concluding that he was no longer in his right mind.

It was his faith which alone upheld him. To death he had long looked forward as to the coming of a friend. And there were moments in which he welcomed the seeming denial of all human aid, as compelling him to rely solely upon God. Yet he knew well that, humanly speaking, Khartoum was doomed, and would reproach himself for the anxiety which never left him for long. " I am torn in two," he told Augusta, " with the thought of my impotence and God's omnipotence. If He is Almighty, He will work His will; and He *is* Almighty, so why should I trouble ? Yet trouble I do, and am worn in the fight." The paradox, for so he considered it, was continually in his thoughts. And in his last letters to Augusta he consoles himself repeatedly with the reflection that whatever happens is the will of God, and therefore inevitably for the best. " I believe ambition put me here in this ruin; however, I trust and stay myself on the fact that not one sparrow falls to the ground without our Lord's permission; also, that enough for the day is the evil." " Our Lord's promise is not for the fulfilment of earthly wishes; therefore, if things come to ruin here He is still faithful, and is carrying out His great plan of Divine Wisdom. What I have to do is to submit my will to His however bitter may be the events which happen to me." " I now take my worries more quietly than before, for all things are ruled by Him for His glory, and it is rebellion to murmur against His will."

[1] Frank Power, *Letters from Khartoum*, 96 f.

2

All through March Gordon continued to expect that Zebehr would be sent to Khartoum, and British troops to Berber. On 13th March the first shot of the siege was fired, and he decided that he must send steamers to extricate the garrison at Halfaya. The Ministers who supposed him to be preparing to ' smash up ' the Mahdi would have been surprised if they could have known how reluctantly he came to this decision; for, as he wrote to Baring, but for the need to rescue the loyal garrison it was doubtful whether they had any right to " fight against those who have thrown in their lot with the only leader they can see." On 22nd March came the Mahdi's answer to the offer of peace sent by Gordon on his way to Khartoum. It bade him adopt the faith of Islam and surrender, or prepare to perish. While Gordon studied the letter the Mahdi's emissaries repeatedly attempted to divert his attention to a bundle which they had brought with them, until, losing patience, he hurled it away from him. Afterwards his clerk, who had returned the bundle to the dervishes, informed him that it was a filthy, patched dervish's coat. Gordon acknowledged the Mahdi's wordy manifesto in a curt note of twenty-five words. It concluded " I cannot have any more communication with you." By the end of the month the dervishes had captured an outpost on the north bank of the Blue Nile and henceforth the Palace was under constant rifle fire.

Baring at least had realised that Khartoum was now in grave danger. He could not know that during a period of approximately nineteen weeks, from the second week in March to the last week of July, only one communication from himself would reach Gordon. But between 20th March and 24th March Gordon's agent at Berber had telegraphed a series of desperate warnings to Cairo, and on 24th March Baring decided that he must do his best to make the Cabinet understand the situation. He was not the man to use alarmist language, although alarmist language would have been abundantly justified, but he went so far as to include the words

" under present circumstances, I think that an effort should be made
to help General Gordon from Suakim, if it is at all a possible military
operation." He succeeded at any rate in alarming the Queen.
" Gordon is in danger," she telegraphed to Hartington, " you are
bound to try and save him. . . . You have incurred fearful responsibility." The Cabinet, however, was not alarmed. Moreover,
the military authorities, none of whom had a tithe of Gordon's
knowledge of conditions in the Sudan, considered an expedition to
Berber too risky to attempt. And next morning Granville's report
to the Queen was full of phrases of an increasingly familiar texture:
". . . anxious as they were to afford every assistance to General
Gordon that was practicable, it would be unjustifiable . . . believed
to be impossible to take Khartoum by assault . . . garrison have six
months' provisions." Hartington, writing to the Queen next day,
hazarded a speculation which showed how far Baring had been
successful in enlightening the Cabinet. " It is possible," he admitted,
" that General Gordon may be surrounded and besieged in
Khartoum."

The Cabinet's refusal reached Baring on 25th March and it is
to his credit that it enraged him greatly. Next day he renewed his
assault upon Ministers. His telegram was a good deal more plain-
spoken than those to which the Foreign Office was accustomed, and
Lord Granville was aghast as he read it during a dinner party at the
Speaker's.

> . . . Let me earnestly beg Her Majesty's Government to place
> themselves in the position of Gordon and Stewart. They have
> been sent on a most difficult and dangerous mission by the British
> Government. Their proposal to send Zebehr, which, if it had
> been acted on some weeks ago, would certainly have entirely
> altered the situation, was rejected. The consequences which they
> foresaw have occurred. If they receive the instructions contained
> in Your Lordship's telegram of the 25th, they cannot but under-
> stand them as meaning that they, and all with them, are to be
> abandoned. . . . No one can regret more than I do the necessity

of sending British or Indian troops to the Sudan, but, having
sent Gordon to Khartoum, it appears to me that it is our bounden
duty, both as a matter of humanity and policy, not to abandon
him.

The Queen hailed with delight this salutary breath of the
common sense, and common morality, which had so long been
absent from the Cabinet's dealings with the Sudan. At last an
official had expressed what she felt, and what would undoubtedly be
felt by the man in the street, whose sentiments she so often unconsciously voiced. " Sir E. Baring only states my own feelings,"
she bade Ponsonby telegraph to Mr. Gladstone. ". . . You told me,
when I last saw you, Gordon must be trusted and supported; and
yet what he asked for repeatedly nearly five weeks ago has been
refused. If not only for humanity's sake, for the honour of the
Government and the nation, he must not be abandoned." And for
Ponsonby's private edification she added the superfluous comment
" Lord Granville is as weak as water."

But Mr. Gladstone was old and very obstinate; moreover,
appeals to humanity were one of his own specialities and he was
not disposed to accept them either from Baring or the Queen. He
was out of town at the moment, convalescent after indisposition,
and Hartington and Granville hurried down, with Baring's startling
dispatch, to consult him. He was unmoved. Next morning he sent
the Queen his verdict. It was evident that he had not relished the
blunt words of the telegram from Cairo. Baring, he told the Queen,
had shown conspicuous ability, " but the difficulties are such that it
is no wonder if occasionally he treads awry." Baring's recom-
mendations, he went on, amounted to a reversal of policy. And soon
he was deep again in the exculpations, the circuitous refusals to
admit ascertained facts, the hints and cloudy ambiguities with which
the Queen was already so familiar. Baring, he said,

. . . proposes to provide for dangers to General Gordon, of the
existence of which at the present moment Your Majesty's

Government do not possess evidence; and he does this in ignorance of what are at the time General Gordon's circumstances, opinions and desires. In conversation here yesterday the joint feeling was that an effort should be made to ascertain these, although it cannot be done with the rapidity which was ensured by the telegraph when it was open to Khartoum. The attainment of this end was contemplated by a telegram drawn yesterday in London and concurred in by Mr. Gladstone. Mr. Gladstone hopes that it will draw from General Gordon valuable information.

Since the message concurred in by Mr. Gladstone naturally did not reach Khartoum it naturally also elicited no information from Gordon, valuable or otherwise. It did, however, enable Ministers to feel that they were still awaiting further communications and that at the worst they had postponed the painful moment when a peace-loving administration would be compelled finally to decide for or against armed intervention. But for the first time there had been serious divisions on policy in the Sudan. Lord Selborne, the Lord Chancellor, had even threatened to resign if the Cabinet did not pledge itself to an expedition in the autumn. It is true that Sir William Harcourt, the Home Secretary, had threatened to resign if it did; it is true, too, that during their differences over Reform Ministers had become too accustomed to threats of resignation to treat them very seriously. Nevertheless, the Lord Chancellor's gesture was at least evidence that the sentiments and standards of common men and everyday non-political life had gained a precarious foothold within the Cabinet.

The Government did not inform the House, or the nation, of its decision to send no troops to Berber, and to withdraw Graham's force from Suakim. But once again it was overruled by events. For on 1st April *The Times* printed a message from Frank Power in Khartoum: "We are daily expecting the British troops," he wrote. "We cannot bring ourselves to believe that we are to be abandoned by the government." 'Abandoned' was an ugly word and Ministers, though in some respects they had shown themselves strangely insensitive, had never been insensitive to public opinion. Next day they decided that the House must be informed at once of their decision. On the morrow Mr. Gladstone would be making his first appearance in the Commons after his recent indisposition and could count on a sympathetic reception. And indeed without such adventitious assistance the old warrior had little doubt that he could make hay of any criticisms on which the Opposition might venture. He had not forgotten how first Baring, and then the Queen, had ventured to invoke humanity, and he positively looked forward to the fray.

Next day saw him at the height of his transcendent powers. 3rd April was a great Parliamentary occasion, albeit one of those great Parliamentary occasions which have but little relation to realities beyond the walls of Parliament. The Prime Minister, who had been received with prolonged cheering, began by reviving the old tendentious misstatement as to the nature of Gordon's mission. The British Government had sent him out to investigate, the Egyptian Government had given him executive powers. They were powers, he was careful to add, as to which the British Cabinet "feel both great interest and responsibility;" nevertheless, the suggestion was unmistakable; Gordon's authority had been unexpectedly extended; morally, the Prime Minister and his colleagues were less responsible than if they had conferred executive powers. themselves. He went on to explain that Gordon was free to withdraw from the Sudan at any moment, if he thought fit; which would have been true if Gordon had received the Government's telegrams of 13th and 16th March, which he had not, and if Khartoum had not been besieged, which it was. Lord Hartington then rose to explain that Khartoum, so far as his information went, was perfectly safe; the Government had considered sending some of Graham's troops to Berber, but for sound military reasons had abandoned the idea. Ministers accepted responsibility for Gordon's safety, but it was far too soon to tell what action, if any, they might find it necessary to take.

Thus far the issue of the day was undecided. For the Opposition was still uneasy at the news that no troops were being sent to assist Gordon, and in the evening Sir Stafford Northcote moved the adjournment of the House. The Conservative leader was by no means an expert Parliamentarian, and Mr. Gladstone, as he listened, must have realised that his enemy was delivered into his hands. For Sir Stafford, like Gladstone blissfully unaware that bullets were even then raining on the Palace walls at Khartoum, had unquestioningly accepted the Government's assurance that Gordon was enviably safe. " I do not say—heaven forbid—he is in actual danger here " he admitted. And he made the further mistake of stressing Power's reference to Khartoum's being abandoned by the Government. The scene which followed was afterwards exultingly described by Sir William Harcourt as unparalleled in his political experience. The Opposition, he told his constituents, " thought they could play tricks with the sick lion, but they were mistaken. He just put out his paw and there was an end of them . . . with his unparalleled eloquence he withered them with the blast of his scornful indignation . . . it was not a defeat, it was a rout." The eloquence of Mr. Gladstone was unquestionably overpowering, but it was not the sort of eloquence which survives in cold print next morning, and as we study the somewhat arid columns of Hansard we are left to imagine the imperious mien of the angry old man, the sharp rap of the signet-ring on the dispatch-box, the " eye like Mars, to threaten and command." But we can at least observe, and wonder at, the arguments which, backed by the tremendous force of the Prime Minister's personality, were sufficient to rout the Opposition.

He began by complaining that in the space of two months this was their seventeenth discussion on Egyptian affairs, that this was unfair to the government, and that Northcote's pessimism as to Gordon's prospects had been unpatriotic. And so he came to the dangerous word ' abandoned.' Gladstone knew of course that just over a week ago Baring had used precisely this word—Gordon and Stewart, he had wired, could not but understand Granville's instructions "as meaning that they, and all with them, are to be abandoned." He knew, too, that the Queen had echoed Baring— "Gordon must not be abandoned." But he knew, too, that of all this his audience was wholly ignorant. So far as Members were aware, there was only the vastly less impressive authority of Frank Power for the ugly word. And so he was free to make effective play with the young man's unofficial status: "What is Mr. Frank Power in relation to us? . . . a temporary Consular Agent. A Consular Agent is not an officer responsible to the government, even if permanently appointed. . . . And yet the right honourable gentleman takes an opinion of Mr. Power . . . as virtually equivalent to an official declaration conveying the mature conviction of General Gordon. Really, sir, it is a farce. . . ." His supporters could not know that the Government had so lately received from its official representatives in Egypt a warning identical with Power's and they broke into delighted cheers. It was evident that the day was already won, and in his peroration the Prime Minister felt able to revert to his complaint of the frequency of debates on the Sudan, but with the added innuendo that this preoccupation had been "out of all proportion to the pressure and urgency of the question," and was obstructing genuinely important public business. The triumph was complete; the debate, which had been expected to last far into the night, collapsed before eight o'clock. The triumph was complete; unfortunately it was one of those triumphs which, as Baring had said of an earlier abnegation of responsibility by the Government, was a mere phantasm of the Parliamentary mind.

3

April drew on, and in Khartoum the increasing pressure of administrative problems was added to the increasing pressure of the besiegers. Money was urgently needed—for grain, for wages, at treble the normal rate to discourage desertion, for pay and gratuities to the troops, for compensation to the owners of buildings destroyed

for military purposes. When Gordon reached Khartoum the treasury
had been, as usual, nearly empty, and the whole of the £100,000
sent by Baring had disappeared between Cairo and Khartoum;
£60,000 of it being purloined by an Egyptian official rewarded on
his return to Egypt with decorations and a life pension of £1,200
per annum. Gordon solved the problem by creating a paper
currency. Without it the defence would have speedily collapsed, but
its value depended solely upon the prestige of his name. Notes of
at least ten different denominations, from 5 to 5,000 piastres, have
survived. Their total value is uncertain, but Mr. Martin Parr has
calculated that it must have reached somewhere about £170,000.
They bore a serial number and an imprint of the seal of both Gordon
and the Government. And amidst the countless distractions of
administration and defence Gordon positively found time to sign
fifty thousand of them with his own hand. As he scrawled the
seemingly unending signatures in the dust and heat of that Khartoum
April, he may have recalled the familiar aphorism as to the deceitful-
ness of riches: it would have amused him if he could have known
that years afterwards collectors and museums all over the world
would be eagerly seeking for " Gordon notes," and that to meet
the demand a plentiful supply of forgeries would be forthcoming.

On 7th April, in a letter which might, or might not, one day
reach Baring, he inserted a characteristic admonition:

> It may be bad taste to say it, but if we get out of this give
> Stewart a K.C.M.G. and spare me at all costs. You will thus
> save me the disagreeableness of having to refuse it. I hate these
> things. If we get out it is the answer to prayer and not by our
> own might and it is a true pleasure to have been here, though
> painful enough at times. . . . The only reinforcements the Sudan
> has received since the 27th November, 1863, date when Hicks's
> defeat was known at Cairo, is seven persons, including myself.

Two days later, on 9th April, an Arab made his devious way
into Khartoum bearing a message dispatched by Baring on 10th

March, the only communication which Gordon was to receive from him during a period of nineteen weeks. It could hardly have been curter. " So far as I know," it ran, " there is no intention on the part of the Government to send an English force to Berber." All Gordon's other questions remained unanswered; it seemed clear that he was to be left not only without assistance but without instructions. He was free to take his own decisions and to seek assistance elsewhere. To Baring he wrote frankly:

> As far as I can understand the situation is this: you state your intention of not sending any relief force up here or to Berber, and you refuse me Zebehr. I consider myself free to act according to circumstances. I shall hold on here as long as I can, and if I can suppress the rebellion, I shall do so. If I cannot, I shall retire to the equator and leave you the indelible disgrace of abandoning the garrisons of Sennar, Kassala, Berber and Dongola, with the certainty that you will eventually be forced to smash up the Mahdi under greater difficulties if you would retain peace in Egypt.

And he explained that he had requested Sir Samuel Baker to appeal to " British and American millionaires " to raise a fund of £300,000 with which to hire three thousand Turkish troops for the Sudan. " This," he said, " would settle the Sudan and Mahdi for ever." Three thousand Turks; he had only asked for two squadrons of British cavalry, for all that would be needed until the eleventh hour was some token of British concern; and the mere knowledge that fifty British soldiers were in the neighbourhood would probably have saved Khartoum.

An Anglo-American subscription list and three thousand Turkish mercenaries to do the work of the British Government—it was a fantastic suggestion, but scarcely more fantastic than the situation in London, where that spring a plan was afoot to collect two thousand big-game hunters to rescue Gordon by way of Suakim and Berber; where a Mrs. Surtees-Alnatt was canvassing Members of

Parliament on behalf of a fund to purchase a safe-conduct for the
garrison of Khartoum; and Baroness Burdett-Coutts would soon
be reporting to *The Times* that she was receiving a flood of contributions to yet another Gordon Rescue Fund, including five
thousand pounds from an English lady and twenty francs from a
French woman in Lyons. " If the will of the people at large," she
wrote, " could penetrate the deadly silence of Khartoum, Gordon
would know that the English nation, misrepresented as it may
have been through its ordinary channels, had sprung to its feet,
and moved by a spirit akin to his own, was eager to strike a blow
on its own account on behalf of a man sent out in his country's
name."

4

Despite his protests at the waste of Parliamentary time on Gordon,
Gladstone's Parliamentary triumph of 3rd April did not immediately
earn him the respite he had demanded. For on 17th April *The Times*
was able to print a fuller message from Power, in which he described
Khartoum as " the centre of an enormous rebel camp." The Palace
was under rifle fire, he said, and the situation was critical. On 21st
April Parliament reassembled after the Easter recess and a fusillade of
questions opened on the Prime Minister. The lion, no longer sick,
once again raised a menacing paw. " There is no apprehension at all
of danger," he assured the House; and again " there is no military
or other danger now threatening Khartoum." But he knew that
Members had been troubled by Power's description of the city
surrounded by a huge army of rebels, and that Power, though but
a temporary Consular agent, might be supposed to be better supplied
with first-hand information on Khartoum than himself. He prepared
accordingly to efface the disquieting impression which the young
man's dispatch must have produced. It cannot be said that he was
successful. Mr. Gladstone was not infrequently over-subtle, but
seldom indeed was he troubled by a sudden sense that his case was

less convincing than it should have been. On this occasion, however, a combination of both embarrassments seems to have betrayed him into a sentence to which it must have been difficult even for Sir William Harcourt to attach any intelligible significance. Gordon, Gladstone endeavoured to explain to the House, was not, according to the information available to Ministers, surrounded:

> The general effect being, according to the expression used, that he is hemmed in—that is to say, that there are bodies of hostile troops in the neighbourhood forming more or less of a chain around it. I draw a distinction between that and the town being surrounded, which would bear technically a very different meaning.

" Of course," he added a little later, " the question of sending help and assistance to General Gordon will relate to some wholly different state of things." It is not difficult to sympathise with Ashmead-Bartlett, Baroness Burdett-Coutts's husband, who, on being reproved by Gladstone on the following afternoon for laughing, explained that he had involuntarily laughed " at the extraordinary discrepancy between the Prime Minister's statements and the well-known facts of the case."

These episodes strengthened a sense, which had begun to gain on some Ministers, that their leader's grasp of the Sudanese problem was inadequate, and at a meeting of the Cabinet next day there were heated differences of opinion. The outcome, however, was, as usual, to defer any decision. Only, the Prime Minister drafted a verbose catalogue of interrogations for Gordon (which did not reach him for more than three months) and in Parliament next day set himself to strike a somewhat more conciliatory note. He stoutly repeated, it is true, that " we see no reason to modify, in any respect, the statements previously made, that there is no military or other danger threatening Khartoum," but he admitted that the country felt " a profound interest and likewise a strong sense of obligation" as to the safety of Gordon, whom he described as " that gallant and heroic officer." And he assured the House that Ministers shared these sentiments, and " have been careful to put themselves in a position to fulfil this obligation in the sense in which they believe the country, in common with themselves, recognise it." The precise position into which Ministers, fresh from their stormy and indecisive discussions, had in fact put themselves it would have been difficult for Mr. Gladstone to particularise further, and he contented himself by concluding dexterously " having made that statement, which I hope is sufficiently explicit and significant, it would not be possible, consistently with my public duty, to enter on any further explanations."

Meanwhile, in Khartoum, Gordon, who had at last abandoned hope of any help from the British Government, was drafting a direct request to the Sultan for a Turkish expedition, and another to the Pope and the consuls of the European powers for funds to finance it. He did not expect the messages to reach their destination (and in fact the nearest they got to it, years later, was the Royal Engineers' Museum at Chatham), but he felt that his duty to the Egyptian garrisons required him to make a last appeal for help. This done, he devoted himself to designing armour for his steamers, wire entanglements and primitive land mines for the ramparts, and medals of silver-gilt, silver and pewter, for those who distinguished themselves in the siege. Before the end of April the Nile had begun to rise, and to form to the south-west a wide lagoon which, for a time, would greatly strengthen the defences. But before the end of April, too, the garrison of Messalemia, about seventy miles to the south-east, had surrendered, and with it went large stores of food and rifles, and one of Gordon's steamers.

6

On 29th April, two days after this ominous news reached Gordon, John Morley was conversing with another Radical Member, Sir Wilfred Lawson, and Wilfrid Scawen Blunt, the champion of the

Arabs, in the smoking-room of the House of Commons. Gordon, all three agreed, was "past praying for," and Morley, to whom the fate of Khartoum presented itself naturally in terms of Parliamentary votes, delivered the reassuring verdict that "people were tired of Gordon," and that his death, which two months ago must certainly have involved the fall of the government, would now only entail "a row."[1] Of such aspects of public affairs John Morley was a shrewd judge, but on this occasion he had not reckoned with the publication, two days later, of a voluminous, though ill-arranged, Blue Book containing the bulk of the Sudan correspondence, and in particular the reference, in Gordon's latest telegram, to "indelible disgrace."

The Opposition promptly put down another motion of censure, and during the brief interval before it was debated there was evidence that for once John Morley had misjudged the temper of the public. On 8th May the vicar of St. Ives in Huntingdonshire wrote to The Times to say that on the previous Sunday he had invited his congregation to pray "for General Gordon in imminent peril at Khartoum," and to suggest that all churches should follow his example—a proposal which, since the Prime Minister had so recently declared that no military or other danger was threatening Khartoum, must have been embarrassing to some of the clergy as well as irritating to Mr. Gladstone. On the same day the Patriotic Association held a crowded meeting in St. James's Great Hall, Piccadilly, "to protest against the abandonment of General Gordon." Earl Cadogan presided, and was supported by the Duke of Portland and a number of peers and Members of Parliament, including the indomitable Ashmead-Bartlett. Hard words were used, the tone of the meeting being set by the Chairman's opening reference to the government's conduct as "devoid of all principles, of all moral courage and all statesmanship." But worse was to come. For on 9th May a Health Exhibition in South Kensington was formally opened by the Duke of Cambridge, and the Prime Minister, making his way to the royal dais, was publicly hissed. At the close of the

[1]Wilfrid Scawen Blunt, Gordon at Khartoum, 232.

ceremony he left the gallery by a different route, but was again hissed and booed. Nor did *The Times* hesitate to attribute this " loud expression of dissatisfaction " to " the intensity of popular feeling among all classes with regard to the fate of General Gordon."

When four days later Gladstone rose to resist the vote of censure he must have known that public opinion regarded him as a defendant on trial, and he had evidently decided that attack would be the most effective form of defence. A relief expedition, he declared, would mean a war of conquest against a people struggling to be free. " Yes," he repeated, as if deliberately to evoke the hallowed memories of the *Risorgimento*, " struggling rightly to be free." He could not of course know that within ten years the dervish hordes, whom this unexpected tribute appeared to rank with Garibaldi and Kossuth, would have exterminated three-quarters of the population of the Sudan, but he cannot have forgotten how lately his own government had dispatched Graham and his army against them, and it would have puzzled even him to explain how the legitimate targets of British rifles at El Teb and Tamaii had at Khartoum suddenly become an inviolable people pursuing the sacred rights of nationality. Indeed, Lord Selborne, Gladstone's Lord Chancellor, afterwards confessed that he could attach no meaning to the Prime Minister's words.[1] But Mr. Gladstone had always maintained that all political action should be founded upon principle, and although the particular principle on which he now justified political inaction would scarcely bear close inspection it was at least a principle.

The Prime Minister turned with growing confidence upon the Opposition. Would *they* send an expedition to Khartoum, he demanded, glaring at Sir Michael Hicks Beach, the mover of the motion. Wilfrid Blunt, who, with Canon Scott Holland, was listening from the Diplomatic gallery, recorded the scene in his diary: " having said this, he waited a moment, and then pointing to Beach, turned to the House and screamed ' Look! Dumb! ' "

And now the Prime Minister revived, for the first time whole-heartedly and in public, his own original illusions as to the nature

[1] *Memorials, Personal and Political*, ii, 136.

of Gordon's mission. The action of the government, he said, had
been " limited to sending him for the purpose of reporting on the
evacuation of the Sudan." And for the first time, too, he hinted
that Gordon was disobeying, or about to disobey, his orders: " his
mission was an absolutely pacific one and it was nothing else as far
as we were concerned. He may detach himself from his mission,
he may undertake another line of action. . . ." These assertions as
to the original instructions were baseless, and the suggestion as to
Gordon's present conduct were founded upon a complete mis-
conception of what was happening at Khartoum, but though they
seem to have had surprisingly little effect upon the House they were
embraced, and perpetuated, by John Morley and other less celebrated
apologists. The most effective passage in the Prime Minister's speech
was a series of quotations of reassuring phrases in Gordon's dispatches. Of these there had been plenty, for Gordon was fond of
insisting paradoxically on his safety and had declared, soon after he
reached Khartoum, that it was as safe as Kensington Park. Ministers
did not know Gordon; and they could hardly be expected to understand that, since he still believed that Khartoum would be saved as
by a miracle—" that by some means not clear God will give us an
issue "—he did consequently also firmly believe that it was not,
and could not be, in danger. The phrases, such as " we are all right
up here," with which the Prime Minister made play would have
provided more telling evidence if they had come from a conventional
general, and, in fact, they seem to have misled hardly anybody but
Mr. Gladstone.

Indeed, next day his speech was virtually demolished by the
much respected W. E. Forster, who reminded the House that
Gladstone's last telegram, which he had just described as " a cove-
nant " with Gordon, had in fact done little more than ask Gordon
at great length whether he was in danger. Forster then declared,
with sudden and shocking simplicity " I believe everyone but the
Prime Minister is convinced of that danger." This statement by a
former Liberal Minister came so near to being the exact truth that
misgivings began to spread far and wide in the Liberal ranks.

Indeed, it was afterwards generally agreed that Forster and a number
of Liberals would have voted for the motion, and that the government would consequently have been overthrown, had it not been
for a speech by Hartington which, despite its numerous convolutions,
qualifications and saving clauses, wavering supporters of the
government were nevertheless able to regard as foreshadowing an
eventual relief expedition at an unspecified date.

Hartington's speech had led the world as well as the House to
believe that in the autumn at least a relief expedition would be sent
to Khartoum, and for a while public agitation died down. Ministers,
however, had in fact decided nothing whatever, and apart from some
dilatory and half-hearted investigations as to the alternative military
routes to Khartoum they confined themselves to dispatching on
17th May yet another characteristic telegram, suggesting that
Gordon should bribe neighbouring tribesmen to escort Egyptian
civilians to safety. Meanwhile, as though to emphasise the relative
unimportance of the Sudan, Ministers had summoned Baring to a
financial conference in London and replaced him for the time being
with a newly arrived member of his staff, known to his friends as
Topsy Egerton. When some three months later the government's
telegram of 17th May found its way into Khartoum, Gordon
attributed it to Egerton, and commented sardonically in his *Journal*:

Egerton's telegram, carefully written in cypher (and equally
carefully without date, but which we ascribe to June) respecting
the contracts to be entered into with the Bedouin tribes to escort
us down (" and be sure and look after *yourself!* ") might have
been as well written in Arabic; it would have produced hilarity
with the Mahdi. . . . The pomp of Egerton's telegram, informing
me " that Her Majesty's Government would (really!) pay on
delivery so much a head for all refugees *delivered* on Egyptian
frontier and would (*positively*, it is incredible!) *reward* tribes with
whom I might contract to escort them down." It was too
generous to believe! Egerton's chivalrous nature must have got
the better of his diplomatic training when he wrote it!

7

Grateful both for their narrow escape from Parliamentary defeat and for the relaxation of public anxiety induced by Hartington's ambiguous half-pledges, Ministers turned with relief from Khartoum to concentrate upon their Reform Bill and preparations for the conference on Egyptian finance, subjects which most of them considered to be a good deal more important, and which they certainly understood a good deal better. During the whole of this 'Conference period,' from May to August, it was rare for Gordon and Khartoum to be accorded more than five minutes hasty discussion at the fag-end of a Cabinet meeting. In the Sudan, however, the unrolling of the scroll proceeded inexorably. On 26th May the Mahdi's forces captured Berber, Khartoum's gateway to the north, and with it Gordon's agent Cuzzi who, to save himself and his family from the prolonged massacre which ensued, was compelled to adopt the dervish dress and the faith of Islam. A month later, the Mahdi sent him, with a flag of truce and a summons to surrender, to Khartoum. When he reached the camp of the besiegers and gazed across the Nile it was with a bitter pang of remorse that he perceived the figure of Gordon, alone at his Palace window, surveying the enemy through a telescope. But Gordon, who sternly disapproved of apostasy, refused to see Cuzzi. And to the Mahdi's summons he sent a curt refusal, adding " If you have letters to send me again, do not send a European."

8

On 27th June, while Cuzzi was carrying the summons of surrender to Khartoum, the Cabinet learned for certain that Berber had fallen. But the Reform Bill had now deeply embroiled Ministers in a constitutional struggle with the Lords, and they had little attention to spare for Khartoum. Most of them had for some while been uneasy, and in particular Hartington, who could not forget the speech with which he had turned the tide of debate on 13th May. But the Prime Minister was resolutely opposed to action in the Sudan, and the imperious old man, as Sir Donald Currie had recently reported to Wilfrid Blunt, "had it all his own way in the Cabinet." Both Currie, who was an intimate of Gladstone's, and Arthur Godley (afterwards Lord Kilbracken), who had lately been his Private Secretary, had also assured Blunt that Gordon was out of his mind.

The weeks drew on, without word from Khartoum. And then, on 20th July, came sudden news that a scrap of paper had been brought into Dongola, with a brief message from Gordon. Khartoum, it said, was still uncaptured; what news was there of a relief expedition? The Cabinet felt compelled to reply, but the telegram which it dispatched to Egerton four days later bore every mark of having been drafted by Mr. Gladstone, and suggested not so much a message of encouragement and instruction to a hard-pressed general as one of the Prime Minister's more evasive answers to an awkward Parliamentary question. The government, Gordon was to be informed, "continue to be anxious to learn from himself his views and position, so that, if danger has arisen or is likely to arise in the manner they have described, they may be in a position to take measures accordingly." It is satisfactory to know that Gordon never had to read this remarkable communication.

But the strange domination which the Prime Minister had so long exercised over his colleagues was at last nearing its end. For several weeks their misgivings as to Khartoum had been steadily increasing, and he had quelled them one and all, partly indeed, by his overpowering personality and immense prestige, but chiefly perhaps because he was the only one of them who had altogether made up his own mind. For Mr. Gladstone hated war and he distrusted Gordon, and he had convinced himself that in defiance of his orders Gordon was doing his best to involve him in war. And because he believed this he persisted in believing that Gordon was not in danger. For as Forster had so lately observed, in that speech which the Prime Minister had described to the Queen as being " of remarkable bitterness and hostility," Mr. Gladstone, who could persuade most people of most things, could, when necessary, persuade himself of almost anything. " He lives completely," noted Lord Acton, " in what for the moment he chooses to believe."

On 25th July the rising tide of the Cabinet's anxiety almost breached the Prime Minister's defences. Nine Ministers were for an expedition and only three against, Granville characteristically declining to express an opinion. But of the three one was Mr. Gladstone, and the three prevailed. A day or two later the Press, as if suddenly realising that the session would soon be over and that the government had decided nothing, resumed its agitation. But in his present mood Mr. Gladstone was prepared to ignore even a Press agitation. The sudden recrudescence of excoriating criticism in journals which had faithfully supported them in their campaign against the Lords was, however, too much for some of his colleagues. And in particular for Hartington, who had been wrestling with his conscience even before his speech of 13th May. As early as 24th April he had written " I don't think I can agree in the course which is now being taken; " yet now, at the end of July, the course had not been altered. Hartington's was not a particularly sensitive conscience, or it would have driven him to decisive action much sooner; but it had troubled him like a nagging tooth, and whenever by dexterous evasion or fierce assertion of authority the Prime Minister had foiled his ponderous attempts to convince his colleagues of their duty it had been left a trifle sorer. On 15th July he had written to Granville " At the last Cabinet when it [the expedition] was mentioned, summoned, as I hoped, to decide on it, I got five minutes at the fag end, and was as usual put off." And now the public accusations of bad faith had goaded him to desperation.

On 29th July two Cabinet Ministers circulated separate memoranda on Gordon to their colleagues. One was Selborne, the Lord Chancellor. In a brief but luminous indictment he set forth the arguments which in Cabinet had so often been forestalled or silenced, demolishing one by one the moral sophistries on which the Prime Minister's case for inaction had so long been founded. Was Gordon, he asked, " to be condemned for operating actively against those who have attacked or threatened him, as we ourselves did near Suakim ? " As for that notorious phrase, " crushing the Mahdi," it was " perfectly intelligible, if he was attacked or threatened by the Mahdi's followers," and by no means justified the Prime Minister in arguing that Gordon had sought to achieve his objects " by other than peaceable means. I am still more averse," he wrote,

> to acting towards a public servant, in whose reputation and safety all England, and (I might almost say) the world, is interested—who has accepted at our instance a mission of extraordinary difficulty—as if we had no real sense of the responsibilities which we have publicly acknowledged, as if something (of which I can see no evidence at all) had happened to absolve us from those responsibilities.

Selborne was Lord Chancellor, and he could hardly have drawn up a more damaging indictment of the conduct of the Cabinet of which he was a member, and by implication of its chief. But Selborne was not essential to the Cabinet, and Mr. Gladstone was prepared to ignore or crush him. Hartington was less able than Selborne, but he was the acknowledged leader of the Whigs, and his massive respectability and powerful connections ensured to the Cabinet, despite its suspect Radical wing, the solidity without which it could not hope to survive. And Hartington, too, circulated a memorandum. It was not so powerful as Selborne's, but it came from the head of the house of Cavendish. Even so at first Mr. Gladstone believed that he could dispose of it. He appended comments before it went the round of the Cabinet, which made it all too clear that he was still unconvinced. Had Mr. Gladstone yielded to argument that day, for such are the ironies of history, Gordon would yet have been saved. Unfortunately Mr. Gladstone had not yet realised that Hartington, too, had at last made up his mind. Two days later he knew the truth. For on 31st July Hartington, perceiving that the Prime Minister was still obstinately resisting, sent in his ultimatum. He no longer argued as to the duty of the Cabinet; he simply explained what he took to be his own. For the first time he had occupied ground from which neither subtle manœuvre nor frontal assault could expel him. He recalled his speech of 13th May, and declared bluntly that no explanation by anyone else could relieve him of the obligations which he believed himself to have incurred. "It is a question of personal honour and good faith," he concluded, "and I don't see how I can yield upon it." The leader of the Whigs was positively threatening resignation. The Prime Minister perceived at once that something much more important than the life of Gordon or the safety of Khartoum was now imperilled. The existence of his government was at stake. And for the first time in the long chapter of procrastinations he acted swiftly. He did not argue. He did not summon a Cabinet. That very day he let Granville know that he would himself propose a grant of money for a relief expedition to Parliament.

Mr. Gladstone's sudden concession has been generally represented as a swift and final capitulation to the threat, from the leading Whig nobleman, to that for which Mr. Gladstone cared most, his own administration. But it was nothing of the kind. Even now the indomitable old man had not been driven from the field. He had but yielded a few hotly-contested yards. Even now he did not despair of staving off an expedition. The well-tried weapons of ambiguity and procrastination were still to hand, why should they not even now prevail? On 5th August, it is true, he would himself move in Parliament for a sum "not exceeding £300,000" (a ridiculously inadequate figure as Hartington subsequently told Granville[1]) "to enable Her Majesty to undertake operations for the relief of General Gordon, should they become necessary." And it is true that, despite the conditional clause, the House and the public understood this to mean that the government had at last made up

---

[1] Holland, *Life of the Eighth Duke of Devonshire*, ii, 22, 3.

its mind. What Gladstone, however, understood by it he made clear in a characteristically worded note to Granville: " I do not consider the evidence as to Gordon's position requires or justifies, in itself, military preparations for the contingency of a military expedition. There are, however, preparations, perhaps, of various kinds which might be made, and which are matters simply of cost and do not include necessary consequences in point of policy."[1]

The motion, in other words, might serve to persuade the House and the public that action was intended, but the Prime Minister himself still had every hope that no action would result from it. Dilke put the position more succinctly. " A way out of the difficulty," he noted, " was found in an agreement that we should ask for a small vote of credit, which we were to use or not as should be thought right later."[2] For Mr. Gladstone still insisted on believing that it was Gordon's duty to abandon the garrison of Khartoum and somehow effect his own escape. " I have never," he would tell Granville four years later, when the tragedy was long over, " heard his power to do so disputed." But Gordon had been explicitly instructed to ensure the safe retreat both of the inhabitants of Khartoum and of the Egyptian garrisons elsewhere in the Sudan, and his instructions had never been cancelled. Moreover, as Joseph Chamberlain's biographer observes[3], " if you send out a soldier to run away from those at whose head you have placed him you must not send a Gordon." But perhaps the biographer of Hartington may be allowed the last word.

If, for political reasons, he dared not openly and explicitly recall Gordon, what *right* had Gladstone to believe that it was Gordon's duty to desert his post? Was Gordon, then, to abandon to slavery or the sword those who put their trust in him in order that the Prime Minister might satisfy his Radicals without offending the rest of the Liberal party?[4]

---

[1] *Ibid.*, i, 480.
[2] Gwynn and Tuckwell, *Sir Charles Dilke*, ii, 61.
[3] J. L. Garvin, *Life of Joseph Chamberlain*, i, 512.
[4] Holland, *Life of the Duke of Devonshire*, i, 423.

The unhappy Hartington soon discovered that he had under-
estimated the resources of his sinuous opponent. On the very day
of the motion, it is true, Wolseley and his staff had flung themselves
on the task of preparation now so many weeks overdue. But
preparations for what? To send troops, surely, at least as far as
Dongola. But no; on 19th August, a fortnight after his motion,
the Prime Minister is reminding his Secretary of State for War,
in all the cautious convolutions of Gladstone prose, that nothing so
far-reaching has been yet decided, that perhaps after all it would
be somewhat precipitate to decide anything whatever for the
present.

> While I entirely sympathise with your anxiety that we should
> not mar any operation which may be proper by delay, I think
> you would admit that, unless there is a necessity of time, the
> moment is more unfortunate than not for a decision.

And, since he could never quite bring himself to believe that a siege
interrupts communications, Mr. Gladstone could not resist adding:

> And Gordon's renewed communication with the Mudir, while
> nothing is sent to us, seem to strengthen the presumption that
> he purposely refrains from communicating with us.

And Ministers, he hinted, would yet have to be assured that they
" were not about to become unawares the slaves of Gordon's
(probably rebellious) ideas."

As he studied the guarded phrases, the ambiguities and in-
nuendos Hartington must have come near to despair. Indeed, writing
to the Queen on 23rd August, he felt bound to speak of the plan of
operations on which he had decided " in the event of its becoming
necessary to send an expedition for the relief of General Gordon."
And he soon found that there were other weapons in the Prime
Minister's armoury of obstruction. For whenever Hartington pressed
for a definite decision Mr. Gladstone would insist that every member

of the Cabinet, now dispersed for the summer recess to the four corners of the United Kingdom, should be separately consulted.[1] Sir William Harcourt might be in the Highlands, and have intimated that, so far as he was concerned, Hartington would be allowed *carte blanche*, but somehow or other a formal verdict must be elicited from him. On 26th August Hartington was desperately pointing out to the Prime Minister, what the Prime Minister, it must be presumed, knew only too well, that such methods of conducting business must result in fatal delay. His only consolation, he admitted to Granville, was that he had already so greatly overspent the Parliamentary grant that it will eventually " appear almost absurd not to send the expedition."

This, indeed, was Hartington's one trump card. As Marquis of Hartington he was far too slow, too simple and too straightforward to be a match for his subtle and powerful antagonist, but as Secretary of State for War he presided over the military machine, now at length launched upon its cumbrous preparations. And sooner or later the mere momentum of the machine, the instinctive assumption of the military mind that military preparations must have a military objective, would be too much even for Mr. Gladstone. And so it fell out. At length the dispute between the advocates of the Nile route and their opponents was settled, and Wolseley, the protagonist of the former, was given the command. And at last there came a moment when it was generally understood that the expedition was to proceed, if necessary, as far as Khartoum. Whether it could compensate by rapid movement for having started several months too late was another question. Later history has shown that even with the iron determination of a Churchill at the heart of the war-machine delay and frustation is possible; the impulse to unrelenting haste was hardly to be expected from a Prime Minister who regretted and mistrusted the whole project, and himself, outside the sheltered arena of domestic politics, possessed none of the qualities of the man of action.

---

[1] Holland, *Life of the Eighth Duke of Devonshire*, i, 490.

9

Meanwhile, Gordon toiled desperately to defend the sprawling town with his half-trained troops who, like the terrified civilians, drew their only strength from his spirit. The half-moon of fortifications to east and south from the Blue to the White Nile, was complete with its redoubts, its improvised land mines and wire entanglements. The Nile was still running deep, and his steamers, with their improvised armour, could steam north and south, harrying the besiegers and collecting supplies. On 29th July, while Hartington and Selborne were circulating their fateful memoranda to the Cabinet, a three-day action cleared a stretch of the Blue Nile, and it was on 29th July, too, that Gladstone's message of 23rd April reached Gordon. Even Dilke had described it as a string of silly questions and it brought little comfort to Khartoum. But Gordon sent a patient answer to Baring next day, and only permitted himself one touch of irony. " You ask me," he wrote, " ' to state cause and intention in staying in Khartoum, knowing government means to abandon Sudan,' and in reply I say ' I stay at Khartoum because Arabs have shut us up and will not let us out.' " On 5th August, while in the House of Commons Gladstone was moving for the beggarly £300,000 for an expedition which he still believed he could prevent from making for Khartoum, Gordon wrote for Baring the first sketch of an optimistic plan (fated to add one more link to the chain of misunderstandings between himself and Mr. Gladstone) for sending Stewart downstream to recapture Berber, hold it for fifteen days, burn it and return to Khartoum. And later in August his ablest subordinate, Mohammed Ali, with an armed flotilla won victories on the Blue Nile which resulted in the capture of guns, ammunition and grain. On 24th August, elated by the success, Gordon wrote to a naval friend: "We are going to hold out here for ever." But it was the last gleam of sunlight before the clouds closed down.

Before sending Stewart to attack Berber, Gordon decided to

dispose of an enemy threat twenty-five miles up the Blue Nile.
Mohammed Ali won a first engagement on 4th September, but on
5th September, disobeying Gordon's instructions, he left the river
and made off through wooded country in an attempt to capture
the dervish sheikh. He was ambushed, and perished with a thousand
of his men. Moreover, the Nile was about to fall, and soon Khartoum would once more be exposed to the south-west. Gordon was
compelled to abandon his plan for recapturing Berber. He could
not now spare troops for Stewart. He would send him to force his
way by steamer downstream to Dongola with dispatches, and let
the world know the true plight of Khartoum. And so he sat down
to write his last letter to Baring.

> How many times have we written asking for reinforcements? . . .
> No answer at all has come to us . . . and the hearts of men have
> become weary at this delay. While you are eating and drinking
> and resting on good beds, we and those with us . . . are watching
> night and day, endeavouring to quell the movement of this
> false Mahdi. . . . The reason why I have now sent Colonel
> Stewart is because you have been silent all this while and
> neglected us, and lost time without doing any good. If troops
> were sent, as soon as they reach Berber, this rebellion will cease.

The " you " to whom these mild reproaches were addressed was
of course the government which Baring represented.

Stewart and young Power left Khartoum, with the French
Consul, on 8th September in the steamer *Abbas*. The venture had
been planned by Gordon with his usual meticulous care. He had
even fitted the *Abbas* with submerged buffers to protect it from
hidden rocks. Two other steamers were to escort it past the two
chief danger points. And Gordon had repeatedly warned Stewart
never to land, save to collect fuel in some lonely spot. Disastrously,
after safely passing Berber, Stewart sent the escorting steamers back.
And then, within two days of Dongola, the *Abbas* struck a rock in
mid-stream. Two sailing boats which Gordon had provided against

just such an emergency had already been cut adrift. Natives appeared on the bank with a white flag, and once again Stewart disregarded his instructions. The three Europeans landed, agreed, unarmed, to enter the house of a local sheikh and were instantly murdered. Another hundred miles and they would have reached Dongola and would have found there a certain Major Kitchener, destined in course of time to be the victor of Omdurman. And if Kitchener had learned from them of Gordon's straits he would doubtless have contrived to hasten the relief of Khartoum. It was two months before Gordon himself learned of this crowning disaster.

10

On 18th September, the day on which Stewart and Power were slaughtered on the banks of the Nile, Mr. Gladstone was staying at Brechin Castle, near Aberdeen, as guest of a Liberal peer, the Earl of Dalhousie. He had been touring Scotland, conducting an agitation against the House of Lords, which had received his Franchise Bill unfavourably. On the previous day he had driven into Aberdeen under a triumphal arch amidst the plaudits of the citizens. Khartoum, it may be supposed, was far from his thoughts. But when he picked up the local Liberal newspaper on the morning of the 18th he saw that, in addition to ecstatic accounts of his own tumultuous reception and stirring speeches, it contained a column of news from Khartoum. A telegram from Cairo gave what purported to be a translation of the first messages to be received from Gordon after four months' silence. It was a garbled version of his plan for sending steamers to raid and burn Berber. This in itself made alarming reading for Mr. Gladstone. For he could not be expected to know that since the defeat of Mohammed Ali the plan had perforce been abandoned; and though he might have been expected to know that Sudanese towns consisted of mud huts " which if burnt one day can be rebuilt the next," he was in fact very ignorant of the Sudan. His suspicions had never been ex-

tinguished, and they were instantly fanned into a flame. Gordon
was rebelliously " smashing up the Mahdi " and launching a reckless
offensive against a people rightly struggling to be free, whom by
now the Prime Minister had almost come to envisage as an as-
semblage of dark-skinned Midlothian Radicals. And as Mr. Gladstone read on, a fellow-guest observed that " his face hardened and
whitened, the eyes burned as I have seen them once or twice in the
House of Commons—burned with a deep fire as if they would have
consumed the paper on which Gordon's message was printed." For
Gordon had added to his dispatch a proposal as to the future administration of the Sudan. Turkish troops, he suggested, should be
sent there. It was not a particularly shocking suggestion, for in
January the government itself had been agreed that the Red Sea
coast and the interior of the Sudan should be handed over to
Turkey after the withdrawal of the Egyptians.

But Mr. Gladstone had changed his mind frequently since
January and was in any case hardly in a mood to reflect upon the
past. And by yet another of the fatalities which had so consistently
dogged Gordon's correspondence with the government the message
had confused the estimated cost of a Turkish contingent, £200,000,
with its numbers, 2000, and spoke of 200,000 Turkish troops. With
a brow like thunder Mr. Gladstone rose, strode from the room and
was seen no more that morning.[1] But he must have acted swiftly,
for next day Granville was instructing Baring, who had by now
returned to Cairo, that Gordon was to be placed under the orders
of Wolseley, and that his Governor-Generalship was to be reduced
to the Governorship of Khartoum and its neighbourhood. But
though in his wrath Mr. Gladstone had for once acted promptly
he was once again too late. The wasted months rendered him as
impotent now to strike at Gordon as to succour him. The Khedive's
version of Granville's instructions did not reach Khartoum till
25th November, and no one there understood it.

[1] Lytton Strachey in *Eminent Victorians* refers this scene to an earlier telegram from
Gordon despatched in April. Allen (*Gordon and the Sudan*, 350) makes it clear that this was
a mistake.

II

Wolseley had arrived in Cairo on 9th September. He was an able soldier and a close friend of Gordon's since their subaltern days; for a long while the two had remembered each other daily in their prayers. Moreover, he trusted Gordon. On 20th October he would write to Colonel Goodenough " I am a great believer in Gordon, and his views, which some scoff at, are always to me full of sound common sense unfettered by routine and red tape." But Wolseley was a cautious general, unlikely to compensate by reckless speed for the apathy in Downing Street. And now that the river route had been chosen, 1650 miles from Cairo to Khartoum, the expedition may be said to have been doomed from the outset. If a younger general, Sir Frederick Roberts, already famous for his brilliant dash to Kandahar, had been sent to cross the desert with a flying force of cavalry from Suakim he might perhaps have been in Khartoum by November. Nobody could prophesy how long Wolseley, who was now laboriously assembling Canadian boatmen and a flotilla of Canadian flat-bottomed boats, might need to complete his laborious journey. And indeed it is difficult to believe that, whoever the commander and whatever the route, the expedition could have been successful. Mr. Gladstone, and subsequently John Morley, in his *Life*, ascribed much of the delay to what Morley called " the battle of the routes." But the plans for a river expedition were in Hartington's hands before any expedition had been agreed on by the government. Moreover, as Hartington bitterly remarked to Granville after the final tragedy, the apologia was in any case ridiculous, since at any time, if the government had genuinely wanted a decision, it could have had one in a week. The expedition was doomed because the government which had authorised it six months too late never wholeheartedly desired or believed in it.

On 29th September *The Times* was able to publish further letters from Power, which carried the story of the siege down to the end of July. No Englishman, said its leading article, would read it without a thrill of pride and a flush of shame. " In the long roll of Englishmen who have spent themselves in the service of England there is no brighter name than that won for himself by General Gordon, nor in the glorious catalogue of their exploits is there any that can outshine his defence of Khartoum." Others, *The Times* pointed out, had faced equally formidable odds, but only Gordon and his two companions (who were supposed still to be alive and in Khartoum) had had to fight on " under the chilling influence of growing indifference and final desertion on the part of those whose first duty was their relief." Had *The Times* had later news from Khartoum it would have written in even more sombre strains.

12

For on 22nd August the Mahdi himself had set forth for Khartoum from his camp fifty miles south of El Obeid. With him, like a swarm of locusts, a vast horde moved slowly across the desert—upwards, thought Father Ohrwalder, who was a prisoner in the Mahdi's hands, of two hundred thousand souls. It was the rainy season, camels were scarce and there were no roads. But the Mahdi had not so far to travel as Wolseley, and he and his followers were fanatics. Even so, he would have preferred to avoid a direct assault upon Khartoum, and as he journeyed he renewed his attempts to induce Gordon to surrender. Once more he sent him a summons, and a dervish dress. Gordon rejected the summons and returned the dress. Again the Mahdi sent Cuzzi, and again Gordon declined to see him. A Greek emissary and a threatening message from the Mahdi's generalissimo he treated with the same contempt. But he knew that the climax of the siege was at hand. In a sense the approach of the Mahdi was a relief. " I have always felt we were doomed to come face to face ere the matter was ended " he wrote in his *Journal*.

For now Gordon had no European companions; it had long been impossible to correspond with his friends; and so on 10th

September, the day after Stewart and Power left him, he had commenced his *Journal*, that strange volume into which he poured night
after night whatever was uppermost in his mind, as in the old days
in Equatoria he had so often sat late scribbling page after page by
the light of a hurricane lamp, to Augusta, to Henry, to Mr. Waller,
to some former Scuttler, to a score of heterogeneous correspondents.
He knew that, if his *Journal* ever reached the outer world, it would
in all probability be published; indeed, he himself suggested in a
note on its cover that if published it would certainly require
" pruning." Nevertheless, save that it touches more seldom on
religious topics, he wrote in the *Journal* precisely as he used to write
to Augusta. With the same discursive abandon, and in the same
colloquial torrent, trivial facts and obscure reflections, theology
strategy, politics, prophecy and expert advice on the Sudan jostled
each other amid quotations from the Bible, facetious imaginary
telegrams from Kitchener, notes on the behaviour of the turkey-
cock in the Palace yard, sardonic pleasantries at the expense of
Granville or Baring and a masterly day-to-day record of the events
of the siege. Once or twice he would even insert in the margin a
satiric pen-and-ink sketch of some imaginary diplomat or editor.

To meet Gordon for the first time in the pages of his Khartoum
Journal would certainly be an astonishing experience, but what
astonishes one already familiar with his correspondence with his
family is the simple fact that the *Journal* resembles the letters so
closely. " I dwell on the joy of never seeing Great Britain again,
with its horrid, wearisome *dinner* parties and miseries;" to Augusta
such outbursts were familiar enough, though in a state paper
addressed to an army commander they certainly wore an exotic air.
Yet even more remarkable than the numerous similarities between
the *Journal* and the letters is the one contrast. Alone Gordon was
directing the defence of a huge perimeter with seven thousand
inferior troops against twenty times as many fearless fanatics, alone
he bore up the civilian population, for ever trembling on the verge
of panic; every decision, military or civil, was his and his alone;
every day his own hopes sank lower, yet every day he must convince

Khartoum anew that help was close at hand; he had no staff, no confidante, no companion. The nervous stress would have driven most men to insanity. Yet the one marked difference between the *Journal* and the letters from Equatoria is that the temper of the *Journal* is more serene.

No doubt he was still frequently impatient. "I have led the officers and officials the lives of dogs while I have been up here" he admitted in his *Journal*, reproducing, almost word for word, numerous similar confessions to Augusta; "it is quite painful to see men tremble so when they come and see me, that they cannot hold the match to their cigarette." And he seems to have developed a kind of obsession with regard to the execution, some six months previously, of two Pashas who had been convicted on overwhelming evidence of flagrant treason, gradually persuading himself that, because he had not intervened to reprieve them, he was guilty of judicial murder. By 13th September, as he pondered on the terror which he inspired, he could even write "Yet I have cut off no heads; I only killed two Pashas." And thereafter he was always tempted to ascribe a major disaster to "Nemesis on the death of the two Pashas."

He mentions, too, that after months of constant explosions from guns, mines and musketry "any loud noise, in this clear air makes me jump (i.e. be, for a moment, afraid)." But in general what is surprising is that there should be so little evidence in the *Journal* of the almost unparalleled nervous strain to which its author was being subjected. And of the self-pity which is so conspicuous in some literary autobiographies there is not a trace. When he mentions "dire anxiety" he is careful to add "but that I have had to undergo a tithe of what any nurse has to undergo, who is attached to a querulous invalid, is absurd, and not to be weighed together." Whatever he said in public, he put little faith as yet in the rumours that a relief expedition was on its way. "I have the strongest suspicions," he noted on 17th September, ". . . that if you wanted to find H.M. forces you would have to go to Shepheard's Hotel at Cairo." But on the nature of the eventual catastrophe which every day seemed to make more certain he would speculate with the most matter-of-fact composure.

> I toss up in my mind whether, if the place is taken, to blow up the palace and all in it, or else to be taken, and, with God's help, to maintain the faith and, if necessary, suffer for it (which is most probable). The blowing up of the palace is the simplest, while the other means long and weary suffering and humiliation of all sorts. I think I shall elect for the last, not from fear of death, but because the former has more or less the taint of suicide, as it can do no good to anyone, and is, in a way, taking things out of God's hands.

Often, however, he would break off a computation of the ammunition his troops had expended, or some disquisition on the inadequate grounds on which the Victoria Cross was awarded nowadays, to draw satiric pictures of pompous politicans and bewildered officials in England struggling with the problems of the Sudan. "Eureka," he imagines one exclaiming triumphantly, "I have found it out; there is a *man* called El Obeyed and a *town* called El Obeyed. When a movement occurs, it is the *man*, not the *town*, which has moved!"

13

On 20th September several unofficial letters were brought into Khartoum, containing chance references to the assembling of a relief expedition, and next day a salute of a hundred and one guns was duly fired from the ramparts. But Gordon was seized with a sudden suspicion as to the official object of the expedition. Whatever else it might be, he insisted with passionate underlinings and capitals, it was not an expedition to relieve *him*.

> I altogether decline the imputation that the projected expedition

has come to *relieve me*. It has *come to* SAVE OUR NATIONAL HONOUR *in extricating the garrisons, etc., from a position our action in Egypt has placed those garrisons. I was relief expedition No.* 1. They are *relief expedition No.* 2. . . . We the *first* and *second* expeditions are equally engaged for the honour of England. This is fair logic. *I came up to extricate the garrisons and failed. Earle comes up to extricate garrisons and (1 hope) succeeds. Earle does not come to extricate me.* . . . I am not the *rescued lamb*, and I will not be.

And thereafter the *Journal* constantly recurs to his unanswerable case against the government. At the beginning of the siege, when he had made no commitments to the people of Khartoum, the government had expressly forbidden him to withdraw to the Equator: why should it now expect him to abandon Khartoum " when I am in honour bound to the people after six months' bothering warfare ?" Ministers, he had begun to suspect, had secretly hoped that the town would fall, and spare them the necessity of coming to a decision. " They did not dare say ' abandon the garrison' so they prevented me leaving for the Equator, with the determination not to relieve me, and the *hope* (well! I will not say what their hope was) (' March, April . . . August, why! he ought to have surrendered, he said six *months*')." " Therefore," he declared passionately, " if any emissary or letter comes up here ordering me to come down, I WILL NOT OBEY IT, BUT WILL STAY HERE AND FALL WITH THE TOWN, AND RUN ALL RISKS."

Meanwhile, the odds against the defenders continued to lengthen. Before the end of September a new dervish generalissimo had brought up artillery. Henceforth the usefulness of Gordon's hitherto invaluable steamers would be sadly diminished. Nevertheless, he sent three of the six which remained to him downstream to meet the relieving force, and with them the first two volumes of his *Journal*. As the slow days passed Gordon began to find garrison and people less trustworthy. He had always known that the Egyptian troops were worthless—" a more contemptible soldier than the Egyptian never existed "—and that the only means of inducing their officers to obey a standing order was to repeat it daily. But now thefts and neglect of duty increased, and there was evidence that treachery was afoot. Not that evidence was easy to come by. For he was his own intelligence service and his knowledge of Arabic was most imperfect, so that he always felt that he was groping in the dark, and on occasion could exclaim despairingly " I am ignorant of all that goes on." Nevertheless, by 12th October he had resolved to make " a sort of general arrest to-night (similar to that made by Napoleon III on the night of the 1st December) of all who are supposed to be in communication with the Mahdi. I shall not hurt them, but shall send them out to the Mahdi. (Query, was it on the night of the 1st and 2nd December . . . or on the night of the 2nd-3rd December ? . . .") Even this, however, troubled his conscience, and three days later he notes that " when once one begins this detestable practice, one can never stop. . . . I wonder how any man can possibly wish to enjoy despotic power."

Most of the day, and a great part of the night, Gordon spent on the roof of the palace with his telescope. He slept little.

> One tumbles at 3 a.m. into a troubled sleep; a drum beats— tup! tup! tup! It comes into a dream, but after a few moments one becomes more awake, and it is revealed to the brain that *one is in Khartoum.* The next query is, where is this tup, tupping going on. A hope arises it will die away. No, it goes on, and increases in intensity. The thought strikes me, ' Have they enough ammunition ? (The last excuse of bad soldiers.) One exerts oneself. At last, it is no use, up one must get, and go on to the roof of the palace. . . .

And now the Mahdi himself was nearing Khartoum, and he renewed his attempts to persuade Gordon to surrender. Rudolf Slatin was now a prisoner of the dervishes, and the Mahdi ordered him to compose an appropriate letter. It was an imprudent choice for, like Cuzzi, the unfortunate Austrian had perforce become a Mahomedan. His letters, in French and German, were full of apologies for this conversion—his religious education, he pleaded, had been neglected in youth—and offers of his services. But as an apostate Slatin was, by Gordon's standards, now beyond the pale. "What can be more strong," he had remarked in the course of the first entry in the *Journal*, "than these words: 'He who denies Me on earth, I will deny him in Heaven?'" And he ignored Slatin's letters, which reached him on 16th and 22nd October, and declined to countenance any breaking of parole, "which should be as sacred when given to the Mahdi as to any other power." But if Slatin eventually escaped, he added, "I shall take him to the Congo with me; he will want some *quarantine*; one feels sorry for him."

Slatin's second letter had reported the wreck of the *Abbas* and the death of Stewart and Power. And on the same day arrived a long letter from the Mahdi, summarising message after message from the documents captured on the steamer, as evidence of Stewart's fate. Even so, Gordon continued for some while to hope that Stewart himself might have escaped, and warned the world that relief might come too late. He could not know that the indecision and inertia in Whitehall was already being reflected on the Nile, or that at this very time an officer who had just joined Wolseley's expedition would be writing bitterly to Colonel Goodenough: "The expedition is planted and taking root here. There are so many people to advise, suggest and plan impracticable schemes that most valuable time is frittered and wasted. . . . We had literally to fight our way through lazy and apathetic people from Alexandria to this, and there is nothing but confusion."

He could, however, ensure that there was neither indecision nor inertia at Khartoum. The Mahdi's letter had concluded with a final summons to apostasy and surrender. Gordon dispatched his final refusal on the same day, through the commander of his fort at Omdurman.

Sheikh Mahomed Achmed[1] has sent us a letter to inform us that Lupton Bey, Mudir of Bahr Gazelle, has surrendered to him,

[1] The Mahdi.

and that the small steamer in which was Stewart Pasha has been captured, together with what was therein. And he demands that we should surrender to him. But to me it is all one whether Lupton Bey has surrendered or not surrendered. And whether he has captured twenty thousand steamers like the *Abbas*, or twenty thousand like Stewart Pasha; it is all one to me. I am here, like iron, and hope to see the newly-arrived English; and if Mahomed Achmed says that the English die, it is all the same to me. . . . . It is impossible for me to have any more words with Mahomed Achmed, only lead.

But Gordon cannot have failed to notice that the Mahdi's letter had concluded with a sentence which he might have written himself: *there is no succour or strength but in God, and peace be upon those who have followed the Guidance.*

14

And so November came. The Mahdi and all his host were now encamped before Khartoum. In July Gordon had calculated that he could hold out till the middle of November. On 24th October he had noted " if they do not come before 30th November the game is up, and Rule Britannia." But since then there had been fresh discoveries of grain, and on 2nd November he reckoned that food might now last for six weeks. On the following day the *Bordein* steamed back from Shendi through a dervish cannonade, bringing with her letters from the relief expedition. There were some private letters too, one, dated 7th August, from Augusta (to whom a War Office official had been sending almost daily reports on Khartoum since early that summer), and two days later Gordon was scribbling to her the last letter but one in their lifelong correspondence. He told her briefly of the " terrible news " of Stewart's catastrophe, which had been confirmed in the official letters, and how he supposed that " H.M.G. are in a precious rage with me for holding out and

forcing their hand." Nevertheless, " all is for the best, and is overruled for good. I am very well, but very grey with the continual
strain on my nerves." He wrote to Mr. Barnes too: " He is not
unfaithful if we fall; for it may be for His greater glory and He does
not promise everything we ask if it is not good for us to have it.
I am content He will enable me to keep my faith and not deny
Him."

On the day on which Gordon wrote to Augusta a clerk discovered some newspapers, in which the letters brought by the
Bordein had been wrapped, blowing about in the palace garden.
Their latest date was actually 15th September and Gordon devoured
them greedily, for they told him far more than he had learned from

1 *Daily News*   2 *Times*   3 *Standard*   4 *Pall Mall Gazette*
A pen and ink sketch from Gordon's Khartoum ' Journal '

the official letters. Much to his irritation he found in them a description of Wolseley leaving Victoria Station for " the Gordon
relief expedition." " No! " he scrawled angrily. " *For the relief of
Sudan garrison.*" Moreover, when leaving England on 31st August
Wolseley was reported to have declared ominously that he hoped
to relieve Khartoum before " many months " had elapsed. If
Wolseley had indeed said that, wrote Gordon, " he must have a
wonderful confidence in our powers of resistance, considering that
when he is said to have made this utterance, we had been blockaded
six and a half months, and are now in our ninth month."

On the whole Gordon had not found the newspapers cheerful
reading. For there was still no evidence that the government had

begun to grasp the urgency of his plight; and during November
the pages of his *Journal*, which he was filling with detailed plans for
the advance of the relieving force, and for the subsequent administration of the Sudan, were still occasionally diversified by satiric
comment on the politicians and potentates in Cairo or London.
For there was no one with whom he could converse, and although
in moments of impatience he could write a dozen lines of " abuse
of Baring " and then scratch them out, with the reflection that " I
dare say Baring is doing his duty better than I am," it was also some
relief to imagine Granville lounging in Walmer Castle in blissful
ignorance that Khartoum had not yet fallen, or the cautious Baring
in an unguarded moment for once disclosing his true opinions.
" Can one imagine a greater farce," he demands on 8th November,
" than Lord Northbrook asking Tewfik for ' assistance of Egyptian
Government to carry out this, or that?' I expect the two roared
with laughter over it (sorry I cannot manage a sketch of the
scene). (Baring would *never* laugh, *it is too serious*, like jesting in
church.)."

In much the same vein a fortnight earlier he had imagined the
protest of the government's spokesman in the House of Lords at a
member's demand for a statement of government policy in the
Sudan. " It was as if he asked the policy of a log floating downstream" he makes the noble lord complain.

> It was going to the sea, as any one who had an ounce of brain
> could see. Well, that was the policy of it; only it was a decided
> policy, and a straightforward one to drift along and take
> advantage of every circumstance. His lordship deprecated the
> frequent questioning on subjects which, as his lordship had said,
> he knew nothing about, and further did not care to know
> anything about.

On the whole, what is surprising about these passages is that there
are so few of them and that they are so good-tempered. Rarely,
indeed, is there a genuine touch of asperity, as when the diarist

confesses " I must say I hate our diplomatists. I think with few exceptions they are arrant humbugs, and I expect they know it. I include the Colvin class."

A letter from Kitchener, among the official communications brought by the *Bordein*, had given Gordon reasonable grounds for expecting the relief force in Khartoum by 10th November, or perhaps 15th November. But Kitchener had been over-optimistic. When he wrote, he did not yet know Wolseley's cautious plans, nor had he allowed for the inertia of Mr. Gladstone and his Cabinet. Wolseley, too, for other reasons, was dangerously optimistic, for in Cairo there had been hopeful rumours, which he was too ready to believe, as to the fortunes of Khartoum. And even when, on 17th November, word reached him from Gordon himself that Khartoum could hold out for another forty days from 4th November he does not seem to have been unduly disturbed; an officer on his staff indeed remarked airily that there was no need for anxiety, since if Gordon had said he could hold out for six weeks he could undoubtedly do so for six months. Such were the misconceptions of the high command as the expedition moved cumbrously forward.

15

But on 12th November the dervishes delivered a fierce attack on the fort at Omdurman across the river. Gordon reported the fortunes of the battle hour by hour in his *Journal*. " What a six hours of anxiety for me," he wrote, " when I saw the shells strike the water near the steamers . . .; imagine my feelings." For he now had only two steamers left in Khartoum—the rest he had sent downstream and of these one, the little *Husseinyeh*, was soon aground. Had he lost the other, the *Ismailia* (on which two thousand bullet marks and five shell holes were counted after the engagement) he would have lost, he reckoned, first Omdurman and then Khartoum. " I have lived *years*," he wrote, when at length the firing had ceased, " in the last *hours*! " Though the fort had not been captured it was cut off from Khartoum. Its fall, and the consequent fall of Khartoum, could only be a question of weeks. And all because his telegraph clerk had not reported news of the impending attack, which had been received on the previous evening.

> I boxed the telegraph clerk's ears for not giving me the telegram last night (after repeated orders that no consideration was to prevent him coming to me); and then my conscience pricked me and I gave him $5. He said he did not mind if I killed him —I was his father (a chocolate-coloured youth of twenty). I know all this is brutal . . . but what is one to do? If you cut their pay you hurt their families. I am an advocate for summary and quick punishment, which hurts only the defaulter.

As the painful days passed, each with its own tale of crisis and frustration, against their common background of ever-increasing anxiety, Gordon's thoughts returned again and again to the problem of the future of the Sudan. The government, so far as he could fathom its intentions, would withdraw speedily, after the relief of Khartoum, leaving the country to its fate. As for him, he could not in conscience carry out such orders, " for I should be a scoundrel if I accepted any proposition which would eventually give trouble to our country." He would resign his Governor-Generalship and, in all probability, his commission, report to King Leopold in Brussels and never set foot in England again. But who should take over the Sudan? The Sultan of Turkey, for choice; but failing him Kitchener, of whom Baker had spoken highly, or perhaps, even now, Zebehr. And so his thoughts would turn wearily back to the old controversy and the opportunities now lost for ever. If he had been allowed Zebehr at the outset Khartoum would not now be besieged. If Zebehr were with the relief expedition it would have been in Khartoum by now. " It does seem ridiculous that when our apparent policy is to hand over the Sudan to the Mahdi, who with his people are far more slave hunters than Zebehr ever would be, we should not have utilised this man in this expedition." It was some consolation, when a new small steamer was launched and the townspeople wished it to be named *Gordon Pasha*, to reply that having bullied them so much he had no fear of their forgetting *him*, and that the steamer was to be called *Zebehr*—and to reflect that the Anti-Slavery Society would be furious.

Zebehr, whatever his faults, would have taken some of the almost intolerable burden from Gordon's shoulders. As it was, after " $8\frac{11}{30}$ months " of siege (as he put it, on 21st November), his subordinates were more unreliable than in the old days in Equatoria.

What has been the painful position for me is that there is not one person on whom I can rely; also, there is not one person who considers that he ought to do anything except his routine duty. We have now been months blockaded, and things are critical; yet not one of my subordinates, except the chief clerk and his subordinate, appears to-day. I had to send for them, and wait till they came, perhaps an hour. ' It is Friday, and it is unreasonable to expect us at the office,' is what they say. My patience is almost exhausted with this continuous apparently never-ending trial; there is not one department which I have not to superintend as closely as if I was its direct head. . . . Nearly every order, except when it is for their interest, has to be repeated two, and even three, times. I may truly say I am weary of my life; day and night, night and day, it is one continual worry.

Suddenly at about one o'clock in the afternoon of 25th November the smoke of steamers was sighted, and all Khartoum thrilled with a wild surmise. The British had arrived! A few minutes, and firing began. A few more minutes, and the familiar *Bordein* was visible—alone, struggling on through a fusillade of bullets and shells. At least, hoped Gordon, some officer from the relieving force might be on board, and acquiring first hand experience of " what it is to be in a penny! boat under cannon fire." But even this modest hope was to be disappointed. No British were on the vessel, nor had she brought any fresh news from the relieving force—as to whose progress he could only deduce, from a letter sent by the commander of his steamers downstream, that it had not advanced beyond Ambukol; "which," he commented sardonically, "is LIVELY!"

All that the *Bordein* had brought him was a few private letters, and two official messages. One of these was the Cabinet's all too characteristic communication of July, with its airy inquiry whether " danger has arisen or is likely to arise." This fortunately, since it was in code and the key had gone down the Nile with Stewart, he could not decipher. The other was the dispatch which the wrath of Mr. Gladstone, during his Scottish campaign, had compelled the Khedive to compose. It was in Arabic, and neither Gordon nor his clerk ever fully grasped its purport. Indeed, he understood it merely to presage the appointment of various British officials to take charge of certain portions of the Sudan, and the abandonment of the rest of it. This, since there could be no peace while the Mahdi was at large, appeared to Gordon to be perverse and disastrous, and did but set his thoughts turning wearily in the familiar circle—the Sultan, Zebehr, his own resignation. The Khedive's dispatch appeared, however, to contain one touch of comic relief. For Gordon understood its promise that he should receive instructions from Wolseley and Baring to imply that Baring himself was positively " bumping his way up here" on a camel. And from time to time the sombre later pages of the *Journal* are enlivened by imaginary descriptions of the Agent General's tribulations *en route*.

Baring to Egerton—' Metemma! at last, after the most fearful sufferings, every bone in my body dislocated with those beastly camels. Found here his *Journal*, from which it appears that that duffer, the Mahdi, has at last roused himself, but I fear it is too late. As to the tone of the *Journal*, it is *simply deplorable*, and (do not mention it, please) he has actually made a sketch (brace yourself up to bear it) of our high priest. Excuse more, for what with the bumping of the camel and the depravity shown by this scoffer, I am more dead than alive.'

However, Gordon seldom cherished ill-feelings for long, and he decided that "if Baring does bump his way up here as British Commissioner, I shall consider he has expiated his faults and shall forgive him." Moreover, even Baring was a transient phenomenon.

In ten or twelve years' time Baring, Lord Wolseley, myself, Evelyn Wood, etc., will have no teeth, and will be deaf; some of us will be quite *passé*; no one will come and court us; new Barings, new Lord Wolseleys will have arisen, who will call us ' bloaks ' and ' twaddlers.' ' Oh! for goodness' sake come away, then! Is that dreadful bore coming? If once he gets alongside you, you are in for half an hour,' will be the remark of some young captain of the present time on seeing you enter the Club. This is very humiliating, for we, each one, think we are immortal.

Gordon at least had never supposed that he was immortal, and there were fewer temptations than ever to suppose so now. The arrival of the *Bordein*, and its evidence that the expeditionary force was still far off, had been a bitter disappointment. Nevertheless, next day, 26th November, a proclamation was posted in Khartoum, announcing that relief was at hand. " If God will, in the next few days the siege will be raised and your alarm will pass away." And had Gordon been in Wolseley's place the siege doubtless would have been raised within a few days, for Gordon had long since learned that in the desert those who are prepared to take risks can travel swiftly. But unlike Gordon, Wolseley was neither familiar with the desert nor a master of irregular warfare. Nor, unfortunately, had he even now understood the full urgency of his task. By now he should have been thinking in terms of days, and almost of hours. Yet on 30th November, four days after Gordon's proclamation, he issued a general order in which, after a tribute to the defence of Khartoum, he warned his troops that Gordon could not be expected to hold out " for many months longer."

16

Ever since September the Nile, whose waters during the summer flood season had served to protect Khartoum, had been steadily falling. And as it fell it became necessary to rebuild some fifteen hundred yards of the ramparts where the White Nile had overflowed them. Despite a systematic bombardment the reconstruction was still going on, but Gordon was anxious, for he knew that " the White Nile end of the Lines is our weakest part." Indeed, there was no aspect of the defence as to which he was not anxious now. The new battery on the right bank of the Blue Nile which fired day and night on the Palace did not trouble him unduly, though it sometimes induced " judicious bobbing." But whenever he heard a gun fire he felt " a twitch of the heart of gnawing anxiety for my penny steamers." And he was haunted by the thought of his dwindling supplies. " Truly I am worn to a shadow by the food question; it is one continual demand." In his last letter to Watson, written on 26th November, he betrayed for once a trace of bitterness.

I am not ill-treated, I consider, but the Cairo people up here— they are the ill-used. I will accept *nothing whatsoever* from Gladstone's government. I will not even let them pay my expenses. I will get the King [of the Belgians] to pay them. I will never set foot in England, but will (D.V., if I get out) go to Brussels and so on to Congo.

On 13th December he recorded in his *Journal* " the 276th day of our anxiety." And he decided to send the *Bordein* to join the flotilla downstream on the 15th. With it would go his *Journal*, which would certainly perish if, as appeared more certain every day, Khartoum fell. Even now, all that was needed to save the town was visible proof that the British were indeed on their way. " All that is absolutely necessary," Gordon wrote on the 13th, " is for fifty of the Expeditionary Force to get on board a steamer and come up to Halfeyeh, and thus let their presence be felt; this is not asking much, but it must happen *at once*; or it will (as usual) be too late." Indeed, it is likely that the arrival of a dozen British soldiers, in red coats, in Khartoum would have induced the Mahdi to withdraw to El Obeid. And Bordeini Bey, a merchant in Khartoum, remembered Gordon saying to him that if a couple of British soldiers from the relief force could be displayed in the town he would have no fear of an attack by the dervishes.

Next day, Sunday, 14th December, came the final entry in Gordon's *Journal*:

> Now MARK THIS, if the Expeditionary Force, and I ask for no more than two hundred men, does not come in ten days, *the town may fall*; and I have done my best for the honour of our country. Goodbye.
> C. G. GORDON

With the *Journal* went his last short letter to Augusta.

> This may be the last letter you will receive from me, for we are on our last legs, owing to the delay of the expedition. However, God rules all, and as He will rule to His glory and our welfare, His will be done. I fear, owing to circumstances, that my affairs pecuniarily are not over-bright. . . .
> Your affectionate brother,
> C. G. GORDON

> P.S. I am quite happy, thank God, and like Lawrence, I have 'tried to do my duty.'

17

On the following day on which Gordon closed his *Journal*, and with it his reckoning with the outer world, now growing more shadowy every day, he sent off a messenger with a final appeal for help. Lest the man should be captured he gave him a small slip of paper, on which he had written "Khartoum all right. 14.12.84. C. G. Gordon." But he had charged the bearer with an urgent verbal message: "We are besieged on three sides. Fighting goes on day and night. . . . Food we still have is little—some grain and biscuit. We want you to come quickly. . . . Do not leave Berber in your rear. . . ." The messenger left Khartoum on 15th December, the extreme limit of the forty days for which Gordon had told Wolseley that he could count on holding out.

On that same day, 15th December, Sir Herbert Stewart arrived in Korti, near Ambukol, to take command of the column which was to strike across 170 miles of desert for Metemma.

A fortnight later, on 30th December, when Gordon's last urgent summons reached them, Stewart and his column were still at Korti. For the journey of the light craft up the Nile and through the rapids had been arduous in the extreme, and as always there had been unforeseen delays. It was on the afternoon of the 30th that the Desert Column rode out of Korti, to strike across the Bayuda wastes for Metemma. Sir Herbert Stewart was in command and Major Kitchener went to lead the way. But still there were delays. For Wolseley had decided that the column must establish supply posts in the desert, and guards at the precious water-holes; and for these precautions they had not collected a sufficient number of camels. A double journey must be made. Stewart did not leave Korti for the second time until 8th January. On this day Lord Granville had an audience of the Queen. He was no longer agitated over the knotty problem of Franchise and Redistribution, as to which Government and Opposition had recently reached substantial agreement. Lord Granville, however, was usually agitated about something, and he spoke long and anxiously about Egyptian affairs. But it was the finances of Egypt which were troubling him. There was no evidence that he was in any way concerned about Khartoum.

18

We have no record from Gordon himself of the last dreadful weeks in Khartoum. But there can be no doubt that his simple creed survived unshaken; and that from it he drew strength to bear his monstrous burdens, and serenity to await disaster without flinching. He had often complained that he possessed many contradictory selves, and now he had manifestly become two distinct beings, one toiling ceaselessly, and often impatiently, at his hopeless tasks, the other resting calmly upon the eternal. " I am learning to be content in whatever state I am," he had written in November, in his last letter to Mr. Barnes at Heavitree. " Thoughts have deepened in me, but nothing new." And then he repeated the faith in which he faced the dark confusion about him.

> We have had in detail nothing but disaster on disaster, yet in general we are successful. God will not let this solution give any glory to man. I always felt that if we got through, it would be a scramble. There would be no glory to man. Our deliverance (if it happens) is due to prayer of others. He is not unfaithful, if we fall. For it may be for His greater glory, and He does not promise everything we ask, if it is not good for us to have it. I am content, He will enable me to keep my faith and not deny him.

He had written much the same *credo* often enough before. It was the faith of a child, but all the stronger, and indeed all the truer, for that.

There is not much reliable evidence as to what happened in Khartoum during the final stages of the siege. Slatin and Father Ohrwalder have left accounts, but, being prisoners of the Mahdi, they were not themselves in the town, while as for the stories of certain Egyptians and Sudanese, who were, they are demonstrably inaccurate at numerous points where they can be tested. Thus the merchant Bordeini Bey retailed a picturesque anecdote of how when urged

to sandbag the Palace windows Gordon ordered a lantern of twenty-four candles to be lit and placed in the window of his room, and then declared that " When God was portioning out fear . . . at last it came to my turn, and there was no fear left to give me. Go, tell all the people of Khartoum that Gordon fears nothing. . . ." In Gordon, however, such theatrical panache would have been hopelessly out of character, and the words ascribed to him figure in countless traditional oriental tales. The story in fact is no more plausible than Bordeini's other tale of Gordon crying in despair on the last day of the siege that he had told the people that help was at hand so often that they would no longer believe him, that he could do no more, and that Bordeini had better leave him to smoke his cigarettes. Moreover, there is unfortunately sound evidence[1] that Bordeini did not enter the Palace during the last weeks of the siege.

We do know, however, that by finds of grain on private premises Gordon was able to prolong the final agonies for a few days longer. But by 15th January food and ammunition in the fortress of Omdurman was exhausted and it had capitulated. And by now there were no rations to issue in Khartoum. Men were eating donkeys, dogs and rats; gum and the pith of date trees was being served out in place of rations, dysentery was rife, and many of the soldiers on the ramparts were too weak to stand. Gordon himself repeatedly toured the fortifications and visited the hospital daily. Indomitably he assured the despairing populace that the British were close at hand. And on 20th January a spy brought word that a great victory had been won by the British downstream. For once the news was accurate, and it was confirmed by the wailing of women in the Mahdi's camp.

[1] The statements of two of Gordon's personal staff, interviewed by Dr. Allen (*Gordon and the Sudan*, 420).

19

On 17th January Stewart's column, of sixteen hundred British troops, had found ten thousand dervishes barring its path at the wells of Abu Klea. What followed was a soldiers' battle. The British could always count on being outnumbered, but thanks to the Gladstone administration they were also outmatched in weapons. Their naval gun and some of their rifles jammed, and the leading dervishes broke through the front line. But the disciplined courage of the British square saved the day after savage hand-to-hand fighting. The enemy was driven off, leaving more than a thousand dead upon the sands. But among the British dead was Colonel Burnaby, who was to have taken over the command at Metemma. The impetuous Burnaby, a fervent admirer of Gordon's, who had proposed to organise a volunteer force to relieve Khartoum, would doubtless have brought to his command that sense of urgency and appetite for risks which had hitherto been so sadly lacking. But it was not to be. Moreover, two days later, on 19th January, soon after the weary troops had glimpsed the Nile, Sir Herbert Stewart was severely wounded by a stray bullet, and the command devolved upon Sir Charles Wilson, an Intelligence officer even less fitted than Stewart for a race against time. The square moved slowly forward to the river, sweeping a dervish onslaught aside. It was not till the 21st that Wilson advanced upon Metemma, and as the attack opened four steamers hove in sight from the south. They were Gordon's steamers from Khartoum, and the troops rushed cheering to the river bank.

The steamers had brought with them not only the six volumes of Gordon's *Journal* but three letters which he had written on 14th December. In one of them, addressed to the Chief of Staff, Wilson read: " I own I consider the position extremely critical, almost desperate, and I say this without any feeling of bitterness to H.M. Government but merely as a matter of fact." In another Gordon had written: " I think the game is up. . . . We may expect a catas-

The Gordon Statue at Khartoum

trophe in the town on or after ten days' time." These letters had
been written on 14th December; it was now 21st January. Like a
previous messenger the commander of the steamers had also been
given a scrap of paper intended to mislead the enemy, should he
be captured, and perhaps representing also Gordon's recurrent sense
that pessimism was lack of faith. Dated 29th December, it bore the
words 'Khartoum all right. Could hold out for year.' But Sir
Charles Wilson was an Intelligence officer, the very Arabs on the
steamers, who could tell him all he needed to know of the plight
of the town, were urging haste, and he cannot have been misled.
Indeed, when subsequently defending himself against charges of
procrastination he made no mention of the scrap of paper. Had
Burnaby lived he would certainly have made a rush for Khartoum
on the steamers that afternoon. But Wilson wasted three days in
reconnaissances up and down the river. It was not until the morning
of the 24th that with two of the steamers he moved off upstream.

20

On the night of the 20th the Mahdi held a council of war. The news
of the defeat at Abu Klea had shaken his confidence in his heaven-
sent invincibility, and he was for withdrawing to El Obeid before
the victorious British could reach Khartoum. One Emir, and one
only, was for holding on. The council broke up without a decision.
Then came news of the second reverse on the banks of the Nile,
and the dervish host stood poised on the verge of striking camp.
But the next day passed, and the next and the next, and the British
had not advanced. The solitary counsellor of courage had, it seemed,
been right; the British were not so formidable after all. Even now,
however, there was hope for Khartoum. For the Mahdi had no
stomach for a direct assault, and was still minded to starve the town
into surrender. And since Gordon would never have surrendered,
even though he had been the only defender left alive, Wilson and
his steamers, despite the long succession of delays, must have

reached Khartoum before it was too late, had the Mahdi not
abandoned caution. For all the testimony from within the dervish
camp is agreed that had " one Englishman " been seen at this last
crucial moment, there would have been no assault.

But now a fatal change came over the scene. For between the
ramparts and the White Nile the ground rises slightly and the
receding river had left a stretch of shallow water and a ridge of
muddy earth. And a deserter had brought word into the Mahdi's
camp of the gap in the defences, where the shallow pool had
prevented the rebuilding of the ramparts or the laying of the much-
feared mines. On Sunday 25th January unwonted movements
could be seen in the dervish camp. Gordon toured the lines, calling
on the despairing troops for a final effort. But the men had ceased
to hope; Bordeini had heard them saying to each other " the
Pasha has deceived us at last." That evening, as twilight fell, the
Mahdi himself crossed stealthily from the west bank of the White
Nile to the dervish camp at Kalakala, a mile south of the defences.
He blessed the troops, bade the Emirs attack that night and assured
them, in the name of God and the Prophet, that victory should be
theirs. It is said that on this last night of the siege in order to hearten
the populace Gordon had ordered the band to play, and rockets to
be discharged, in Khartoum. At about three in the morning, when
the moon had set, and all was silent in Khartoum, the attackers crept
towards the path into the defences opened by the Nile. As they
reached the ramparts a fierce bombardment opened from the Arab
guns. Within a few minutes the feeble defenders in the gap had
been swept aside and the dervishes were inside Khartoum. By four
the town had fallen.

21

Gordon had not had a redoubt built round his headquarters in the
centre of the town, for he had wished it to be clear that he was not
concerned for his own safety. For the same reason there had never

been a strong guard at the Palace. But no guard would have availed now. The men of whom in the remote security of Downing Street Mr. Gladstone had been able to think as a people rightly struggling to be free were loose in the town, and massacre, rape and plunder would continue unchecked for days. There was no more that Gordon could do. Soon there was a tumult in the Palace garden and dervishes were bounding up the stairs which led to his room. He came out in his white uniform and stood at the head of the stairs, peering forward in a characteristic pose, his left hand resting on his sword hilt. The leading dervish plunged his long spear into his breast. Gordon, who had not attempted to defend himself, fell forward on his face. It was almost dawn.

His body was dragged to the foot of the stairs, where hundreds pressed round to stain spears or swords in his blood. The head was cut off and carried in triumph to the Mahdi's camp. The prisoner Slatin at his tent door saw a group of shouting dervishes carrying a bloody cloth. They unwrapped its contents and displayed the head of Gordon. The blue eyes were half-open and the hair was quite white. " Is not this," they cried exultantly, " the head of your uncle, the unbeliever ? " " What of it ? " replied Slatin. " A brave soldier who fell at his post. Happy is he to have fallen; his sufferings are over." Two days later Wilson's two steamers struggled into sight of Khartoum. They were sixty hours too late.

22

When Wolseley heard of the catastrophe on 4th February, his first action was to fall on his knees and pray that Gordon might have been swiftly killed. At three in the morning of 5th February Wolseley's telegram reached Whitehall, and Brett went off at once to inform Lord Granville. But Lord Granville was not to be found. His servants insisted that he was at Walmer, but this, Brett felt certain, was untrue. The news spread through London and the country with uncanny speed. The nation was first stunned, then angry. There was no exaggeration in a statement in the Press next morning that " the shock caused by the news of the fall of Khartoum has no parallel in the experience of the present generation." " No words of ours," it continued, " can adequately express the mingled feelings of dismay, consternation and indignant disgust universally evoked by this lamentable result of a long course of disregard of the elementary maxims of statesmanship." When the Queen heard the news at Osborne she hurried to Sir Henry Ponsonby's cottage, a quarter of a mile away, and terrified his wife by appearing suddenly, pale and trembling, in the dining-room with the ejaculation " Too late!" That morning she dispatched Sir John and Lady Cowell with her personal condolences to Augusta. In her *Journal* she dashed down " It is too fearful. The Government is alone to blame, by refusing to send the expedition till it was too late." And then, abandoning the use of cipher, and therewith all the constitutional proprieties, she telegraphed *en clair* to Hartington, Granville and Mr. Gladstone: " These news from Khartoum are frightful, and to think that all this might have been prevented and many precious lives saved by earlier action is too frightful."

But Mr. Gladstone was unrepentant. That same day he returned a respectful seven-hundred-word protest, on the theme that he was not " altogether able to follow the conclusion which your Majesty has been pleased thus to announce." Gordon himself, he hinted, had been responsible for the fall of Khartoum since he had recommended that Wolseley should take the precaution of capturing Berber *en route*. Alternatively, he submitted, Khartoum had probably been taken by treachery—in which event nobody, of course, unless perhaps Gordon once again, would be to blame. The one error, he suggested in conclusion, which his own government had certainly committed was in allowing any of its troops ever to cross the Egyptian frontier. This remarkable communication appeared to John Morley to be a vindication of government policy well fitted to remain as the last word in " an unedifying and a tragic chapter."

The inscription on the Gordon monument in St. Paul's, to one *who at all times and everywhere gave his strength to the weak, his substance to the poor, his sympathy to the suffering, his heart to God*, is noticeably more accurate than most lapidary tributes. *He saved an Empire by his warlike genius, he ruled vast provinces with justice, wisdom and power.* It is not difficult, however, to picture the sardonic amusement with which that resounding epitaph, and the whole process of popular canonisation, would have been regarded by one who a few weeks before his death had written in his *Khartoum Journals* " The fact is that, if one analyses human glory, it is composed of nine-tenths twaddle, perhaps ninety-nine hundredths twaddle."

THE END

Bibliography

I. UNPUBLISHED LETTERS AND PAPERS

The Barnes Papers (lent by Sir Kenneth Barnes)
The Blunt Papers (lent by Brigadier Gordon Blunt)
The Bredin Papers (lent by G. R. F. Bredin, Esq., C.M.G.)
The Donnelly Papers (lent by Major Gordon H. Donnelly)
The Freese Papers (lent by Mr. Freese-Pennefather)
The Maund Papers (Rhodes House Library)
The Moffitt Papers (lent by the late Lt.-Col. F. W. Moffitt, D.S.O.)
Notes by Lt.-Col. F. W. Moffitt, D.S.O., and Mr. William F. Scott
The Waller Papers (Rhodes House Library)

Also smaller collections and individual letters lent by owners and institutions listed in the Foreword

II. GORDON'S WRITINGS

Colonel Gordon in Central Africa (1874-1879), from original letters documents. Edited by Dr. Birkbeck Hill. De La Rue, 1881-83
General Gordon's Letters from the Crimea, the Danube and Armenia. C man, 1884
Journals at Khartoum. Edited by A. Hake. Kegan Paul, 1885
Letters to his Sister. Macmillan, 1888
Observations on the Holy Communion (Southampton). Vickers, 188
Reflections in Palestine. Macmillan, 1884

III. WORKS ON GORDON

ALLEN, BERNARD M., *Gordon and the Sudan.* Macmillan, 1931
ANON., *A Woman's Memories of General C. G. Gordon.* Remingt
ANON., *Gordon Memoirs.* Privately printed, 1895
ANON., *More About Gordon, by One Who Knew Him Well.* Bent
ANON., *Three Martyrs of the Nineteenth Century.* S.P.C.K., 18

BARNES, R., and BROWN, C., *Sketch, with Facsimile Letter*. Macmillan, 1885

BLUNT, W. S., *Gordon at Khartoum*. Swift, 1911

BOULGER, D. C., *Life of Gordon*. Unwin, 1896

BUCHAN, JOHN, *Gordon at Khartoum* (Great Occasions). R. Davies, 1934

BUTLER, SIR W. F., *Charles George Gordon*. Macmillan, 1889

COE, C. C., *General Gordon in a New Light*. Simpkin, 1885

GORDON, HENRY, W., *Events in the Life of General C. G. Gordon* 1886-87. Kegan Paul, 1896

GRAHAM, SIR G., *Last Words with Gordon*. Chapman, 1887

HAKE, A. E., *The Events of the Taiping Rebellion*. W. H. Allen, 1891

HAKE, A. E., *The Story of Chinese Gordon*, 2 vols. Remington, 1884

HOPE, EVA, *Life of General Gordon*

HUTCHINSON, H. G., *Portraits of the Eighties*. Unwin, 1920

LILLEY, W. E., *The Life and Work of General Gordon at Gravesend*. Kingdom, 1885

MACAULAY, JAMES, M. D., *Gordon Anecdotes*. Religious Tracts Society, 1887

MOSSMAN, S., *Private Diary of Exploits in China*. Low, 1885

STRACHEY, LYTTON, *Eminent Victorians*. Chatto & Windus, 1918

WILSON, H. G., *General Gordon at Gravesend*. 1885

WORTHAM, H. E., *Gordon, An Intimate Portrait*. Harrap, 1933

IV. GENERAL WORKS

BELL, E. H. C. M., *The Life and Letters of C. F. Moberly Bell*. Gran Richards, 1927

BOULGER, D. C., *The Life of Sir Halliday Macartney*. Lane, 1908

BROOKES, E. H., *The History of Native Policy in South Africa from 1850 the Present Day*. Nasionale Pers., 1924

BULLOCH, J. M., *Bibliography of the Gordons*, Section 1. Aberdee University Press, 1924

BURDETT-COUTTS, BARONESS, *A Sketch*. Unwin Bros., 1893

CHAILLE-LONG, M., *My Life in Four Continents*. Hutchinson, 1912

CHAILLE-LONG, M., *The Three Prophets*. D. Appleton, New York, 18

CHIROL, SIR VALENTINE, *Fifty Years in a Changing World*. Jonathan Ca 1927

CHINLY, COLONEL, *Essays in Modern Military History*. 1874

23

It was not, however, by any means the last word for history, or for the nation. The apologia under three heads which Mr. Gladstone sat down so promptly to pen on that February day has long since vanished into the limbo of forgotten political special pleading. While as for the public, it signified its verdict by speedily establishing a nation-wide cult of Gordon for which the only precedents must be sought in the middle ages. Gordon windows were dedicated in cathedrals and parish churches. Gordon clubs for boys sprang up in industrial towns, and Gordon statues in Trafalgar Square and elsewhere. Pamphlets, books and sermons on the soldier-saint poured from press and pulpits. A national day of mourning was observed, a national subscription established the Gordon Boys' Homes, and Parliament voted a handsome sum to the family whose finances had caused him so many anxious calculations.

In his stubborn contention that if Zebehr had been with him there need have been no siege of Khartoum, there can be little doubt that Gordon was right; and that he was right in his long-term view, that if there was to be peace for Egypt the Upper Nile must be effectively controlled, history itself has long since proved. For although, after the curtain had fallen on the tragedy of Khartoum, Mr. Gladstone's government evacuated the Sudan, the strength for its reconquest was steadily accumulated in Egypt. A succession of British officers drilled the Khedive's spiritless troops into the semblance of an army. In 1885 a Mahdist invasion was repulsed; by 1889 the forward movement had begun; and in 1897 Kitchener broke the dervish hordes for ever at Omdurman. When it conferred on him an honorary degree Cambridge hailed Kitchener as *Gordonis ultor*, the avenger of Gordon. But Gordon needed, and would have desired, no avenger. Sufficient that the whole reconquest had cost but 60 British and 160 Egyptian lives. Sufficient that therewith peace came to the Sudan, with the Rule of Law, prosperous tillage where once the slavers had raided and a Gordon College in Khartoum.

CROMER, EARL OF, *Modern Egypt*, 2 vols. Macmillan, 1908

DURNFORD, A. W., *A Soldier's Life and Work in South Africa*, 1872–79. Low, 1882

ESHER, VISCOUNT, *To-day and To-morrow*, 2 vols. John Murray, 1910

FITZMAURICE, E. G. P., *The Life of Granville George Leveson-Gower*, 2 vols. Longmans, 1905

Golgotha and the Garden of the Resurrection, 2nd ed. The Garden Tomb Association, 1944

GARDENER, A. G., *The Life of Sir William Harcourt*. Constable, 1923

GESSI, ROMOLO, *Seven Years in the Sudan*. Sampson Low, 1892

GRAHAM, SIR G., *The Life, Letters and Diaries of*, edited R. H. Vetch Blackwood, 1901

GWYNN, S. M. and TUCKWELL, M., *The Life of Sir Charles Dilke*. John Murray, 1917

HOLLAND, B. H., *The Life of Spencer Compton, 8th Duke of Devonshire*. Longmans, 1911

HOPKINS, THE REV. EVAN H., *Calvary and the Tomb*. Marshall Bros., 1899

HUXLEY, LEONARD, *The Life and Letters of Thomas Henry Huxley*, 3 vols. Macmillan, 1903

LEON, E. DE., *The Khedive's Egypt*. Sampson Low, 1877

LI HUNG CHANG, *The Memoirs of Li Hung Chang*, with an Introduction by J. W. Foster. Constable, 1913

MALET, SIR E. B., *Shifting Scenes*. John Murray, 1901

MALLET, SIR B., Book title, Publisher and date to follow in proof.

MAURICE, SIR F. D. and ARTHUR, SIR G., *The Life of Lord Wolseley.* Heinemann, 1924

MORLEY, JOHN, *The Life of William Ewart Gladstone*. Macmillan, 1903

MORLEY, VISCOUNT, *Recollections*, 2 vols. Macmillan, 1917

NEUFELD, CHARLES, *A Prisoner of the Khalifa*. Chapman & Hall, 1899

OLIPHANT, LAURENCE, *Haifa*, 2nd edition. Blackwood, 1887

OLIVER, F. S., *The Endless Adventure*, Vol. III. Macmillan, 1935

POWER, FRANK, *Letters from Khartoum*. Sampson Low, 1885

REDMAYNE, SIR RICHARD, *Mines, Men and Memories*. Eyre & Spottiswoode, 1942

RENDEL, LORD, *The Personal Paper of Lord Rendel*, edited by F. E. Hamer Benn, 1931

ROUNDELL PALMER, EARL OF SELBOURNE, *Memorials*, 4 vols. Macmillan, 1896–98

SLATIN PASHA, RUDOLF C., *Fire and Sword in the Sudan.* Arnold, 1906

STANLEY, SIR HENRY M., *Autobiography.* Samson Low, 1909

TYLDEN, G., *The Rise of the Basuto.* Juta, Cape Town, 1950

QUEEN VICTORIA, *Letters,* Second Series, Edited G. Buckle, Vol. III. John Murray, 1928

VETCH, R. H., *The Life of General the Hon. Sir Andrew Clarke.* John Murray, 1905

WHYTE, F., *The Life of W. T. Stead,* 2 vols. Jonathan Cape, 1925

WILLIAMS, BASIL, *Cecil Rhodes.* Constable, 1921

WILKINS, W. H., *The Romance of Isabel, Lady Burton,* 2 vols. Hutchinson, 1897

WILSON, SIR C. RIVERS, *Chapters from My Official Life.* Arnold, 1916

WINGATE, SIR F. REGINALD, *Mahdiism and the Egyptian Sudan.* Macmillan, 1891

WINGATE, SIR F. REGINALD, *The Sudan, Past and Present. Royal Artillery Institution,* 1892

WOLF, LUCIEN, *The Life of the First Marquess of Ripon,* 2 vols. John Murray, 1921

WOODHAM SMITH, CECIL, *Florence Nightingale.* Constable, 1950

V. PERIODICALS

The Academy, July, 1865
The Daily News
The Dundee Advertiser, 18th September, 1884
The Fortnightly Review
The Friend of China
The Nineteenth Century, May, June, July, 1884
The Pall Mall Gazette
The Sudan Diocesan Review
The Times

VI. OFFICIAL DOCUMENTS

Blue Books
Cape Government Papers
Parliamentary Debates (Hansard)

23

It was not, however, by any means the last word for history, or for the nation. The apologia under three heads which Mr. Gladstone sat down so promptly to pen on that February day has long since vanished into the limbo of forgotten political special pleading. While as for the public, it signified its verdict by speedily establishing a nation-wide cult of Gordon for which the only precedents must be sought in the middle ages. Gordon windows were dedicated in cathedrals and parish churches. Gordon clubs for boys sprang up in industrial towns, and Gordon statues in Trafalgar Square and elsewhere. Pamphlets, books and sermons on the soldier-saint poured from press and pulpits. A national day of mourning was observed, a national subscription established the Gordon Boys' Homes, and Parliament voted a handsome sum to the family whose finances had caused him so many anxious calculations.

In his stubborn contention that if Zebehr had been with him there need have been no siege of Khartoum, there can be little doubt that Gordon was right; and that he was right in his long-term view, that if there was to be peace for Egypt the Upper Nile must be effectively controlled, history itself has long since proved. For although, after the curtain had fallen on the tragedy of Khartoum, Mr. Gladstone's government evacuated the Sudan, the strength for its reconquest was steadily accumulated in Egypt. A succession of British officers drilled the Khedive's spiritless troops into the semblance of an army. In 1885 a Mahdist invasion was repulsed; by 1889 the forward movement had begun; and in 1897 Kitchener broke the dervish hordes for ever at Omdurman. When it conferred on him an honorary degree Cambridge hailed Kitchener as *Gordonis ultor*, the avenger of Gordon. But Gordon needed, and would have desired, no avenger. Sufficient that the whole reconquest had cost but 60 British and 160 Egyptian lives. Sufficient that therewith peace came to the Sudan, with the Rule of Law, prosperous tillage where once the slavers had raided and a Gordon College in Khartoum.

The inscription on the Gordon monument in St. Paul's, to one *who at all times and everywhere gave his strength to the weak, his substance to the poor, his sympathy to the suffering, his heart to God,* is noticeably more accurate than most lapidary tributes. *He saved an Empire by his warlike genius, he ruled vast provinces with justice, wisdom and power.* It is not difficult, however, to picture the sardonic amusement with which that resounding epitaph, and the whole process of popular canonisation, would have been regarded by one who a few weeks before his death had written in his *Khartoum Journals* " The fact is that, if one analyses human glory, it is composed of nine-tenths twaddle, perhaps ninety-nine hundredths twaddle."

THE END

Bibliography

I. UNPUBLISHED LETTERS AND PAPERS

The Barnes Papers (lent by Sir Kenneth Barnes)
The Blunt Papers (lent by Brigadier Gordon Blunt)
The Bredin Papers (lent by G. R. F. Bredin, Esq., C.M.G.)
The Donnelly Papers (lent by Major Gordon H. Donnelly)
The Freese Papers (lent by Mr. Freese-Pennefather)
The Maund Papers (Rhodes House Library)
The Moffitt Papers (lent by the late Lt.-Col. F. W. Moffitt, D.S.O.)
Notes by Lt.-Col. F. W. Moffitt, D.S.O., and Mr. William F. Scott
The Waller Papers (Rhodes House Library)

> Also smaller collections and individual letters lent
> by owners and institutions listed in the Foreword

II. GORDON'S WRITINGS

Colonel Gordon in Central Africa (1874-1879), from original letters and
documents. Edited by Dr. Birkbeck Hill. De La Rue, 1881-83
General Gordon's Letters from the Crimea, the Danube and Armenia. Chapman, 1884
Journals at Khartoum. Edited by A. Hake. Kegan Paul, 1885
Letters to his Sister. Macmillan, 1888
Observations on the Holy Communion (Southampton). Vickers, 1885
Reflections in Palestine. Macmillan, 1884

III. WORKS ON GORDON

ALLEN, BERNARD M., *Gordon and the Sudan.* Macmillan, 1931
ANON., *A Woman's Memories of General C. G. Gordon.* Remington, 1885
ANON., *Gordon Memoirs.* Privately printed, 1895
ANON., *More About Gordon, by One Who Knew Him Well.* Bentley, 1894
ANON., *Three Martyrs of the Nineteenth Century.* S.P.C.K., 1885

BARNES, R., and BROWN, C., *Sketch, with Facsimile Letter.* Macmillan, 1885

BLUNT, W. S., *Gordon at Khartoum.* Swift, 1911

BOULGER, D. C., *Life of Gordon.* Unwin, 1896

BUCHAN, JOHN, *Gordon at Khartoum* (Great Occasions). R. Davies, 1934

BUTLER, SIR W. F., *Charles George Gordon.* Macmillan, 1889

COE, C. C., *General Gordon in a New Light.* Simpkin, 1885

GORDON, HENRY, W., *Events in the Life of General C. G. Gordon* 1886-87. Kegan Paul, 1896

GRAHAM, SIR G., *Last Words with Gordon.* Chapman, 1887

HAKE, A. E., *The Events of the Taiping Rebellion.* W. H. Allen, 1891

HAKE, A. E., *The Story of Chinese Gordon,* 2 vols. Remington, 1884

HOPE, EVA, *Life of General Gordon*

HUTCHINSON, H. G., *Portraits of the Eighties.* Unwin, 1920

LILLEY, W. E., *The Life and Work of General Gordon at Gravesend.* Kingdom, 1885

MACAULAY, JAMES, M. D., *Gordon Anecdotes.* Religious Tracts Society, 1887

MOSSMAN, S., *Private Diary of Exploits in China.* Low, 1885

STRACHEY, LYTTON, *Eminent Victorians.* Chatto & Windus, 1918

WILSON, H. G., *General Gordon at Gravesend.* 1885

WORTHAM, H. E., *Gordon, An Intimate Portrait.* Harrap, 1933

IV. GENERAL WORKS

BELL, E. H. C. M., *The Life and Letters of C. F. Moberly Bell.* Grant Richards, 1927

BOULGER, D. C., *The Life of Sir Halliday Macartney.* Lane, 1908

BROOKES, E. H., *The History of Native Policy in South Africa from 1850 to the Present Day.* Nasionale Pers., 1924

BULLOCH, J. M., *Bibliography of the Gordons,* Section 1. Aberdeen University Press, 1924

BURDETT-COUTTS, BARONESS, *A Sketch.* Unwin Bros., 1893

CHAILLE-LONG, M., *My Life in Four Continents.* Hutchinson, 1912

CHAILLE-LONG, M., *The Three Prophets.* D. Appleton, New York, 1884

CHIROL, SIR VALENTINE, *Fifty Years in a Changing World.* Jonathan Cape, 1927

CHINLY, COLONEL, *Essays in Modern Military History.* 1874

CROMER, EARL OF, *Modern Egypt*, 2 vols. Macmillan, 1908

DURNFORD, A. W., *A Soldier's Life and Work in South Africa*, 1872-79. Low, 1882

ESHER, VISCOUNT, *To-day and To-morrow*, 2 vols. John Murray, 1910

FITZMAURICE, E. G. P., *The Life of Granville George Leveson-Gower*, 2 vols. Longmans, 1905
Golgotha and the Garden of the Resurrection, 2nd ed. The Garden Tomb Association, 1944

GARDENER, A. G., *The Life of Sir William Harcourt*. Constable, 1923

GESSI, ROMOLO, *Seven Years in the Sudan*. Sampson Low, 1892

GRAHAM, SIR G., *The Life, Letters and Diaries of*, edited R. H. Vetch Blackwood, 1901

GWYNN, S. M. and TUCKWELL, M., *The Life of Sir Charles Dilke*. John Murray, 1917

HOLLAND, B. H., *The Life of Spencer Compton, 8th Duke of Devonshire*. Longmans, 1911

HOPKINS, THE REV. EVAN H., *Calvary and the Tomb*. Marshall Bros., 1899

HUXLEY, LEONARD, *The Life and Letters of Thomas Henry Huxley*, 3 vols. Macmillan, 1903

LEON, E. DE., *The Khedive's Egypt*. Sampson Low, 1877

LI HUNG CHANG, *The Memoirs of Li Hung Chang*, with an Introduction by J. W. Foster. Constable, 1913

MALET, SIR E. B., *Shifting Scenes*. John Murray, 1901

MALLET, SIR B., Book title, Publisher and date to follow in proof.

MAURICE, SIR F. D. and ARTHUR, SIR G., *The Life of Lord Wolseley*. Heinemann, 1924

MORLEY, JOHN, *The Life of William Ewart Gladstone*. Macmillan, 1903

MORLEY, VISCOUNT, *Recollections*, 2 vols. Macmillan, 1917

NEUFELD, CHARLES, *A Prisoner of the Khalifa*. Chapman & Hall, 1899

OLIPHANT, LAURENCE, *Haifa*, 2nd edition. Blackwood, 1887

OLIVER, F. S., *The Endless Adventure*, Vol. III. Macmillan, 1935

POWER, FRANK, *Letters from Khartoum*. Sampson Low, 1885

REDMAYNE, SIR RICHARD, *Mines, Men and Memories*. Eyre & Spottis-woode, 1942

RENDEL, LORD, *The Personal Paper of Lord Rendel*, edited by F. E. Hamer Benn, 1931

ROUNDELL PALMER, EARL OF SELBOURNE, *Memorials*, 4 vols. Macmillan, 1896-98

SLATIN PASHA, RUDOLF C., *Fire and Sword in the Sudan.* Arnold, 1906

STANLEY, SIR HENRY M., *Autobiography.* Samson Low, 1909

TYLDEN, G., *The Rise of the Basuto.* Juta, Cape Town, 1950

QUEEN VICTORIA, *Letters,* Second Series, Edited G. Buckle, Vol. III. John Murray, 1928

VETCH, R. H., *The Life of General the Hon. Sir Andrew Clarke.* John Murray, 1905

WHYTE, F., *The Life of W. T. Stead,* 2 vols. Jonathan Cape, 1925

WILLIAMS, BASIL, *Cecil Rhodes.* Constable, 1921

WILKINS, W. H., *The Romance of Isabel, Lady Burton,* 2 vols. Hutchinson, 1897

WILSON, SIR C. RIVERS, *Chapters from My Official Life.* Arnold, 1916

WINGATE, SIR F. REGINALD, *Mahdiism and the Egyptian Sudan.* Macmillan, 1891

WINGATE, SIR F. REGINALD, *The Sudan, Past and Present. Royal Artillery Institution,* 1892

WOLF, LUCIEN, *The Life of the First Marquess of Ripon,* 2 vols. John Murray, 1921

WOODHAM SMITH, CECIL, *Florence Nightingale.* Constable, 1950

V. PERIODICALS

The Academy, July, 1865
The Daily News
The Dundee Advertiser, 18th September, 1884
The Fortnightly Review
The Friend of China
The Nineteenth Century, May, June, July, 1884
The Pall Mall Gazette
The Sudan Diocesan Review
The Times

VI. OFFICIAL DOCUMENTS

Blue Books
Cape Government Papers
Parliamentary Debates (Hansard)

INDEX

Abbas, s.s., 402-3, 412
Abu Hamed, 355, 365
Abu Klea, 426, 427
Abu Saoud (slave-trader), 156, 167, 186
Abyssinia, 237, 239, 249-50, 263-4;
  campaign in, 127-8, 132
Aden, 284
Ain Karim, 313, 318
Alexandra, Queen (as Princess of
  Wales), 270
Alexandria, 266, 267
Allen, Dr. Bernard, 206, 208, 270, 360
Aloula (Abyssinian general), 264
Anson, Willie (nephew), 180, 181
Arabi Pasha, 197, 328
Ararat, Mount, 38
Armenia, 35, 36, 37, 38
Ashanti expedition, 144
Ashmead-Bartlett, William, 294, 387,
  389
Athens, 33

Bahr el Ghazal: campaign in, 256-9;
  Gordon's plans for, 353, 362
Baker, Julian, 209
Baker, Sir Samuel, 141, 146, 152, 156,
  162, 332, 333, 385; Gordon on,
  147-8, 149, 164, 166, 171; Sudan
  "hatred" of, 171; Gordon rebuffs,
  218-9
Balaclava, 23, 25, 26, 30, 31
Bantry, 287

Baring, Sir Evelyn, 253-4, 265, 328,
  329, 383, 392, 404; Gordon's verdict
  on, 253, 260; and Gordon's Khartoum expedition, 331, 332-3, 335,
  336-7, 339, 340-3, 347-9, 350, 360,
  363-4, 369-71, 384-5, 401; conference with Gordon, 348-9; realises
  desperate situation, 377-80; Gordon's
  last letter to, 402; Gordon's comments on, 415, 419-20
Barnes, Rev. R. H., 272, 314,
  320, 321, 333, 340, 345, 351, 414,
  424
Basutoland, 302-7
Beach, Sir Michael Hicks, 390
Beaconsfield, Lord, 260, 269, 272, 273,
  275, 276
Bedden, 214
Bell, C. F. Moberly, 155, 356, 363
Benson, Edward White, Archbishop of
  Canterbury, 319
Berber, 164, 172, 250, 355-6, 369;
  keypoint for Khartoum evacuation,
  364, 365; Cabinet refuses troops for,
  370, 371, 377, 380, 381, 385; cap-
  tured by Mahdi, 393; attempt to
  recapture, 401, 402, 403
Beresford, Lord William, 278
Berlin, 143
Bernhardt, Sarah, 297
Berzati Bey (Arab secretary), 287
Bessarabia, 35, 36, 43

James, Sir Henry, 219

Jerusalem, 312-23; Gordon's Biblical researches in, 314-19, 321-2; his routine in, 321-2

Johannis, King of Abyssinia, 237, 239, 263-4

Juba river, 216

Kabarega, King of Unyoro, 227-8, 231

Kahding, 51

Kahpu, 65

Kalakala, 428

Kandahar, 288-9

Kassala, 239

Katarif, 239, 258

Keir, Father, 278

Keppel, Admiral Sir Henry, 294

Keppel, Lady, 294, 295

Keren, 239, 250

Kerri, 223, 228

Khartoum, 163, 190, 232, 237, 249, 260, 262; Gordon first arrives at, 164-7; he returns from Gondoroko, 171-3; he enters as Governor-General, 239; his palace routine, 255-6; Government decision to evacuate, 326-7, 332, 334, 336-7, 344; Gordon's reception at, 356, 357; his plan for evacuation, 362, 364, 367, 369; his warnings about, 369-72; siege of, 372 et seq.; administrative problems, 383; relief expedition to, 400, 401, 405, 409, 412, 414, 420; fall of, 428

Khedive, s.s., 193, 215

Kimberley, Lord, 304

Kimburn, 34

Kingsley, Charles, 139

Kintang, 85-6

Kismayu, 196

Kitchener, Lord, 403, 416, 417, 423, 431

Kordofan, 237, 258, 328

Korosko, 349, 353, 354

Korti, 423

Kung, Prince, 89, 90

Lado, 190-1, 200, 202, 204, 205

Lake Albert, 190, 195, 215, 227-9, 230

Lake Kioga, 227, 228, 230

Lake Victoria, 195, 227, 229, 230, 237

Lanarkshire, 107, 130-1

Lar Wang (Taiping rebel): Gordon's offer of safety to, 73-5; murder of, 77-82, 277, 281

Lausanne, 271-2

Lawson, Sir Wilfrid, 388

Leeku, 57, 72

Leopold II, King of the Belgians: suggests Congo expedition, 271, 284, 310-11, 322-3, 334, 338; Gordon's plan to hand over negro provinces to, 353, 362

Lesseps, Count Ferdinand de, 161, 253

Li Hung Chang, 52, 64-5, 66, 280; Gordon under his orders, 54; on Gordon, 55-6, 57-9; and Wang massacre, 73-82; reconciled with Gordon, 83-5; at Changchow, 87; letter from, 133; Gordon prevents his rebellion against Peking, 281-3

Lilley, Mr. (Presbyterian minister), 225; on Gordon, 41; letters to, 139-41

Linant, Ernest, 190, 195, 214, 223, 227

INDEX

447

Tientsin, 44, 282, 283; Gordon on engineering duties, 46-7
Times, The: on Wang massacre, 82; and Gordon's letter on Ireland, 288; on Gordon and the Congo, 325; supports him on Khartoum, 355-6, 363, 390; Power's dispatches to, 380, 382, 383, 386, 405-6
Tsingpu, 51
Tupper, Martin, 139
Twywell, 211, 289-90, 297, 299

Uganda, 190; Long's mission to King of, 171, 181, 188; Gordon's proposal to recognise independence, 230

Vanity Fair, cartoon of Gordon in, 285-6
Victoria, Queen: tribute to Gordon, 13; "very anxious about Egypt," 332; on dilatory Sudan policy, 344; supports Gordon, 364, 370, 371, 378-9, 383; and fall of Khartoum, 430
Vivian, H. C., 265-6, 271

Wade, Sir Thomas, 282
Wadi Halfa, 369
Waissoo, 86
Waled-el-Michael, 237, 239, 250
Walker and Pasquali, Messrs., 253
Waller, Rev. Horace, 211, 226, 235, 236, 245, 247, 259, 289-90, 303, 313, 323, 336

Walungchiao, 72
Wanti, 72
Ward, Frederick T., 50, 51-2
Wardle, Mr. (Manchester City Mission) 104, 109
Watson, Colonel C. M., 183-4, 190, 207, 347, 350
Weymouth, 108
Wilson, Sir Charles, 163-4, 426-7, 429
Wilson, Rivers, 260, 262, 275
Wokong, 65, 67-8
Wolseley, Field-Marshal Viscount: with Gordon in Crimea, 29, 40; leads Ashanti expedition, 144, 145; interviews with Gordon, 334-5, 338, 340; sees him off on Khartoum expedition, 345-6; and relief expedition, 400, 404, 405, 414, 416, 420, 429
Wood, Sir Evelyn, 344, 348
Woolwich, 15-21

Yakub Khan, 279

Zanzibar, proposed expedition to, 235, 271, 284
Zebehr (slave-trader), 241, 256; growing power of, 163; not allowed to join Gordon's Sudan mission, 350-1, 354, 378; Gordon suggests as Sudan ruler, 362-3, 366, 368, 369, 370, 417